A Guide to

Collecting Cookbooks
and
Advertising Cookbooks

A History of People, Companies and Cooking

Col. Bob Allen

COLLECTOR BOOKS
A Division of Schroeder Publishing Co., Inc.

The current values in this book should be used only as a guide. They are not intended to set prices, which vary from one section of the country to another. Auction prices as well as dealer prices vary greatly and are affected by condition as well as demand. Neither the Author nor the Publisher assumes responsibility for any losses that might be incurred as a result of consulting this guide.

Additional copies of this book may be ordered from:

COLLECTOR BOOKS
P.O. Box 3009
Paducah, Kentucky 42002-3009

@ $14.95. Add $2.00 for shipping and handling.

Copyright: Col. Bob Allen, 1990

This book is dedicated to two women who collected everything and threw nothing away. Both women cut out and kept recipes from newspapers and magazines and sent for all kinds of recipe advertising publications. They both lived into their ninetieth year before they passed away.

There was an estate auction by the heirs in both families and we were at each auction. The results of our purchases added greatly to our collection and knowledge.

This book is also dedicated to Jo Ellen's mother, Henrietta Schweiss, who purchased a used copy of "The Story of Crisco," copyright 1914, at a rummage sale, brought it home and gave it to Jo when she was in high school. Jo attributes her interest in collecting to the gift of this book.

I also dedicate this book to my very patient and dearest wife.

Credits and Acknowledgments

The content of this book has been greatly enhanced by the contributions of the following cookbook collectors:

Velma Scott of Hagerstown, Maryland
Roberta "Bobbi" Deal of Mecklenburg, New York

And thanks to the following companies:

The Hulman Company of Terre Haute, Indiana
General Mills, Inc. of Minneapolis, Minnesota
Gerneral Foods Corp. of White Plaines, New York
The Pillsbury Company of Minneapolis, Minnesota
Church & Dwight Co., Inc. of Princeton, New Jersey
William B. Reily & Co. of New Orleans, Louisiana
Pevely Dairy Company of St. Louis, Missouri
International Multifoods of Minneapolis, Minnesota
Thomas J. Lipton, Inc. of Englewood Cliffs, New Jersey

About The Author

For the past ten years, Bob Allen has been a collector, eight of which he has been an avid collector of fruit jars and fruit jar go-withs including the *Ball Blue Books* and *Kerr Home Canning Books*. At one time his collection totaled 1,600 jars. He has been in the furniture refinishing profession for almost 20 years and has owned shops in locations in southern California and Missouri. The two locations in Missouri also included antique shops.

Bob attended the Missouri Auction School in Kansas City and has been auctioning for nine years and is now known as Col. Bob Allen. He has given many talks on fruit jars and closures and on the history of collecting cookbooks and cook booklets. He has also authored articles for monthly publications of two collectors clubs.

Bob has been host for two radio programs on antiques and collectibles. He and his wife have traveled extensively to antique shows throughout the Midwest and California and enjoy attending antique seminars.

Before the winter of 1986-87, Bob volunteered to organize the cookbook collection of his wife, Jo Ellen. About six weeks into the organizing, he stated that she could write a book with all of the information contained in her collection. Jo Ellen declined the suggestion, saying that she would keep changing it and never get it done.

That explains why Bob is the author of this book. Please feel free to contact him at P.O. Box 85, St. James, Missouri 65559.

About The Collector

Jo Ellen Allen has raised four children and enjoys baking very much. There are always baked goods of some kind in the house. On the holidays, cookies, pies and Swedish bread rings are gifts to friends and relatives.

Jo Ellen's mother purchased a 1914 edition of "The Story of Crisco" at at rummage sale and gave it to Jo Ellen who was then a teenager. This book has real sentimental value and became the basis to collect other baking recipe books and booklets.

When all the children were grown and on their own,

Bob started collecting fruit jars and Jo Ellen collected with him, Bob searching for jars and Jo Ellen searching out baking item cookbooks. After about eight years, Bob tired of fruit jar collecting and was slowly getting interested in Jo Ellen's collection.

Jo Ellen states, "Not only do I collect the cookbooks and cook booklets for the recipes, I also collect them for the wonderful artwork on the front of them and contained in them."

Happy Collecting!

Table Of Contents

Chapter 1

About This Book

What is a Cookbook?

A cookbook can be many different things, depending on its author and its purpose. The one element all are sure to possess is recipes. It is many things - years of knowledge, preparation, serving, its role in family life. It is a loving compilation of favorite recipes from culinary experts to home economists. It is what to do with those leftovers to have a new and exciting meal. It is how to cook for that magic number. It is cooking with utmost confidence because the recipes have been tested and approved.

A cookbook is the tremendous contribution of the food industry to our country and the zealous care of and protection of our governmental agencies. Most important, it is the American woman. It is the mother who writes from a small town in the country to a daughter in the city. It is the young bride who valiantly copes with the complexities of a new marriage. It is the older woman who, now that her budget is bigger, can truly enjoy and use all of those wonderful recipes. It is the young graduate that can learn how to cook.

A cookbook is the culinary expert and home economist that almost defies belief in their dedication and devotion, its enthusiasm and creativity.

Also perhaps more important of all, a cookbook is the spirit, the caring, the untiring giving of the magnificent, great and gracious ladies of the culinary arts cookery world.

More than anyone, the collector needs to spend some money on the reference books and materials that give them some clues to what they are collecting and their prices in the market place.

As you become acquainted with this book you will be fascinated by the early dates, and such terms as "cookery," "culinary expert," "school of cookery" and "The Art of Cookery." You may even be surprised that there were cooking schools as early as the 1800's. Material in this book includes cooking schools and culinary experts dating in the 1870's and 1880's. (Don't forget that the Civil War was 1861-1865.) Shortly after 1900, *The Boston Cooking School Magazine* became *The American Cookery Magazine*.

As you settle down and become used to this book, you will realize that you are seeing such terms as "home economist," "Department of Home Economics," and "test

kitchens." Food companies had their own spokesladies (if you will) such as Martha Lee Anderson of Arm & Hammer Baking Soda, Ann Pillsbury of Pillsbury Flour, Betty Crocker for Washburn Crosby Company, makers of Gold Medal Flour, later in 1928 becoming General Mills, Inc.

From the turn of the century and through the 1920's and 30's was a time of change. Rural areas were receiving electricity, cooking stoves were being changed from wood-burning, coal burning and kerosene to carbide gas, natural gas, and electric. Small electrical appliances such as toasters and waffle irons were coming into use. Carbide gas systems were installed into the home for the cooking stove, clothes ironing and even for lighting. The chafing dish appeared and ovens were coming equipped with heat regulators. The early refrigerators were becoming popular.

At the same time that all of this was happening, less and less was heard about the school of cookery or the cooking school. Suddenly women were going to college and majoring in Home Economics and becoming a professional to teach or be employed by a food company. Some food companies employed as many as 35 home economists. Some graduates chose to be in the employ of a magazine and eventually became the food editor.

All of these changes required revising exisiting recipes such as the oven temperature of low, medium or high to degrees Fahrenheit, and what speed and how long to beat a mixture with an electric mixer. The culinary experts and home economists were kept busy trying to keep food company recipe publications up to date and author new up-to-date cookbooks.

Some of the food company cookbooks were hard-cover but the majority were soft-cover. The hard-cover ones are so marked in our listings; any unmarked publication is a soft-cover publication. Three-ring or two-ring hard-covers are so indicated and soft-cover spiral and hard-cover spiral books are so indicated. Some have wood covers and two-ring binders and these are so marked.

About the time that the "modern" changes were going on, the manufacturers of kitchen items and equipment such as cast iron cookware, aluminum cookware, cook stoves, refrigerators, electric mixers, even vacuum cleaner manufacturers all started publishing cookbooks and recipe books to advertise their products and to help keep their name before the housewife. These had to be kept up-to-date with many revisions and newer editions.

In 1903 Good Housekeeping published their first cookbook edited by their magazine food editor and by the 1940's other magazine publications began publishing cookbooks. By the 1950's more magazines were publishing cookbooks and newspapers such as the *New York Times* and the *New York Herald-Tribune* began publishing cookbooks by their food editors. Later, Time-Life entered the cookbook field.

By the 1960's the same publishing companies that had been publishing cookbooks for everyone else suddenly began to see where the additional profits were. They put in test kitchens and hired their own home economists and food editors and began publishing their own cookbooks. As the market was being inundated with cookbooks and recipe books, our population was growing fast enough to absorb all of this.

You will find later food company recipe publications using the terms "Home Service Center," "Customer Service Center," "Consumer Services Department" and "Research Kitchens." There are no longer companies, so it seems, but corporations and incorporations or a subsidiary of a corporation. The earlier company address was Chicago U.S.A. or New York, N.Y. U.S.A. The address then changed to Chicago 22, Ilinois and then changed to a five-digit zip code number, and as if that wasn't enough, they came out with a nine-digit zip code. We have certainly progressed in the last 100 years and rightly so.

This book is by no means a complete compilation of what's out there in cookbooks or advertising recipe books. We have collected only enough pocket cookbooks, fund raising, charity, regional and political and other canning, preserving and curing to show a good cross-section. We have passed up a lot of them because this was not our main interest. The *Ball Blue Books* are the result of a national survey of Ball Fruit Jar collectors.

Our main interest is reflected in the chapters with a baking ingredient title, such as flour, baking powder, yeast, etc. If we found one from this category we did not have, we would try to bring it home unless the condition was really bad or it was horribly over priced. The chapters are as complete as we could collect and research.

The cookbooks listed in the chapters Hard-cover Cookbooks and Soft-cover Cookbooks are fairly complete except that we didn't collect all of the manufacturers of kitchen items, just a token amount. There must be a ton of these out there.

This book is based on four collections and this makes it more complete and knowledgeable. We have corresponded with many of the food companies and manufacturers to learn of publications that we have not found or were not known to us.

This book is just a guide to go by and a sampling of the market place. You have to use your own judgment as to age, condition, and quality compared to some of the items listed herein. Our earliest hard-cover cookbook is 1859 and our earliest soft-cover cookbook is 1867. The oldest advertising cookbook referred to in this book is 1859. The hard-cover and soft-cover cookbooks in our

collection include those through 1988. The baking chapters of this book have been brought up to date to show the company history and change in ownership and to reflect the various mergers. Cookbooks produced after 1969 are not valued as many are still available and hold their original face value. You will see some of the companies in this book as originally founded and you will be able to follow the development and progress as other companies were merging or purchasing their competitor.

I would like to mention here some things about the White House Cookbooks. They are quite old and difficult to come by in good to very good condition. The following are the copyright editions:

    1887 - first edition
    1894 - copyright edition
    1899 - copyright edition
    1914 - copyright edition
    1915 - copyright edition
    1924 - copyright edition

The reprint of 1983 was of the 1915 copyright edition, not the original as advertised. There are many printings of each copyright. We have collected the following White House Cookbooks:

    1890 - edition of the 1887 copyright
    1904 - edition of the 1899 copyright
    1905 - edition of the 1899 copyright
    1911 - edition of the 1899 copyright
    1923 - edition of the 1915 copyright
    1925 - edition of the 1924 copyright
    1926 - edition of the 1924 copyright

I would like to make you aware of the Capital Cookbook which is a take-off from The White House Cookbook and some people are trying to make it worth a lot more than it really is valued.

The one that I saw was a 1912 take-off of the 1911 White House Cookbook with a picture of President Taft's wife. They appeared the same except for the cover.

Definitions of Condition

Mint - As though you went to the bookstore, bought it and brought it home

Very Fine - Near mint

Fine - Almost as good as very fine, but with a little soil or fingerprint or a slightly turned corner

Very Good - Relatively clean, no damage, eveything in tact, very few turned corners, no rounded corners, no tears

Good - Some soil on cover, minor damage, a few turned corners, no tears and no missing pages

Fair - Soiled cover, some corner damage, a little mice nibbling but not too much, maybe a tear or two, some discoloration acceptable and no pages missing

Bad - Very soiled, lots of corner damage, mice damage, tears, discolorations, missing pages. You should not want to buy it in this condition unless it is really old and there is hope to update it in the future.

Poor - Missing cover and title page, other missing pages, mouse eaten, soiled. You should not want it in this condition.

The values given in this book are for cookbooks and recipe books in Good to Very Good condition. For publications that are in Fine condition to Mint condition please add to the value indicated. For publications in Fair to Bad condition please deduct from the value indicated.

I hope that you will use this book as a guide to your collecting. You may want to specialize in a particular category. Some collectors just collect Jell-O, Pillsbury and Pillsbury Bake Offs and Pillsbury Classics. Other collectors specialize in Betty Crocker, Arm & Hammer Baking Soda or the trade card Bird series.

The values given here are based on an age of two generations which would be 40 years, a generation being 20 years. A new book will no doubt depreciate in value when you bring it home because it is a used book and after ten years of use it is not very resalable, usually soiled and showing wear.

Inflation is and has been upon us for many years now. The 1961 price index tells us that what cost $1.00 in 1961 now costs $3.65 to $4.25. Yes, the dollar is shrinking.

A cookbook at the turn of the century sold for $1.25 to $2.00 for a hard-cover cookbook and by 1910 the cost was $2.25 to $2.50. If you were to figure in today's cost of publishing that cookbook would be $36.50. This is close because today many sell for $19.95 to $29.95.

Enjoy your collecting!

NCV denotes No Collector Value
▸ denotes titles found in photo section

Photos

Hard-cover Cookbooks

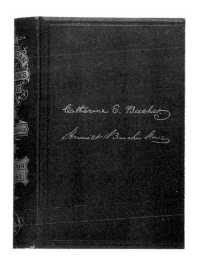

American Woman's Home. 1869. $300.00

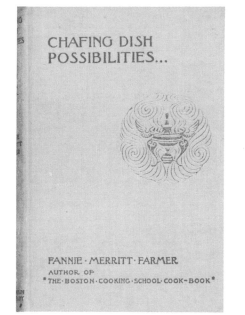

Chafing Dish Possibilities. 1898. $250.00

Chez Maxim's. 1962. $25.00

Come into the Kitchen Cook Book. 1969. $25.00

Esquire Cook Book. 1955. $5.00

The Fireside Cook Book. 1949. $25.00

The First Ladies Cook Book. 1969. $10.00

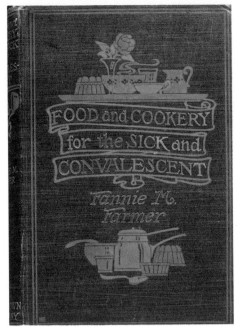

Food and Cookery for the Sick and
Convalescent. 1905. $20.00

Good Housekeeping Everyday
Cook Book. 1903. $50.00

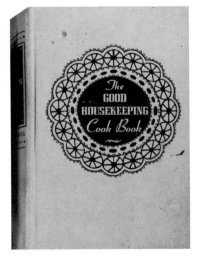

The Good Housekeeping
Cook Book. 1943. $7.50

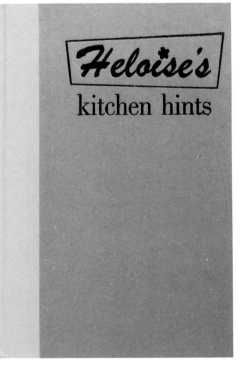

Heloise's Kitchen Hints. 1963. $5.00

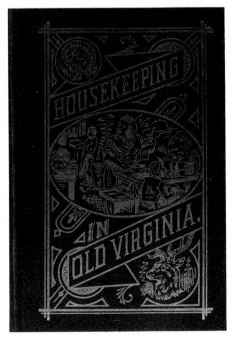

Housekeeping in Old Virginia.
1879. $70.00

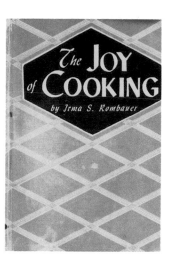

The Joy of Cooking.
1946. $10.00

The I Hate To Cook Book. 1960.
$10.00

Italian Regional Cooking. 1969. $15.00

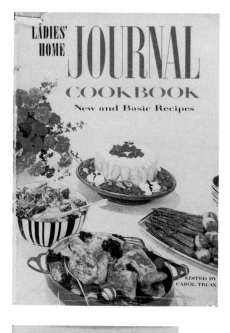

Ladies Home Journal Cook Book.
1960. $10.00

The Margaret Rudkin Pepperidge
Farm Cookbook. 1963. $10.00

The Mystery Chef's Own Cook
Book. 1945. $12.50

The Presidential Cook Book. 1907. $12.50

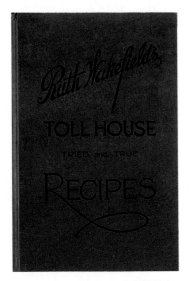

**Ruth Wakefield's Toll House
Tried and True Recipes.
1945. $7.50**

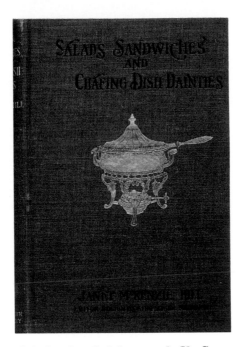

**Salads, Sandwiches and Chafing
Dish Dainties. 1899. $50.00**

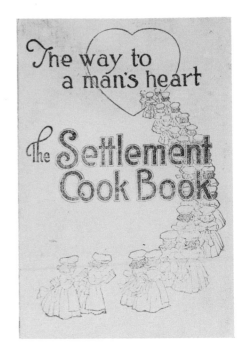

**The Settlement Cook Book. 1925.
$25.00**

**When You Entertain. 1932.
$25.00**

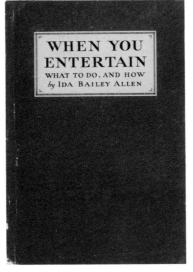

**St. Louis Symphony of Cooking.
1954. $15.00**

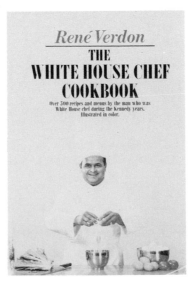

**The White House Cook Book.
1889. $60.00**

**The White House Chef
Cookbook. 1967. $10.00**

Wolf in Chef's Clothing. 1950.
$12.00

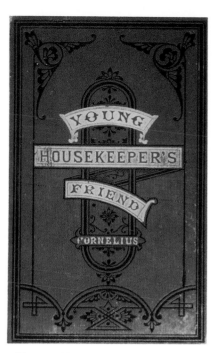

Young Housekeeper's Friend.
1871. $75.00

═══ Soft-cover Cookbooks and Booklets ═══

The Ad-Ven-tur-ous Billy and Betty.
1923. $12.00

American Beauty Recipes Using
Macaroni Products. Circa 1930.
$8.00

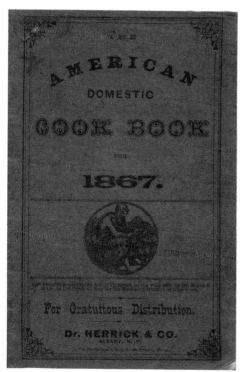

The American Domestic Cook Book
For 1867. 1867. $35.00

Around the World
Cook Book. 1951.
$6.00

The Art and Secrets of Chinese Cookery.
1942. $8.00

Aunt Sammy's Radio
Recipes. 1927. $12.00

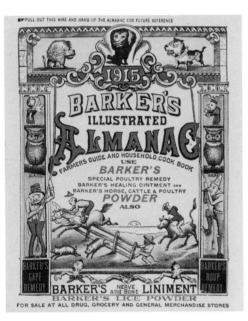

Barker's Illustrated Almanac. 1915.
$20.00

Better Meals for Less.
1930. $10.00

Cakes and Desserts. 1927.
$12.00

Candy Making in the Home.
1913. $14.00

Celebrity Recipes.
1961. $3.00

Clementine Paddleford's
Cook Young Cookbook.
1966. $6.00

Cooking Club Magazine.
1917. $14.00

The Dining Room Magazine.
1876. $30.00

Dr. King's New Guide To
Health. 1909. $20.00

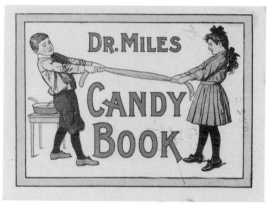

Dr. Miles Candy Book. 1910. $16.00

The Enterprising Housekeeper.
1902. $16.00

Fireless Cooking.
1920's. $12.00

Food And Fun.
1953. $6.00

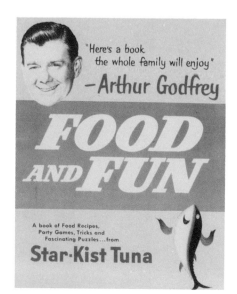

15

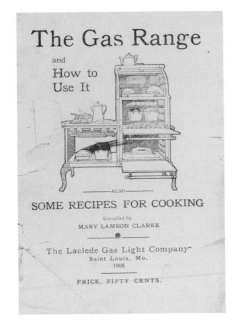

**Good Pies - Easy To Make.
1920. $12.00**

**Hess Happy-Home Cook
Book. 1920. $12.00**

The Gas Range. 1906. $16.00

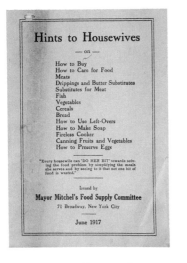

**Hints to Housewives.
1917. $14.00**

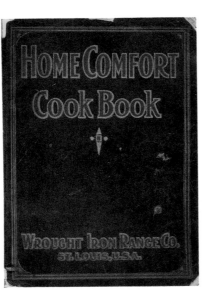

**Home Comfort Cook Book.
1925. $12.00**

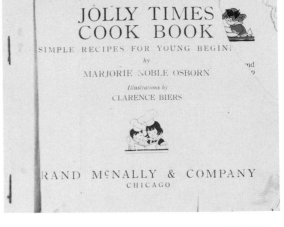

Jolly Times Cook Book. 1934. $10.00

**Kate Smith's Favorite
Recipes. 1939. $10.00**

**Kraft
Cheese And Ways to
Serve It. 1921. $12.00**

Cheese recipes for wartime meals

HOW TO MAKE YOUR CHEESE GO FURTHER

Kraft
Cheese Recipes
For Wartime
Meals. 1943.
$8.00

MENUS AND RECIPES

Tested and Approved by
THE KROGER FOOD FOUNDATION

...... to help you plan
your meals for contrasts of

texture,
flavor
and color

Kroger
Menus and Recipes. Circa 1930.
$5.00

CANNING "DO'S" AND CANNING "DON'TS"

Prepared by
THE KROGER
FOOD FOUNDATION

Bulletin No. 11   © 1931, The K. G. & B. Co.

Kroger
Canning "Do's" and Canning
"Don'ts." 1931. $5.00

Three R's
to remember in
Feeding School Children

Prepared by
THE KROGER
FOOD FOUNDATION

Bulletin No. 13   © 1931, The K. G. & B. Co.

Kroger
Three R's To Remember in
Feeding School Children. 1931.
$5.00

HOW to MAKE the MENU
PLEASE the CROWD
— AND PAY A PROFIT

THE KROGER FOOD FOUNDATION
talks quantity and quality—tells you what
to serve...how much to buy...what to
charge...how much you'll make

(E)

Kroger
How to Make The Menu Please the
Crowd - And Pay A Profit. 1933.
$10.00

THE LARKIN IDEA
JUNE 1916

The Larkin Idea.
1916. $14.00

Libby's
FANCY RED ALASKA
SALMON
Libby, McNeill & Libby, Chicago, U.S.A.

Libby's Fancy Red Alaska Salmon.
1935. $10.00

Leibig Company's Cook
Book. 1893. $20.00

Majestic Cook Book. 1899.
$20.00

Marion Harland's
Recipe Calendar.
1924. $24.00

McCall's
Time-Saving Cookery. 1922.
$12.00

McCall's
What To Serve At Parties.
1923. $12.00

McCall's Basic Cake Book. 1956.
$6.00

Meletio's Home Cook
Book and Encyclopedia.
1925. $12.00

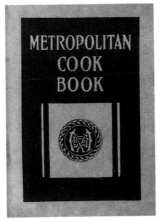

Metropolitan Cook
Book. 1918. $14.00

Metropolitan Cook
Boook. 1922. $12.00

**Metropolitan
The Family Food
Supply. 1928. $12.00**

**Modern Household Helps.
1903. $20.00**

**Mrs. Winslow's
Domestic Receipt
Book For 1873.
$28.00**

**Mrs. Winslow's Domestic
Receipt Book For 1878.
$28.00**

**My Meat Recipes.
1926. $12.00**

**New Art Refrigerator
Recipe Book. 1940. $8.00**

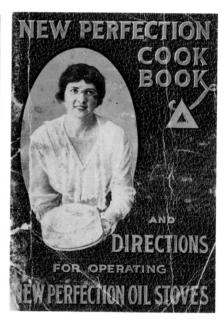

**New Perfection Cook Book.
1895. $20.00**

**The New Perfection
Cook Book. 1923.
$12.00**

**100 Old Fashioned
Cooking Recipes. 1910.
$16.00**

19

101 Ways To Prepare
Macaroni. 1949. $8.00

One Man's Family -
Mother Barbour's Favorite
Recipes. 1952. $15.00

Original Menus. 1908.
$16.00

Papa Cribari in Cucina.
Circa 1950. $6.00

Peanut's Cook Book. 1969. $6.00

Pennsylvania Dutch
Cooking. 1960. $6.00

The Peter Pan Peanut Butter
Cook Book. 1963. $3.00

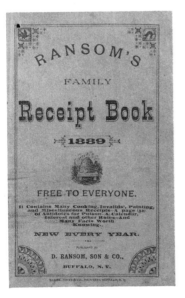

Ransom's Family Receipt
Book. 1889. $24.00

Ransom's Family Receipt
Book. 1906. $16.00

Ransom's Family
Receipt Book.
1907. $16.00

Ransom's Family Receipt
Book. 1908. $16.00

The Recipe Book for Club
Aluminum Ware. 1925.
$12.00

Recipes For Trade Mark Pureed
Fruits and Vegetables. 1930.
$10.00

Recipes For War Breads.
1917. $14.00

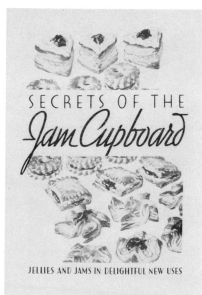

Secrets of the Jam Cupboard.
1930. $10.00

Tables and Favors.
1922. $12.00

Three Hundred and Ten Daily
Recipes and Menus For Home
and For Guests. 1930. $10.00

Treasured Recipes
of the Old South.
1941. $8.00

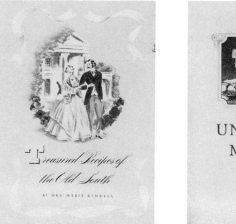

Unusual Meats. 1919.
$14.00

Victory Cook Book.
1943. $8.00

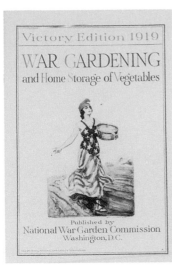

War Gardening and Home
Storage of Vegetables.
1917. $14.00

Warner's Safe Cook Book.
1889. $24.00

Warner's Safe Cure
Telephone Book and
Cooking Recipes. 1893.
$16.00

Westinghouse
Refrigerators.
1948. $8.00

The Wilken Family Home Entertaining Album. 1937. $10.00

Woman's Day Cook Book of
Favorite Recipes. 1963.
$2.00

The Wonder Sandwich Book.
1928. $12.00

Yacht Club Manual of Salads.
1914. $14.00

Confessions of 211 St. Louis Housewives and Bob Hope...or, What's
Going On In Their Kitchens! 1967.
$4.00

Golden Anniversary Cook
Book. 1949. $8.00

Hood's High Street Cook
Book. 1887. $24.00

The Ladies' Delight Cook
Book. 1889. $24.00

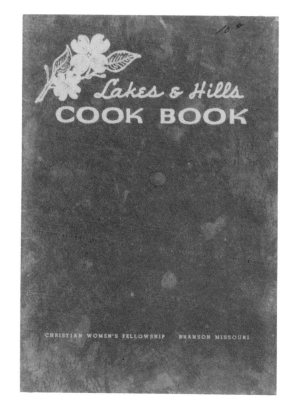

Lakes & Hills Cook Book. 1936. $10.00

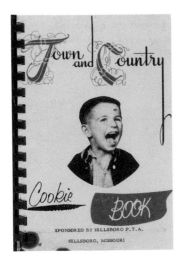

Town and Country Cookie
Book. 1953. $6.00

Electric Cook Book.
1910. $16.00

Murphy's Pets. 1899. $10.00

Favorite Recipes from
The United Nations.
1956. $6.00

KTTR Problems & Solutions Cook
Book. 1969. $4.00

Your Neighbor Lady Book. 1956.
$6.00

Ball Blue Book. 1915.
$25.00

Ball Blue Book. 1916.
$25.00

Ball Blue Book.
1926. $20.00

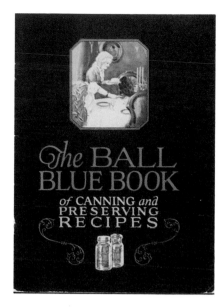

Kerr
Modern Home
Canning in Economy
Jars. 1905. $16.00

Kerr
Economy Jar Home
Canning Recipes.
1909. $16.00

Kerr
Home Canning Book. 1916. $14.00

**Kerr Home Canning Book.
1935. $20.00**

**Kerr Home Canning Book.
1942. $8.00**

**Finer Canned & Frozen
Fruits. 1946. $8.00**

**Home Freezing of Fruits
and Vegetables.
Circa 1947. $8.00**

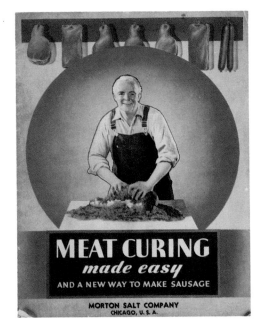

Recipes for Meat Dishes. 1950. $6.00

**Meat Curing Made Easy.
1933. $10.00**

**The Salties.
Circa 1920.
$12.00**

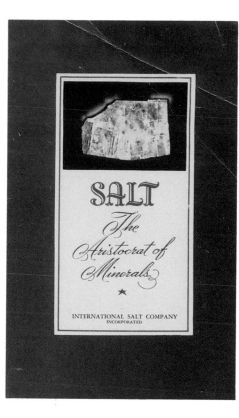

Salt, The Aristocrat of Minerals.
Circa 1940.
$8.00

Home Pickling and Salting Vegetables.
1943. $4.00

Chocolate

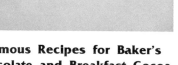

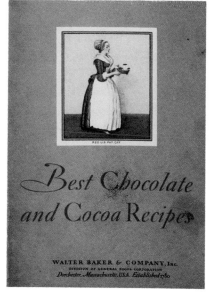

**Baker's Chocolate
Choice Receipts By
Miss Parloa. 1897.
$20.00**

**Baker's Chocolate.
Choice Recipes. 1901.
$16.00**

**Famous Recipes for Baker's
Chocolate and Breakfast Cocoa.
1928. $12.00**

**Baker's Chocolate
Best Chocolate and Cocoa
Recipes. 1931. $10.00**

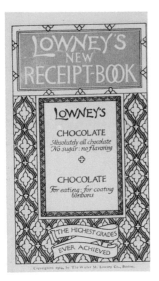

Lowney's New Receipt-
Book. 1904. $16.00

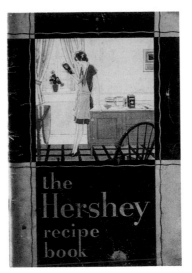

The Hershey Recipe Book.
1930. $10.00

Nestlés Semi-Sweet
Chocolate Kitchen
Recipes. 1959. $6.00

Baking Powder

Dr. Price's
Table and Kitchen.
1893. $20.00

Dr. Price's
Table and Kitchen.
1908. $16.00

The New Dr. Price
Cook Book. 1921.
$12.00

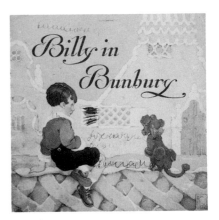

Dr. Price's
Billy in Bunbury. 1925. $12.00

Royal Baker And Pastry
Cook. 1898. $24.00

Royal Baker And Pastry
Cook. 1902. $16.00

28

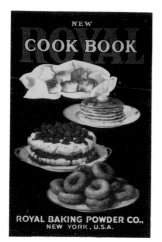

New Royal Cook
Book. 1922. $12.00

The Little Gingerbread Man.
1923. $20.00

The Horsford Almanac
and Cook Book.
1879. $28.00

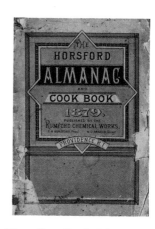

Rumford
The New Horsford's Bread
and Pastry Cook. Circa
1865. $30.00

The Horsford Almanac
& Cook Book. 1883.
$24.00

Cozinhados Saudaveis
Com O Po´ De Levedura.
Circa 1890. $30.00

Rumford, The Wholesome
Baking Powder. 1907.
$16.00

Rumford, The Whole-
some Baking Powder.
1913. $14.00

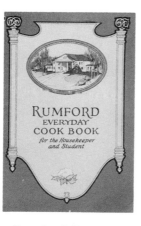

Rumford Everyday
Cook Book For The
Housekeeper and
Student. Circa 1919.
$14.00

Rumford Nya Bakbok.
1922. $25.00

Rumford
Several New Things
Under The Sun.
1929. $25.00

Clabber Girl
The Old, Healthy,
Family Baking Powder.
1923. $12.00

Clabber Girl - The
Healthy Baking Powder.
1931. $10.00

Calumet
Reliable Recipes. 1914.
$14.00

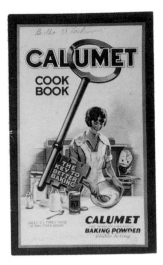

Calumet Cook Book.
1922. $12.00

Calumet
Happy Times Recipe Book. 1934.
$10.00

Cook Book, Dry Yeast
Baking Powder. Circa
1880's. $25.00

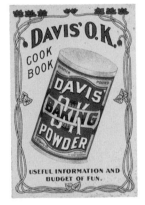

Davis' O.K. Cook
Book. 1907. $16.00

KC Cook's Book.
1942. $8.00

Cleveland's Superior
Receipts. 1895.
$20.00

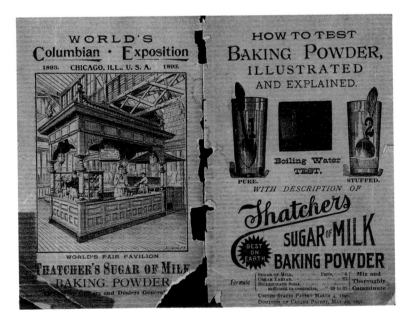

Thatchers
How To Test Baking
Powder. 1894.
$24.00

New Reducing Diet Menus With Domino Sugar. 1954. $6.00

Sugar Spoon Recipes From the Domino Sugar Bowl Kitchen. 1962. $4.00

So You're Canning... Circa 1950. $4.00

Old Favorite Honey Recipes. 1945. $6.00

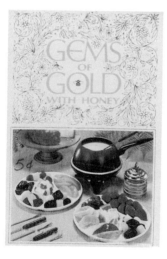

Gems of Gold With Honey. 1963. $4.00

Brer Rabbit's Modern Recipes for Modern Living. Circa 1930. $10.00

Corn Products Cook Book. 1915. $14.00

Corn Products Cook Book. 1916. $14.00

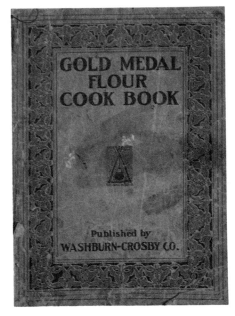

Gold Medal Flour Cook Book.
1904. $16.00

Swans Down
Igleheart's Cake
Secrets. 1915.
$14.00

Swans Down
Igleheart's Cake
Secrets. 1922.
$12.00

How to Bake by the Ration
Book. 1943. $8.00

The Pillsbury Cook Book.
1914. $14.00

Pillsbury's Cook
Book. 1929. $12.00

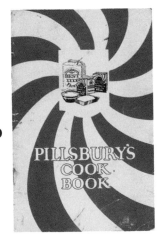

Swans Down
Cake Secrets. 1953.
$6.00

The Talking Millstones.
1945. $25.00

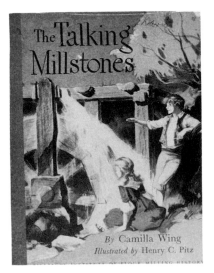

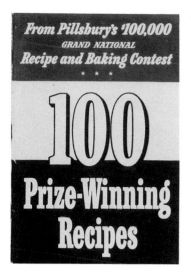

100 Prize-Winning
Recipes. 1950. $20.00

100 Prize-Winning
Recipes. 1951. $15.00

Kate Smith Chooses Her 55 Favorite
Cake Recipes. 1952. $6.00

100 Prize Winning
Recipes. 1953. $15.00

100 Prize Winning
Recipes. 1953. $10.00

Standard-Tilton
War Time Recipes.
1917. $20.00

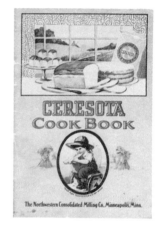

Ceresota Cook Book.
Circa 1880. $30.00

Larabee's Best Flour.
1931. $10.00

The Town Crier
Baking Guide. 1932.
$10.00

Aristos Flour Cook
Book. 1911. $25.00

Occident Flour
Tested Recipes.
1936. $10.00

Occident Flour
Tested Recipes.
1939. $10.00

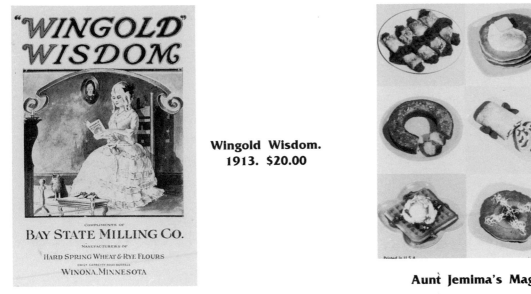

Wingold Wisdom.
1913. $20.00

Aunt Jemima's Magical Recipes. 1952. $6.00

Arm & Hammer Baking Soda

Book of Valuable
Recipes. 1916. $14.00

Arm & Hammer Almanac.
1920. $12.00

Good Things To Eat.
1924. $12.00

It's All In Knowing How.
1934. $10.00

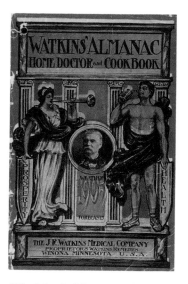

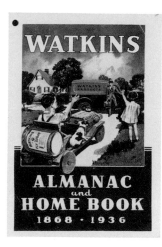

Watkins' Almanac Home Doctor and Cook Book. 1905. $16.00

Watkins' Almanac Home Doctor and Cook Book. 1907. $16.00

Watkins Almanac Home Doctor & Cook Book. 1915. $14.00

Watkins Almanac and Home Book. 1936. $10.00

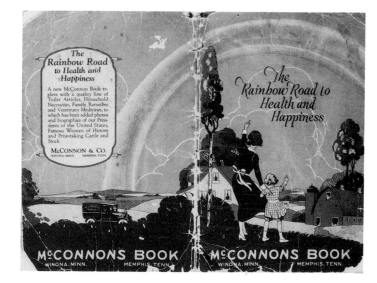

The Rainbow Road to Health and Happiness. 1926. $12.00

Aunt Jane's Cook Book. 1939. $10.00

Quality Helps For Home Makers. 1923. $12.00

Rawleigh's Good Health Guide Almanac Cook Book.
1922. $12.00

Rawleigh's Good Health Guide and Cook Book.
1929. $12.00

Rawleigh's Good Health
Guide Cook Book and Year
Book. 1932. $10.00

Tested Recipes with
Blue Ribbon Malt
Extract. 1927. $12.00

Burnett's
What's Cooking? 1940's.
$8.00

F.W. McNess' Cook Book
and Health Hints. 1915.
$14.00

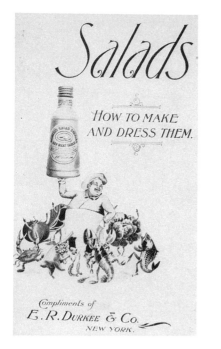

Salads - How To Make And Dress Them. 1907. $16.00

Golden Rule Foods...The Golden Rule Way. Circa 1920. $12.00

Receipts For Cakes, Creams, Custards, Candies, Etc. 1890's. $20.00

Yeast

Fleischmann's Bake It Easy! 1961. $3.00

Fleischmann's The Young Cook's Bake-A-Bun Book. 1967. $3.00

Northwestern The Art of Baking Bread. Circa 1920. $12.00

Maca The Art of Making Bread at Home. 1939. $20.00

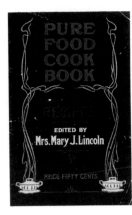

Cottolene
600 Selected Recipes.
1892. $24.00

Cottolene
Pure Food Cook
Book. 1907. $20.00

Home Helps - A
Pure Food Cook
Book. 1910. $20.00

Spry
Aunt Jenny's 12 Pies
Husbands Like Best.
1952. $5.00

Spry
Home Baking Made Easy
For Beginners and
Experts. 1953. $5.00

Spry 20th Anniversary
Cookbook of Old and
New Favorites. 1955.
$7.00

Mazola Recipes.
1915. $14.00

Better Foods With
This Pure Oil.
1923. $12.00

Wesson Oil
Recipes. 1911.
$16.00

Planter's Peanut Oil
They Taste So-o-o
Good! 1955. $4.00

Staley's
Children's Party Book. 1935.
$10.00

Good Luck Recipes.
1916. $14.00

Three Meals A Day -
With Nucoa. 1930.
$10.00

Nucoa
My Special Date Bake
Book. 1931. $10.00

Silver Churn Butterine
Cook Book. Circa 1880.
$24.00

Silver Churn
Veribest Economy.
1918. $14.00

Nuts And Fruits

Baker's Cocoanut
Recipes. 1911.
$16.00

Baker's Coconut
Recipes. 1926. $14.00

A Few of the Delicious
Desserts Made With
Dunham's Original Shred
Cocoanut. Circa 1890.
$20.00

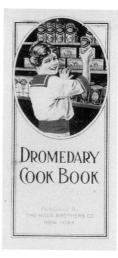

Dromedary Cook
Book. 1914.
$14.00

**Dromedary Cocoanut
Food From Sunny Lands.
1925. $12.00**

**United Fruit Company
The New Banana.
1931. $10.00**

**Fruit Dispatch Co.
Banana Salad Bazar.
1940. $8.00**

**Chiquita Banana's Recipe
Book. 1950. $6.00**

**Sun-Maid Raisins. 1921.
$12.00**

**Sunkist Recipes,
Oranges-Lemons.
1916. $14.00**

**Busy-Day Salads
and Desserts. Circa
1919. $14.00**

**Downright Delicious Sun-
Maid Raisin Recipes.
1949. $8.00**

**Dole Pineapple
The Kingdom That Grew Out
Of A Little Boy's Garden.
1930. $18.00**

**Florida Citrus Commission.
Favorite Recipes from Florida. 1960. $4.00**

Cox's Manual of
Gelatine Cookery.
1914. $14.00

Royal Desserts. 1932.
$10.00

The Story of Plymouth
Rock. 1901. $16.00

Plymouth Rock
Gelatine Dainties
and Household
Helps. 1910.
$16.00

Dainty Desserts For
Dainty People. 1924.
$12.00

Knox Gelatine
Dainty Desserts-
Salads-Candies.
1927. $12.00

JELL-O. 1904. $100.00

JELL-O The Dainty
Dessert. 1905. $75.00

JELL-O Ice Cream
Powder. 1906.
$65.00

JELL-O The Dainty
Dessert. 1908.
$60.00

JELL-O
Desserts of the World.
1909. $60.00

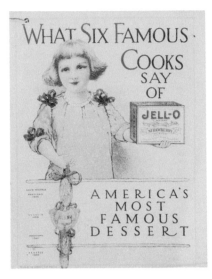

What Six Famous Cooks Say
of JELL-O. 1912. $55.00

"Yes, JELL-O, Please, All
Seven Flavors." 1912.
$55.00

"Even If You Can't Cook, You
Can Make a JELL-O Dessert."
1913. $55.00

The JELL-O Girl Entertains.
1914. $55.00

The JELL-O Girl Gives A Party.
1914. $55.00

JELL-O and the Kewpies.
1915. $55.00

JELL-O America's
Most Famous Dessert.
1916. $50.00

All Doors Open To
JELL-O. 1917. $50.00

New Talks About JELL-O.
1918. $14.00

For Economy Use JELL-O.
$12.00

"It's So Simple." 1922.
$15.00

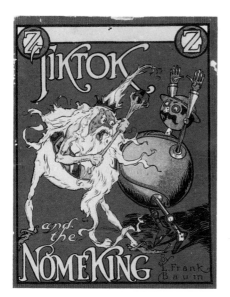

Polly Put The Kettle On
We'll All Make JELL-O.
1924. $45.00

Untitled. 1925.
$15.00

Tiktok and the Nome King.
1933-1934. $50.00

All Eyes On The New Creation.
Circa 1890. $2.50

Jack & Mary's JELL-O Recipe
Book. 1937. $35.00

**New York Condensed
Milk Company. 1892.
$25.00**

**Borden's Evaporated
Milk Book of Recipes.
Circa 1919. $14.00**

**Borden's
New Magic In The
Kitchen. 1931. $10.00**

**108 World's Fair Recipes
From Borden's. 1933-1934.
$10.00**

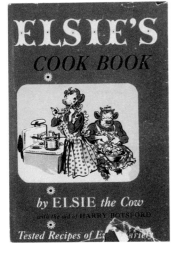

**Elsie's Cook Book. 1952.
$20.00**

**Borden's
Starlac Presents Food In
Fiction. 1953. $6.00**

**Pet Milk Company
Recipe Book. 1923.
$12.00**

**Pet Milk
Tempting Low Cost Meals
for 2 or 4 or 6. 1940.
$6.00**

**Pet Milk
Cookbook for
Young Moderns.
1957. $4.00**

**Carnation
100 Glorified Recipes.
1934. $10.00**

**Growing Up With Milk.
1942. $8.00**

**Carnation
Baking Secrets. 1953.
$6.00**

**Teen-Time Cooking with
Carnation. 1959. $6.00**

**Fun To Cook Book.
1967. $3.00**

**Quality Dairy
King Quality Presents
the VIP Stand-Up
Cook Book. 1964.
$3.00**

**Aunt Sally's Favorite
Recipes. 1935. $10.00**

Desserts

**Frozen Dainties.
1899. $20.00**

**White Mountain
Frozen Dainties.
1905. $16.00**

**North Brothers
Dainty Dishes For
All The Year
Round. 1897.
$20.00**

Dainty Dishes For All The Year Round. 1905. $16.00

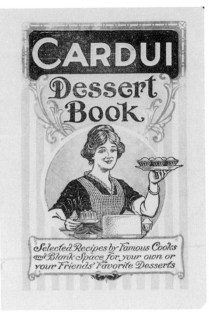

North Brothers Cardui Dessert Book. 1914. $14.00

HAVE SOME JUNKET.

Have Some Junket. 1902. $16.00

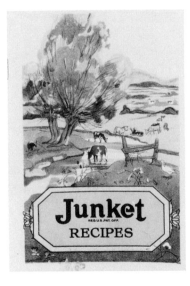

Junket Recipes. 1926. $12.00

Junket How To Make Tempting Nutritious Desserts. 1941. $8.00

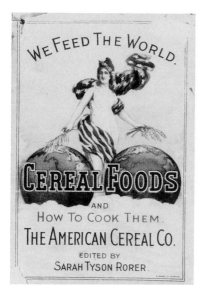

**We Feed The World. 1899.
$25.00**

**Shredded Wheat
More Light. 1898. $20.00**

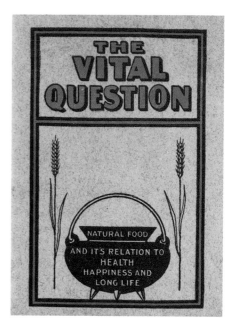

The Vital Question. 1906. $16.00

**Fifty Ways of Serving
Shredded Wheat.
1924. $12.00**

**Recipes For New and
Delicious Energy Dishes.
1933. $10.00**

Cerealine Flakes. 1886. $25.00

**Cream of Rice, The
World's Best Food. Circa
1890. $25.00**

Kellogg's
The Sunny Side of Life Book.
1934. $10.00

Ralston Purina
Breakfast Around The World.
Circa 1940. $8.00

Better Homes & Gardens

In July of 1922 a magazine was published titled *Fruit Garden And Home.* It was a new monthly full of practical advice. By the latter part of 1924 the name was changed to *Better Homes & Gardens* and included such information as: decorating help, electric refrigerators, a new way to keep foods fresh, electric kitchens, new appliances making cooking easier, families and their cars, the new auto industry, the home front, Victory gardens, and more. The following is what we have been able to collect or have knowledge of:

1930, 1937 - *Better Homes and Gardens Cook Book.* The Home Service Bureau, three-ring binder. **$25.00**

1930, 1931, 1932, 1933, 1935 - *Better Homes and Gardens Cook Book.* 13th printing, The Home Service Bureau, three-ring binder. **$20.00**

1938 - *My New Better Homes and Gardens Cook Book.* Three-ring binder. **$20.00**

1940 - *My New Better Homes and Gardens Cook Book.* Fifth edition, sprial. **$17.50**

1949 - *Better Homes & Gardens Cook Book.* Spiral. **$15.00**

1953 - *Better Homes and Gardens New Cook Book.* Myrna Johnston, Director of Foods Department, five-ring binder. **$12.00**

1955 - *Better Homes and Gardens Junior Cook Book.* 78 pages. **$12.00**

1958 - *Salad Book.* 156 pages. **$12.00**

1959 - *Holiday Cook Book.* 160 pages. **$12.00**

1959 - *Meat Cook Book.* 160 pages. **$12.00**

1959, 1961 *Holiday Cook Book.* 160 pages. **$10.00**

1959, 1962 - *Meat Cook Book.* 160 pages. **$10.00**

1955, 1963 - *Better Homes and Gardens Junior Cook Book.* 78 pages. **$10.00**

1963 - *Bread Cook Book.* 160 pages. **$10.00**

1963 - *Best Buffets.* 62 pages. **$10.00**

1963 - *So-Good Meals.* 62 pages. **$10.00**

1963 - *Meals In Minutes.* 62 pages. **$10.00**

1952, 1962, 1965 - *Meat Cook Book.* 160 pages. **$5.00**

1965 - *Vegetable Cookbook.* 160 pages. **$7.50**

1965 - *Barbecue Book.* 156 pages. **$7.50**

1965 - *Better Homes & Gardens New Cook Book.* 394 pages. **$10.00**

1966 - *Pies and Cakes.* 96 pages. **$7.50**

1966 - *Cookies and Candies.* 72 pages. **$7.50**

1958, 1966 - *Salad Book.* 156 pages. **$5.00**

1963, 1967 - *Bread Cookbook.* 160 pages. **$5.00**

1966, 1967 - *Cookies and Candies.* 92 pages. **$5.00**

1967 - *Jiffy Cooking.* **$5.00**

1968 - *Better Homes & Gardens New Cook Book.* 400 pages. **$10.00**

1968 - *Casserole Cook Book.* 160 pages. **$5.00**

1968 - *Cooking For Two, Menus and Recipes for Every Occasion.* **$5.00**

1966, 1967, 1968 - *Cookies and Candies.* 90 pages. **$5.00**

1958, 1966, 1969 - *Salad Book.,* 156 pages. **$2.50**

1969 - *Dessert Cookbook.* 160 pages. **$2.50**

1969 - *Holiday Cook Book - Special Occasions.* Ninth printing, 160 pages. **$2.50**

1969 - *Meat Cookbook.* Over 400 meat recipes, 160 pages. **$2.50**

1969, 1970 - *Dessert Cookbook.* 160 pages. **NCV**

1965, 1970 - *Barbecue Book.* 156 pages. **NCV**

1968, 1970 - *Casserole Cookbook.* 160 pages. **NCV**

1968, 1970 - *Better Homes & Gardens New Cookbook.* Three-ring binder, 400 pages. **NCV**

1970 - *Better Homes & Gardens New Cookbook.* Sixth printing, three-ring binder, 400 pages. **NCV**

1970 - *Better Homes and Gardens Encyclopedia of Cooking.* Volume 1-20. **NCV**

1970, 1971 - *Better Homes and Gardens Encyclopedia of Cooking.* Volume 1-20. **NCV**

1966, 1967, 1968, 1971 - Cookies and Candies. 90 pages. **NCV**

1968, 1970, 1973 - Better Homes & Gardens New Cookbook. Sixth printing, 400 pages. **NCV**

1970, 1971, 1973 - Better Homes & Gardens Encyclopedia of Cooking. Volume 1-20, special edition, second printing. **NCV**

1973 - Homemade Bread Cook Book. 90 pages. **NCV**

1974 - Christmas-Time Cookbook. **NCV**

1975 - Better Homes & Gardens New Cookbook. 400 pages. **NCV**

1977 - All Time Favorite Beef Recipes. First edition. **NCV**

1978 - Better Homes & Gardens Complete Step-by-Step Cookbook. **NCV**

1988 - Better Homes & Gardens Best Barbecue Recipes. **NCV**

1989 - Better Homes & Gardens Quick & Easy Recipes - Good Food and Good Ideas from Kraft. Soft-cover. **NCV**

1989 - Better Homes & Gardens Eating Healthy Cook Book. 288 pages. **NCV**

1989 - Better Homes and Gardens Tasty Timesaving Cooking. 466 recipes. **NCV**

◊◊◊◊

Better Meals for Less Money. 1931, Green. **$15.00**

Betty Crocker's Kitchen Gardeners, A Year Round Guide to Growing & Using Herbs & Vegetables. 1971, Mary M. Campbell, illus. by Tasha Tudor, Universal Publications, INc., 170 pages. **NCV**

The Betty Furness Westinghouse Cook Book. First printing, 1954, Julia Kiene, 496 pages. **$12.00**

Beverages and Sandwiches for your Husband's Friends. 1893, 48 pages. **$25.00**

The Bible Cook Book. 1958, Marian Maeve O'Brien, The Bethony Press, St. Louis. **$12.00**

Biblical Garden Cookery. 1976, Eileen Gaden, Christian Herald Books, 214 pages. **NCV**

The Blender Cookbook. 1961, Seranne and Gaden, New York. **$5.00**

The Blue Book of Cookery. Second priting, 1926, 650 pages. **$25.00**

Blue Book of Cooking. 1938, University of Michigan Alumnae, spiral, 204 pages. **$20.00**

Blueberry Hill Cookboook. 1959, Elsie Masterton. **$12.00**
Blueberry Hill Menu Cookbook. 1963, Elsie Masterton, 374 pages, **$10.00**

The Bon Appetit Dinner Party Cook Book. 1984, Knapp Publishers. **NCV**

The Bontempi Cook Book. 1965, Fedora Bontempi. **$10.00**

A Book of Appetizers. 1958, Helen Evans Brown. **$10.00**

The Book of Entrees. First edition, 1911, Janet M. Hill, 366 pages. **$35.00**

The Book of Entrees. 1911, 1915, Janet M. Hill, 366 pages. **$25.00**

Book of Entrees. 1927, Lucy G. Allen. **$25.00**

A Book of Good Dinners For My Friend or What to Have for Dinner. 1905, 1914, Fannie Merritt Farmer, Dodge Publishing Company, stiff covers, 259 pages. **$30.00**

A Book of Hors d'Oeuvres. 1941, Lucy G. Allen. **$17.50**

A Book of Middle Eastern Food. 1968, Claudia Roden, Britain. **$10.00**

A Book of Middle Eastern Food. 1972, American Edition. **NCV**

A Book of Practical Recipes For The Housewife. 1934, Detroit Times. **$20.00**

A Book of Unusual Soups. 1923, 1930, Mary D. Chambers, 162 pages. **$20.00**

Books & My Food - Original Recipes with Little Quotations for Every Day in the Year. 1906, E.L. Cory & A.M. Jones. **$30.00**

Boston Cook Book. 1883, 1887, 1902, Mrs. D.A. Lincoln (Mary J.). **$35.00**

The Boston Cooking-School Cook Book. 1896, 1897, Fannie Merritt Farmer, Boston: Little Brown & Company, 1897 printing of 1896 copyright, 567 pages. **$250.00**

The Boston Cooking-School Cook Book. 1896, 1900, 1901, 1902, 1903, 1904, 1905, 1906, Fannie Merritt Farmer, Boston, 1912 printing of 1906 copyright, 648 pages. **$100.00**

The Boston Cooking-School Cook Book. 1896, 1900, 1901, 1902, 1903, 1904, 1905, 1906, 1914, Fannie Merritt Farmer, copyright 1914 by Fannie Merritt Farmer, 648 pages. **$100.00**

The Boston Cooking-School Cook Book. 1896, 1900, 1901, 1902, 1903, 1904, 1905, 1906, 1914, 1918, Fannie Merritt Farmer, copyright 1918 by Mary W. Farmer, 656 pages. **$75.00**

The Boston Cooking-School Cook Book. 1896, 1900, 1901, 1902, 1903, 1904, 1905, 1906, 1914, 1918, Fannie Merritt Farmer, 1919 printing of Mary W. Farmer's copyright of 1918, 656 pages. **$50.00**

The Boston Cooking-School Cook Book. 1896, 1900, 1901, 1902, 1903, 1904, 1905, 1906, 1914, 1918, Fannie Merritt Farmer, 1920 printing of Mary W. Farmer's copyright of 1918. **$50.00**

The Boston Cooking-School Cook Book. 1896, 1900, 1901, 1902, 1903, 1904, 1905, 1906, 1914, 1918, Fannie Merritt Farmer, 1921 printing of Mary W. Farmer's copyright of 1918. **$40.00**

The Boston Cooking-School Cook Book. 1896, 1900, 1901, 1902, 1903, 1904, 1905, 1906, 1914, 1918, 1923, Fannie Merritt Farmer, 1923 copyright by Cora D. Perkins, 806 pages. **$30.00**

The Boston Cooking-School Cook Book. 1896, 1900, 1901, 1902, 1903, 1904, 1905, 1906, 1914, 1918, 1923, 1924, Fannie Merritt Farmer, 1924 copyright by Cora D. Perkins, 808 pages. **$25.00**

The Boston Cooking-School Cook Book. 1896, 1900, 1901, 1902, 1903, 1904, 1905, 1906, 1914, 1918, 1923, 1924, 1927, 1928 copyrights by Cora D. Perkins; 1930, 1931, 1932, 1933, 1934 copyrights by Dexter Perkins; Fannie Merritt Farmer, 1934 printing of the 1934 copyright, 831 pages. **$20.00**

The Boston Cooking-School Cook Book. 1896, 1900, 1901, 1902, 1903, 1904, 1905, 1906, 1914, 1918, 1923, 1924, 1927, 1928, 1930, 1931, 1932, 1933, 1934 by Dexter Perkins; Fannie Merritt Farmer, 1935 printing of the 1934 copyright, 831 pages. **$15.00**

The Boston Cooking-School Cook Book. 1896, 1900, 1901, 1902, 1903, 1904, 1905, 1906, 1914, 1918, 1923, 1924, 1927, 1928, 1930, 1931, 1932, 1933, 1934, 1936 by Dexter Perkins; Fannie Merritt Farmer, 1937 printing of the 1936 copyright, 838 pages. **$15.00**

The Boston Cooking-School Cook Book. 1896, 1900, 1901, 1902, 1903, 1904, 1905, 1906, 1914, 1918, 1923, 1924, 1927, 1928, 1930, 1931, 1932, 1933, 1934, 1936 by Dexter Perkins; Fannie Merritt Farmer, 1938 printing of the 1936 copyright, 838 pages. $12.00

The Boston Cooking-School Cook Book. 1896, 1900, 1901, 1902, 1903, 1904, 1905, 1906, 1914, 1918, 1923, 1924, 1927, 1928, 1930, 1931, 1932, 1933, 1934, 1936, 1941, 1942 by Dexter Perkins; Fannie Merritt Farmer, 1942 printing of the 1942 copyright, 830 pages. **$12.00**

The Boston Cooking-School Cook Book. 1896, 1900, 1901, 1902, 1903, 1904, 1905, 1906, 1914, 1918, 1923, 1924, 1927, 1928, 1930, 1931, 1932, 1933, 1934, 1936, 1941, 1942, by Dexter Perkins; Fannie Merritt Farmer, 1943 printing of 1942 copyright claimed by Wilma Lord Perkins, seventh edition, revised by Wilma Lord Perkins, **$10.00**

The Boston Cooking-School Cook Book. 1896, 1900, 1901, 1902, 1903, 1904, 1905, 1906, 1914, 1918, 1923, 1924, 1927, 1928, 1930, 1931, 1932, 1933, 1934, 1936, 1941, 1942, by Dexter Perkins; Fannie Merritt Farmer, 1945 printing of 1942 copyright claimed by Wilma Lord Perkins, seventh edition, completely revised by Wilma Lord Perkins. **$10.00**

Boston School Kitchen Text Book. 1887, Mrs. D.A. (Mary J.) Lincoln, 237 pages. **$45.00**

Boston School Kitchen Text Book. 1887, 1909, Mrs. D.A. (Mary J.) Lincoln, 237 pages. **$30.00**

Boston's Locke-Ober Cafe. Ned & Pam Bradford, 1978. **NCV**

Bread and Bread Making. 1887, S.T. Rorer, Arnold & Co., Philadelphia. **$50.00**

Breads, Cakes and Pies in Family Meals. 1971. **NCV**

Breakfasts, Luncheons, Dinners. 1928, Mary D. Chambers. **$25.00**

The Bride's Book of Recipes and Household Hints. 1947, Carleton J. West, publisher, spiral, stiff cover. **$12.50**

The Bride's Cook Book. First edition, 1954, Poppy Cannon, 400 pages. **$12.00**

Bride's Favorite Receipts. 1960, gift of Clerk of Marion County, Indianapolis, Indiana. **$10.00**

Bride's View of Cooking Cookbook. 1974, Elise Maclay, G.R. Gibson Company, publishers, 121 pages. **NCV**

Bronxville War Cook Book. 1917, by The Thrift Committee of the National League for Women's Service in Bronxville, New York. **$25.00**

The Brown Bag Cookbook. 1974, John A. Gould, Doubleday, 154 pages. **NCV**

Brunches and Coffees. 1969, Marion Courtney. **$7.50**

Buckeye Cookery and Practical Housekeeping. 1877, Buckeye Publishers. **$75.00**

Buckeye Cookery With Hints on Practical Housekeeping. 1877, 1883, Buckeye Publishers. **$45.00**

The New Buckeye Cook Book. 1888, 1890, a revised and enlarged edition of Practical Housekeeping, sold only by subscription, The Home Publishing Co., Dayton, Ohio, copyright by Estelle W. Wilcox, 1,288 pages. **$35.00**

Bull Cook and Authentic Historical Recipes and Practices. 1960, 1961, 1962, 1963, 1964, 1965, E. Herter, 352 pages. **$10.00**

The Butterick Book of Recipes and Household Helps. 1927, Butterick Publishing Co., 256 pages. **$25.00**

The Butterick Cook Book. 1911, The Butterick Publishing Co. **$30.00**

Cafeteria Recipes. 1925, Mable E. Schadt, small limited edition. **$30.00**

Cake and Food Decorating. 1956, by Wecolite. **$12.00**

Cake-Art-Craft - Learn How to Decorate. 1930, Fred Abuer, Chicago. **$20.00**

Cakes, Pastry and Dessert Dishes. 1917, 1925, Janet M. Hill, 276 pages. **$30.00**

A Calendar of Dinners with 616 Recipes. 18th edition, 1921, Marion Harris Neil, Story of Crisco. **$25.00**

Calorie Book of Recipes. 1909. **$30.00**

Calories Don't Count. 1961, Herm Taller, M.D. **$10.00**

Camp Cookery. 1878, Maria Parloa. **$60.00**

Camp Cookery. 1910, Horace Kephart, New York, 170 pages. **$30.00**

◊ ◊ ◊ ◊

Campbell's Soup

In 1869 Joseph Campbell and Abram Anderson began their small canning operation in Camden, New Jersey, making preserves, salad dressing, ketchup and canning vegetables. Anderson left the company in 1876. Joseph Campbell retired in 1894 and the company was incorporated as Joseph Campbell Company in 1905. In 1922, the name was changed to Campbell Soup Company.

By 1900, Campbell's was involved mainly with the canning of concentrated soup. 1904 was the birth of Campbell's pork and beans, and that was also the year that the Campbell kids were introduced. The following is what we have collected from Campbell's:

1963 - *A Campbell Cookbook - Cooking with Soup.* Home Economics Department, spiral, 200 pages. **$10.00**

1965 - *A Campbell Cookbook - Cooking with Soup.* 608 skillet dishes, casseroles, stews, etc., spiral, 200 pages. **$10.00**

1968 - *A Campbell Cookbook - Cooking with Soup.* Home Economics Department, 608 skillet dishes, casseroles, stews, sauces, gravies, dips, soup mates and garnishes, spiral, 200 pages. **$5.00**

1968 - *A Campbell Cookbook - Cooking with Soup.* A revised edition, Home Economics Department, 608 skillet dishes, casseroles, stews, sauces, gravies, dips, soup mates and garnishes, 200 pages. **$5.00**

1975 - *A Campbell Cookbook - Most-For-The-Money Main Dishes.* First edition, Home Economists of Campbell Kitchens, spiral, 136 pages. **NCV**

◊ ◊ ◊ ◊

Campbell's Great Restaurant Cook Book. 1969, Doris Townsend, Rutledge Books, 160 pages. **$8.00**

The Canape Book. 1935, Maiden. **$20.00**

The Can Opener Cook Book. 1952, Poppy Cannon. **$12.00**

Candies & Bon Bons, How To Make. 1913, Marion Harris Neil. **$30.00**

Candy and Candy Making. 1929, Mary B. Bookmeyer, 127 pages. **$25.00**

Cape Cod Cook Book. 1931, Suzane Cary Gruver. **$20.00**

Cape Cod Cook Book. First edition, 1954, Peter Hunt, 181 pages. **$15.00**

Cassell's Cookery. First edition, 1912, A.G. Payne, Cassell & Co., 360 pages. **$25.00**

Casserole. 1914, Olive M. Hulse, Hopewell Press, Chicago, 97 pages. **$25.00**

Casserole Specialties. 1955, Nedda Cason Anders. **$15.00**

Casserole Treasury. 1964, Lousene R. Brunner, 310 pages. **$8.00**

Catering for Special Occasions, with Menus and Recipes. 1911, Fannie Merritt Farmer. **$30.00**

Catering for Two - Comfort & Economy for Small Households. First edition, 1898, Alice L. James, New York, 345 pages. **$35.00**

Catering For Two. 1898, 1906, Alice L. James. **$30.00**

The Centennial Cook Book. 1876, Ella Myers, published in Philadelphia, rare. **$500.00**

Century Cook Book. 1895, Mary Ronald, The Century Company. **$35.00**

Century Cook Book. 1895, 1900, Mary Ronald, The Century Comany. **$30.00**

The Century Cook Book and Home Physician. 1894, Dr. N.T. Oliver & Jennie Hausley. **$40.00**

▸ *Chafing Dish Possibilities.* First edition, Dec. 1898, Fannie Merritt Farmer, autographed, 161 pages. **$250.00**

Chafing Dish Possibilities. 1898, 1909, Fannie Merritt Farmer, 161 pages. **$125.00**

Chafing Dish Possibilities. 1898, 1909, 1910, Fannie Merritt Farmer, 161 pages. **$50.00**

Chafing-Dish Specialties. 1954, Nedda Cason Anders. **$12.00**

Charging the Human Battery - 50 New Recipes with Iceberg Lettuce. 1929, Iceberg Head Lettuce Institute. **$20.00**

Cheese & Cheese Cookery. 1967, T.A. Layton, 254 pages. **$10.00**

Cheese Cook Book. 1942, Mary Dahnke. **$17.50**

Chef's Magic. 1973, Nancy and Arthur Hawkins, Prentice-Hall. **NCV**

▸ *Chez Maxim's Secrets and Recipes from the World's Most Famous Restaurant in Paris.* First edition, 1962, by The Countess of Toulouse, Lautrec, 8½x12", 253 pages. **$25.00**

The Chicago Daily News Cook Book. 1930, Edith G. Shuck, Editor of Cookery. **$20.00**

A Child's First Cook Book - For Boys and Girls From 7-12. 1950, Alma S. Lach, 96 pages. **$12.00**

Chinese Cooking. 1974, Kenneth Lo. **NCV**

Choice Candy From Your Own Kitchen. 1970, 1971, *Farm Journal,* 94 pages. **NCV**

Choice Candy Recipes. 1929, Lucy G. Allen, Little, Brown & Co. **$25.00**

Choice Recipes for Clever Cooks. 1929, Lucy G. Allen. **$25.00**

Choice Recipes to Cook Ahead. 1980, Katharine Hiam. **NCV**

The Christmas Cook Book. First edition, 1953, Zella Boutell, Vail-Ballou Press, 269 pages. **$12.00**

The Christmas Cookie Book. 19459, Virginia Pasley, Little, Brown & Co. **$17.50**

Christmas Entertaining. 1980, Barbara Myers. **NCV**

Classical Recipes of the World. 1955, Henry Smith. **$12.00**

Clayton's Quaker Cook-Book. 1883, H.J. Clayton, San Francisco, rare. **$400.00**

Clean Plates. 1964, Cooking for Young Children. 1964, Mitzi F. Perry-Miller. **$10.00**

Cocktail Supper Cookbook. 1955, Marion W. Flexner. **$12.00**

Coconut - The Tree of Life. 1976, Carolyn. **NCV**

Coffee Cookbook. 1981, Maxwell House. **NCV**

Coffee and Waffles. 1926, Alice Foote MacDougall. **$25.00**

Coffee Cookery. 1940, Helmut Ripperger. **$17.50**

Come Cook With Me. First edition, 1967, Maurice Brockway, introduction by Pauline Trigere, 176 pages. **$10.00**

Come For Cocktails, Stay For Supper. 1970, Marian Burres & Lois Levine. **NCV**

The Comfort of Cooking and Heating by Gas. 1898, Marion Harland. **$40.00**

▸ *Come Into The Kitchen Cook Book.* First edition, 1969, Mary and Vincent Price, 7½x11", 212 pages. **$25.00**

The Common Sense Cook Book. 1939, Ida Bailey Allen, 125 pages. **$25.00**

Common Sense in the Household; A Manual of Practical Houseswifery. First edition, 1871, Marion Harland, 556 pages. **$250.00**

The Compendium of Cookery and Reliable Recipes. 1890, Mrs. E.C. Blakeslee and Emma Leslie & Dr. Hughes, revised and enlarged, two complete volumes in one, rules for cooking and the book of Knowledge. **$50.00**

Complete American Cook Book. 1957, Stella Stanard, revised, 512 pages. **$12.00**

The Complete Book of Cheese. 1955, Bob Brown with an introduction by Clifton Fadiman, a feast of cheese recipes, legends, antedotes and history, 314 pages. **$12.00**

The Complete Book of Food and Nutrition. First edition, 1961, J.I. Rodale and Staff, publisher Rodale Books, Inc., 1,054 pages. **$10.00**

The Complete Book of Freezer Cookery. 1953, 1966, Ann Seranne, Doubleday, 350 pages. **$8.00**

The Complete Book of Table Setting. 1982, Amelia Levitt Hill. **NCV**

The Complete Book of World Cookery. 1972, Crescent Books. **NCV**

The Complete Chocolate Chip Cookie Book. 1982, Bob & Suzanne Stat, 128 pages. **NCV**

The Complete Family Cook Book. 1970, Curtin Promotions, Inc., New York, three-ring binder, indexed, 416 pages. **NCV**

The Complete Family Cook Book. 1970, 1972, Curtin Promotions, Inc., New York, 416 pages. **NCV**

The Complete Home Dissertation on Domestic Life & Affairs. 1903, 503 pages. **$30.00**

A Complete House-wifes Guide. 1886, Marion Harland, 529 pages. **$40.00**

The Complete Menu Book. First edition, 1939, Gladys T. Lang, Houghton Mifflin Co., 399 pages. **$20.00**

The Complete Scandinavian Cookbook. 1964, Alice B. Johnson. **$10.00**

Complete Round The World Meat Cookbook. 1967, Myra Waldo, 492 pages. **$15.00**

The Complete Western Cookbook. 1964. **$10.00**

Confessions of a Sneaky Organic Cook. First edition, 1971, Jane Kinder Leher, 255 pages. **NCV**

The Congressional Club Cook Book. 1927, The Congressional Cabinet, Washington, D.C., forward by Mrs. Herbert C. Hoover, signed and serial numbered. **$50.00**

Consolidated Library of Modern Cooking. First edition, 1904, five volumes, Christine T. Herrick and Marion Harland. Each volume **$35.00**

The Conspirators Cookbook. First American edition, 1966, 1967, Paul Palmer, 258 pages. **$10.00**

Cookbook. 1972, Cecil Brownstone, Associated Press Food Column Reporter. **NCV**

Cook Book For All Occasions. 1936, Jessie Marie DeBoth, spiral. **$20.00**

A Cook Book For Diabetics. 1959, Leonard Louis Levinson, plastic spiral. **$12.00**

A Cook Book in Greek. 1915, Makis Guinis, recipes are in the Greek language. **$25.00**

Cook Book of Left-Overs. 1935, Carroll Ann Rylon. **$20.00**

A Cook Book of Left-overs. 1941, Clara Newman & Bell Whiley, 421 pages. **$17.50**

The Cookbook of the United Nations. First printing, 1970, Brabara Kraus, 128 pages. **NCV**

The Cook Book "Oscar" of the Waldorf. 1896, 900 pages. **$50.00**

The Cook is in The Parlor. 1947, Marguerite Gilbert McCarthy. **$17.50**

Cook Book Taste of Texas. 12th printing, 1949, Jane Trahey editor. **$17.50**

Cook It In A Casserole. Ninth printing, 1943, 1950, Florence Brobeck. **$8.00**

Cook It Outdoors. 1953, James Beard. **$17.50**

Cook It Quick - 203 Delicious Half-Hour Recipes. 1971, 1981, Arthur Hawkins, 127 pages. **NCV**

Cook Until Done. 1962, George Bradshaw & Ruth Norman. **$8.00**

Cookery for 1 or 2. 1978, Barbara Swain. **NCV**

The Cookie Cookbook. 1977, John F. Carofoli. **NCV**

Cooking As Men Like It. 1935, J. George Frederick. **$20.00**

Cooking Fondue. 1970, from Doubleday Little Cookbook Shelf. **NCV**

Cooking For Beginners. 1884, Marion Harland. **$50.00**

Cooking For One. 1949, Elinor Parker. **$17.50**

Cooking For Profit. 1933, Alice Bradley. **$25.00**

Cooking For Two. 1909, 1910, Janet M. Hill, 407 pages. **$35.00**

Cooking For Two. 1909, 1924, Janet M. Hill. **$25.00**

Cooking For Two. 1909, 1924, 1930, Janet M. Hill, completely revised, 407 pages. **$20.00**

Cooking For Two. 1909, 1924, 1944, Janet M. Hill, new revised edition by Marjorie Mills & Sally Larken, 407 pages. **$10.00**

Cooking For Two. 1947, 1957, Ida Bailey Allen. **$12.00**

The Cooking of Provincial France. 1968, M.F.K. Fisher. **$15.00**

The Cooking of Scandinavia. 1968, D. Brown & editors of *Time-Life.* **$8.00**

Cooking On A Ration. 1943, Mills. **$17.50**

Cooking The British Way. 1963, Joan Clibbon. **$10.00**

Cooking The French Way, 1960, Spring Books, London, revised. **$10.00**

Cooking The Indian Way. 1962, Atlia Hasain & Sita Pasrisha. **$10.00**

Cooking The Middle East Way. 1962, Irfan Orga, Czechoslovakia. **$10.00**

Cooking in The New South. 1984, Anne B. Phillips. **NCV**

The Cooking of India. 1969, *Time-Life* recipes. **$10.00**

Cooking The French Way. 1982, Lynne Marie Waldee. **NCV**

Cooking The Norwegian Way. 1982, Sylvia Munson. **NCV**

Cooking Way Down South in Dixie. 1949, A. Monroe Aurand, Jr., limited publication, private printing. **$17.50**

Cooking With A Foreign Accent. Second edition, 1959, ring bound, A Sunset Book. **$12.00**

Cooking with Craig Clairborne & Pierre Francy. 1983, more than 600 recipes from the New York Times. **NCV**

Cooking With Helen McCully Beside You. 1970, Helen McCully. **NCV**

Cooking with Hougen. 1960, Richard T. Hougen. **$10.00**

Cooking With Miracle Whip Salad Dressing. Second printing, 1983, by The Kraft Kitchens, Consumer Affairs Department, Kraft, Inc., spiral, 160 pages. **NCV**

Cooking With The Cuisinart Food Processer. 1977, Roy Andries de Groot, 218 pages. **NCV**

Cooking Within Your Income. 1936, Ida Bailey Allen, published exclusively for F.W. Woolworth, this is #1 of the Kitchen Book Shelf Series Planned, hard cover binder, 144 pages. **$20.00**

Cooking Without a Grain of Salt. 1964, Elma W. Bagg, Doubleday, 224 pages. **$10.00**

Cooking Without Mother's Help. First edition, 1920, Clara Ingram Judson, 103 pages. **$25.00**

Cooking Without Recipes. 1965, Helen Worth, 259 pages. **$8.00**

Cook's Tour of San Francisco's Best Restaurants. 1963, Doris Muscatine, recipes interspersed with text. **$8.00**

The Copco Pots and Pans Cookbook. 1968, Sann Seranne and Joan Wilson. **$8.00**

Copper Kettle Cook Book. 1963, Marth Dixon. **$8.00**

Cottage Kitchen. 1907, Marion Harland. **$35.00**

Country Food. 1982, Miriam Ungerer. **NCV**

The Country Kitchen. 1936, Della T. Lutes, 259 pages. **$20.00**

The Country Kitchen. 1936, 1938, Della T. Lutes, 266 pages. **$10.00**

Cream City Recipe Book. 1930, Cream City Ware, Geuder, Paschke & Frey & Co., Milwaukee, Wisconsin. **$20.00**

Creole Book Book. 1930. **$20.00**

Cross Creek Cookery. First edition, 1942, Marjorie Kinman Rawlings, 254 pages. **$20.00**

The Cruising Cook Book. 1949, Jones & McKim. **$15.00**

Culinary Arts Institute Encyclopedia Cook Book. 1950, Ruth Berolzheimer, thumb indexed. **$12.00**

Culinary Gems from the Kitchens of Old Virginia. 1952, Irene Lawrence King, 500 recipes, 224 pages. **$15.00**

The Cuisine of Hungary. 1971, George Lang publisher, Atheneum. **NCV**

Cutco Cook Book - Meat and Poultry Cookery. First edition, 1961, World's finest cutlery, Margaret Mitchell, Director Home Economics, Wear-Ever Aluminum, Inc. **$8.00**

Daily Food For Christians. 1898, DeWolfe Fiske Co. **$35.00**

A Dainty Cook Book. 1901, Mrs. Nelson Oliphant. **$30.00**

Dairy Products, Milk & Butter Substitutes, Fats & Deep-Fat Frying, Cheese, Eggs. 1929, International Correspondence Schools, Scranton, Pennsylvania, 145 pages. **$25.00**

Delectable Dinners. 1939, Peterson-Badenoch. **$30.00**

Delineator Cook Book. 1934, 1937, edited by Mildred Maddocks Bently, Director Butterick Publishing Co., published by Delineator Institute. **$30.00.**

Denmark From A to Z with Recipes. 1950's, The Danish Agricultural Marketing Board, stiff cover, 56 pages. **$15.00**

The Derrdale Game Cook Book. 1937, 1950, Master Chef Louis De Gouy of the Waldorf-Astoria Hotel, New York, limited edition of 1,250 copies, 308 pages. **$200.00**

Desserts and Salads. 1932, Lemcke. **$20.00**

The Detroit News Menu Cook Book. 1933, Myrtle Calkins, "The Home Newspaper." **$17.50**

The Diabetic's Cook Book. 1955, C.B. Strachan, Medical Arts Publishing Foundation, 304 pages. **$10.00**

Diabetic Menus, Meals and Recipes. 1949, Betty M. West, Doubleday. **$17.50**

The Dairy Cook Book. 1941, edited by Ruth Berolzheimer, Culinary Arts Institute. **$17.50**

Dig That Dish. 1967, Ruth Chier Rosen. **$8.00**

The Dinah Shore Cook Book. 1973. **NCV**

The Diner's Club Cook Book - Great Recipes from Great Restaurants. 1959, Myra Waldo. **$17.50**

Dining Out in Any Language - Many Countries Heard From. First edition, 1956, Myra Waldo, 152 pages. **$17.50**

Dinner At My Place. 1979, South Carolina's First Lady Cookbook. **NCV**

Dinner at Omar Khay Yams. 1944, George Mardikian, Dominion of Canada. **$17.50**

Dinners That Wait: A Cook Book. 1954, Betty Wason, 216 pages. **$10.00**

Dinner Year-Book. 1878, Marion Harland, New York. **$125.00**

Directions for Cooking. 1841, Eliza Leslie. **$250.00**

The Dixie Cook Book. 1883, 1885, A.G. Wilcox, Atlanta, Georgia, 688 pages. **$65.00**

Domestic Receipt Book. 1849, 1850, Catherine Beecher. **$250.00**

Down on the Farm Cook Book. 1943, Helen Worth. **$17.50**

◊ ◊ ◊ ◊

Dr. Chase's Recipes

Dr. Chase began in 1856 to publish his twenty years of recipes in a pamphlet of only a few pages. By 1863, after traveling between New York and Iowa selling the work, over 23,000 copies had been sold. The following are the listings we have collected or have knowledge of.

1863, 1865 - *Dr. Chase's Recipes or Information for Everybody.* 25th edition, A.W. Chase, M.D., about 800 practical recipes, contains preface to the 10th edition of 1863, 384 pages. **$125.00**

1863, 1865, 1866 - *Dr. Chase's Recipes or Information for Everybody.* 35th edition, A.W. Chase, M.D., about 800 practical recipes, 384 pages. **$100.00**

1863, 1865, 1866 - *Dr. Chase's Recipes or Information for Everybody; About Eight Hundred Practical Recipes.* 37th edition, A.W. Chase, M.D., 384 pages. **$100.00**

1863, 1865, 1866, 1867, 1872 - *Dr. Chase's Recipes or Information for Everybody.* 71st edition, A.W. Chase, M.D., about 800 practical recipes, 400 pages. **$75.00**

1863, 1865, 1866, 1867, 1872, 1875 - *Dr. Chase's Recipes.* Dr. A.W. Chase, M.D., R.A. Beal. **$60.00**

1863, 1865, 1866, 1867, 1872, 1875, 1879 - *Dr. Chase's Family Physician, Farrior, Bee-Keeper & Second Receipt Book.* Dr. A.W. Chase, Toledo, Ohio. **$60.00**

1879, 1885 - *Dr. Chase's Second Receipt Book.* 662 pages. **$45.00**

1884, 1887, 1893 - *Dr. Chase's Last and Complete Receipt Book and Household Physician.* Memorial edition, F.B. Dickerson & Co., 865 pages. **$25.00**

1888 - *Dr. Chase's Receipt Book.* Published by F.B. Dickerson & Co. after Dr. Chase's death. **$40.00**

1905 - *Dr. Chase's Recipe Book.* Memorial edition, Dr. A.W. Chase, F.B. Dickerson & Co. **$30.00**

◊ ◊ ◊ ◊

The Duncan Hines Dessert Book. 1955, Duncan Hines Company. **$10.00**

Duncan Hines Food Odyssey. 1955, 266 pages. **$12.00**

The Dutch Cook Book. 1953, Heller. **$12.00**

Easter Idea Book. 1954, Charlotte Adams, Lenten dishes, etc. **$15.00**

Easy Meals. First edition, 1913, Caroline French Benton, 325 pages. **$25.00**

Eat Italian Once a Week. 1967, Vernon Jarratt. **$10.00**

Eat Well and Stay Well. 1963. **$8.00**

Eating and Cooking Around The World - Fingers Before Forks. 1963, Erick Berry (pseud), Allena Champlin Best. **$10.00**

Eating The Russian Way. 1963, Berytl Gould Marks. **$8.00**

The Economy Cook Book. 1948, 1949, compiled by the staff of the *Journal of Living*. **$17.00**

Edgewater Beach Hotel Salad Book. 1928, Arnold Shircliffe. **$25.00**

Edith Barber's Cook Book. 1940, Edith M. Barber. **$17.50**

Edith Barber's Cook Book. 1940, 1946, 1955, Edith M. Barber. **$10.00**

Eggs, Beans & Crumpets. First edition, 1940, P.G. Wodehouse. **$17.50**

Eggs; Facts and Fancies About Them. 1890, Anna Barrows. **$35.00**

Electric Refrigerator Recipes and Menus - Specially Prepared for the General Electric Refrigerator. First edition, 1927, General Electric Co., Miss Alice Bradley, 144 pages. **$25.00**

Electric Refrigerator Recipes and Menus - Specially Prepared for the General Electric Refrigerator. Third edition, 1927, 1927, 1928, General Electric Company, Miss Alice Bradley, 144 pages. **$15.00**

Electric Refrigerator Menus & Recipes. Fifth edition, 1927, 1927, 1928, General Electric Co., Alice Bradley, 144 pages. **$5.00**

Elementary Home Economics. 1926, Mary Lockwood Mathews, recipes, home management and sewing. **$20.00**

Elsie DeWolfe's Recipes for Successful Dining. 1934, Elsie DeWolfe (Lady Mendl), 102 pages. **$25.00**

Encyclopedia of World Cookery. 1955, Czechoslavakia. **$12.00**

The Enterprising Housekeeper. 1897, 1898, Helen Louise Johnson. **$25.00**

1000 Entertainment Ideas. 1928, The Modern Pricilla, Boston. **$25.00**

Escoffiers' Cookbook of Desserts, Sweets and Ices. 1966, A. Escoffier. **$10.00**

▶ *Esquire's Cook Book For the Pioneering Male with a Taste for Fine Food and the Woman who wants to be The Perfect Hostess.* 1935, 1948, 1954, 1955, over 750 delicious recipes, 322 pages. **$5.00**

Esquire's Handbook for Hosts. 1949, 1953, Lucy J. Allen, Grosset & Dunlap, New York, 288 pages. **$10.00**

Esquire's Handbook For Hosts. 1967, 1968, 1969, 1971, 1973, Roy Andries de Groot, 476 pages. **NCV**

Everyday Cook Book. 1889, Mrs. E. Neil, Chicago. **$50.00**

Everyday Cook Book. 1889, 1892, Mrs. E. Neil, Chicago. **$40.00**

Everyday Foods. 1930, 1932, Harris and Lacy, Houghton Mifflin Co., 550 pages. **$20.00**

Everyday Foods. Fifth edition, 1930, 1932, 1933, 1949, Jessie W. Harris, Elizabeth Lacy Speer, 494 pages. **$10.00**

Eve's Daughters. 1884, Marion Harland. **$45.00**

The Experienced English Housekeeper Cook Book. 1790, Elizabeth Raffald. **$1,500.00**

Fabulous Fondues. 1970, Dorothy Becker and Nancy Wallace. **NCV**

Factory's Easy-As-Pie Cookbook. 1964, Owings Mills, Maryland. **$8.00**

The Family and Householders Guide. 1859, mostly medicines and cooking, 238 pages. **$100.00**

The Family Circle Dessert and Fruit Cook Book. First edition, 1954, 144 pages. **$15.00**

Family Circle Outdoor Cooking. 1978. **NCV**

Family Cook Book. 1962, Gertrude Wilkerson, 640 pages. **$10.00**

Family Favorites From Country Kitchens. 1973, *Farm Journal,* 278 pages. **NCV**

The Family Nurse. 1837, Mrs. Lydia Child. **$325.00**

The Family's Food. 1931, Lauman, McKay & Zuill. **$20.00**

The Family Save-All. Pre-1873, Hannah Mary Peterson. **$70.00**

The Fannie Farmer Junior Cook Book. 1942, Wilma Lord Perkins, 208 pages. **$25.00**

The New Fannie Farmer Boston Cooking-School Cook Book. 1951, 1952, completely revised by Wilma Lord Perkins, 878 pages. **$17.50**

The New Fannie Farmer Boston Cooking-School Cook Book. Ninth revised edition, 1951, 1952, 1959, 1964, Dexter Perkins Corporation, revised by Wilma Lord Perkins, seventh printing, 878 pages. **$6.00**

The Fannie Farmer Cookbook. 11th edition, 1959, 1964, 1965, Dexter Perkins Corporation, 12th printing, revised by Wilma Lord Perkins, 624 pages. **$6.00**

The Fannie Farmer Cookbook. 12th edition, 1986, revised by Marion Cunningham with Jeri Laber, 14th printing, copyright by Alfred A. Knopf, Inc., 811 pages. **NCV**

The Farm & Home Cook-Book & Housekeepers Assistant. 1909, by *Farm & Home* magazine. **$35.00**

Farm Journal's Complete Pie Cookbook. 1965, 308 pages. **$5.00**

The Farmers & Imigrants Complete Guide, Hints, Recipes & Table Settings. 1849, Josiah Marshall. **$130.00**

The Farmers & Imigrants Complete Guide or A Hand Book Hints, Recipes & Table Settings. 1849, 1856, Josiah Marshall. **$100.00**

Fascinating Foods from the South. 1963, Alline P. Van Duzon, Gramarey Publishers, 117 pages. **$8.00**

Fashions in Foods in Beverly Hills. Second edition, 1930, Beverly Hills Women's Club, foreword by Will Rogers (two recipes by him). **$35.00**

The Favorite Medical Receipt and Home Doctor. 1908, Josephus Goodenough, M.D. **$35.00**

Favorite Recipes. 1936, Charlotte E. Fritz, The Record Herald, Waynesboro, Pennsylvania. **$20.00**

Favorite Recipes from Royal Neighbor Kitchens. First printing, 1960, Harriet S. Jeanes, editor and fraternal advisor, Royal Neighbors of America since 1895, spiral. **$8.00**

Favorite Recipes of America - Desserts. 1968, Favorite Recipes Press, Louisville. **$5.00**

Favorite Recipes of America - Salads. First edition, 1968, Favorite Recipes Press, Louisville, 384 pages. **$5.00**

Favorite Recipes of Famous Women. 1925, Florence Stratton, 119 pages. **$25.00**

Fearless Cooking for One. 1980, Michele Evans, Simon & Shuster, 388 pages. **NCV**

Feast Day Cook Book - The Traditional Feast Day Dishes. 1951, **$12.00**

Feasts for All Seasons. 1966, Roy Andreis de Groot, 730 pages. **$8.00**

Feeding the Family. 1925, M.S. Rose. **$25.00**

Festive Salads & Molds. 1966, Evelyn Loeb. **$8.00**

Festive Snacks & Canapes. 1967, Evelyn Loeb, small booklet. **$8.00**

Fifty Great Buffet Parties. 1969, 1973, 1974, Ruth Conrad Bateman, Doubleday, 224 pages. **NCV**

The Fifty Two Sunday Dinners. 1924, *Woman's World Magazine.* **$25.00**

The Findhorn Cook Book. 1976, Barbara Friedlander, Findhorn, Scotland. **NCV**

The Fine Art of Chinese Cooking. 1962, Dr. Lee Su Jan, Gramery Publishing, 234 pages. **$8.00**

The Fine Art of Roman Cooking. 1960's, Alexander Lenard, the authentic recipes of the Eternal City, by the creator of Wimmie Ille Pu, 192 pages. **$10.00**

The Finnish Cookbook. 1964, Beatrice A. Ojakangas, 250 pages. **$8.00**

▶ *The Fireside Cook Book.* 1949, James A. Beard, fifth printing, 322 pages. **$25.00**

The First Ladies Cook Book - Favorite Recipes of All the Presidents. 1965, Smithsonian Institution-National Trust for Historic Preservation, Home Library Press, under Lyndon B. Johnson's term of office, 224 pages. **$25.00**

▶ *The First Ladies Cook Book - Favorite Recipes of All the Presidents.* 1965, 1969, Smithsonian Institution-National Trust for Historic Preservation, Home Library Press, under Lyndon B. Johnson's term of office, 228 pages. **$10.00**

The Fitness Connection. 1983, Family Circle, Mazola Oil, Best Foods of CPC International. **NCV**

The 5 Minute Dessert. 1961, Marie Buynon Roy. **$6.00**

Fondue, Chafing Dish and Casserole Cookery. 1969, Margaret Deeds Murphy, New York. **$6.00**

Food and Cookery for the Sick and Convalescent. 1904, 1905, Fannie Merritt Farmer, 289 pages plus ads. **$45.00**

Food and Cookery for the Sick and Convalescent. 1904, 1905, 1907, Fannie Merritt Farmer, 289 pages plus ads. **$35.00**

Food and Cookery for the Sick and Convalescent. 1904, 1905, 1907, 1909 printing, 289 pages plus ads. **$25.00**

▶ *Food and Cookery for the Sick and Convalescent.* 1904, 1905, 1907, 1911 printing, 289 pages plus ads. **$20.00**

Food and Cookery for the Sick and Convalescent. 1904, 1904, 1907, 1913 printing, 289 pages plus ads. **$15.00**

Food & Flavor - Gastronomic Guide to Health & Good Living. First edition, 1913, H.T. Finck, New York, 612 pages. **$25.00**

Food and Nutrition. 1967, Life Science Library, 200 pages. **$6.00**

Food For Better Living. 1960, McDermott, Trilling & Nicholas. **$8.00**

Food For the Settler. 1982, Bobbie Kalman. **NCV**

Food For Two. First edition, 1947, Ida Bailey Allen, 339 pages. **$17.50**

Food For Us All. 1969, The Yearbook of Agriculture, United States Government Printing Office, 360 pages. **$6.00**

Food From Famous Kitchens. 1961, English. **$8.00**

Food is More Than Cooking. 1968, Jean Henderson. **$6.00**

Food is More Than Cooking - Basic Guide for Young Cooks. 1968, 1969, Jean Anerson. **$6.00**

Foods and Cookery. 1917, Emma Matteson and Ethel Newlands. **$25.00**

Foods and Household Management - A Text-Book of the Household Arts. Seventh edition, 1914, 1916, Helen Kinne and Anna M. Cooley, B.S., 401 pages. **$25.00**

For Men Only, A Cook Book by Achmea Audullah and John Kenny. 1937. **$20.00**

For Love of Cooking. 1975, Lena Sturges, 415 pages. **NCV**

The Ford Treasury of Favorite Recipes from Famous Eating Places. First edition, 1950, Nancy Kennedy, 252 pages. **$12.50**

The Ford Treasury of Favorite Recipes from Famous Eating Places. 1905, 1954, 1955, Nancy Kennedy, 252 pages. **$5.00**

The Forgotten Art of Flower Cookery. 1973, Leona Woodring Smith. **NCV**

Ford Times Cook Book...by Nancy Kennedy. 1967, 1974, Ford Motor Co., volume 6, 144 pages. **NCV**

The Forget-About Meat Cookbook. 1974. **NCV**

The Four Seasons Cook Book. 1971, Charlotte Adams, James Beard, special consultant, 319 pages. **NCV**

Francatelli's Modern Cook Book - A Practical Guide to the Culinary Art. Pre-1873, Charles Elme Francatelli, pupil to the celebrated Careme and Maitre-d' Hotel and Chief Cook to her Majesty, the Queen of England, reprinted from the ninth London edition, 600 pages. **$300.00**

The Frances Parkinson Keyes Cook Book. First edition, 1955. **$12.00**

Franco-American Soups and other Specialties. 1900, A. Biardot, president, American Food Company. **$30.00**

French-American Cooking. 1967, Morton G. Clark. **$6.00**

The French Chef Cookbook. 1968, Julia Child. **$25.00**

The French Cook Book for American Families. 1930, Xavier Raskin. **$20.00**

French Cooking. 1972, Round the World Books. **NCV**

French Cooking For All. 1932, Voison. **$20.00**

French Cooking For American Kitchens. 1932, Bonney. **$20.00**

French Pastry Book. 1932, Crippen. **$20.00**

The French-Kosher Cookbook. 1960, Ruth & Bob Grossman. **$8.00**

French Dishes For American Tables. 1885, 1887, Pierre Caron, translated and edited by Mrs. Frederic Sherman, New York, 231 pages. **$45.00**

Frozen Dainties. 1905, Mrs. Mary J. Lincoln, author of the *Boston Cook Book,* for The White Mountain Freezer Company. **$35.00**

Frigidaire Recipes. 1928, copyright Union 1910, 77 pages. **$15.00**

Frigidaire-Frozen Delights. 1929, Frigidaire Corp. **$15.00**

Frigidaire Recipe Book. 1931. **$12.00**

The Frugal Gourmet. 1984, Jeff Smith. **NCV**

The Frugal Gourmet Cooks American. 1988, Jeff Smith. **NCV**

Fun With Cooking - Easy Recipes for Beginners. First edition, 1947, Mae Blacker Freeman, Random House, 58 pages. **$17.50**

The Galley Guide Cook Book. 1947, A.W. Moffat. **$17.50**
The Garden Way Bread Book - A Baker's Almanac. First edition, 1979, Ellen Foscue Johnson, 192 pages. **NCV**

Gardening for Gourmets - Good Eating from a Small Garden Plot. 1959, Ruth A. Watson. **$12.00**

The Garrulous Gourmet. First edition, 1952, William Wallace Irwin, foreword by Fred Allen, 208 pages. **$17.50**

General Foods Cook Book. First edition, 1932, 370 pages. **$25.00**

General Foods Cook Book. 1932, 1934, 370 pages. **$10.00**

The General Foods Kitchens Cook Book. 1959, women of General Foods Kitchens, 436 pages. **$15.00**

Genuine German Cooking and Baking. 1930, Lina Meier, cloth cover. **$22.50**

German Cook Book in German. 1869, Mrs. Henriette Davidus, Milwaukee. **$60.00**

German National Cookery for American Kitchens. 1904, Henriette Davidus, Milwaukee, second American edition (from the 35th German publication). **$35.00**

Gesunde Kost Ein Kochbuch. 1928, Mary Hahn, in German. **$25.00**

A Gift to the Bride. 1937, 230 pages. **$20.00**

Gifts From Your Kitchen. 1955, Carli Laklanand and Frederic Thomas. **$12.00**

The Gingerbread Boy. 1932, Platt & Munk, illustrations on each page. **$25.00**

Ginnie and Geneva Cook Book. 1975. Catherine Woolley, 96 pages. **NCV**

The Glamour Magazine Party Book. 1965, Eleanor Elliott. **$8.00**

Going Wild in The Kitchen. 1965, Gertrude Parke, David McKay Company, Inc., 329 pages. **$8.00**

The Gold Cook Book by Louis P. DeGouy. 1947, 1948, intro by The "Oscar" of the Waldorf Astoria Hotel, New York, 1256 pages. **$25.00**

The Gold Cook Book by Louis P. DeGouy. 1947, 1948, 1951, intro by The "Oscar" of the Waldorf Astoria Hotel, New York. **$12.50**

Good Cheap Food. 1973, Miriam Ungerer. **NCV**

Good Cooking Made Easy and Economical. 1934, Haseltine & Dow. **$20.00**

Good Food & How To Cook It. 1939, Phyllis Kraft Newill, 555 pages. **$25.00**

Good Food & How To Cook It. 1920, George Conforth, 224 pages. **$30.00**

Good Food & How To Prepare It. 1920, 1930, George E. Conforth, 228 pages. **$15.00**

◊◊◊◊

Good Housekeeping

▶ 1903 - *Good Housekeeping Everyday Cook Book.* Arranged by Isabel Gordon Curtis, associate editor of *Good Housekeeping,* The Good Housekeeping Library Number One, their first publication of a cookbook, Phelps Publishers, 4⅛"x9⅜", 320 pages. **$50.00**

1922 - *Book of Menus, Recipes & Household Discoveries.* Good Housekeeping, New York, 253 pages. **$25.00**

1922, 1924 - *Good Housekeeping Book of Menus, Recipes & Household Discoveries.* Eighth edition, *Good Housekeeping* Magazine Department, Department of Cookery, 254 pages. **$15.00**

1926 - *Good Housekeeping's Book on Business of Housekeeping.* Mildred M. Bently, 194 pages. **$25.00**

1927 - *Good Housekeeping Book of Good Meals.* First edition, Katherine Fisher, Director, 256 pages. **$30.00**

1927 - *Good Housekeeping Book of Good Meals.* Fifth edition, Katherine Fisher, Director, 256 pages. **$5.00**

1930 - *Good Housekeeping Institute Meals Tested and Approved.* Fifth edition, 254 pages. **$5.00**

1931 - *Meals Tested, Tasted and Approved - Favorite Recipes and Menus from Our Kitchens to Yours.* Fourth edition, Good Housekeeping Institute, 254 pages. **$5.00**

1933 - *Book of Meals, Tested & Approved.* Good Housekeeping, New York, 256 pages. **$10.00**

1933 - *Good Housekeeping Cook Book.* First edition, Dorothy B. Marsh, Katherine Norris, Adeline Mansfield, Katherine Fisher, Director, 254 pages. **$10.00**

1933, 1934 - *Good Housekeeping Cook Book.* Second edition, Dorothy B. Marsh, Katherine Norris, Adeline Mansfield, Katherine Fisher, Director. 254 pages. **$7.50**

▶ 1942, 1943 - *The Good Housekeeping Cook Book.* Dorothy B. Marsh, Katherine Fisher, 949 pages. **$7.50**

The Good Housekeeping Cook Book. 1949, Dorothy B. Marsh, Katherine Fisher. **$5.00**

Good Housekeeping Cook Book. 1955, Dorothy B. Marsh. **$7.50**

Good Housekeeping Party Book. 1949, 1950, 1951, 1952, 1953, 1954, 1955, 1956, 1957, 1958, Dorothy B. Marsh, Director of Foods and Cookery, 278 pages. **$2.00**

Good Housekeeping Cook Books. 1958, a collection of cookbooks in soft-cover put into a hard-cover binder. **$6.00**

Good Housekeeping's Around the World Cook Book. 1958, Consolidated Book Publishers, Chicago. **$12.00**

Good Housekeeping's Quick and Easy Cook Book. 1958, Consolidated Book Publishers. **$12.00**

Good Housekeeping Book of Cake Decorating. 1961, Dorothy B. Marsh, 8"x11", 199 pages. **$10.00**

Good Housekeeping Cookbook. 1955, 1963, Dorothy B. Marsh. **$5.00**

Good Housekeeping's Cooking For Company. 1967, by the Food Editors of *Good Housekeeping* magazine. **$6.00**
◊◊◊◊

Good Living. 1890, 1908, Sara Van Buren, household edition, 643 pages. **$30.00**

Good Things To Eat and How To Prepare Them. Seventh edition, 1909, Larkin Company, Est. 1875. **$15.00**

Good Neighbor Recipes. 1952, Erickson and Rock. **$12.00**

Good Ways in Cooking. 1889, Mrs. S.T. Rorer. **$50.00**

Gordon Bleu Cook Book. 1947, Dione Lucas, 322 pages. **$17.50**

Gordon Bleu Cook Book. 1947, 1974, Dione Lucas. **NCV**

The Gourmet Cook Book. 1951, 1954, Robert Miller, two volumes, 1500 pages. **$15.00**

Gourmet Cooking Confidential. 1975, Ralph Varhetta. **NCV**

Gourmet Cooking Without Salt. 1981, Eleanor P. Brenner, 432 pages. **NCV**

Gourmet, The Magazine of Good Living. 1944, 12 issues bound in hard cover. **$12.00**

Gourmet Meals for Easy Entertaining. 1960, Martha Nemes Fried. **$8.00**

Gourmet's Menu Cook Book. Third printing, 1967, 676 pages. **$6.00**

The Graham Kerr Cookbook. 1966, 1969, The Galloping Gourmet. **$6.00**

Grand Daughter's Inglenook Cook Book. 1942, Elgin, Illinois. **$17.50**

Grand Union Cook Book. 1902, Margaret Compton, Grand Union Tea Company, 322 pages. **$30.00**

Grandma's Cooking. 1956, Allan Keller, New England recipes. **$15.00**

The Grange Cook Book. 1970, Virginia State Grange. **NCV**

The Great American Ice Cream Book. 1973, Paul Dickson, New York, third printing, 206 pages. **NCV**

Great Recipes from the World's Great Cook. 1964, Peggy Harvey, Gramarey Publishers. **$6.00**

The Green Thumb Cookbook. First edition, 1977, Anne Moyer, Rodale Press, Inc., 316 pages. **NCV**

Greek Cooking. 1977, Ruth Kershner. **NCV**

Griswold-Aunt Helen's Delicious Dutch Oven Dishes as Prepared in the Griswold Kitchen. 1927, Griswold Mfg. Co. **$25.00**

The Grocer's Answer Book. 1927, Crouse Grocery. **$15.00**

Mrs. Hale's New Cook Book. 1851, Mrs. Sarah J. Hale. **$250.00**

Mrs. Hale's New Cook Book. 1851, 1859, Mrs. Sarah J. Hale. **$110.00**

Mrs. Hale's Receipts for the Million - Containing 4545 Receipts. 1851, Mrs. Sarah J. Hale, 800 pages. **$250.00**

Mrs. Hale's Receipts for the Million - Containing 4545 Receipts. 1851, 1857, 800 pages. **$110.00**

Hamilton Ross Modern Cook Book. 1940, K. Camille & Den Dooven, 238 pages. **$17.50**

Handbook of Food and Diet. 1912, 1914, 1915, Chicago American School of Home Economics, 254 pages. **$17.50**

Harper's Cook Book. 1902, editors of *Harper's Bazaar.* **$35.00**

Harpers Universal Recipe Book. 1869, Boston. **$175.00**

Harvest of Yesterdays. First edition, 1976, Gladys Tabor. **NCV**

Hawaii Kai Cookbook. 1970, Roma and Gene Schindler. **NCV**

Hawaiian and Pacific Foods. 1915, 1967, Katherine Bazore. **$6.00**

Health in the Household or Hygenic Cookery. 1886, Susanna W. Doods, A.M., D.D. **$50.00**

Health and Cooking and Eating for Health, Happiness and Success. 1935, Health Department Cookware Company, Michigan. **$20.00**

Heinz Recipe Book. 1939, H.J. Heinz Company, Pittsburgh, spiral. **$20.00**

Helen Corbitt Cooks for Company. 1974, Helen Corbitt, Houghton-Mifflin, 434 pages. **NCV**

▶ *Heloise's Kitchen Hints.* 1963, third printing, 186 pages. **$5.00**

The Highlander's Cookbook. 1966, recipes from Scotland. **$6.00**

Hints to Housewive's. 1917, Mayor Mitchell's Food Committee. **$25.00**

Hobby Horse Cookery. 1950, Marjory Hendricks, Watergate Inn, Washington, D.C. (site of the Watergate Scandal). **$15.00**

Holiday Book of Food and Drink. 1952, chapters were food features in *Holiday* magazine. **$12.00**

Holiday Cookbook - Home Economics Teachers Favorite Recipes. 1970, Montgomery, Alabama, spiral. **NCV**

Holiday Party Casseroles. 1956, Edna Beileyson, Peter Pauper Press, 60 pages. **$12.00**

Home Candy Making. 1869, 1889, Mrs. S.T. Rorer, Arnold and Company. **$100.00**

Home Candy Making. 1977, Beekman House, New York. **NCV**

Home Comfort Cook Book. 1924, Wrought Iron Range Company, St. Louis, U.S.A., established in 1864, book reads "This Book is not for sale at book stores, however, the company will be pleased to forward a copy to any address upon receipt of cost of postage and mailing - 10 cents," 213 pages. **$25.00**

The Home Cook Book. 1874, J. Fred Waggoner. **$70.00**

The Home Cook Book. 1874, 1875, 1876, 1877, 1882, J. Fred Waggoner. **$45.00**

The Home Garden Cook Book. 1970, Ken and Pat Kraft. **NCV**

The Home Has A Heart. 1968, Thrya Ferre Bjorn, Swedish recipes, second printing. **$5.00**

Home and Health and Home Economics. 1880, C.H. Fowler, Phillips and Hunt Home Remedies and Helpful Hints. **$35.00**

Home Partners - Certified Bread. 1924. **$15.00**

The Home Queen Cook Book. 1898, contributed by 200 World's Fair Ladies (1893 plus), Fort Dearborn Publishers, 608 pages. **$40.00**

Home Science Cook Book. 1909, Mrs. D.A. (Mary) Lincoln and Anna Barrows. **$35.00**

The Homekeeper. 1872, S.D. Farrar, Boston. **$70.00**

Homemaker's Handbook. 1939, Dorothy Myerson, Economical Standard Practice Manual for Cook and Housekeeper, 576 pages. **$20.00**

The Hood Basic Cook Book. 1949, Marjorie Heseltime. **$17.50**

Hood's Book of Home Made Candies. 1888, C.I. Hood and Company, Proprietors of Hood's Sarsaparilla, Lowell, Massachusetts. **$50.00**

The Horizon Cook Book & Illustrated History of Eating & Drinking Through The Ages. 1968, William H. Hale, 768 pages. **$8.00**

The Horizon Cook Book. 1968, American Heritage Cooking from Biblical Times On, two volumes, 760 pages. **$12.00**

The Hospitality Cook Book. 1960. **$8.00**

Hot Dog Cookbook. 1966, William Kaufman, autographed. **$6.00**

Hot Weather Dishes. Pre-1886, Mrs. S.T. Rorer, Arnold and Company. **$50.00**

The House Book or A Manual of Domestic Economy. 1840, Miss Eliza Leslie, Philadelphia. **$325.00**

House & Garden's Cook Book. 1958, Simon & Shuster, first printing, 8"x11", 324 pages. **$15.00**

Household Discoveries and Mrs. Curtis's Cook Book. 1908, 1909, Disney Morse, The Success Company, Isabel Gordon Curtis, black cover, 1,205 pages. **$35.00**

Household Discoveries and Mrs. Curtis's Cook Book. 1908, 1909, red cover, 1,205 pages. **$35.00**

Household Discoveries and Mrs. Curtis's Cook Book. 1908, 1909, 1914, Sidney Morse, Success Company, Isabel Gordon Curtis, 1,205 pages. **$25.00**

Household Receipts. Fourth edition, 1886, Joseph Burnett And Company (extracts), Boston. **$40.00**

The Household Searchlight Cook Book. 1942, 1943, 1946, Ida Miglierio and others, *The Household* Magazine. **$10.00**

The Household Searchlight Homemaking Guide. 1937, 1938, Ida Migliario and others, *The Household* Magazine. **$12.50**

The Household Searchlight Recipe Book. 1931, 1937, 1938, *The Household* Magazine, 320 pages. **$12.50**

The Housekeepers Cook Book. 1894, The Housekeeping Publishing Company, 687 pages. **$45.00**

▸ *Housekeeping in Old Virginia.* 1879, Marion Cabell Tyree, 528 pages plus ads. **$70.00**

Housekeeping Made Easy. 1842, Mrs. Ellis (pseudonym), Anna Cora Mowatt, friend of Marion Harland. **$275.00**

Housewifery: Manual Practical Housekeeping. 1919, Lydia Ray Balderston, 175 pages. **$30.00**

How America Eats. 1960, Clementine Paddleford, 495 pages. **$25.00**

How Famous Chefs Use Marshmallows. 1929, 1930, Marca Camp, The Angelus-Campfire Company. **$12.50**

How Mama Could Cook - Old Fashioned Recipes. 1946, Dorothy Malone. **$17.50**

How I Feed My Family on $16.00 A Week (And Have Meat, Fish or Poultry on the Table Every Night). 1975, Jo Ann York with Jerome Agel and Eugene Boe, first printing, 160 pages. **NCV**

How The Shakers Cook and The Noted Cooks of the Country. 1889, A.J. White. **$35.00**

How To Cook. 1973, Raymond Sokolov. **NCV**

How To Cook a Wolf. 1944, M.F.K. Fisher, 261 pages. **$20.00**

How To Cook A Pig & Back-to-the-Farm Recipes. 1977, Betty Talmadge. **NCV**

How to Entertain at Home - 1,000 Entertainment Ideas. 1928, The Modern Priscilla Publishing Co., Boston. **$25.00**

How To Gorge George Without Fattening Fanny. 1970, Nancy Gould, Hawthorne Books, Inc., 203 pages. **NCV**

Hows & Whys of Cooking. 1938, Evelyn Halliday & Isabel Noble, University of Chicago Principal, 252 pages. **$20.00**

Hows & Whys of French Cooking. 1974, Alma Lach, University of Chicago, 635 pages. **NCV**

▸ *The I Hate To Cook Book - More Than 180 Quick and Easy Recipes.* 1960, Peg Bracken, drawings by Hilary Knight, first printing, 176 pages. **$10.00**

The I Love America Diet. 1983, Phyllis George and Bill Alder, 248 pages. **NCV**

Ida Bailey Allen's Modern Cook Book. 1924, 1008 pages. **$25.00**

Ida Bailey Allen's Money-Saving Cook Book. First edition, 1940, 481 pages. **$17.50**

The Ideal Cookery Book - 1349 Useful Unique Recipes. 1891, Mrs. Annie Clark, Edgewood Publishing Co. **$35.00**

Illustrated History of French Cuisine. 1962, Christian Guy Charle Magne to Charles de Gaulle (translated), 243 pages. **$8.00**

The Institute Cook Book. 1913, 1917, Helen Cramp, 507 pages. **$25.00**

The Intelligent Person's Guide to Calories & Sodium. 1980, The Jeffrey Weiss Group, Inc., 128 pages. **NCV**

The International Cook Book. 1906, Alexander Fillippini, former Chef at Delmonicos of New York, 1,059 pages. **$30.00**

The International Cook Book. 1929, M.W. Heywood, World's Famous Chefs Merhandiser's, Inc., first printing 11/1/29, 383 pages. **$30.00**

The International Cook Book. 1929, M.W. Heywood, World's Famous Chefs Merchandiser's, Inc., second printing 11/15/29, 383 pages. **$20.00**

International Cook Book - Edition of the American Woman's Cook Book. 1938, 1939, 1940, Ruth Berolzheimer, Culinary Arts Press. **$10.00**

Invalid Cookery. 1880, Mrs. Julia A. Pye, Chicago. **$45.00**

Imperial Cook Book. 1894, Mrs. Grace Towsend. **$35.00**

Israeli Cookery. 1962, Cornfield. **$6.00**

The Italian Cook Book - An Italian Expert's Collection of more than 420 Authentic Recipes for the American Homemaker and Hostess. 1955, Maria Luisa Taglienti, 310 pages. **$15.00**

Italian Desserts and Antipasto, Ala Mama Mia. 1958, Angela Catanzaro, 314 pages. **$12.50**

Italian Family Cooking. 1974, Mary Reynolds. **NCV**

▶ *Italian Regional Cooking.* 1969, Ada Boni, printed in Italy, translated from Italian to English in 1969, 9¼"x11¾", 302 pages. **$15.00**

It's A Picnic. First edition, 1969, Nancy Fair McIntyre, 150 pages. **$6.00**

Jack Bailey's What's Cookin'. First edition, 1949, Jack Bailey, World Publishers, 187 pages. **$17.50**

The Jack Sprat Cookbook. First edition, 1965, Paris Leary & Muriel DeGre. 240 pages. **$8.00**

The James Beard Cook Book with Isabel E. Callvert. 1959, 1961, 456 pages. **$20.00**

James Beard Menus For Entertainment. 1965. **$10.00**

James Beard's Outdoor Cooking. 1960. **$15.00**

James Beard's Treasury of Outdoor Cooking. 1960, New York, 282 pages. **$15.00**

Jolly Times Cook Book. 1934, Marjorie Noble Osborn, Rand McNally & Company, Chicago. **$20.00**

The Joy of Cooking. 1931, 1936, 1941, 1942, 1943, Irma. S. Rombauer, illus. by Marion Rombauer Becker, Bobbs-Merrill Company, 684 pages. **$17.50**

▶ *The Joy of Cooking.* 1931, 1936, 1941, 1942, 1943, 1946, Irma S. Rombauer, illus. by Marion Rombauer Becker, Bobbs-Merrill Company, 884 pages. **$10.00**

The Joy of Cooking. 1931, 1936, 1941, 1942, 1943, 1946, 1952, Irma S. Rombauer, illus. by Marion Rombauer Becker, Bobbs-Merrill Company, 1,011 pages. **$7.50**

The Joy of Cooking. 1931, 1936, 1941, 1942, 1943, 1946, 1952, 1953, Irma S. Rombauer, illus. by Marion Rombauer Becker, Bobbs-Merrill Company, 1,013 pages. **$5.00**

The Joy of Cooking. 1931, 1936, 1941, 1942, 1943, 1946, 1952, 1953, 1962, 1963, 1964, 1975, Irma A.

Rombauer, Marion Rombauer Becker, illus. by Marion Rombauer Becker, Ginnie Hofman and Ikki Matsumoto, first printing, May 1975, 39th printing, September 1985, 915 pages. **NCV**

The Joy of Eating Natural Foods - 2,000 Recipes. 1962, 1971, Agnes Toms, complete organic cookbook. **NCV**

June Platts New England Cook Book. First edition, 1971, June Platt, intro by James Beard, McClelland and Stewart Publishers, 240 pages. **NCV**

Junior League of Charleston, South Carolina. 1953, seventh printing, 330 pages. **$15.00**

Just For Two Cookbook. 1942, 1949, Lily Haxworth Wallace, 322 pages. **$10.00**

The Kate Smith Cook Book. 1958, Kate Smith. **$15.00**

The Kate Smith Company's Coming Cook Book. 1958. **$15.00**

The Keep Calm Cookbook. 1963, Adele & David Kweder, M.D. **$6.00**

The Kenmore Cook Book - The United States Regional Cook Book. 1939, 1940, 1947, Ruth Berolzheimer for Sears Roebuck and Company, Consolidated Publishers. **$10.00**

The Kentucky Home Cook Book. 1899, compiled by Ladies of Maysville, Kentucky, 387 pages. **$35.00**

Kentucky Housewife Cook Book. 1839. **$325.00**

Key West Cook Book. 1949, Farrar Straus, by members of Key West Women's Club. **$17.50**

Kids Cooking - A First Cookbook for Children. 1970, Aileen Paul and Arthur Hawkins, 128 pages. **NCV**

Kindergarten Chef - Miss Wenthen's Students. First edition, 1974, Maureen Wenthen, Dodd, Mead & company, New York, 64 pages. **NCV**

Kings In The Kitchen. 1961, Gertrude Booth. **$8.00**

The Kitchen Book. 1973, K. Paradies, 464 pages. **NCV**

Kitchen Fugue. First edition, 1945, Sheila Kaye Smith, New York, Harper country life in wartime Sussex with recipes, 215 pages. **$17.50**

Kitchen Companion. 1887, Maria Parloa. **$45.00**

Kitchenette Cookery. 1917, Anna Merritt East, Little, Brown & Co., Boston, 116 pages. **$25.00**

Konfekt: Swiss Confectionery Specialties. 1950's, Sillman, London. **$17.50**

Recipes from 50th Anniversary Cookbook. 1982, Kraft, Inc. **NCV**

La Cucina - The Complete Italian Cook Book. 1953, Rose L. Sorce. **$12.00**

La Cuisine Creole. First edition, 1885, Lafcadio Hearn, devoted to New Orleans dishes, rare. **$400.00**

▶ *Ladies Home Journal Cook Book.* First edition, 1960, Carol Truax, Doubleday. **$10.00**

The Large Type Cook Book - 300 Easy-To-Prepare Recipes. First edition, 1968, Avanelle S. Day, 342 pages. **$8.00**

Larkin Housewives Cook Book - Good Things to Eat, How To Prepare Them. 1915, 1916, 1917, 1923, 140 pages. **$10.00**

Larusse French Home Cooking. 1980, J. Gerard & M. Kamman, 320 pages. **NCV**

Larusse Gastronomque Encyclopedia of Food, Wine & Cookery. 1961, New York. **$8.00**

Larousse Treasury of Country Cooking. 1978, New York, 512 pages. **NCV**

Leone's Italian Cookbook. 1967, Gene Leone. **$6.00**

Les Plaisirs De La Table. 1926, Edouard Nigon. **Rare**

Lets Ask The Cook. 1970, Nan Wiley. **NCV**

Lets Cook It Right. 1947, 1962, Adelle Davis, Harcourt, Brace & World, Inc., New York, 10th printing, 597 pages. **$6.00**

Let's Eat Right to Keep Fit. 1954, Adelle Davis, 322 pages. **$10.00**

Liberal Living, Narrow Means. 1890, C.T. Herrick. **$50.00**

Liberace Cooks. 1970, edited by Carol Truax. **NCV**

Library of Home Economics: Principles of Cookery. 1934, 12 volumes, only edition on cooking. **$15.00**

Lifetime Cooking Fun and Eating Pleasure. 1945, Ann Williams Heller. **$17.50**

Light Desserts. 1981, Deborah Kidushim-Allen. **NCV**

The Lily Wallace New American Book Book. 1941, 1942, Lily Haxworth Wallace, 930 pages. **$12.50**

The Lily Wallace New American Cook Book. 1941, 1942, 1943, 1947, 1949, 1960, Lily Haxworth Wallace. **$5.00**

Lorain Cooking. 1924, 1925, 1926, 1927, 1928, 1929, The Research Kitchen of American Stove Co., seventh edition, 171 pages. **$5.00**

Look Who's Cooking. 1974, Marce and John Carafoli. **NCV**

Low-Fat Cookery. 1959, Evelyn Stead & Gloria Warren. **$8.00**

The Low Fat, Low Cholesterol Diet. 1951, Gofman Dobbin, 371 pages. **$8.00**

Lowney's Cook Book. 1907, 1908, 1912, Maria Willet Howard, Walter M. Lowney Company, Boston, 421 pages. **$12.50**

Lowney's Cook Book. 1907, 1908, 1912, 1921, Maria Willet Howard, Walter M. Lowney Company, Boston, 412 pages. **$10.00**

Luchow's German Cook Book - Favorite Dishes of America's Most Famous German Restaurant. First edition, 1952, Leonard Jan Mitchell, 224 pages. **$17.50**

Luchow's German Cook Book - Favorite Dishes of America's Most Famous German Restaurant. 1952, Leonard Jan Mitchell, second printing, 224 pages. **$12.50**

Luchow's German Cook Book - The Story and The Favorite Dishes of America's Most Famous German Restaurant. 1952, 1952, 1953, 1954, 1954, 1955, 1956, 1957, 1958, 1959, Leonard Jan Mitchell, 224 pages. **$5.00**

Luchow's German Cook Book - The Story and the Favorite Dishes of America's Most Famous Restaurant. 1952, 1952, 1953, 1953, 1954, 1955, 1956, 1957, 1958, 1959, 1963, Leonard Jan Mitchell, 224 pages. **$3.00**

Made Over Dishes. 1898, Sarah Tyson Rorer. **$35.00**

Magic Chef Cooking. 1924, 1934, 1935, Dorothy E. Shank, American Stove Company, 204 pages. **$10.00**

Magic Chef Cooking. 1924, 1934, 1935, 1936, Dorothy E. Shank, American Stove Company, 204 pages. **$7.50**

The Magic Menu Cookbook. 1970, Edmond C. Longarini and Marion Dee Longarini, C. Nichols. **NCV**

Mama Mia Italian Cook Book. 1955, Angela Catanzaro, Liveright Publishing Corp., 286 pages. **$15.00**

Marion Burros - You've Got It Made. 1984. **NCV**

Margaret Mitchell's Magic. 1951, meat and poultry cooking. **$15.00**

Margaret Mitchell's Cooking. 1932, Aluminum Cooking Utensil Company. **$20.00**

▶ *The Margaret Rudkin Pepperidge Farm Cookbook.* First edition, 1963, 440 pages. **$10.00**

Marguerite Patten's Fruit and Vegetable. 1962, Paul Hamlin. **$8.00**

Marguerite Patten's Savoury Cooking. 1962. **$8.00**

Marion Harland's Complete Cook Book. 1903, 1906, Bobbs-Merrill co., 781 pages. **$35.00**

Martha Washington Log Cabin Cook Book. 1924, M.W. Guild, Valley Forge. **$30.00**

The Marvel Cook Book. 1925, Georgette MacMillan, Street & Smith Corp. **$25.00**

Mary Hunt's Salad Bowl. 1936, 1939, 1945, Mary Hunt Altfillisch, fourth printing, 102 pages. **$10.00**

Mary Meade's Magic Recipes For The Osterizer. 1952, 1966, Ruth Ellen Church, 256 pages. **$6.00**

Mastering The Art of French Cooking. 1961, Simone Beck, Louisette Bertholle & Julia Child, Alfred A. Knopf Publishers, second printing, 716 pages. **$10.00**

Mastering The Art of French Cooking. 1961, 1965, S. Beck, L. Bertholle & J. Child. **$6.00**

Mastering The Art of French Cooking. 1961, 1965, 1966, S. Beck, L. Bertholle & J. Child, 684 pages. **$4.00**

Maurice Brockway - Come Cook With Me. 1967. **$6.00**

The Maxwell House Coffee Cookbook. 1964, Ellen Sattoustall. **$8.00**

McCall's Illustrated Dinner Party Cook Book. 1961. **$8.00**

McCall's Cookbook. 1963, Random House, 785 pages. **$8.00**

McCall's Book of Wonderful One Dish Meals. 1972. **NCV**

McCall's Cooking School Mistake-Proof Recipes. 1986, McCall's Publishing Company, not available through bookstores, hard-cover three-ring binder. **NCV**

M'Kenzies 5,000 Receipts. 1835, recorded in 1836 in *The Farmer's Mechanic's* and *Gentleman's Almanac* by Nathan Wild, contains "Instructions Respecting Diet" from

M'Kenzies 5,000 Receipts, Quantity of Food, and Quality, Dietic substances. **$350.00**

A Meal in Itself - A Book of Soups. 1944, Mary Frost Mabon. **$17.50**

Meal Planning & Table Service - For The American Home Without Servants. 1955, Beth Bailey Mclean, 20th printing. **$5.00**

Men In Aprons. 1944, Lawrence A. Keating, 186 pages. **$15.00**

Mennonite Community Cook Book. 1950, Mary Emma Showalter. **$12.00**

Menu Cook Book. 1924, Alice Bradley. **$25.00**

375 Menu Cookbook. 1973, Marguerite Patten. **NCV**

Menus for Every Occasion. 1931, Tipton. **$20.00**

Meta Given's Modern Encyclopedia of Cooking. 1947, first printing, 2 volumes, 1724 pages. **$17.50**

Meta Given's Modern Encyclopedia of Cooking. 1947, 1948, 1949, 1952, 1953, 15th printing, 2 volumes, 1724 pages. **$10.00**

Mickey Mouse Cook Book. 1975, Golden Press. **NCV**

The Mid-Atlantic Recipe Swap with General Foods Kitchens. 1970, Washington, D.C., three-ring binder. **NCV**

Mirro-Matic Pressure Pan Recipes. 1952, Aluminum Goods Mfg. Co., Manitowac. **$6.00**

Miss Leslie's New Cook Book - A Complete Manual of Domestic Cookery. Pre-1871, Eliza Leslie, her last cookbook. **$275.00**

Miss Leslie's New Cookery Book. 1851, Eliza Leslie, T.B. Peterson Publishing Co., Philadelphia, 662 pages. **$250.00**

Miss Leslie's New Cookery Book. 1851, 1857, Eliza Leslie, T.B. Peterson Publishing Co., Philadelphia, 662 pages. **$250.00**

Miss Leslie's New Receipts Cook Book - Over One Thousand Receipts. 1850, 1851, 1854, Eliza Leslie. **$200.00**

Mixer and Blender Cookbook. 1972, Myra Street. **NCV**

The Modern Cake Baker, Pastry Cook and Confectionery. First edition, 1894, Fred M. Yanner, 262 pages. **$45.00**

The Modern Cook Book and Kitchen Guide for the Busy Woman. 1932, Mabel Claire. **$20.00**

The Modern Family Cook Book. 1942, Meta Given. **$17.50**

The Modern Family Cook Book. 1942, 1953, 1958, 1961, Meta Given, 632 pages. **$5.00**

Modern Priscilla Cook Book. First edition, 1924, The Priscilla Publishing Company, 352 pages. **$25.00**

Modern Priscilla Cook Book. 1924, 1928, 1929, 1930, 1932, The Priscilla Publishing Company, 442 pages. **$7.50**

Modern Priscilla Standard Cook Book - Methods and Recipes. 1929, the new 1930 subscription edition, The Priscilla Publishing Company. **$25.00**

Modernistic Recipe-Menu Book of the DeBoth Homemaker's Cooking School. 1929, Jessie Marie De-Both. **$25.00**

The Molly Goldberg Cook Book. 1955, 1959, Molly Goldgerg & Myra Waldo. **$10.00**

Monarch Cook Book. 1905, Malleable Iron Range Co. **$30.00**

Money Saving Cook Book. 1940, Ida Bailey Allen, 481 pages. **$15.00**

Monstrous Depravity - A Jeremiad & A Lamentation About Things to Eat. 1963, John Gould, 224 pages. **$6.00**

Morgantown Temple Sister's Cook Book. 1942, West Virginia, some recipes by Eleanor Roosevelt. **$17.50**

Motherly Talks with Young Housekeepers. 1873, Mrs. Harriet Beecher Stowe. **$75.00**

Mother's Book. 1831, 1844, Mrs. Lydia Child. **$325.00**

Mrs. Allen's Cook Book. 1920, Lucy G. Allen. **$25.00**

Mrs. Apple Yard's Kitchen. 1942, Louise Andrews Kent. **$17.50**

Mrs. Caldwell's Cook Book. 1925, J.H. Sears & Company, Inc. New York, 118 pages. **$25.00**

Mrs. Coffman's Cook Book. 1889, copyright applied for first edition, Mrs. Eva M. Coffman, 72 pages. **$45.00**

Mrs. Gillette's Cook Book. 1905, Mrs. F.L. Gillette, Saalfield Publishing Co., 605 pages. **$35.00**

Mrs. Goodfellow's Cookery as It Should Be - A New Manual of the Dining Room and Kitchen. Pre-1873, **$90.00**

Mrs. Lincoln's Boston Cook Book. 1889, Mrs. D.A. Lincoln (Mary J.). **$45.00**

Mrs. Mander's Cook Book. 1968, Olga Sarah Manders. **$6.00**

Mrs. Olson's Get-Together Recipes. 1973, Meredith Publishers, give-away with coffee purchase. **NCV**

Mrs. Parker's Complete Housekeeper. 1888, 1894, 473 pages. **$25.00**

Mrs. Putman's Receipt Book; And Young Housekeepers Assistant. 1849, 1954, Boston. **$200.00**

Mrs. Rasmussen's Book of One-Arm Cookery. 1946, **$17.50**

Mrs. Rorer's Philadelphia Cook Book - A Manual of Economics. First edition, 1886, Mrs. S.T. Rorer, Arnold and Company, 581 pages. **$75.00**

Mrs. Rorer's Philadelphia Cook Book - A Manual of Home Economics. 1886, 1887, 1914, Mrs. S.T. Rorer, Arnold and Company, 581 pages. **$25.00**

Mrs. Rorer's Every Day Menu Book. 1905, Mrs. Sarah T. Rorer, Philadelphia, Arnold & Company, 300 pages plus ads. **$35.00**

Mrs. Rorer's New Cook Book - A Manual of Housekeeping. First edition, 1902, Sarah Tyson Rorer, Arnold and Company, 731 pages. **$35.00**

Mrs. S.T. Rorer's Ice Creams, Water Ices and Frozen Puddings. 1913. **$25.00**

Mrs. Scott's North American Seasonal Cook Book. First edition, 1921, Mrs. Anna B. Scott, 252 pages. **$25.00**

Mrs. W.H. Wilson's New Cook Book. First edition, 1914, Foster and Parker Company. **$25.00**

Mrs. William Vaughn Moody's Cook Book. 1931, Harriet C. Moody, Scribner's & son, 475 pages. **$20.00**

Murder On The Menu. 1972, Jeanine Larmoth and Charlotte Turgeon, 268 pages. **NCV**

My Favorite Recipe - By 500 of the World's Best Cooks. 1938, S. Claire Sondheim, Culinary Arts Institute. **$20.00**

My Nameday, Come For Dessert. 1962, Helen McLoughlin, 320 pages. **$8.00**

My Own Cookbook. First edition, 1972, Gladys Tabor, 312 pages. **NCV**

My Own Cookbook. 1972, Gladys Tabor, second printing, 312 pages. **NCV**

The Mystery Chef's Own Cook Book. 1934, 1943, Longman Green, 366 pages. **$20.00**

▶ *The Mystery Chef's Own Cook Book.* 1934, 1943, 1945, Longman Green, 366 pages. **$12.50**

The Nancy Drew Cookbook - Clues to Good Cooking. 1977, Carolyn Keene, first printing, 160 pages. **NCV**

The National Cook Book - By A Lady of Philadelphia. Eighth edition, 1857, Hannah Mary Peterson. **$110.00**

National Cook Book. 1904, Marion Harland and Mrs. Christine Terhune Herrick. **$35.00**

The National Cook Book. 1935, Shiela Hibben. **$20.00**

National Cooking the Finnish Way. 1974, Ulla Kakonen. **NCV**

Never in the Kitchen When Company Arrives. 1964. **$6.00**

The New American Cook Book. 1941, Lily Haxworth Wallace, The American Stores Company, 930 pages. **$17.50**

The New American Cook Book. 1941, 1942, Lily Haxworth Wallace, The American Stores Company. **$12.50**

The New Art of Simplified Cooking. 1940. **$17.50**

The New Art of Buying, Preserving and Preparing Foods. 1934, General Electric Kitchen Institute. **$20.00**

A New Book of Cookery. First edition, 1912, Fannie Merritt Farmer, Little, Brown & Co., Boston, 440 pages. **$35.00**

A New Cook of Cookery. 1912, 1915, Fannie Merritt Farmer, by Mary W. Farmer, 440 pages. **$30.00**

The New Butterick Cook Book. 1924, Flora Rose, The Butterick Publishing Company, 734 pages. **$30.00**

The New Buckeye Cook Book. 1888, Home Publishing Company, 1,288 pages. **$50.00**

The New California Cook Book. 1946, 1955, Genevieve Callahan. **$17.50**

New Casserole Cookery. 1968, Marian Tracy, 220 pages. **$6.00**

New Cook Book and Marketing Guide. 1880, 1881, 1883, Maria Parloa. **$50.00**

The New Cookery. 1916, 1922, Lenna Francis Cooper, Head Dietitian of Battle Creek Sanitarium, Director of Battle Creek Sanitarium School of Home Economics, 449 pages. **$25.00**

The New Cook's Cookbook. 1969, Carol Guilford, 262 pages. **$6.00**

The New Connecticut Cook Book. First edition, 1947, The Woman's Club of Westport, 338 pages. **$17.50**

A New Cruising Cook Book - Easy To Cook Meals on A Two-Burner Stove. 1960, Russell K. Jones and C. McKin Norton. **$8.00**

New Dishes from Left Overs. 1935, Coral Smith. **$20.00**

New Delineator Recipes. 1929, Butterick Publishing Company, 222 pages. **$30.00**

New Delineator Recipes. 1929, 1930, Ann Batchelder's ten recipes, Butterick Publishing Company, 222 pages. **$25.00**

The New England Cook Book. 1905, 1906, Mary J. Loncoln, Maria Parloa, Marion Harland, 286 pages. **$30.00**

New Housekeeper's Manual. 1873, Catherine Beecher and Harriet Beecher Stowe, New York, **$70.00**

The New Idea Cookbook. 1965. **$6.00**

The New New Can-Opener Cookbook. 1951, 1952, 1959, 1968, Poppy Cannon, 314 pages. **$6.00**

The New Pennsylvania Dutch Cook Book. 1958, 240 pages. **$12.00**

New Receipts for Cooking - Miss Leslie of Philadelphia. 1954, Eliza Leslie. **$325.00**

New Standard Domestic Science Cook-Book. 1908, 1911, Jennie A. Hansey, Ella M. Blackstone, London, England, 1,400 recipes. **$30.00**

The New World Encyclopedia of Cooking. 1975, Culinary Arts Institute, 800 pages. **NCV**

The New York Cook Book. 1880, Mrs. Jane Astor. **$45.00**

The New York Times Cook Book. First edition, 1961, Craig Claiborne, Harper & Bros., 718 pages. **$9.00**

The New York Times Cook Book. 1961, Craig Claiborne, Harper & Bros., 718 pages. **$5.00**

The New York Times Large Type Cookbook. 1968, Jean Hewlitt, 446 pages. **$6.00**

The New York Times Natural Foods Cookbook. 1968, Jean Hewlitt. **$6.00**

The New York Times Natural Foods Cookbook. 1968, 1971, Jean Hewlitt. **NCV**

The Newlywed's Handbook. First edition, 1937, Rogers Publishing Company, Inc., Chicago, 104 pages. **$20.00**

Nothing Fancy. 1984, Diana Kennedy. **NCV**

Nutrition in Health & Disease. 1928, Lenna F. Cooper, Edith M. Barber, Helen Mitchell, J.B. Lippincotte Co. **$25.00**

Nutrition in Health & Disease. 1928, 1929, 1930, 1931, 1935, 1938, 1941, 1943, Lenna F. Cooper, Edith M. Barber, Helen S. Mitchell. **$7.50**

Official Handbook for the National Training School for Cookery. 1879, London, England, 416 pages. **$60.00**

The Official Cook Book of the Hay System. 1934, 1943, Wm. Howard Hay, M.D. by Esther Smith. **$12.50**

Old World Foods For New World's Families. 1946, spiral. **$10.00**

Old Southern Recipes. 1932. **$17.50**

One Hundred Luncheon Dishes. 1932, Larned. **$17.50**

One Hundred Picnic Suggestions. 1932, Larned. **$17.50**

One Hundred Salads. 1932, Larned. **$17.50**

One Hundred and One Desserts. 1907, May E. Southworth. **$30.00**

One Hundred and One Entrees. 1904, 1906, Paul Elder, compiled by May E. Southworth, San Francisco. **$30.00**

One Hundred and One Entrees. 1904, 1906, 1907, Paul Elder, compiled by May E. Southworth, San Francisco. **$20.00**

One-Piece Dinners. 1925, Mary D. Chambers. **$25.00**

Onions In The Stew. 1955, Betty Macdonald, 256 pages. **$12.00**

The Original Picayune Creole Cook Book. 1901, 1906, 1916, 1922, 1928, 1936, 1938, 1942, 1947, 1954, *New Orleans Times,* Picaynne Publishing Company. **$7.50**

Our Candy Recipes. 1932, Van Arsdale. **$17.50**

Out of Kentucky Kitchens. 1949, Matian Flexner, Duncan Hines recipes. **$12.00**

Outdoor Picture Cook Book. 1954. **$12.00**

The Outdoorsman's Cook Book. 1944, Arthur H. Carhart, first printing. **$17.50**

Out of This World Cook Book. 1978, favorite recipes of astronauts, by wives and others of the space program, spiral. **NCV**

Overseas Press Club Cookbook. 1962, Sigrid Schultz. **$6.00**

Palmer House Cook Book. 1935, Ernst E. Amiet. **$17.50**

Papa Rossis Secrets of Italian Cooking. 1969, Victor Bennett with Antonia Rossi, Prentice-Hall, Inc., 236 pages. **$6.00**

Party Sandwiches. 1928, Butterick Publishing Company by Delineator Home Institute. **$20.00**

Patty Pans: A Cook Book for Beginners. 1929, 1938, Florence LaGanke. **$20.00**

Paula Peck's Art of Good Cooking. 1961. **$8.00**

Peach Cookbook. 1974, Cynthia and Jerome Rubin. **NCV**

The Pennsylvania Dutch Cook Book. 1949, Ruth Hutchinson, 213 pages. **$17.50**

Pennsylvania State Grange Cook Book. Sixth edition, 1928, Pennsylvania State Home Economics Committee. **$25.00**

Pennsylvania State Grange Cook Book. 1928, 1934, Pennsylvania State Home Economics Committee. **$20.00**

The Pennypincher's Book of Fine Food. 1968, Caroline Hightower, a collection of delectable recipes, 126 pages. **$6.00**

Peoples Home Library, Cooking Vetinary, Medical Allopathic-Homeopathic. 1911, Ritter. **$25.00**

The Peoples Home Medical Book and The Peoples Home Recipe Book. 1911, Mrs. Alice Gitchell Kirk, two books in one, 3½" thick. **$25.00**

Pearl's Kitchen. 1973, Pearl Bailey. **NCV**

Peter Hunt's Cape Cod Cookbook. 1957, 1962, Peter Hunt, 181 pages. **$8.00**

Peterson's National Cook Book. 1891, Hannah Mary Peterson. **$50.00**

Peterson's New Cook Book - Useful and Practical Receipts for Housewife's. 1857, Hannah Mary Peterson. **$175.00**

Physical Culture Cook Book. 1901, Mrs. Mary Richardson under direction of Bernarr McFaddan, 249 pages. **$35.00**

Physical Culture Cook Book. 1929, Bernarr McFadden with collaboration of Milo Hastings, director of Physical Culture Food Research Laboratory. **$20.00**

Pictorial Review Standard Cook Book - A Sure Guide for Every Bride. 1926, 1934, Chester H. Smith. **$15.00**

Picture Cook Book. 1951, 1958, Mary Hamman, Time-Life, 10"x14", 292 pages. **$12.00**

Picture Cook Book. 1951, 1958, 1959, Mary Hamman, Time-Life, 292 pages. **$7.50**

The Pleasures of the Table. An Account of Gastronomy from Ancient Days to Present Times. 1902, 477 pages. **$30.00**

The Pleasure of Your Company. First edition, 1976, Diane & Paul Von Welanetz, 300 pages. **NCV**

The Pooh Cook Book. 1975, V.H. Ellison, illus. by E.H. Shepard. **NCV**

Potluck Party Recipes. 1960, Thora H. Campbell. **$8.00**

The Practical American Cook Book. 1855. **$110.00**

Practical Cake and Confectionery Art. 1932, Bauer. **$17.50**

Practical Candy Making. 1930, Porter. **$17.50**

Practical Cooking And Dinner Giving. 1890, Mrs. Mary F. Henderson. **$35.00**

Practical Cooking & Serving. 1902, 1912, 1916, Janet McKenzie Hill, Doubleday, 679 pages. **$20.00**

Practical Cooking & Serving. 1902, 1912, 1916, 1923, Janet McKenzie Hill, Doubleday, 679 pages. **$12.50**

Practical Dietetics, Diet in Health & Disease. 11th edition, 1917, Alida Frances Pattee. **$12.50**

Practical Dietetics, Diet in Health & Disease. 1917, 1929, Alida Frances Pattee. **$7.50**

Practical Housekeeping - A Compilation of Tried and Approved Recipes. 1881, 1887. **$45.00**

Practical Housekeeping - Tried and Approved Recipes. 1881, 1887, 1893. **$35.00**

Practical Suggestions for Young Housekeepers. 1883, Mrs. T. J. Kirkpatrick, Cosy Nest Cottage, Springfield, Ohio. **$50.00**

The Presidential Cook Book. First edition, 1895, adapted from the White House Cook Book. The Werner Company, 440 pages. **$40.00**

The Presidential Cook Book. 1895, 1896, adapted from the White House Cook Book, The Saalfield Publishing Company. **$30.00**

The Presidential Cook Book. 1895, 1896, 1901, adapted from the White House Cook Book. **$20.00**

▶ *The Presidential Cook Book.* 1895, 1896, 1901, 1904, 1907, 1909, adapted from the White House Cook Book. The Saalfield Publishing Company, 440+ pages. **$12.50**

The Presidents Cookbook. 1968, Poppy Cannon & Patricia Brooks, Funk & Wagnalls, 545 pages. **$6.00**

Pressure Cookery Perfected. 1978, Roy Andries De Grout. **NCV**

Pressure Cooking. 1947, Ida Bailey Allen, 403 pages. **$17.50**

Principals of Cookery. 1906, 1910, 1914, 1922, Anna Barrows, Library of Home Economics, American School of Home Economics, Chicago, 234 pages. **$12.50**

Prinicipals of Domestic Science. Pre-1869, Miss Catherine E. Beecher, Mrs. Harriet Beecher Stowe, J.B. Ford & Co. Publishers. **$225.00**

Principles of Food Preparation. 1930, Mary D. Chambers. **$17.50**

Prize Essay of American Public Health Association - Practical Sanitary and Economic Cooking Adapted To Persons of Moderate and Small Means. 1889, Mrs. Mary Hinman Able, 190 pages. **$45.00**

Prudence Penny's Cook Book. 1947, Home Economics editor of Los Angeles *Examiner* newspaper, second printing. **$17.50**

Putnam's Household Handbook. 1916, Mae Savell Croy, G.P. Putnam. **$25.00**

Pyrex Prize Recipes. 1953, Corning Glass Works. **$10.00**

The Pyromaniac's Cookbook, The Best in Flaming Food and Drink. 1968, John J. Poister. **$6.00**

Quantity Cookery, Menu Planning and Cooking for Large Numbers. 1925, L. Richards and N. Treat, 200 pages. **$25.00**

Quantity Cookery, Menu Planning and Cooking for Large Numbers. 1951, 1952, 628 pages. **$12.00**

Quick and Easy Desserts. 1965, William Kaufman. **$6.00**

Rangoon International Cook Book. 1954, Woman's Society of Christian Service Rangoon, Burma Methodist English Church. **$24.00**

Rational Cookery: Cookery Made Practical and Economical. Fifth edition, 1870, Hartelaw Reid, Edinburgh, England. **$70.00**

Receipts. Second edition, 1898, Louise D. Speer, 208 pages. **$35.00**

Recipe Book - Beard on Bread. 1974, James Beard. **NCV**

Recipes and Menus for Fifty. 1922, Francis L. Smith, 237 pages. **$20.00**

Recipes at Moderate Cost. Second edition, 1943, Constance C. Hart, spiral. **$17.50**

Recipes for Successful Dining. 1934, 117 pages. **$20.00**

Recipes From the Kitchens of West Virginia. 1969. **$6.00**

Recipes From The Old Country and The New. 1910, Maria E. Martin, 309 pages. **$30.00**

Recipes From The Old South. 1961, Martha L. Meade, 185 pages. **$8.00**

Recipes from Pasquale's Kitchen. 1984, Pasqual Carpino, Judith Dryman. **NCV**

Recipes From the Regional Cooks of Mexico. First edition, 1978, Diana Kennedy. **NCV**

Recipes from Scotland. Second edition, 1947, F. Marion McNeill, Edinburgh, Scotland. **$15.00**

Recipes of All Nations. 1945, Countess Morphy. **$25.00**

Recipes Out of Bilibid, Japanese POW Camp. 1946, Col. H.C. Fowler, 93 pages. **$30.00**

500 Recipes by Request from Andersons Famous Dutch Kitchens. 1948, Jeanne M. Hall & Belle Anderson Ebner. **$17.50**

Recipes, Valuable and Tried. 1898, Louise D. Speer. **$35.00**

Recouts in Herb Cookery. First edition, 1933. **$20.00**

The Rector Cook Book. 1928, George Rector, compliments of Cribben & Sexton Company, manufacturers of Universal Gas Ranges. **$25.00**

The Redbook Timesaver Cookbook. 1960, 1961, 1962, 1963, 1964, 1965, 1966, 1967, 1968, 1969, 1970, 1971, 1972, by the editors of *Redbook,* compiled by Ruth Fairchild Pomeroy, Saturday Review Press, New York, 328 pages. **NCV**

The Red & White International Cook Book. 1930's, Red & White Corp. Grocery Stores. **$25.00**

The Rodale Cookbook. 1973, 1974, 1975, 1976, 1977, Nancy Albright, Chef-Manager of the Rodale Press Dining Room, 486 pages. **NCV**

Round The World Cook Book. 1936, 1956, Culinary Arts Institute, Kay Morrow, Hazel Himminger, Pauline Dubins, S. Calire Soundheim, four plastics rings, wood covers. **$5.00**

Ruth Wakefield's "Toll House Tried & True Recipes." First edition, 1936, Ruth G. Wakefield. **$25.00**

▶ *Ruth Wakefield's "Toll House Tried and True Recipes."* 1936, 1937, 1938, 1939, 1940, 1945, Ruth G. Wakefield, Viking Press, 21st printing, 269 pages. **$7.50**

Salads. 1911, Olive M. Hulse, Hopewell Press, Chicago. **$20.00**

▶ *Salads, Sandwiches and Chafing Dish Dainties.* First edition, 1899, Janet McKenzie Hill, 250+ pages. **$50.00**

Salads, Sandwiches & Chafing Dishes. 1907, 1911, Janet McKenzie Hill. **$25.00**

Salads, Sandwiches and Chafing Dish Recipes. First edition, 1916, Marion H. Neil, 262 pages. **$25.00**

Salads, Sandwiches and Specialty Dishes. 1932, Emory Hawcock. 1932, **$20.00**

A Salute To American Cooking. 1968, Stephen & Ethel Longstreet. **$10.00**

Salute to Cheese. 1966. **$6.00**

The Saturday Evening Post Christmas Book. 1976, illus. by Norman Rockwell and others, stories, carols, poems, crafts, recipes, 148 pages. **NCV**

The Sausage Book - Being a Compendium of Sausage Recipes. 1969, Richard Gehman's. **$6.00**

Savarin Cook Book. 1930, Allevi. **$20.00**

School and Home Cooking Textbook. First edition, 1920, Carlotta C. Greer, 554 pages. **$20.00**

School and Home Cooking Textbook. 1920, 1925, Carlotta C. Greer, revised edition. **$15.00**

The School Kitchen Textbook. 1915, 1916, Mary J. Lincoln, 308 pages. **$25.00**

The Science of Food and Cookery. 1921, H.S. Anderson, 297 pages. **$25.00**

The Science of Food & Cookery. Seventh edition, 1921, 1938, H.S. Anderson, 297 pages. **$20.00**

The Sea Food Cook Book - Classic to Contemporary. 1986, Pierre Francy & Bryan Miller. **NCV**

Sea Food Cookery. 1949, Wallace, Blue Ribbon Books. **$12.00**

Season To Taste. 1957, Peggey Harvey. **$12.00**

The Service Cook Book. 1933, Mrs. Ida Bailey Allen, published exclusively for F.W. Woolworth Co., N.R.A. symbol, spiral, stiff cover, 188 pages. **$20.00**

The Settlement Cook Book. 1901, 1915, Mrs. Simon Kander, Liberty edition. **$75.00**

▶ *The Settlement Cook Book.* 14th edition, 1901, 1915, 1925, Mrs. Simon Kander, Tested Recipes, etc. The Settlement Cooking Classes, The Milwaukee Public School Kitchens, The School of Trades for Girls, and Experienced Houewives, 614 pages plus ads. **$25.00**

The Settlement Cook Book. 21st edition, 1901, 1915, 1925, 1931, 1936, compiled by Mrs. Simon Kander, tested recipes, etc., no ads, 624 pages. **$15.00**

The Settlement Cook Book. 29th edition, 1901, 1915, 1925, 1931, 1936, 1940, 1949, compiled by Mrs. Simon Kander, tested recipes, etc., 624 pages. **$10.00**

The Settlement Cook Book. 1901, 1915, 1925, 1931, 1936, 1940, 1949, 1965, compiled by Mrs. Simon Kander, tested recipes, etc., 535 pages. **$6.00**

Seven Hundred Sandwiches. 1929, 1930, Florence A. Cowles. **$20.00**

Shaker Recipes and Formulas For Cooks and Homemakers. 1969, William Lawrence Lassiter. **$6.00**

Show Me Missouri Heritage Cookbook. 1980, Mrs. Margaret Lawler. **NCV**

The Silent Hostess Treasure Book. 1931, Electric Ref. Dept., General Electric Company, 101 pages. **$12.50**

The Silent Hostess Treasure Book. 1931, 1932, Electric Ref. Dept, General Electric Company, 103 pages. **$10.00**

The Simon's Handy Receipt Book or Simon's Complete Cook Book. 1894, W.E. Simons Manufacturing Company, Fine Flavoring Extracts, Bacon and Gaul, Binghampton, New York, 127 pages. **$35.00**

Simple French Cookery. 1958, Edna Beilenson, Peter Pauper Press, 60 pages. **$12.00**

Simple New England Cookery. 1962, Edna Beilenson, 62 pages. **$8.00**

Simple Oriental Cookery. 1960, Edna Beilenson. **$8.00**

Singers & Swingers in the Kitchen. 1967, Roberta Ashly, Barbara Streisand to Mike Jagger. **$6.00**

The Six-Couple Dinner. 1922, Alice Bradley. **$25.00**

600 Receipts Cook Book. 1867. **$80.00**

Six Hundred Suggestions For Serving Meat. 1935, Alice Bradley, principal of Miss Farmer's School of Cookery, Inc., Boston, 91+ pages. **$20.00**

The 60 Minute Chef. 1947, Lillian Beuno McCue and Carol Truax, **$17.50**

Slade's Cooking School Recipes. 1916, Slade's Cooking School, Maine. **$25.00**

Smorgasbord and Scandinavian Cookery. 1948, Florence Brobeck & M. Kiellerg, 341 pages. **$17.50**

Some Favorite Southern Recipes of the Duchess of Windsor. 1942. **$20.00**

Someone's in the Kitchen with Dinah - Dinah Shore's Personal Cookbook. 1971, eighth printing 1973, 179 pages. **NCV**

The Something-Went-Wrong-What-Do-I-Do-Now-Cookbook. 1970, John & Marina Baer, 158 pages. **NCV**

The Soup Book. 1949, Louis De Gouy, Chef of the Waldorf-Astoria Hotel, New York. **$17.50**

South Florida Cookery. 1964, Alex D. Hawkes. **$6.00**

Southern Cooking. 1941, 1949, Mrs. S.R. Dull. **$17.50**

Spanish Cooking. 1957, 1959, Eliz Cais, 1957 was the first American edition. **$10.00**

Specialties of the House. 1960, Elizabeth H. Grossman, Simon Schuster, 96 pages. **$8.00**

The Split-Level Cookbook - Family Meals to Cook Once & Serve Twice. 1967, Louann Gaeddert & Thomas Y. Crowell. **$6.00**

▶ *St. Louis Symphony of Cooking.* First editon, 1954, The Woman's Association of the St. Louis Symphony Society, compiled by Mrs. J. Eldred Newton, 472 pages plus index. **$15.00**

The Standard Cook Book. 1948, Anne Director. **$12.00**

Start To Finish. 1954, Ann Batchelder. **$12.00**

Stella Standard's Cook Book. 1952, Stella Standard, 512 pages. **$12.00**

Stillmeadow Cook Book. Third edition, 1947, Gladys Tabor. **$17.50**

Stillmeadow Cook Book. 1947, 1965, Gladys Tabor, 335 pages. **$7.50**

Stillmeadow Sampler. 1959, Gladys Tabor. **$20.00**

Stillroom Cookery. 1977, Grace Firth. **NCV**

The Story of a Cook. First edition, 1942, Herman Smith, illus. Eleanor Sense by Anna Barrows. **$17.50**

The Stouffer Cook Book of Great American Food & Drink. 1973. **NCV**

Streamlined Cooking. First edition, 1939, Irma S. Rombauer, Bobbs-Merrill Company, 239 pages. **$25.00**

Strength From Eating - How & What To Eat & Drink. 1901, Bernar McFadden, Physical Culture Publishing Company, 194 pages. **$35.00**

The Summer Cookbook. First edition, 1966, Lousene Rousseau Brunner, 200 pages. **$6.00**

Sun Country Mexican Cookbook II. 1981, Old El Paso Pet, Inc., spiral, 128 pages. **NCV**

The Sunset Cookbook. 1960, Annabel Post, Home Economics editor, 215 pages. **$8.00**

The Supper of The Lamb - A Culinary Entrtainment. 1967, 1969, Robert Farrar Capon, 272 pages. **$6.00**

Swedish Food - 200 Selected Swedish Dishes. Sixth edition, 1946, 1954, published by Esselte-Gothenburg-Sweden, 151 pages. **$7.50**

Swedish Cooking. 1960, Marianno Gronwall Van Der Turk. **$8.00**

Sweet Home Cook Book. 1888. **$45.00**

The Swiss Cookbook. First edition, 1967, Nika Hazelton. **$6.00**

Table Etiquette. 1930, Mary D. Chambers. **$20.00**

Table Service. 1915, Lucy G. Allen, intro by Fannie Farmer. **$25.00**

Table Service. 1915, 1921, 1926, Lucy G. Allen, teacher of the Boston Cooking School, dedicated to Fannie Merritt Farmer, 128 pages. **$15.00**

The Taste of Country Cooking. 1976, 1978, 1982, Edna Lewis, Alfred A. Knopf, New York, 268 pages. **NCV**

201 Tasty Dishes for Reducers. 1948, 128 pages. **$17.50**

Tasty Cooking For Good Health. 1973, Anne Marshall. **NCV**

Tea-Time at the Masters. 1977, collection of recipes for golfer & cook. 291 pages. **NCV**

The Teenager's Menu Cookbook. 1969, Charlotte Adams. **$6.00**

The Temperance Cook Book. 1889, adapted from the White House Cook Book, free from all references to liquors, Saalfield Publishing Co., manilla cover. **$50.00**

Tested Tasties. 1967, Naylor. **$6.00**

The Texas Cookbook. First edition. 1965, Mary Faulk, Koock Bros. Publishers, 499 pages. **$6.00**

Things You Have Always Wanted to Know about Cooking. 1932, Margaret Mitchell, The Aluminum Cooking Utensil Company, bound in aluminum covers, 80 pages. **$25.00**

Thomas Jefferson's Cook Book. 1938, Marie Kimball, Richmond, Virginia, 11 pages. **$25.00**

Thomas Jefferson's Cook Book. 1938, 1949, Marie Kimball. **$10.00**

Thoughts For Buffets. 195448, William Barass. **$12.00**

Thoughts For Feastive Foods. 1964, Hougton-Mifflin Co. **$6.00**

A Thousand Ways to Please A Family. 1922, Louise Bennett Weaver & Helen Cowles LeCron, 397 pages. **$25.00**

A Thousand Ways to Please A Husband with Bettina's Best Recipes. 1917, Louise Bennett Weaver & Helen Cowles LeCron, 480 pages. **$75.00**

A Thousand Ways to Please A Husband. 1917, 1932, Louise Bennett Weaver & Helen Cowles LeCron, 480 pages. **$25.00**

Three Easy Pieces - The Quick Menu Cookbook. 1985, mix and match to create over 20,000 meals, General Foods Corporation, 96 pages. **NCV**

365 Ways To Cook Hamburgers. 1958, 1960, Doyne Nickerson, Doubleday, 189 pages. **$8.00**

Three Meals a Day - Collection of Valuable and Reliable Recipes in all Classes of Cookery. 1887, 1890, Miss M.C. Cooke, Acme Publishers, 544 pages plus ads. **$45.00**

Time-Life Recipes - The Cooking of India. 1969. **$6.00**

The Time Readers Book of Recipes. 1949, Florence Arfmann. **$17.50**

Time-Saving Cookery. 1922, Sarah Field Splint. **$25.00**

Trader Vic's Book of Food & Drink. 1946, Trader Vic. **$17.50**

Treasury of Good Food Ideas from the Kraft Kitchens. 1957, Kraft Foods, Inc., sold for $2.00 to hold the Kraft Kitchen Treasury Recipes, three-ring binder. **$10.00**

Treasury of Good Ideas From The Kraft Kitchens. 1957, 1960's, Kraft, Inc., sold for $2.00 to hold the Kraft Kitchen Treasury Recipes, three-ring binder. **$5.00**

A Treasury of Great Recipes. First edition, 1965, Vincent & Mary Price, Doubleday, 455 pages. **$20.00**

Treasury of Outdoor Cooking. 1960, James Beard. **$8.00**

A Treasury of White House Cooking - Washington to Nixon. 1972, Francois Rysavy. **NCV**

The Twelve Days of Christmas Cookbook. 1965, Suzanne Huntley, **$6.00**

Universal New Revised Cook Book with Advice to Housewives. 1930, Mary Ellen Quinlan, University of Chicago, 752 pages. **$30.00**

The United States Regional Cook Book. 1939, 1940, 1947, Ruth Berolzheimer, 752 pages. **$7.50**

The Vegetable Cook Book. 1939, Cora Rose and Bob Brown. **$20.00**

The Vegetarian Epicure. 1972, Anna Thomas. **NCV**

The Victory Binding of the American Woman's Cook Book. 1943, Ruth Berolzheimer, Wartime edition, Culinary Arts Institute. **$10.00**

Viko Cook Book - Recipes from the Viko Aluminum Test Kitchen. First edition, 1936, Aluminum Goods Manufacturing Company. 252 pages. **$20.00**

Virginia Cookery. 1930, Velma Moeschlein. **$30.00**

Visions of Sugarplums - A Cookbook of Cakes, Cookies, Candies & Confections From All the Countries that Celebrate Christmas. First edition, 1968, Mimi Sheratin, Random House, New York. 205 pages. **$6.00**

Vita Craft Instruction Book. 1948, Vita Craft Corporation. **NCV**

Waiting for Dessert. 1982, Valdimir Estrogon. **NCV**

The Waldorf Cook Book by "Oscar," Maitre de Hotel, The Waldorf Astoria. 1896, Louis DeGouy, Saalfield Publishing Company, nearly 4,000 recipes, 900 pages. **$50.00**

War Food: Practical and Economical Methods of Keeping Vegetables and Fruits and Meats. 1917, Amy L. Hardy, Boston. **$25.00**

War-Time Breads and Cakes. 1918, Amy L. Hardy, Boston, 66 pages. **$25.00**

Wear Ever New Method Cooking Instruction. 1946, by Aluminum Cooking Utensils Company, with recipes. **$12.00**

Weight Watchers Cook Book. First edition, 1966, Jean Nidetch, Hearthside Press, 288 pages. **$6.00**

Weight Watchers Program Cookbook. 1974, Jean Nidetch, eighth printing, 320 pages. **NCV**

The Well-Fed Bridegroom. 1957, 1966, Margaret Williams, an informal, fool-proof culinary guide to help young brides and new homemakers outfit the kitchen, stock the larder, plan and cook meals, 192 pages. **$6.00**

West Coast Cook Book. Helen Evans Brown, 1952 reprint, 437 pages. **$8.00**

What's Cooking in Rome. 1960, Ava Maria Sodality Church of St. John Baptist, volume two. **$6.00**

What Cooks at Stillmeadow. First edition, 1958, Gladys Tabor, Philadelphia, 250 pages. **$20.00**

What One Can Do With A Chafing Dish. 1890, H.L.S., John Ireland Publishers. **$35.00**

What Shall I Eat. 1935, Edith M. Barber. **$20.00**

What to Eat, How To Serve It. 1891, C.T. Herrick. **NCV**

When You Entertain - What To Do And How. 1932, Ida Bailey Allen, published by Coca-Cola Company, Atlanta, Georgia, 124 pages. **$25.00**

▶ *The White House Chef Cookbook.* First edition, 1967, Rene Verdon (Kennedy's Chef in the White House), 288 pages. **$10.00**

The White House Chef Cookbook. 1967, 1968, Rene Verdon (Kennedy's Chef in the White House), 288 pages. **$5.00**

▶ *The White House Cook Book.* 1887, 1889, Mrs. F.L. Gillette and Hugo Ziemann, 1889 printing of the 1887 copyright, 562 pages. **$60.00**

The White House Cook Book. 1887, 1890, Mrs. F.L. Gillette and Hugo Ziemann, copyright by R.S. Peale for The Werner Company, 570 pages. **$60.00**

The White House Cook Book. 1887, 1890, 1894, Mrs. F.L. Gillette and Hugo Ziemann, The Werner Company, 1898 printing of the 1894 copyright. **$50.00**

The White House Cook Book in German - Das Weisze Haus Kochbuch. 1887, 1890, 1894, 1899, Mrs. F.L. Gillette and Hugo Ziemann, copyright by The Werner Company, 649 pages. **$50.00**

The White House Cook Book. 1887, 1890, 1894, 1899, Mrs. F.L. Gillette and Hugo Ziemann, The Saalfield Publishing Company, 1904 printing of the 1899 copyright, 590 pages. **$40.00**

The White House Cook Book. 1887, 1890, 1894, 1899, Mrs. F.L. Gillette and Hugo Ziemann, The Saalfield Publishing Company, 1905 printing of the 1889 copyright, 590 pages. **$30.00**

The White House Cook Book. 1887, 1890, 1894, 1899, Mrs. F.L. Gillette and Hugo Ziemann, The Saalfield Publishing Company, 1911 printing of the 1899 copyright, 590 pages. **$20.00**

The White House Cook Book. 1887, 1890, 1894, 1899, 1914, 1915, Mrs. F.L. Gillette and Hugo Ziemann, The Saalfield Publishing Company, 1923 printing of the 1915 copyright, 609 pages. **$20.00**

The White House Cook Book. 1887, 1890, 1894, 1899, 1914, 1915, 1924, Mrs. F.L. Gillette and Hugo Ziemann, revised by Mary E. Dague, Saalfield Publishing Company, 1925 printing of the 1924 copyright, 605 pages. **$20.00**

The White House Cook Book. 1887, 1890, 1894, 1899, 1914, 1915, 1924, Mrs. F.L. Gillette and Hugo Ziemann, revised by Mary E. Dague, The Saalfield Publishing Company, 1926 printing of the 1924 copyright, 606 pages. **$20.00**

The White House Cook Book. 1887, 1890, 1894, 1914, 1915, 1924, 1964, Janet Halliday Ervin, Follett Publishing Company, first printing, pictures of Lyndon B. Johnson & Claudia Alta (Lady Bird) Johnson. **$10.00**

The White House Family Cookbook. 1988, Henry Waller, White House Executive Chef for more than 20 years shares more than 250 best-loved recipes of the past five presidential households. **NCV**

Who Says We Can't Cook. 1955, Women's National Press Club. **$12.00**

Widdifield's New Cook Book or Practical Receipts for the Housewife. 1851, Hannah Widdifield. **$275.00**

Widdifield's New Cook Book or Practical Receipts For The Housewife. 1851, 1856, Hannah Widdifield. **$200.00**

Widdifields' New Cook Book. 1851, 1856, 1873, Hannah Widdifield, revised edition, 396+ pages. **$100.00**

The Williamsburg Art of Cookery. Third edition, 1942, Mrs. Helen Bullock, signed. **$10.00**

The Williamsburg Art of Cookery. 1942, 1958, 1965, 1972, Mrs. Helen Bullock. **NCV**

Wilson's Meat Cookery. 1919, Eleaner Lee Wright, Wilson & Company. **$25.00**

The Wise Encyclopedia of Cookery. 1948, Wm. H. Wise & Company, 1,329 pages. **$17.50**

The Wise Encyclopedia of Cookery. 1948, 1951, 1952, 1954, Wm. H. Wise & Company, 1,329 pages. **$5.00**

Wines & Spirits. First edition, 1961, William E. Massee, 427 pages. **$10.00**

With A Saucepan Over the Sea. 1903, Adelaide Keen, Little & Borwn, recipes of many foreign countries. **$30.00**

▶ *Wolf in Chef's Clothing - The Picture Cook and Drink Book for Men.* 1950, Robert H. Loeb, Jr., 123 pages. **$12.00**

The Woman's Book. 1907, intro by Margret E. Sangster, recipes by Fannie Merritt Farmer, author of *Boston Cooking School Cook Book*, Woman's Home Companion, Cromwell Publishing Company, 352 pages. **$35.00**

Woman's Day Encyclopedia of Cookery. 1965, hard-cover binder to hold 12 soft-cover publications. **NCV**

Woman's Day Encyclopedia of Cookery. 1966, 22 volumes - Volume 1, 157 pages. **$3.00**
Volume 2, 157 pages. **$3.00**

Woman's Day Encyclopedia of Cookery. 1973, 22 volumes, 157 pages. **NCV**

Woman's Day Oriental Cooking - The Fast Wokery. 1971, Jacquelne Heiteay. **NCV**

Woman's Exchange Recipes. 1946, Stella V. Hough in collaboration with Kay Kopera. **$17.50**

Woman's Favorite Cook Book. 1906, Annie R. Gregory, three volumes in one, 678 pages. **$30.00**

Woman's Home Companion Cook Book. 1946, intro. by Dorothy Kirk. **$17.50**

Woman's Institute Library of Cookery. 1918 in Great Britain, 1928 Scranton, Pennsylvania, one volume. **$25.00**
   Part One - 53 pages plus vegetables.
   Part Two - 53 pages plus milk, butter and cheese.

Woman's Own Book of Cake Decorating and Cake Making. 1966, George Newnes. **$6.00**

Woman's World Cook Book. 1940, Ruth Berolzheimer, Consolidated Publishing Co. **$20.00**

Wonderful Ways to Prepare Stews & Casseroles. 1978, Jo Ann Shirly. **NCV**

The Working Girl Must Eat. 1938, Hazel Young. **$20.00**

The Working Wive's (Salaried or Otherwise) Cook Book. 1963, Theodora Zavin and Freda Stuart, 164 pages. **$6.00**

A World of Good Eating, Recipes from Around The World. 1951, Jack Frost Studio's, spiral. **$12.00**

World of Menus & Recipes. 1970, Gertrude Crum. **NCV**

World Wide Cook Book, Menus and Recipes of 75 Nations. 1944, Pearl V. Metzelthin. **$17.50**

The World's Modern Cook Book and Kitchen Guide For The Busy Women. 1932, 1941, 1942, 1943, Mabel Claire, The World Syndicate Publishing Company. **$7.50**

Wurlitzer Centennial Cook Book. 1856, 1956, a collection of recipes covering three generations of the Farney and Wurlitzer family and the wives of the present business associates, 172 pages. **$30.00**

The Yankee Cookbook. 1963, I. Wolcott, 398 pages. **$6.00**

Yankee Hill Country Cooking - Heirloom Recipes from Rural Kitchens. 1963, 202 pages. **$6.00**

Yanner Baking. 1894, F.M. Yanner, 250 pages. **$35.00**

The Year-Round Holiday Cookbook. 1969, Suzanne Huntley, 244 pages. **$6.00**

200 Years of Charleston Cooking. 1934, Blanche S. Rhett, Lettie Gay, 305 pages. **$25.00**

You Can Cook For One. 1966, Louise Pickoff. **$6.00**

The Young French Chef. First edition, 1969, Denise Perret & Mary Eckley, 71 pages. **$6.00**

Young Housekeepers' Friend. 1845, 1846, 1859, 1863, Mrs. Mary Hooker Cornelius. **$90.00**

▶ *Young Housekeeper's Friend.* 1845, 1846, 1859, 1863, 1868, 1871, Mrs. Mary Hooker Cornelius, preface in part: "I wish gratefully to acknowledge the favor with which it has been regarded during the twenty-five years since its first publication," 312 pages. **$75.00**

The Young Wife's Cook Book. 1857, "with receipts of all the best dishes to be prepared for breakfast, dinner and tea as well as a large number of new receipts for cooking," 700 pages. **$130.00**

Your Foods And You or *The Role of Diet.* 1924, Ida Bailey Allen. **$25.00**

Your Mexican Kitchen. 1935, Natalie V. Scott. **$20.00**

The Zane Grey Cookbook. First edition, 1976, Barbara & George Reiger. **NCV**

Chapter 6

Soft-cover Cookbooks and Booklets

Paper cover or soft-cover books of a sort appeared in America as early as 1829 in Boston. During the Civil War years of 1861-1865, the famous Beadle dime novels flourished. By 1865 the house of Beadle and Adams had produced 4,000,000 copies of cheap literature.

With the development of high speed rotary presses and a drop in paper prices beginning in 1873, the time was right for the increase of soft-cover publications. It was at this time that the food companies and the manufacturers of kitchen items commenced advertising with soft-cover cookbooks and booklets to promote their wares or products and to include recipes.

The next step in the evolution of the soft-cover occurred in 1914 but not with soft covers as such. Small leather-bound books were produced to be sold for 25 cents.

Advertising cookbooks and bookets have been used for many years to introduce new food products and build brand loyalty or recognition. Not only does one learn about foods but also about advertising, health concerns, fashions, furniture, lifestyles and financial conditions of the times. These cookbooks and booklets from the 1870's through the 1890's are very scarce in good to very good condition. They were not published with the intent to last 100 years. They were published for use by the housewife in her daily cooking and if used everyday they lasted ten years or so then they would be ready to be pitched. The ones that survived were not used very much and were put away and handed down from generation to generation and preserved. I love to go to an estate auction of someone that lived into their nineties. Most homemakers accumulated these cookbooks, used them and valued them enough to save at house cleaning time. They are fun to read and enjoy and a pleasure to display.

Some companies and their advertising grew together. The Quaker Oats Company was the first to register a cereal trademark - the full-figured Quaker man with a scroll in hand emblazoned with "Pure." Also Quaker was the first to use the package as a sales tool and symbol of recognition.

At the turn of the century Quaker cookbooks deluged the mail; week long cooking schools were held in the larger cities and samples were left at every doorstep. Today history is revealed through these booklets and their changes from year to year.

A tiny booklet, "The Vital Question," was distributed in 1899 by the manufacturers of Shredded Whole-Wheat Biscuits, granulated wheat shread. The "perfect" food was heralded as bread without flour, yeast, germs, baking powder gasses, greasy shortening or salt, yet a light short bread. Shredded wheat was the basic ingredient in the booklet's salads, puddings, pies, beverages and sandwiches.

When baking powders were commercially produced in the middle 1800's, no one could have foreseen the controversy that would develop over the merits of the three types. They were the phosphate, cream of tartar and alum.

While baking powder and soda were being promoted to replace yeast in baking, Fleischmann's promoted yeast with recipes and rhymes. In 1907-1908, Fleischmann's published *The Teddy Bear Baking School* booklets, appealing to young and old through rhymes. A yellowed 1920 booklet, *Excellent Recipes for Baking Raised Bread* convinced homemakers that the essential ingredient was yeast, a standard of excellence since 1868. Interspersed among the recipes were simple sketches to add to the attractiveness of the pages.

Among the most appealing and colorful bookets to be discovered are those promoting Jell-O. While urban shoppers found nationally-advertised foods in the stores, rural homemakers waited at home for the Watkins man, the Raleigh man or the Jewel Tea man who brought products direct from the factory or the manufacturer. He came first by horse and buggy and then in the very early 1900's he came by auto car with a box in the rumble seat to hold his merchandise. These men would also bring any news with them such as Mrs. Jacobs a couple of miles away was in good health. By 1930 he carried 150 necessities including extracts, spices, salves, soaps and premiums.

The Larkin Company, established in 1875 in Buffalo, New York, entered the household via magazine advertising, semiannual; mail-order catalogs, and the cooperation of the railroads. The customers themselves became the salespeople. Neighbors and friends met in clubs to order household necessities and select premiums such as furniture, dishes, silverware and other necessities and luxuries. Some of today's very desired collectibles such as the Larkin desk, Haviland china, Deldare pottery and Noritake's Azalea pattern dinnerware were among Larkin premiums.

Larkin Housewives Cook Book, published in 1915, contained recipes specifying Larkin products such as tomato soup, flour leavening agents, crackers, and prepared pudding mixes. They were to be turned with a Larkin spatula, frozen in a Larkin ice cream freezer or baked in a Larkin casserole.

Your search will produce a wide variety of cookbooks, booklets and advertising recipe booklets distributed by food companies and kitchen equipment manufacturers. Appreciation will grow for the exciting development of industrial America. Memories will be awakened as pages

open up to disclose food-stained, mouse-eaten, often-used recipes.

Many of the following soft-cover cookbooks and booklets can be found rather easily, however, some we have searched for ten years and have only recently found. Many are still in use and can be found by the collector. I hope that you enjoy the following list and find them interesting, amusing, and yes, even surprising.

NCV denotes No Collector Value

▶ **Denotes titles found in the photo section**

The Abbotts Hostess Handbook. 1950's, The Abbotts milkman, creamed cottage cheese, butter, light cream, half & half, heavy cream, grape drink, etc., 22 pages. **$6.00**

Adventures in San Francisco Sourdough Cooking & Baking. 1973, Charles D. Wilford, Gold Rush Sourdough Co. **NCV**

Adventures in Sourdough Cooking & Baking. 1977, Charles Wilford, Gold Rush Sourdough Co. **NCV**

▶ *The Ad-ven-tur-ous Billy and Betty.* 1923, Van Camps Products Co., Van Camps Canned Foods. **$12.00**

Albertson's Slim Down With Low-Calorie Beef Recipes. 1982, recipes courtesy of Beef Industry Council, 24 pages. **NCV**

All About Eggs. 1956, Ida Bailey Allen, Bell Telephone Laboratories, Booklet Rack Service, 15 pages. **$6.00**

All American Way of Cooking and Canning with All American Pressure Cookers. 1948, Wisconsin Aluminum Foundry Co. **$8.00**

All-Season Cookies from the Kitchens of Mirro Aluminum Company. 1970's, Manitowoc, Wisconsin, 16 pages. **NCV**

American Beauty Selected Recipes. 1930's, American Beauty Macaroni Products. 20 pages. **$10.00**

▶ *American Beauty Recipes Using Macaroni Products.* 1930's, The American Beauty Macaroni Company, 16 pages. **$8.00**

American Beauty Recipes Using Macaroni Products. 1953, Glen G. Hoskin, American Beauty Macaroni Company. **$6.00**

American Beef Cookouts. 1984, Meat Board Test Kitchens & Beef Industry Council, Chicago. **NCV**

American Cooker Recipe Book. 1926. **$12.00**

American Waterless Cooker Recipe Book - Roasting, Cooking, Preserving. 1927, West Bend Aluminum Co. **$12.00**

▶ *The American Domestic Cook Book For 1867.* For Gratuitous Distribution. 1867, Dr. Herrick & Co., Albany, New York, Manufacturing Chemists, 32 pages. **$35.00**

The American Domestic Cook Book - for Gratuitous Distribution. 1869-1870, Dr. Herrick's Family Medicines, New York, New York, 32 pages. **$35.00**

The American Way Cooking School Recipes. 1941, *Joplin Globe and News Herald,* last session, 12 pages. **$8.00**

The American Way Cooking School Recipes. 1941, presented by *The Warren Tribune,* second session, 12 pages. **$8.00**

The American Way Cooking School Recipes. 1941, presented by *The Warren Tribune,* third session, 12 pages. **$8.00**

Americana Cookery. 1971, plastic spiral. **NCV**

America's Favorite Recipes. 1941, published by Capper's Reader Service, volume 14, 16 pages. **$8.00**

Any Bride Can Cook. 1965, 1968, Maudie Owens, 81 pages. **$3.00**

The A & P News. 1929, week of Dec. 2, No. 27, by Ann Page, published weekly in the interst of the customers of The Great Atlantic & Pacific Tea Company, established in 1859, 4 pages. **$6.00**

Apporved Recipes For Cooking with Gas. 1936, by A-B Stoves, Inc. Battle Creek, Michigan, Dorothy K. Harris, Director Home Economics Dept., 64 pages. **$10.00**

Armour's Extract of Beef - Richest, Strongest, Best. 1880, Prof. C.F. Pfau, Armour & Co., Chicago, 32 pages. **$28.00**

Armour's Star Ham - 60 Ways To Serve. 1920's, prepared by Dept. of Food Economics, Armour & Co., Chicago, Star, Veribest and Cloverbloom brands, 26 pages. **$12.00**

Armour's Monthly Cook Book. 1912, May, volume one, No. 7. **$14.00**

▶ *Around The World Cook Book.* 1951, Kalamazoo Stove & Furnace Company, 50th year, 1901-1951, Culinary Arts Press, Reading, Pennsylvania, 48 pages. **$6.00**

The Art and Secrets of Chinese Cookery. 1932, La Choy Food Products, Inc. 15 pages. **$10.00**

▶ *The Art and Secrets of Chinese Cookery.* 1942, La Choy Food Products, Inc. 27 pages. **$8.00**

The Art of Rosette Cooking. 1945, Ursula Kaiser, owner of Kalkus-Hirco, Inc. which manufactures Rosette Irons, Tartmaster and Krimput Sealer, a special thanks to Kelly's Kitchen, 90 pages. **$8.00**

The Art of Rosette Cooking. First edition, 1980, Kalkus-Hirco Rosette Irons. **NCV**

The Art of Serving Bread. 1935. Taystee Bread, Purity Bakeries Service Corp., 32 pages. **$10.00**

Atlas Book of Recipes. 1943, Hazel Atlas Glass Co. **$8.00**

Aunt Chick's Pies, Tarts, Ravioli, Cookies, Doughnuts. 1941, Nettie McBirney, The Chicadees, Tulsa, Oklahoma, 39 pages. **$8.00**

The Aunt Ellen Booklet on Waterless Cooking. 1928, Griswold, Mfg. Co., Erie, Pennsylvania. **$12.00**

▶ *Aunt Sammy's Radio Recipes.* 1927, United States Dept. of Agriculture, 142 pages. **$12.00**

Aunt Sammy's Radio Recipes Revised. 1931, Ruth Van Deman and Fanny Walker Yeatman, bureau of Home Economics, 142 pages. **$10.00**

The Automatic Cook Book - Selected Recipes for Time and Temperature Oven Cooking. 1927, Robert Shaw Thermostat Company. **$12.00**

The Avocado Bravo. 1975, California Advisory Board, Newport Beach, California, 48 pages. **NCV**

Azteca Tortillas, The Sun Tortilla - Bright New Recipes for Family Food. 1982, Azteca Corn Products Corporation. **NCV**

Baby's Recipe Book. 1972, Linda McDonald, 126 pages. **NCV**

Backpack Cookery. 1966, Ruth Dyar Mendenhall, Las Siesta Press, 40 pages. **$3.00**

Bake-Rite Oven Thermometer with Recipes. 1931, American Thermometer Co., St. Louis, Missouri, U.S.A. **$10.00**

Bakers Review - The National Monthly of the Baking Industry. 1958, August, 70 pages. **$6.00**

Ball Steam Pressure Cookers-Canners Cook Book. 1934, Ball Brothers Company Recipes. **$20.00**

Barker's Illustrated Almanac, Farmers Guide and Household Receipts. 1879, 34 pages. **$30.00**

▶ *Barker's Illustrated Almanac, Farmers Guide and Household Cook Book.* 1915, 32 pages. **$20.00**

Be An Artist At The Gas Range - Successful Recipes. 1935, The Mystery Chef, Laclede Gas & Light Co., St. Louis, Missouri, 96 pages. **$10.00**

Be An Artist At The Gas Range - Successful Recipes. 1935, The Mystery Chef Longmans, Green & Co., publishers of the *Mystery Chef's Own Cook Book*, 96 pages. **$10.00**

Be An Artist At The Range. 1935, the "Mystery Chef," a complete cook book of successful recipes, Tetly Tea, 96 pages. **$10.00**

The Beech-Nut Book of Menus & Recipes. 1923, Ida Bailey Allen, 32 pages. **$12.00**

Beef Cook-Off Winners. 1987, Missouri Cattlewomans Beef Recipes, 8-pages fold out. **NCV**

Beef Is A Brunch Favorite. 1983, Meat Board Test Kitchens & Beef Industry Council, 12-page fold out. **NCV**

Beef Is A Microwave Favorite. 1987, The Meat Board and Meat Board Test Kitchens, Beef Industry Council. **NCV**

Belles Vignes. 1959, Vins Joyeus, Paris, France, and New York, 106 pages. **$6.00**

Bently Farm Cook Book. 1974. **NCV**

The Best Bon Apetit. 1975, 1976, Bon Appetit Publsihing Company, volume two, 112 pages. **NCV**

Better Homes & Gardens - So Good Luncheons for Bridge & Other Occasions. 1942, 31 pages. **$8.00**

Better Homes & Gardens - Table Settings and Accessories. 1944, 50 pages. **$8.00**

▶ *Better Meals for Less.* 1930, George E. Cornforth, Chef for the New England Sanitarium, 128 pages. **$10.00**

Better Meals for Less Money. 1915, Josephine Headen, Haldeman-Julius Publications, Girard, Kansas, 64 pages. **$14.00**

Better Wartime Meals. 1940's, Ruth F. Hatheway, Director of Home Economics Dept., compliments of the Bakers of Wonder Bread, Continental Baking Co., Inc., 21 pages. **$8.00**

The Bicentennial Beef Cookbook, The Greatest Beef Dishes of America's First 200 Years. 1975, Beef Industry Council. **NCV**

Big Boy Barbecue Book. 1956, 1957, shows how easy it is to cook on spit or grill, Tested Recipe Institute, Inc. **$6.00**

Blu Star Creations Presents Recipes For Thrifty Families. 1880's Blu Star Creations, No. 2, 32 pages. **NCV**

Bon Appetit. 1975 monthly, The Art and Culinary Treasures of China, Cruise Ship Cuisine, 70 pages. **NCV**

Bond Bread Cook Book. 1933, General Baking Company, Barbara Hoyt, Director Bond Bakers Service Kitchen. **$10.00**

Bond Bread - Name Your Favorite Recipe Book. 1935. **$10.00**

Bond Bread Cook Book. 1935, Barbara Hoyt, General Baking Company. **$10.00**

Book of Cookies. 1958, No. 2, 68 pages. **$6.00**

Bread, The Most Important of All Foods. 1925, Spaulding Bread. **$12.00**

Breast O Chicken and Tuna Recipes. 1949. **$8.00**

Bridal Shower Ideas. First edition, 1956, Ruby Chatham, a variety of themes and ways of gift presentation. **$6.00**

The Budget Gourmet. 1962, Sylvia Vaughn Thompson. **$3.00**

Busy-Day Salads and Desserts. 1920, Alice Bradley, principal, Miss Farmer's School of Cookery, California Fruit Growers Exchange. **$12.00**

Cakes and Cookies with Personality. 1939, Nucoa, published by The Best Foods Inc., New York, New York, fourth printing. **$10.00**

▶ *Cakes and Desserts.* 1927, a collection of 150 tested recipes for home cookery, *Woman's World* magazine Co. Inc., Lillian Dynever Rice of Forest Hills, Long Island, New York, 50 pages. **$12.00**

Cakes and Pies - A 2 In 1 Cookbook. First edition, 1978, Arlene Mueller, Nitty Gritty Productions. **NCV**

Calendar of Desserts. 1916, Elizabeth O. Heller, 365 answers. **$14.00**

A Calendar of Desserts. 1940, Consumer Services Dept., General Foods, Corp. **$8.00**

The Calendar of Luncheons with 52 Practical Sunday Evening Suppers - 365 Answers to What Shall We Have for Luncheon. 1916. **$14.00**

Calendar of Meats. 1930's, Dorothy Stuart, Mayrose Test Kitchen, Mayrose Brand, St. Louis Independent Packing Company, 18 pages. **$10.00**

Calorie Saving Recipes with Sucary. 1955. **$6.00**

Camp Cookery. 1926, Horace Kephart. **$12.00**

▶ *Candy Making in the Home.* 1913, Christine Terhune Herrick, 32 pages. **$14.00**

Candy Making. 1929, Women's Institute of Domestic Arts and Sciences, Inc., Scranton, Pennsylvania. **$12.00**

Cashing In On Lamb. 1928, National Livestock & Meat Board, Chicago. **$12.00**

Casseroles And Compliments with Minute Rice. 1966, General Foods Corp., first printing. **$3.00**

Casseroles Cookbook. 1982, Favorite Recipes Press, 128 pages. **NCV**

Catering To A Crowd. 1981, Standard Brands. **NCV**

CBS Radio Booklet - Kate Smith's Favorite Recipes. 1939. **$10.00**

Celebrate The Four Seasons Cookbook. 1979, Hallmark, volume 11, 80 pages. **NCV**

▶ *Celebrity Recipes.* 1961, Helen Dunn. **$3.00**

The Centayr Almanac and Cook Book. 1886, makers of Castoria. **$24.00**

Charging The Human Battery - 50 New Recipes with Iceberg Lettuce. 1929, Iceberg Head Lettuce Western Growers Protective Assoc. **$12.00**

The Charles A. Bogeler Co. Cookery Book and Book of Comfort and Health. 1897. **$20.00**

The Chafing Dish. 1900, Sternau. **$16.00**

Chafing Dish Recipes. Circa 1910, Vinol (tonic). **$14.00**

Cheaper Cuts of Meat And How To Prepare Them. 1919, The Griswold Mfg. Co., Erie, Pennsylvania, U.S.A., City Gas & Electric Co., Sioux City, Iowa. **$14.00**

The Chef's Standby - Blue Ribbon Mayonnaise. 1922, John Behrmann, Inc., Chicago, Richard-Hellmann's, 14 pages. **$12.00**

Chefster 7 In 1 Deep Frying. 1950's, Knapp-Monarch Company, St. Louis. **$6.00**

A Child's Christmas Cookbook. 1984, Betty Chancellor, Illus. Thomas Nast and the St. Nicholas Books, 40 pages. **NCV**

Children's Party Book. 1929, *Woman's World* Magazine Co. Inc., Lily Haxworth Wallace and Lillian Dynever Rice. **$12.00**

Choice Recipes of Fish and Seafoods. 1947-1948, a Public Service by The Boston Post, New England, 47 pages. **$8.00**

Chuckwagon Cooking from Marlboro - Country Range Recipes and Chuckwagon History. 1981, Philip Morris, Inc., 28 pages. **NCV**

Classic American Pies. 1984, Ready Crust brand pie curst, Keebler, spiral, 64 pages. **NCV**

Classic American Recipes for Preserves. 1914, Parawax. **$8.00**

▶ *Clementine Paddleford's Cook Young Cookbook.* 1966, food editor of *This Week* magazine, 124 pages. **$6.00**

Coldspot Operating Suggestions and Recipes. 1930's, Sears Roebuck and Company, 32 pages. **$10.00**

A Collection of The Very Finest Recipes Ever Assembled Into One Cookbook. 1979, Cookbook Publishers, 270 pages. **NCV**

The College Woman's Cookbook. 1923, Evanston, Illinois, 96 pages. **$12.00**

Come Into The Kitchen. 1920's, Lydia E. Pinkham Medicine Company. **$12.00**

Come To Our Barbecue - Taylor Wine Cook Book. 1958. **$6.00**

The Complete Chocolate Chip Cookie Book. First edition, 1982, Bob & Suzanne Stat. **NCV**

The Complete Family Recipe Card Library Series - Recipes from the Kitchens of Dorothy Taylor. 1973, collect all 15 series, A-Series-A-Week, 11 wonderful recipe cards and one series in each envelope. **NCV**

Connecticut Home Record. 1917, County Farm Bureau, small booklet. **$8.00**

Cook Book - Vegex. 1920's, shaped like a jar. **$12.00**

Cook Book and Instructions. 1930, The Standard Electric Stove Co., Toledo, 32 pages. **$10.00**

Cook Book by Reddie Wilcolater. 1946, The Wilcolater Company. **$8.00**

Cookbook Secrets - Gloria Pitzer Presents 400 Recipes for Eating Out At Home Cookbook. 1981, Feb., 10th printing, Book Three, 52 pages. **NCV**

Cook Book - The Malleable Range Made in South Bend Ranks First in the Heart of the Home. 1898, 79 pages. **$24.00**

Cookbook - The Original Junk Food Book - Gloria Pitzer Presents the Secret Restaurant Recipe File Cookbook. 1981, Feb., 17th printing, Book One, 52 pages. **NCV**

The Cookery Calendar. 1925, Woman's World Magazine Co. Inc. **$12.00**

The Cookie Book - Fun to Make Easy to Bake. 1973, Eva Moore, first printing, 64 pages. **NCV**

Cookie Time Favorite Recipes Old and New. 1983, Lorrie De Rose, distributed by Select Magazines, Inc., booklet, 63 pages. **NCV**

Cookies. 1944, Clara Gebhard and Mary Jane Albright, Wheat Flour Institute, Chicago, 16 pages. **$8.00**

Cookies from Kix. 1970's, General Mills, Inc., 6 page fold out. **NCV**

Cookies Galore - Home Baked Are Best. 1956, Francis Barton, Consumer Service Dept., General Foods Corp., 39 pages. **$6.00**

▶ *Cooking Club Magazine.* 1917, Jan., Cooking Club Publishers, edited by Adella Clapp Starr, 19th year. **$14.00**

Cooking for 1 or 2. 1980, 1982, Katherine Hayes Greenberg and Barbara Kanerva Kute. **NCV**

Cooking For Two - With Menus and Recipes. 1936, Katharine Fisher, Director Good Housekeeping Institute, 12 pages. **$10.00**

Cooking Is Fun. 1955, "Gas Range." **$6.00**

Cooking German Style. 1979, International Pub. Co. **NCV**

Cooking Recipes From Warner's Safe Cook Book. 1889, Warner's Safe Cure Kidney and Liver disease. **$24.00**

Cooking the Modern Way. 1948, Planters Peanuts. **$8.00**

Cooking with Cold. 1933, Kelvinator. **$10.00**

Cooking with Gourmet Grains. 1971, Stone-Buhr Milling Co., Seattle, 162 pages. **NCV**

Cook-Less Recipes. 1968, Shirley A. Boie. **$3.00**

Coop Cook Book of Candy. 1930's, General Publishing And Binding, Iowa Falls, Iowa, 30 pages. **$10.00**

Country Gardener's Cookbook - For The Gardener Who Likes To Cook. 1974, Emma Baily, Rodale Press, Inc., 48 pages. **NCV**

Cranberries And How To Cook Them. 1938, Eatmor Cranberries, American Cranberry Exchange. **$10.00**

Cranberry Dishes That Children Love. 1950. **$6.00**

The Cream Top Book of Tested Recipes. 1935, Cream Top Bottle Corp. **$10.00**

Creative Kitchenry - It's Easy. 1973, Homemakers Schools, Rural Gravure Service Inc. **NCV**

Creamette Good Health Cookbook. 1970, Creamette Pasta, Creamette Company, Minneapolis, Minnesota. **NCV**

Creamette Good Health Cookbook. 1980, since 1916 the Creamette Company has been dedicated to providing pasta products made only from 100% durum semolina wheat, 8½"x11", 10 pages. **NCV**

◊ ◊ ◊ ◊

Culinary Arts Institute

The recipe publications of the Culinary Arts Institute were published and sold individually, however, various hard-cover binders with wires were manufactured and sold to hold from 20 to 24 soft-cover recipe publications, like little libraries. The binder had a series of wires to hold the recipe publications. The following binders are known:

1942 - red binder to hold 20 recipe publications, cover title of *Culinary Arts Institute Encyclopedia Cook Book.*

1948 - blue binder to hold 20 recipe publications, cover title of *Culinary Arts Institute Encyclopedia Cook Book.*

1949 - red binder to hold 24 recipe publications, cover title of *The Encyclopedia of Cooking,* Consolidated Publishers.

1956 - white binder to hold 24 recipe publications, cover title of *Cooking Magic,* Culinary Arts Institute.

1948, 1950, 1959, 1962, 1964, 1971 - binder to hold 24 recipe publications, cover title of *Culinary Arts Institute Encyclopedic Cookbook.*

Culinary Arts Institute-Consolidated Book Publishers, copyright by Book Production Industries, Inc. - Ruth Berolzheimer, Director, 1938-1953; Melanie DeProfit, Director, 1954-1970's.

1936 - *Pennsylvania Dutch Cook Book - Fine Old Recipes.* Culinary Arts Press, Reading, Pennsylvania, 48 pages. **$10.00**

1940 - *The Salad Book - 400 Delicious Salads.* Two wood covers, four plastic rings, 48 pages. **$8.00**

1940 - *500 Snacks - Brite Ideas For Entertaining.* No. 1, first printing, green cover, 48 pages. **$8.00**; second printing. **$6.00**

1940, 1949 - *500 Tasty Snacks - Ideas For Entertaining.* No. 1, 48 pages. **$4.00**

1940, 1949, 1950 - *500 Snacks.* No. 1, 48 pages. **$3.00**

1942, 1949, 1950, 1951 - *500 Snacks.* No. 1, 48 pages. **$2.00**

1942, 1949, 1950, 1951, 1952 - *500 Snacks.* No. 1, 48 pages. **$2.00**

1942, 1949, 1950, 1951, 1952, 1954 - *500 Snacks.* No. 1, 48 pages. **$2.00**

1940 - *500 Delicious Dishes from Leftovers.* No. 2, first printing, green cover, 48 pages. **$8.00**; second printing, red cover. **$6.00**

1940, 1949 - *500 Delicious Dishes From Leftovers.* No. 2, 48 pages. **$4.00**

1940, 1949, 1950 - *500 Delicious Dishes From Leftovers.* No. 2, 48 pages. **$3.00**

1940, 1949, 1950, 1951 - *500 Dishes From Leftovers.* No. 2, 48 pages. **$2.00**

1940, 1949, 1950, 1951, 1952 - *500 Delicious Dishes From Leftovers.* No. 2, 48 pages. **$2.00**

1940, 1949, 1950, 1951, 1952, 1954 - *500 Delicious Dishes From Leftovers.* No. 2, 48 pages. **$2.00**

1940 - *250 Classic Cake Recipes - 250 Tempting Cakes and Frostings.* No. 3, first printing, 48 pages. **$8.00**; second printing. **$6.00**

1940, 1949 - *250 Classic Cake Recipes.* No. 3, 48 pages. **$4.00**

1940, 1949, 1950 - *250 Classic Cake Recipes.* No. 3, 48 pages. **$3.00**

1940, 1949, 1950, 1951 - *250 Classic Cake Recipes.* No. 3, 48 pages. **$2.00**

1940, 1949, 1950, 1951, 1952 - *250 Tempting Cakes And Frostings - 250- Classic Cake Recipes.* No. 3, 48 pages. **$2.00**

1940, 1949, 1950, 1951, 1952, 1954 - *250 Tempting Cakes And Frostings.* No. 3, 48 pages. **$2.00**

1940 - *250 Ways to Prepare Poultry and Game Birds.* No. 4, first printing, light orange cover, 48 pages. **$8.00**; second printing. **$6.00**

1940, 1949 - *250 Ways To Prepare Poultry and Game Birds.* No. 4, 48 pages. **$4.00**

1940, 1949, 1950 - *250 Ways To Prepare Poultry and Game Birds.* No. 4, 48 pages. **$3.00**

1940, 1949, 1950, 1951 - *250 Ways To Prepare Poultry and Game Birds.* No. 4, 48 pages. **$2.00**

1940, 1949, 1950, 1951, 1952 - *250 Ways To Prepare Poultry and Game Birds.* No. 4, 48 pages. **$2.00**

1940, 1949, 1950, 1951, 1952, 1954 - *250 Ways To Prepare Poultry and Game Birds.* No. 4, 48 pages. **$2.00**

1940 - *250 Superb Pies And Pastries - America's Favorite Desserts.* No. 5, first printing, orange cover, 48 pages. **$8.00**; second printing, red cover. **$6.00**

1940, 1949 - *250 Superb Pies And Pastries.* No. 5, 48 pages. **$4.00**

1940, 1949, 1950 - *250 Pies And Pastries.* No. 5, 48 pages. **$3.00**

1940, 1949, 1950, 1951 - *250 Pies And Pastries.* No. 5, 48 pages. **$2.00**

1940, 1949, 1950, 1951, 1952 - *250 Superb Pies And Pastries.* No. 5, 48 pages. **$2.00**

1940, 1949, 1950, 1951, 1952, 1954 - *250 Superb Pies And Pastries.* No. 5, 48 pages. **$2.00**

1940 - *250 Delicious Soups.* No. 6, first printing, red & black cover, 48 pages. **$8.00**; second printing, blue & black printing. **$6.00**

1940, 1949 - *250 Delicious Soups.* No. 6, 48 pages. **$4.00**

1940, 1949, 1950 - *Delicious Soups.* No. 6, 48 pages. **$3.00**

1940, 1949, 1950, 1951 - *250 Delicious Soups.* No. 6, 48 pages. **$2.00**

1940, 1949, 1950, 1951, 1952 - *250 Delicious Soup Recipes.* No. 6, 48 pages. **$2.00**

1940, 1949, 1950, 1951, 1952, 1954 - *250 Delicious Soups.* No. 6, 48 pages. **$2.00**

1940 - *500 Delicious Salads and Dressings.* No. 7, first printing, 48 pages. **$8.00**; second printing. **$6.00**

1940, 1949 - *500 Tempting Salads.* No. 7, 48 pages. **$4.00**

1940, 1949, 1950 - *500 Tempting Salads.* No. 7, 48 pages. **$3.00**

1940, 1949, 1950, 1951 - *500 Salads and Dressings.* No. 7, 48 pages. **$2.00**

1940, 1949, 1950, 1951, 1952 - *500 Salads and Dressings.* No. 7, 48 pages. **$2.00**

1940, 1949, 1950, 1951, 1952, 1954 - *500 Salads and Dressings.* No. 7, 48 pages. **$2.00**

1940 - *250 Ways to Prepare Meat.* No. 8, first printing, yellow cover, 48 pages. **$8.00**; second printing, green cover. **$6.00**

1940, 1949 - *250 Ways To Prepare Meat.* No. 8, 48 pages. **$4.00**

1940, 1949, 1950 - *250 Ways To Prepare Meat.* No. 8, 48 pages. **$3.00**

1940, 1949, 1950, 1951 - *250 Ways To Prepare Meat.* No. 8, 48 pages. **$2.00**

1940, 1949, 1950, 1951, 1952 - *250 Ways To Prepare Meat.* No. 8, 48 pages. **$2.00**

1940, 1949, 1950, 1951, 1952, 1954 - *250 Ways To Prepare Meat.* No. 8, 48 pages. **$2.00**

1940 - *250 Fish and Sea Food Recipes.* No. 9, first printing, yellow cover, 48 pages. **$8.00**; second printing, red cover. **$6.00**

1940, 1949 - *250 Fish and Sea Food Recipes.* No. 9, 48 pages. **$4.00**

1940, 1949, 1950 - *250 Fish and Sea Food Recipes.* No. 9, 48 pages. **$3.00**

1940, 1949, 1950, 1951 - *250 Fish and Sea Food Recipes.* No. 9, 48 pages. **$2.00**

1940, 1949, 1950, 1951, 1952 - *250 Fish and Sea Food Recipes.* No. 9, 48 pages. **$2.00**

1940, 1949, 1950, 1951, 1952, 1954 - *250 Fish and Sea Food Recipes.* No. 9, 48 pages. **$2.00**

1940 - *300 Ways to Serve Eggs.* No. 10, first printing, green cover, 48 pages. **$8.00**; second printing, orange cover. **$6.00**

1940, 1949 - *300 Ways To Serve Eggs.* No. 10, 48 pages. **$4.00**

1940, 1949, 1950 - *300 Ways To Serve Eggs.* No. 10, 48 pages. **$3.00**

1940, 1949, 1950, 1951 - *300 Ways To Serve Eggs.* No. 10, 48 pages. **$2.00**

1940, 1949, 1950, 1951, 1952 - *300 Ways To Serve Eggs.* No. 10, 48 pages. **$2.00**

1940, 1949, 1950, 1951, 1952, 1954 - *300 Ways To Serve Eggs.* No. 10, 48 pages. **$2.00**

1940 - *250 Ways to Serve Fresh Vegetables.* No. 11, first printing, blue cover, 48 pages. **$8.00**; second printing, red cover. **$6.00**

1940, 1949 - *250 Ways To Serve Fresh Vegetables.* No. 11, 48 pages. **$4.00**

1940, 1949, 1950 - *250 Ways To Serve Fresh Vegetables.* No. 11, 48 pages. **$3.00**

1940, 1949, 1950, 1951 - *250 Ways To Serve Fresh Vegetables.* No. 11, 48 pages. **$2.00**

1940, 1949, 1950, 1951, 1952 - *250 Ways To Serve Fresh Vegetables.* No. 11, 48 pages. **$2.00**

1940, 1949, 1950, 1951, 1952, 1954 - *250 Ways To Serve Fresh Vegetables.* No. 11, 48 pages. **$2.00**

1940 - *250 Delectable Desserts - Custards, Souffles, Sauces, Puddings, Meringues, Cakes.* No. 12, first printing, green cover, 48 pages. **$8.00**; second printing, red cover. **$6.00**

1940, 1949 - *250 Delectable Desserts.* No. 12, 48 pages. **$4.00**

1940, 1949, 1950 - *250 Delectable Desserts.* No. 12, 48 pages. **$3.00**

1940, 1949, 1950, 1951 - *250 Delectable Desserts.* No. 12, 48 pages. **$2.00**

1940, 1949, 1950, 1951, 1952 - *250 Delectable Desserts.* No. 12, 48 pages. **$2.00**

1940, 1949, 1950, 1951, 1952, 1954 - *250 Delectable Desserts.* No. 12, 48 pages. **$2.00**

1941 - *250 Ways of Serving Potatoes.* No. 13, first printing, red cover, 48 pages. **$8.00**; second printing, green cover. **$6.00**

1941, 1949 - *250 Ways of Serving Potatoes.* No. 13, 48 pages. **$4.00**

1941, 1949, 1950 - *250 Ways of Serving Potatoes.* No. 13, 48 pages. **$3.00**

1941, 1949, 1950, 1951 - *250 Ways of Serving Potatoes.* No. 13, 48 pages. **$2.00**

1941, 1949, 1950, 1951, 1952 - *250 Ways of Serving Potatoes.* No. 13, 48 pages. **$2.00**

1941, 1949, 1950, 1951, 1952, 1954 - *250 Ways of Serving Potatoes.* No. 13, 48 pages. **$2.00**

1941 - *500 Tasty Sandwiches - Party Sandwiches & Fancy Foods.* No. 14, blue cover, 48 pages. **$8.00**; second printing. **$6.00**

1941, 1949 - *500 Tasty Sandwiches.* No. 14, 48 pages. **$4.00**

1941, 1949, 1950 - *500 Tasty Sandwiches,* No. 14, 48 pages. **$3.00**

1941, 1949, 1950, 1951 - *500 Tasty Sandwiches.* No. 14, 48 pages. **$2.00**

1941, 1949, 1950, 1951, 1952 - *500 Tasty Sandwiches.* No. 14, 48 pages. **$2.00**

1941, 1949, 1950, 1951, 1952, 1954 - *500 Tasty Sandwiches.* No. 14, 48 pages. **$2.00**

1941 - *250 Ways To Make Candy.* No. 15, blue cover, 48 pages. **$8.00**; second printing, orange & black cover. **$6.00**

1941, 1949 - *250 Ways To Make Candy.* No. 15, 48 pages. **$4.00**

1941, 1949, 1950 - *250 Ways To Make Candy.* No. 15, 48 pages. **$3.00**

1941, 1949, 1959, 1951 - *250 Ways To Make Candy.* No. 15, 48 pages. **$2.00**

1941, 1949, 1959, 1951, 1952 - *250 Ways To Make Candy*. No. 15, 48 pages. **$2.00**

1941, 1949, 1959, 1951, 1952, 1954 - *250 Ways To Make Candy*. No. 15, 48 pages. **$2.00**

1941 - *250 Luscious Refrigerator Desserts*. No. 16, yellow & black cover, 48 pages. **$8.00**; second printing, red, orange & black cover. **$6.00**

1941, 1949 - *250 Luscious Refrigerator Desserts*. No. 16, 48 pages. **$4.00**

1941, 1949, 1950 - *250 Luscious Refrigerator Desserts*. No. 16, 48 pages. **$3.00**

1941, 1949, 1950, 1951 - *250 Luscious Refrigerator Desserts*. No. 16, 48 pages. **$2.00**

1941, 1949, 1950, 1951, 1952 - *250 Luscious Refrigerator Desserts*. No. 16, 48 pages. **$2.00**

1941, 1949, 1950, 1951, 1952, 1954 - *250 Luscious Refrigerator Desserts*. No. 16, 48 pages. **$2.00**

1941 - *The Cookie Book - 250 Cookie and Small Cake Recipes*. No. 17, green cover, 48 pages. **$8.00**; second printing, yellow cover. **$6.00**

1941, 1949 - *The Cookie Book*. No. 17, 48 pages. **$4.00**

1941, 1949, 1950 - The Cookie Book. No. 17, 48 pages. **$3.00**

1941, 1949, 1950, 1951 - *The Cookie Book*. No. 17, 48 pages. **$2.00**

1941, 1949, 1950, 1951, 1952 - *The Cookie Book*. No. 17, 48 pages. **$2.00**

1941, 1949, 1950, 1951, 1952, 1954 - *The Cookie Book*. No. 17, 48 pages. **$2.00**

1941 - *Dairy Dishes*. No. 18, red cover, 48 pages. **$8.00**; second printing. **$6.00**

1941, 1949 - *Dairy Dishes - 300 New Menu Ideas*. No. 18, 48 pages. **$4.00**

1941, 1949, 1950 - *Dairy Dishes - 300 New Menu Ideas*. No. 18, 48 pages. **$3.00**

1941, 1949, 1950, 1951 - *Dairy Dishes - 300 New Menu Ideas*. No. 18, 48 pages. **$2.00**

1941, 1949, 1950, 1951, 1952 - *Dairy Dishes*. No. 18, 48 pages. **$2.00**

1941, 1949, 1950, 1951, 1952, 1954 - *Dairy Dishes*. No. 18, 48 pages. **$2.00**

1941 - *Breads, Biscuits And Rolls - 250 Recipes*. No. 19, 48 pages. **$8.00**; second printing. **$6.00**

1941, 1949 - *Breads, Biscuits And Rolls - 250 Recipes*. No. 19, 48 pages. **$4.00**

1941, 1949, 1950 - *Breads, Biscuits And Rolls - 250 Recipes*. No. 19, 48 pages. **$3.00**

1941, 1949, 1950, 1951 - *Breads, Biscuits And Rolls - 250 Recipes*. No. 19, 48 pages. **$2.00**

1941, 1949, 1950, 1951, 1952 - *Breads, Biscuits And Rolls*. No. 19. **$2.00**

1941, 1949, 1950, 1951, 1952, 1954 - *Breads, Biscuits And Rolls*. No. 19. **$2.00**

1941 - *Menus For Everyday of the Year - Successful Meal Planning*. No. 20, first printing, green cover, 48 pages. **$8.00**; second printing. **$6.00**

1941, 1949 - *Sauces, Gravies And Dressings*. No. 20, 48 pages. **$4.00**

1941, 1949, 1950 - *250 Sauces, Gravies and Dressings*. No. 20, 48 pages. **$3.00**

1941, 1949, 1950, 1951 - *Sauces, Gravies and Dressings*. No. 20, 48 pages. **$2.00**

1941, 1949, 1950, 1951, 1952 - *Sauces, Gravies and Dressings*. No. 20, 48 pages. **$2.00**

1941, 1949, 1950, 1951, 1952, 1954 - *Sauces, Gravies and Dressings*. No. 20, 48 pages. **$2.00**

1942 - *Meals For Two - For Young Marrieds and Small Families*. No. 21, first printing, 48 pages. **$8.00**

1942, 1949 - *Meals For Two Cookbook*. No. 21, 48 pages. **$4.00**

1942, 1949, 1950 - *Meals For Two Cookbook*. No. 21, 48 pages. **$3.00**

1942, 1949, 1950, 1951 - *Meals For Two Cookbook*. No. 21, 48 pages. **$2.00**

1942, 1949, 1950, 1951, 1952 - *Meals For Two Cookbook*. No. 21, 48 pages. **$2.00**

1942, 1949, 1950, 1951, 1952, 1954 - *Meals For Two Cookbook*. No. 21, 48 pages. **$2.00**

1942 - *Body Building Dishes For Children* - Approximately 200 Recipes. No. 22, 48 pages. **$8.00**

1942, 1949 - *Dishes For Children* - 200 Recipes. No. 22, 48 pages. **$4.00**

1942, 1949, 1950 - *Dishes For Children* - 200 Recipes. No. 22, 48 pages. **$3.00**

1942, 1949, 1950, 1951 - *Dishes For Children* - 200 Recipes. No. 22, 48 pages. **$2.00**

1942, 1949, 1950, 1951, 1952 - *Body Building Dishes For Children* - 200 Recipes. No. 22, 48 pages. **$2.00**

1942, 1949, 1950, 1951, 1952, 1954 - *Body Building Dishes For Children.* No. 22, 48 pages. **$2.00**

1942 - *Facts About Food* - A Complete Handbook of 2,000 Culinary Facts That Belongs In Every Kitchen. No. 23, 48 pages. **$8.00**

1942, 1949 - *Facts About Food* - A Complete Handbook of 2,000 Culinary Facts. No. 23, 48 pages. **$4.00**

1942, 1949, 1950 - *Facts About Food.* No. 23, 48 pages. **$3.00**

1941, 1949, 1950, 1951 - *Facts About Food.* No. 23, 48 pages. **$2.00**

1941, 1949, 1950, 1951, 1952 - *Facts About Food* - A Complete Handbook. No. 23, 48 pages. **$2.00**

1941, 1949, 1950, 1951, 1952, 1954 - *Facts About Food* - A Complete Handbook. No. 23, 48 pages. **$2.00**

1942 - *Menus.* No. 24, contains twelve monthly sections with day to day recipes, 48 pages. **$8.00**

1942, 1949 - *Menus.* No. 24, 48 pages. **$4.00**

1942, 1949, 1950 - *Menus.* No. 24, 48 pages. **$3.00**

1942, 1949, 1950, 1951 - *Menus.* No. 24, 48 pages. **$2.00**

1942, 1949, 1950, 1951, 1952 - *Menus.* No. 24, 48 pages. **$2.00**

1942, 1949, 1950, 1951, 1952, 1954 - *Menus.* No. 24, 48 pages. **$2.00**

1954 - *Quick Dishes For The Woman in a Hurry* - 332 Recipes In 30 Minutes or Less. No. 101, 68 pages. **$6.00**

1954, 1955 - *Quick Dishes For The Woman in a Hurry* - 332 Recipes In 30 Minutes or Less. No. 101, 68 pages. **$3.00**

1954, 1955, 1965 - *Quick Dishes For The Woman in a Hurry* - 332 Recipes In 30 Minutes or Less. No. 101, 68 pages. **$1.00**

1954 - No. 102, 68 pages. **$6.00**

1954, 1955 - No. 102, 68 pages. **$3.00**

1954, 1955, 1965 - No. 102, 68 pages. **$1.00**

1954 - No. 103, 68 pages. **$6.00**

1954, 1955 - No. 103, 68 pages. **$3.00**

1954, 1955, 1965 - No. 103, 68 pages. **$1.00**

1954 - *The Chocolate Cookbook* - 218 Full-Flavored Chocolate Recipes. No. 104, 68 pages. **$6.00**

1954, 1955 - *The Chocolate Cookbook* - 218 Full-Flavored Chocolate Recipes. No. 104, 68 pages. **$3.00**

1954, 1955, 1965 - *The Chocolate Cookbook* - 218 Full-Flavored Chocolate Recipes. No. 104, 68 pages. **$1.00**

1954 - *The Lunch Box Cookbook* - 336 Taste-Tempting Lunch Box Foods. No. 105, 68 pages. **$6.00**

1954, 1955 - *The Lunch Box Cookbook* - 336 Taste-Tempting Lunch Box Foods. No. 105, 68 pages. **$3.00**

1954, 1955, 1965 - *The Lunch Box Cookbook.* No. 105, 68 pages. **$1.00**

1954 - No. 106, 68 pages. **$6.00**

1954, 1955 - No. 106, 68 pages. **$3.00**

1954, 1955, 1965 - No. 106, 68 pages. **$1.00**

1954 - *Brunch, Breakfast and Morning Coffee.* No. 107, 68 pages. **$6.00**

1954, 1955 - *Brunch, Breakfast and Morning Coffee.* No. 107, 68 pages. **$3.00**

1954, 1955, 1965 - *Brunch, Breakfast and Morning Coffee.* No. 107, 68 pages. **$1.00**

1954 - *The Ground Meat Cookbook* - 204 Intriguing Ground Meat Recipes. No. 108, 68 pages. **$6.00**

1954, 1955 - *The Ground Meat Cookbook* - 204 Intriguing Ground Meat Recipes. No. 108, 68 pages. **$3.00**

1954, 1955, 1965 - *The Ground Meat Cookbook* - 204 Intriguing Ground Meat Recipes. No. 108, 68 pages. **$1.00**

1954 - *Elegant Desserts - 220 Deliciously Distinctive Desserts.* No. 109, 68 pages. **$6.00**

1954, 1955 - *Elegant Desserts - 220 Deliciously Distinctive Desserts.* No. 109, 68 pages. **$3.00**

1954, 1955, 1965 - *Elegant Desserts - 220 Deliciously Distinctive Desserts.* No. 109, 68 pages. **$1.00**

1954 - *The French Cookbook.* No. 110, 68 pages. **$6.00**

1954, 1955 - *The French Cookbook.* No. 110, 68 pages. **$3.00**

1954, 1955, 1965 - *The French Cookbook.* No. 110, 68 pages. **$1.00**

1954 - *Dishes Children Love - 264 Favorite Recipes of All Children.* No. 111, 68 pages. **$6.00**

1954, 1955 - *Dishes Children Love - 264 Favorite Recipes of All Children.* No. 111, 68 pages. **$3.00**

1954, 1955, 1965 - *Dishes Children Love - 264 Favorite Recipes of All Children.* No. 111, 68 pages. **$1.00**

1955 - No. 112, 68 pages. **$3.00**

1955, 1965 - No. 112, 68 pages. **$1.00**

1955 - *The Scandinavian Cookbook.* No. 113, 68 pages. **$6.00**

1955, 1965 - *The Scandinavian Cookbook.* No. 113, 68 pages. **$1.00**

1956 - *250 Ways To Prepare Meat.* No. 114, 48 pages. **$6.00**

1956, 1965 - *250 Ways To Prepare Meat.* No. 114, 48 pages. **$1.00**

1956 - *Entertaining Six or Eight - 143 Delectable Recipes for Delicious Foods.* No. 115, 68 pages. **$6.00**

1956, 1965 - *Entertaining Six or Eight - 143 Delectable Recipes for Delicious Foods.* No. 115, 68 pages. **$1.00**

1956 - No. 116, 68 pages. **$6.00**

1956, 1965 - No. 116, 68 pages. **$1.00**

1956 - *Cooling Dishes for Hot Weather, 260 Cooling Recipes for Hot Weather.* No. 117, 68 pages. **$6.00**

1956, 1965 - *Cooling Dishes for Hot Weather, 260 Cooling Recipes for Hot Weather.* No. 117, 68 pages. **$1.00**

1956 - *The New England Cookbook - 191 Favorite All-American Dishes.* No. 118, 68 pages. **$6.00**

1956, 1965 - *The New England Cookbook - 191 Favorite All-American Dishes.* No. 118, 68 pages. **$1.00**

1956 - *Sunday Night Suppers - 161 Chafing Dishes and Other Specialties.* No. 119, 68 pages. **$6.00**

1956, 1965 - *Sunday Night Suppers - 161 Chafing Dishes and Other Specialties.* No. 119, 68 pages. **$1.00**

1941, 1956 - *Menus For Every Day of the Year.* No. 120, 48 pages. **$3.00**

1941, 1956, 1965 - *Menus For Every Day of the Year.* No. 120, 48 pages. **$1.00**

1964 - *250 Ways To Prepare Meat.* No. 4, 48 pages. **$3.00**

1964, 1965 - *250 Ways To Prepare Meat.* No. 4, 48 pages. **$3.00**

1964, 1965, 1969 - *250 Ways To Prepare Meat.* No. 4, 48 pages. **$2.00**

1964 - *300 Delicious Salad Recipes.* No. 7, 48 pages. **$3.00**

1964, 1965 - *300 Delicious Salad Recipes.* No. 7, 48 pages. **$3.00**

1965, 1969 - *300 Delicious Salad Recipes.* No. 7, 48 pages. **$2.00**

1964 - *200 Different Fish and Sea Food Recipes.* No. 9, 48 pages. **$3.00**

1964, 1965 - *200 Different Fish and Sea Food Recipes.* No. 9, 48 pages. **$3.00**

1964, 1965, 1969 - *200 Different Fish and Sea Food Recipes.* No. 9, 48 pages. **$2.00**

1964 - *250 Breads, Biscuits and Rolls.* No. 19, 48 pages. **$3.00**

1964, 1965 - *250 Breads, Biscuits and Rolls.* No. 19, 48 pages. **$3.00**

1964, 1965, 1969 - *250 Breads, Biscuits and Rolls.* No. 19, 48 pages. **$2.00**

1964 - *250 Sauces, Gravies and Dressings.* No. 20, 48 pages. **$3.00**

1964, 1965 - *250 Sauces, Gravies and Dressings.* No. 20, 48 pages. **$3.00**

1964, 1965, 1969 - *250 Sauces, Gravies and Dressings.* No. 20, 48 pages. **$2.00**

1964 - *250 Ways To Serve Eggs.* No. 21, 48 pages. **$3.00**

1964, 1965 - *250 Ways To Serve Eggs.* No. 21, 48 pages. **$3.00**

1964, 1965, 1969 - *250 Ways To Serve Eggs.* No. 21, 48 pages. **$2.00**

1964 - *250 Delicious Dishes From Leftovers.* No. 23, 48 pages. **$3.00**

1964, 1965 - *250 Delicious Dishes From Leftovers.* No. 23, 48 pages. **$3.00**

1964, 1965, 1969 - *250 Delicious Dishes From Leftovers.* No. 23, 48 pages. **$2.00**

1964 - *2,000 Useful Facts About Food.* No. 24, 48 pages. **$3.00**

1964, 1965 - *2,000 Useful Facts About Food.* No. 24, 48 pages. **$3.00**

1964, 1965, 1969 - *2,000 Useful Facts About Food.* No. 24, 48 pages. **$2.00**

1965 - *Pennsylvania Dutch Cookbook - Fine Old Recipes.* Claire S. Davidow and Ann Goodman, 48 pages. **$3.00**

1965 - *Kitchen Companion Series - 200 American Family Recipes.* 48 pages. **$3.00**

1965, 1969 - *Kitchen Companion Series - 200 American Family Recipes.* 48 pages. **$2.00**

1965, 1969, 1975 - *Kitchen Companion Series - 200 American Family Recipes.* 48 pages. **$2.00**

◊ ◊ ◊ ◊

The Daniel Webster Flour Cook Book. 1907, 120 pages. **$16.00**

Delicious Maple Recipes. 1920's, Highland Maple Syrup. **$12.00**

Del Monte Peaches - 11 Food Experts Tell Us How To Serve Them. 1927, California Packing Corporation, San Francisco, 16 pages. **$12.00**

Del Monte Tomato Sauce Recipes. 1930, California Packing Corporation, San Francisco, 24 pages. **$10.00**

Diamond Jubilee Edition to Celebrate 75th Diamond Anniversary of the American Stoves, Inc. 1961, Acme Markets. **$3.00**

Diary by Teddy Barbour. 1937. **$10.00**

Dick Van Patten's Season by Choice Menu Plan. 1980's, written with Nutritionist Audrey Cross, Libby's Natural Pack, S.S. Pierce Company, recipes with no salt or sugar added, 18 pages. **NCV**

Different and Delightful Ways of Using Rose Apples. 1929, Kehoe Preserving Co., Terre Haute, Indiana. **$12.00**

Different Salads Featuuring Rose Apple Recipes. 1930, Kehoe Preserving Co. **$12.00**

▶ *The Dining Room Magazine.* October 1876, Volume 1, No. 10, edited by Mrs. Laura E. Lyman, recipes and cookery topics, The Union Publishing Company, a subsidiary of Royal Baking Powder Company, 18 pages plus ads. **$30.00**

The Dixie Book - 159 Short Cuts To Better Meals and Easier Housework. 1930's, The Capital City Products Co., Columbus, Ohio, 24 pages. **$10.00**

Dormeyer Electric Mix Treasures. 1947, Ethel Allison, prepared especially for your Dormeyer Mixer, 34 pages. **$8.00**

Dormeyer Electric Mix Treasures. 1949, contains Betty Crocker recipes using Softasilk Cake Flour and Gold Medal Flour, Spry "Basic One Bowl" recipes using Spry, MIx-Easy recipes using Swans Down Cake Flour, Ann Pillsbury recipes using Pillsbury's Best Flour, 34 pages. **$8.00**

Dr. Caldwell Syrup Pepsin. 1938. **$10.00**

Dr. King's Guide to Health Cook Book. 1901. **$20.00**

Dr. King's Guide to Health Cook Book. 1902. **$20.00**

Dr. King's Guide to Health Cook Book. 1908. **$20.00**

Dr. King's Guide to Health Cook Book. 1910. **$16.00**

Dr. King's New Beauty Book, Health Guide Cook Book. 1905. **$20.00**

▶ *Dr. King's New Guide to Health - Household Instructor and Family Prize Cook Book.* 1909, H.E. Bucklen & Company, Chicago, Illinois, Windsor, Connecticut, 36 pages. **$20.00**

▶ *Dr. Miles Candy Book.* 1910, Dr. Miles Medical Co., Elkhart, Indiana, distributed by Karl F. Strobach, druggist, St. James, Missouri, 32 pages. **$16.00**

Dr. Miles Cook Book. Circa 1910, Cure All Co. **$14.00**

Duff's Gingerbread. 1930's, made with Duff's Molasses, in the shape of a can, P. Duff & Sons, Inc., Pittsburg, 20 pages. **$10.00**

Duncan Hines Twelve Favorite Dishes with His Nine Magic Rules on How to Be A Good Cook. 1947, *This Week* magazine, edited by Clementine Paddleford, recipes tested by Gertrude Lynn, United Newspapers Magazine Corp. **$8.00**

Duncan Hines Adventures in Good Cooking And The Art of Carving In The Home. 1960. **$3.00**

Desserts With American Dash - One Pan! One Mix! 1982, Duncan Hines, Proctor & Gamble, 12 pages. **NCV**

Duncan Hines Micro Hints. 1986, Duncan Hines Kitchens, Proctor & Gamble, 20 pages. **NCV**

Duplex Cook Book. Circa 1910, Durham Manufacturing Company, Cast Iron Stoves. **$14.00**

Easter Idea Book. 1954, Charlotte Adams, Lenten dishes, ham, eggs, centerpieces. **$6.00**

Easy Meat Recipes. 1946-1947, compliments of Will Doctor & Co., Union Market National Livestock and Meat Board. **$8.00**

"Easy-on-the-cook-book" - Meal Time in Jig Time - Complete Guide to Summer Meals. 1959, Everywoman's Family Circle, part 1, 16 pages. **$6.00**

"Easy-on-the-cook-book" - Whoop-de-do Barbecues. 1959, Everywoman's Family Circle, part 2, 16 pages. **$6.00**

"Easy-on-the-cook-book" - Summer Socialables. 1959, Everywoman's Family Circle, part 3, 16 pages. **$6.00**

Easy-To-Cook Book - Girls & Boys. 1967, 1972, Ann Wainwright, edited by Barbara Zeitz, introduction by Poppy Cannon, over 100 recipes, third printing, 64 pages. **NCV**

75 Easy Yam Recipes With A Romantic Past from the Magic Evangeline Land of Louisiana. 1940's, 36 pages. **$8.00**

Easy Ways to Good Meals - 99 Delicious Dishes Made with Campbell's Soups. 1950, Anne Marshall, Home Economist, Campbell's Soup Company, 48 pages. **$6.00**

Easy Ways to Good Meals - 99 Delicious Dishes Made with Campbell's Soups. 1950, 1951, Anne Marshall, Home Economist, Campbell's Soup Company, 48 pages. **$6.00**

Eat Light With Beef. 1984, Meat Board Test Kitchens & Beef Industry Council, 15 pages. **NCV**

Edgewater Beach Hotel Salad Book. 1928, Arnold Shircliffe, Hotel Monthly, Paris, Chicago, etc. **$12.00**

Ecko Flint Stainless Steel Cookware - The Quality Cookware That Makes A Cook A Chef. 1966, 1967, booklet, 30 pages. **$3.00**

Eggs At Any Meal. 1931, U.S. Dept. of Agriculture, Leaflet No. 39, 8 pages. **$10.00**

Encyclopedia of Cooking. 1959, Mary Margaret McBride, small booklet. **$6.00**

Enterprising Housekeeper. Second edition, 1889, Enterprise Manufacturing Co., Philadelphia, 64 pages. **$24.00**

The Enterprising Housekeeper. 1897, Helen Louise Johnson, The Enterprosing Manufacturing Company of Pennsylvania. **$20.00**

Enterprising Housekeeper. 1900, 200 tested recipes presented at the Pan-American Exposition on back cover, 1901. **$16.00**

Enterprising Housekeeper. 1900, 1901, 200 tested recipes presented at the Pan-Pacific Exposition. **$16.00**

▶ *The Enterprising Housekeeper.* Fourth edition, 1902, Helen Louise Johnson, The Enterprise Mf'g Co. of Pennsylvania, 200 tested recipes, 90 pages plus index. **$16.00**

The Enterprising Housekeeper. 1906, Helen Louise Johnson, he Enterprise Mfg. Co. of Pennsylvania, Philadelphia, 200 tested recipes, 90 pages plus index. **$16.00**

The Enterprising Housekeeper. 1912, new edition containing 200 tested recipes and household helps. **$14.00**

Entertaining Ease From The Makers of Reynolds Metals Company Consumer Division. 1982, Reynolds Metals Company, Richmond, Virginia. **NCV**

Estate Cook Book - Some Extra Good Recipes for Baking and Roasting by "Time and Temperature." 1924, 1925, 1926, Ada Bessie Swann, The Estate Stove Company. **$12.00**

Estate Cook Book - Some Extra Good Recipes. 1924, 1925, 1926, 1928, Ada Bessie Swann, The Estate Stove Company. **$12.00**

Ever Ready Natural Food Recipes. 1973, Castle & Cooke, Inc., Honolulu, 10-page foldout. **NCV**

Exciting World of Rice Dishes. 1959, General Foods Kitchens, General Foods Corp., 20 pages. **$6.00**

Fabulous Fiber Cookbook. 1977, Jeanne Jones, 192 pages. **NCV**

Family Circle's Great Desserts - 250 of The Best Desserts Ever. 1974. **NCV**

Family Fare Food Management and Recipes. 1950 U.S.D.A. Bulletin No. 1, prepared by Bureau of Human Nutrition and Home Economics, 96 pages. **$6.00**

Famous Dishes From Every State. 1936, Frigidare Corp. Dayton, OHio, 40 pages. **$10.00**

Famous Florida Chef's Favorite Citrus Recipes. Fifth edition, 1972, includes Disney Chef's recipes from the Magic Kingdom. **NCV**

Farm Journal's Country Cookbook - More Than 1,000 Tested Recipes. Special edition, 1959, Nell B. Nichols, food editor, *Farm Journal,* 420 pages. **$6.00**

The Farmer's Mechanics, And Gentleman's Almanack. 1836, Nathan Wild, contains "Instructions Respecting Diet" from M'Kenzies 5,000 Receipts, Quanity of Food, Quality, Dietic Substances Under Receipts; For Salting Beef & etc., 46 pages. **$110.00**

Favorite Cookie Cookbook. 1955, Hyla Nelson O'Conner, over 200 tested recipes, 144 pages. **$6.00**

101 *Favorite Freshwater Fish Recipes.* 1979, Duane R. Lund. **NCV**

Favorite Recipes. 1936, Charlotte E. Fity, *The Record Herald,* Waynesboro, Pennsylvania. **$10.00**

Favorite Recipes For All Occasions - 121 Years of Cookery. First edition, 1973, from Heublein Foods Group, Hartford, Connecticut. **NCV**

Favorite Recipes From the United Nations. 1956, published by the United States Committee for the United Nations. **$6.00**

Favorite Recipes in Country Kitchens. 1945, General Foods Corp. **$8.00**

Favorite Recipes Using Williams Chili Seasoning. 1940's, C.L. Williams Food Inc., 2"x3" booklet. **$8.00**

Festive Manna. 1966, Miriam Field, Standard Brands, Inc. **$3.00**

Fifty Good Ways of Serving Woodcock Macaroni. 1919, 15 pages. **$14.00**

Fifty Quick Desserts. 1929, Hostess Cake. **$12.00**

The Fifty Two Sunday Dinners. 1924, *Woman's World* Magazine Co., Inc. **$12.00**

▶ *Fireless Cooking.* 1920's, The Durham Manufacturing Co., Muncie, Indiana, instructions and recipes for use with Duplex Fireless Stoves, 48 pages. **$12.00**

Fish And Other Products of the Sea-Cooking - A Choice Collection of Recipes. Ninth edition, 1890, compliments of Shute & Merchant, Gloucester, Massachusetts, 36 pages. **$24.00**

Fish and Seafood Cookery. 1930's, Mid-Central Fish Co., Kansas City, Missouri. **$10.00**

Flako Recipe Album. 1954, Flako Products Corp., since 1922, pie crust mix, cookie mix, corn muffin mix, biscuit mix, cup cake mix, 52 pages. **$6.00**

The Fondue Party Cookbook. 1971, Beth Merriman, published in association with *Parade Magazine,* 86 pages. **NCV**

▶ *Food And Fun.* "Here's a Book the Whole Family Will Enjoy." 1953, Arthur Godfrey, Star-Kist Tuna, 30 pages. **$6.00**

Food And Nutrition. 1925, 1927, 1934, 1941, 1942, The American Red Cross. **$8.00**

Food Fair - Know-How About Meat. 1963, Food Fair Stores, Inc. Cowles Magazines and Broadcasting, Inc., 32 pages. **$3.00**

Food Fit For A King Recipes. 1939, Majestic Waterless Low-Heat Cookware. **$10.00**

Food Hints. 1925, Durr's Mohawk Valley Products. **$12.00**

Food Styles. 1987, Mid American Harvest, Schnuck's Markets, Inc., Bridgeton, Missouri (St. Louis), Vol. 2, No. 2. **NCV**

Food Surprises From The Mirro Test Kitchen. 1929, 16 pages. **$12.00**

Foods That Made New England Famous. 1945, 1972, Gretchen McMullen, H.P. Hood & Sons, founded in 1845 in Massachusetts. **NCV**

For The Hostess. 1928, by the editors of *Vogue & Vanity Fair* magazines, 72 pages. **$12.00**

Fort Lauderdale News. 1969, 10th Annual All Electric Cooking School, Florida Power and Light Co. **$3.00**

Franco American Soups and Other Specialties. 1900, A. Biardot, Franco American Food Co., Jersey City. **$16.00**

Frank Leslies "Chimney Corner" Cookery Book - Two Hundred Useful Economical Recipes. 1890's, New York, E.R. Durkee & Co. **$20.00**

The French Have A Word For It - Mayonnaise Recipes From Some of the World's Greatest Chefs and the Kitchens of Best Foods. 1967, 48 pages. **$2.00**

French Fried Delicacies. 1926, "Wear-Ever" French Fryer, 16-page foldout. **$12.00**

Fresh Mushroom Cookbook. 1967, 1968, 1971, Sybil Henderson, Henderson Associates, Los Angeles, California. **NCV**

Frigidaire, Frozen Delights. 1929. **$12.00**

Frigidaire Recipe Book. 1931, Miss Vernal L. Miller, Frigidaire Corp., subsidiary of General Motors Corp. **$10.00**

Fridgidaire Recipe Book. 1932, Miss Verna L. Miller, Firgidaire Corp. **$10.00**

Frigidaire Recipe Book. 1933, Miss Verna L. Miller, Frigidaire Corp. **$10.00**

From Soup to Nuts with Real Mayonnaise. The Best Foods, Inc., New York, New York, 16 pages. **$8.00**

Fun With Coffee. 1956, Pan-American Coffee Bureau, New York, 32 pages. **$6.00**

The Garden Way Bread Book - A Baker's Almanac. 1979, Ellen Foscue Johnson, Gardenway Publishing, 192 pages. **NCV**

Gas Cooking With An Oil Stove. 1926, Nesco, National Enameling & Stamping Co., Inc., Milwaukee. **$12.00**

▸ *The Gas Range and How To Use It - Also Some Recipes For Cooking.* 1906, compiled by Mary Lamson Clarke, The Laclede Gas & Light company, St. Louis, Missouri, 96 pages. **$16.00**

Gebhardt's Mexican Cookery for American Homes. 1931, 62 pages. **$10.00**

Gebhardt's Mexican Cookery for American Homes. 1932, Gebhardt's, San Antonio. **$10.00**

Gem Chopper Cook Book. 1890's, Sargent & Co., New York, cloth cover. **$20.00**

Gem Chopper Cook Book. 1902, Sargent & Co., New York. **$16.00**

GE - The New Art of Modern Cooking. 1937, spiral, 112 pages. **$10.00**

General Electric Refrigerator Food Freezer Combination - 76 New-Different-Recipes. 1950's, 48 pages. **$6.00**

General Foods Kitchens. 1967, G.F. Corp., mailer. **$3.00**

Gentleman's Companion or Around The World With Knife, Fork and Spoon. 1946, Chas. H. Baker, Jr., simulated leather covers. **$8.00**

Girl's & Boy's Easy-To-Cook Book. 1967, 1972, Ann Wainwright, edited by Barbara Zeitz, third printing. **NCV**

Gloria Pitzer Presents 400 Recipes for Eating Out at Home Cookbook. 1981, 12 pages. **NCV**

Gloria Pitzer's Presents The Secret Restaurant Recipe File Cookbook. 1981, 12 pages. **NCV**

Go All Out with Stove Top Stuffing - It'll Make Your Holidays Extra-Special. 1981, General Foods Corp., booklet, 12 pages. **NCV**

"Gone With The Wind" Cook Book. 1940, a gift with the purchase of Pebeco Toothpaste, 48 pages. **$8.00**

"Gone With The Wind" Cook Book. 1941, a gift with the purchase of Pebeco toothpaste, 48 pages. **$8.00**

Good Enough To Eat With A Spoon! 1931, Slade's Peanut Butter, 8-page booklet. **$5.00**

Good Food - The Adventurous Eater's Guide to Restaurants Serving America's Best Regional Specialties. 1983, Jane and Michael Stern, 460 pages. **NCV**

Good Housekeeping's Treasury of Family-Time Favorites - The Desserts That Everybody Loves Etc. 1930, 8 pages. **$5.00**

◊ ◊ ◊ ◊

Good Housekeeping

1958 - *Appetizer Book.* No. 1, 68 pages. **$6.00**

1958 - *Book of Cookies.* No. 2, 68 pages. **$6.00**

1958 - *Cake Book With Decorating Ideas.* No. 3, 68 pages. **$6.00**

1958 - *Quick 'n Easy Cook Book.* No. 4, 68 pages. **$6.00**

1958 - *Casserole Book - Oven Dishes.* No. 5, 68 pages. **$6.00**

1958 - *Book of Salads to Heighten Appetites.* No. 6, 64 pages. **$6.00**

1958 - *Party Pie Book - Plain and Fancy.* No. 7, 68 pages. **$6.00**

1958 - *Hamburger & Hotdog Book.* No. 8, 64 pages. **$6.00**

1958 - *Meat Cook Book.* No. 9, 68 pages. **$6.00**

1958 - *Book of Vegetables*. No. 10, 68 pages. **$6.00**

1958 - *Book of Delectable Desserts*. No. 11, 64 pages. **$6.00**

1958 - *Egg and Cheese, Spaghetti and Rice*. No. 12, 68 pages. **$6.00**

1958 - *Book of Breads & Sandwiches*. No. 13, 68 pages. **$6.00**

1958 - *Company Meals and Buffets with Menus*. No. 14, 64 pages. **$6.00**

1958 - *Fish and Shellfish Book*. No. 15, 68 pages. **$6.00**

1958 - *Poultry & Game Book*. No. 16, 68 pages. **$6.00**

1958 - *Book of Ice Creams & Cool Drinks*. No. 17, 64 pages. **$6.00**

1958 - *Ten P.M. Cook Book*. No. 18, 68 pages. **$6.00**

1958 - *Around The World Cook Book - Specialty Recipes*. No. 19, 64 pages. **$6.00**

1958 - *Who's Who Cooks*. No. 20, 68 pages. **$6.00**

A hard-cover binder was sold separately with sold separately with 20 wires to hold the above soft-cover cookbooks titled *Good Housekeeping's Cook Books*.

1967 - *Cooking for Company* - No-Panic, No-Fail. No. 9, 64 pages. **$3.00**

1967 - *Perfect Parties, Birthday, Holiday, 5 P.M.* No. 10, 64 pages. **$3.00**

1967 - *Suppertime Cook Book*. 64 pages. **$3.00**

◊ ◊ ◊ ◊

▶ *Good Pies - Easy To Make*. 1920, Department of Dietetics And Cookery, Merrell-Soule Company, Syracuse, New York, makers of None-Such Mincemeat. **$12.00**

Good Things - The Chas. A. Vogeler Co.'s Cookery Book and Book of Comfort. 1897. **$20.00**

Good Things To Eat. 1904, sent free on request, Libby, McNeill & Libby, Chicago. **$16.00**

Good Things To Eat And How To Serve Them - Delane Brown's Cook Book. 1930, superb brand canned fruits and vegetables, 64 pages. **$10.00**

Gorton's Sea Products. 1909, Gorton-Pew Fisheries Co. **$16.00**

Grandma's Old Fashioned Molasses. 1946, Duffy-Mott Company. **$8.00**

Grandma's Greatest Hits. 1980, Grandma's Molasses, Duffy-Mott Co. **NCV**

The Great American Ice Cream Book. 1973, third printing. **NCV**

Gregory's Elko-Ozark Recipe Book. 1920, also cooking hints, Gregory-Robinson-Speas, Inc., Rogers, Arkansas, 32 pages. **$12.00**

The Griswold Erie Cook Book. 1890, Griswold Mfg. Co., Erie, Pennsylvania. **$16.00**

Guardian Service Tested Recipes. 1940, Betty Gray, Director, Century Food Kitchen, 48 pages. **$8.00**

Hamilton Beach Food Mixer Instructions and Tested Recipes. 1948, all recipes tested at the College of Home Economics, Syracuse University, 50 pages. **$8.00**

Happy Holiday from Duncan Hines - A Special Collection of Holiday Recipe Ideas. 1980, Proctor & Gamble. **NCV**

Health For Victory Meal Planning Guide - Point-Thrifty Menus and Over 200 Recipes. June 1944, Westinghouse Electric & Mfg. Co., 56 pages. **$8.00**

Health For Victory Meal Planning Guide - Ration Point-Thrifty Menus and 227 Recipes. July 1944, Julen Kieye, Westinghouse Electric & Mfg. Co. **$8.00**

Helps For The Hostess - Compliments of the Makers of Campbell's Soups. 1910, Joseph Campbell Company, Camden, New Jersey, 64 pages. **$20.00**

The Heart of the Kernel - Kornlet Recipes. 1896, Fannie Merritt Farmer, Meadow Queen Canned Vegetables, The Haserot Canneries Co., 24 pages. **$20.00**

◊ ◊ ◊ ◊

The H.J. Heinz Company, Pittsburg, Pennsylvania

1925 - *Heinz Book of Salads*. 90 pages. **$12.00**

1925, 1930 - *Heinz Book of Salads*. 90 pages. **$10.00**

1930 - *The Heinz Book of Meat Cookery*. Prepared by The Home Economics Department, 56 pages. **$10.00**

1930's - *The Heinz Salad Book*. **$10.00**

1939 - *Heinz Recipe Book*. Home Economics, spiral, 212 pages. **$10.00**

1940's - *H.J. Heinz Co. - Cookbook for the Wife of the Man Who Works a Nite-Shift*. **$8.00**

1965 - *Heinz Magic of Food Show From The Theatre of Food - Festival of Gas Pavilion.* New York World's Fair 1964-1965, 28 pages. **$6.00**

1970 - *Cook With Ketchup for Variety.* 24 pages. **NCV**

1972 - *Soup Cookery - The Savory Heinz Way.* 45 pages. **NCV**

1977 - *For Variety Cook with Soup.* Home Economics Department. **NCV**

1984 - *Put Your Best Food Forward with Heinz Ketchup - 22 Great Recipes from Heinz.* 20-page booklet. **NCV**

◊ ◊ ◊ ◊

Here's A Book The Whole Family Will Enjoy - Arthur Godfrey Food and Fun. A book of food recipes, party games, tricks and fascinating puzzles. 1953. **$10.00**

Here's How By Stouffers. 1962, Stouffer Foods Corp. **$3.00**

Hess Happy-Home Cook Book for Health, Comfort & Happiness. 1920, compliments of Hess Warming & Ventilating Co., Chicago, 35 pages. **$12.00**

Hints For Food and Health. Circa 1910, Lydia Pinkham's Medicine Co., Lynn, Massachusetts. **$14.00**

Hints to Housewives. June 1917, issued by Mayor Mitchel's Food Supply Committee, New York City, 112 pages. **$14.00**

Hobby Horse Cookery. 1950, Marjary Hendricks, Watergate Inn, Washington, D.C., This is where the famous Watergate Scandal took place. **$10.00**

The Hollywood Salad Bowl. 1930's, Ann Page, A & P Grocery Stores, movie stars' recipes. **$10.00**

Home Comfort Cook Book. 1918, Wrought Iron Range Co., St. Louis, established in 1864, 54th anniversary edition, 168 pages. **$14.00**

Home Comfort Cook Book. 1924, Wrought Iron Range Co., St. Louis, established in 1864. **$12.00**

Home Comfort Cook Book. 1925, Wrought Iron Range Co. **$12.00**

Homemaking a la Carte Cook Book. 1987, Homemakers Schools, Inc. 32 pages. **NCV**

Hood's Cook Book. 1877 reprint, No. 1, C.I. Hood & Co. Apothecaries, Lowell, Massachusetts, reprint refers to a 2nd edition of No. 1 in 1879, 32 pages. **$28.00**

Hoods Book of Home Made Candies. 1888, C.I. Hood & Co., proprieters of Hood's Sarsaparilla, Lowell, Massachusetts, 18 pages. **$24.00**

Hood's Book of Home Made Candies. 1905, No. 2, C.I. Hood & Co. **$16.00**

How Bread Can Help You Make Magic Meals in Minutes. 1956, Betty Baker, Home Economist, Holsum Bread, Kansas City, Missouri. **$6.00**

How To Carve. 1924, Swift & Company, 34-page booklet. **$8.00**

How To Cook for 1 or 2 With Reynolds. 1980, Consumer Products, Consumer Division, Reynolds Metals Co., Richmond, 29 pages. **NCV**

How to Cook with California Wines - 81 Delicious Secrets of Wine Cookery - All Easy. 1940's, Wine Advisory Board, San Francisco, 16 pages. **$8.00**

How To Get The Most Out Of The Food You Buy. 1941, prepared in the interest of the National Nutrition Program, General Electric Consumers Institute, 22 pages. **$8.00**

How To Get The Most Out of the Food You Buy. 1942, prepared in the interest of the National Nutrition Program, General Electric Consumer Institute. **$8.00**

How To Get The Most Out of Your Mixmaster. 1936-1937, Sunbeam Corp. **$10.00**

How To Get the Most Out Of Your Sunbeam Mixmaster. 1950, Home Economics Dept., Sunbeam Corp., 44 pages. **$6.00**

How To Get The Most Out Of Your New Sunbeam Mixmaster. 1957, Home Economics Dept., mixer instruction and recipe booklet. **$6.00**

How To Give Luncheons, Teas and Showers. 1964, Florence Brobeck, The Amy Vanderbilt Success Program for Women, 72 pages. **$3.00**

How To Stay In Love for Years and Years and Years With Your Frigidaire Electric Range - With Recipes. 1947. **$8.00**

How To Use Your General Electric Refrigerator. 1940's, 24 pages. **$8.00**

Howdy Doody Cook Book. 1952, Welch Grape Juice Co. **$20.00**

Hunt's For The Best Tasting Recipes. 1982, The Hunt-Wesson Kitchens, 14 pages. **NCV**

Iced Beverages for Young and Old. 1926, Apollo Beverage Shakers, small booklet. **$6.00**

Ida Bailey Allen's Sandwich Book - 500 Sandwiches You Can Make. 1955, 144 pages. **$6.00**

"I Found It," by Mannetta. 1980's, recipes, 119 pages. **NCV**

Idle Hour Cook Book - How to Cook With The Gas Turned Off. 1939, Chamber's Corporation, manufacturers of Chambers, the original insulated gas range, 64 pages. **$10.00**

◊ ◊ ◊ ◊

Ideals Publishing Corporation, Milwaukee, Wisconsin

1972 - *The Ideals Family Cookbook.* Maryjane Hooper Tonn, editor, seventh printing, 64 pages. **NCV**

1973 - *The Ideals Whole Grain Cookbook.* Maryjane Hooper Tonn, editor, fourth printing, 64 pages. **NCV**

1974 - *The Ideals Family Garden Cookbook.* Maryjane Hooper Tonn, editor, first printing, 64 pages. **NCV**

1974 - *The Ideals Family Cookbook.* Maryjane Hooper Tonn, editor, first printing, vol. 2, 64 pages. **NCV**

1974 - *The Ideals All Holidays Cookbook.* Maryjane Hooper Tonn, editor, first printing, 64 pages. **NCV**

1975 - *Ideals Christmas Cookbook Treasury.* 64 pages. **NCV**

1976 - *From Mama's Kitchen.* Catherine Smith, third printing, 64 pages. **NCV**

1978 - *The Farmhouse Cookbook From Ideals.* Clarice Moon, first printing, 64 pages. **NCV**

Other Ideals Publishing Corp. publications:

Quick & Simple Cookbook
Menus From Around The World
Christmas Gifts From The Kitchen
Simply Delicious
Sophie Kay's Family Cookbook
The Ideals American Cookbook
The Ideals Country Kitchen Cookbook
The Ideals Around The World Cookbook
The Ideals Outdoor Cookbook
Gourmet On The Go
The Ideals Family Dessert Cookbook
The Ideals Complete Family Cookbook
The Ideals Cookie Cookbook
The Ideals Festive Party Cookbook
Soups For All Seasons
The Ideals Junior Chef Cookbook
The Naturally Nutritious Cookbook
Tempting Treasures

◊ ◊ ◊ ◊

Improved Puritan Cook Book. Circa 1910, Sears, Roebuck & Co., Chicago, The Puritan Food Chopper, recipes for all seasons of the year, 58 pages. **$14.00**

Instruction and Recipe Book for Users of Hotpoint Hughs Electric Ranges. 1922, Miss Bernic Lowen, Home Economist, Edison Electric Appliance Co. Inc., Chicago, 48 pages. **$12.00**

Instructions and Recipes. 1940's, Universal Speedliner Electric Ranges, Landers, Frary & Clark, New Britain, Connecticut, 121 pages. **$8.00**

International Entertaining. 1980, Bon Appetit Publications, Zack Hanle, Rita Leinwand Jefferson and Jiny Morgan, The Knapp Press. **NCV**

International Favorites Recipes. 1984, Louis Rich™, 14-pages fold out. **NCV**

International Harvester Refrigerator Recipes. 1949, Irma Harding, Director, Home Economics, International Harvester Company. **$8.00**

◊ ◊ ◊ ◊

International Recipe Series

The International Recipe Series consisted of nine soft-cover recipe books. You could order a "slip-case" at a special price. The slip-case holds complete set of nine books. International Publishing Co., Dallas, Texas.

1979 - *Cooking German Style.* Venture into the exciting world of international cooking, 34 pages. **NCV**

1979 - *Cooking French Style.* 34 pages. **NCV**

1979 - *Cooking Hungarian Style.* 34 pages. **NCV**

1979 - *Cooking Japanese Style.* 34 pages. **NCV**

1979 - *Cooking Mexican Style.* 34 pages. **NCV**

1979 - *Cooking Italian Style.* 34 pages. **NCV**

1979 - *Cooking Chinese Style.* 34 pages. **NCV**

1979 - *Cooking Greek Style.* 34 pages. **NCV**

1979 - *Cooking Hawaiian Style.* 34 pages. **NCV**

◊ ◊ ◊ ◊

International Vegetarian Cookery. 1965, Sonya Richmond, 192 pages. **$3.00**

Iona Electric Mixer Recipes and Instructions. 1969, 8-page fold out. **$1.00**

Introducing Ortega Exciting Recipes. 1980, Heublein, Inc., Clinton, Iowa, Ortega cooks have known for 80 years. **NCV**

Irvin S. Cobb's Own Recipe Book. 1934, Frankfort Distilleries, Inc., Louisville. **$8.00**

It's Easy To Be A Gourmet With Peanuts ... The Good Buys In Many Ways. 1964, Oklahoma Peanut Commission, 29 pages. **$3.00**

It's Easy To Be A Gourmet With Peanuts ... The Good Buys in Many Ways. 1970, Oklahoma Peanut Commission, 29 pages. **NCV**

James Beard Cooks With Corning - Selected Recipes. 1973, Corning Glass Works, Corning, New York, 32 pages. **NCV**

Jams, Jellies & Marmalades - Certo Surejell. 1924, Alice Bradley. **$6.00**

Japanese Deep-Sea Crabmeat. 1933, Japan Canned Crab Packers & Exporters Association, New York, New York. **$8.00**

Jellies - How to Make Perfect Jellies with Sure-Jell. 1940's, 10-pages fold out package insert. **$4.00**

Jewell Chafing Dish. 1893, Jewell Mfg. Co., Buffalo, New York, 46 pages. **$20.00**

▶ *Jolly Times Cook Book - Simple Recipes For Young Beginners.* 1934, Marjorie Noble Osborn, Rand McNally & Company, Chicago, 64 pages. **$10.00**

Julia Child, Lunch & Party Dishes From The French Chef Cookbook. 1961, 1963, 1964, 1965, 1966, 1968, 1972, 90 pages. **NCV**

Kate Smith's Favorite Recipes. 1939, General Foods Corp., advertising Swans Down Cake Flour and Calumet Baking Powder, "On the Air with a new Kate Smith Show." **$10.00**

▶ *Kate Smith's Favorite Recipes.* 1939, General Foods Corp., Swans Down Cake Flour, Calumet Baking Powder, Diamond Crystal Salt, Baker's Coconut, Baker's Chocolate, fourth printing. **$10.00**

Kate Smith Says: "Bake A Cake For Someone in the Service." 1945, General Foods Corp., Swans Down Cake Flour & Calumet Baking Powder, 16 pages. **$8.00**

Keen Kutter Cook Book. 1910, E.C. Simmons Hardware, sold with a Keen Kutter food chopper, 24 pages. **$16.00**
The Kelvinator Book of Delicacies - Kelvinated Desserts, Salads and Other Dainties. 1925, Kelvinator Corp., 20 pages. **$12.00**

The Kelvinator Book of Recipes. 1928, Kelvinator, Division of Nash-Kelvinator Corp., Detroit, 32 pages. **$12.00**

Kitchen Economy Comfort Cooking. 1907, compiled by Miss Catharine E. Parsons especially for The Malleable Steel Range Mfg. Co., South Bend, Indiana. **$16.00**

Kitchen Magic Quick Feats and Family Feasts Starring the Original Carl Budding Smoke-Toasted-Sliced Beef-Corned Beef-Ham-Turkey. 1970's, Carl Budding & Company, Chicago, 32-page booklet. **NCV**

Kitchen Tested Lucky Leaf Recipes for Fruit Products and Pie Fillings. 1982, Knouse Foods, Inc., makers of Lucky Leaf Products, established in 1925 in Peach Glen, Pennsylvania, 29 pages. **NCV**

Kitchen Tested Recipes. 1933, Sunbeam Mixmaster. **$10.00**

Know The Joy of Better Cooking Electrically. 1963, Home Service Department, Kansas City Power & Light Company, 96 pages. **$3.00**

◊ ◊ ◊ ◊

Kraft Cheese

In 1903, James L. Kraft had a horse, a wagon, and a working capital of $65.00. He filled his wagon with cheese at the market and started making the rounds of Chicago grocers to sell the cheese. He soon expanded his business to four routes, calling twice a week. J.L. Kraft soon found himself in the cheese-making business also. In 1916, the method of producing cheese was patented by J.L. Kraft. By 1917, Kraft cheese in tins was ready to market.

In 1917, J.L. Kraft & Bros. Company of Chicago and New York was manufacturing Elkhorn Brand Cheese packaged in tins in eight varieties. During World War I the Kraft Cheese in tins was shipped to the boys overseas. In 1920 the company introduced their first five-pound loaf cheese wrapped in foil. By 1921, the company had added a plant in San Francisco.

By the early 1930's the J.L. Kraft & Bros. Company merged with or acquired The Phenix Cheese Company of New York and Chicago bringing to Kraft the "Philadelphia" brand cream cheese. The company name was changed to Kraft-Phenix Cheese Corporation. During the 1930's the tins were discontinued and replaced with foil-wrapped in carton and glass jars with pry-off lids and when the product was gone, you had juice glasses.

By 1943 the company name was Kraft Cheese Company. During the World War II years, Kraft Cheese Company offered recipe publications to stretch the Ration Points. "In these days of rationed foods, American homemakers are finding many ways to serve appetizing balanced meals at a very low cost in Ration Points." By the 1940's Kraft had developed the packaged Kraft Dinner and had acquired Parkay oleomargarine.

By the 1950's, with the addition of so many other

food products, the company name was changed to Kraft Foods Company. In the 1970's Kraft was operating in Canada as Kraft, Limited. In the 1970's the name on a recipe publication was listed as Kraft Foods, Division of Kraftco Corporation. By 1980 this was changed to Kraft, Inc.

In 1985 Kraft, Inc. purchased the Craig Food Service, the wholesale food distributor in Salem, Missouri, to expand their outlets to restaurants and hotels in Central Missouri. In 1986, there was a leveraged buy-out of Kraft, Inc. by Phillip Morris, General Foods.

We have collected the following publications:

1917 - *Elkhorn Cheese - 8 Varieties in Tins - A Few Choice Recipes, Try Them.* J.L. Kraft & Bros. Co., Chicago, New York, four-page leaflet. **$8.00**

▶ 1921 - *Cheese And Ways To Serve It.* 32 pages. **$12.00**

1920's - *Delicious Cheese Recipes.* Phenix Cheese Company, New York, 32 pages. **$12.00**

1938 - *Favorite Recipes From Mary Dahnke's File.* Kraft-Phenix Cheese Corp., 47 pages. **$10.00**

▶ 1943 - *Cheese Recipes for Wartime Meals - How to Make Your Cheese Go Further.* Mary Dahnke, Director, Home Economics Kitchen, Kraft Cheese Company, 16 pages. **$8.00**

1950's - *44 Wonderful Ways to Use Philadelphia Brand Cream Cheese.* From the Kraft Kitchen, 20 pages. **$6.00**

1955 - *Treasury of Good Food Ideas.* From the Kraft Kitchen, 3-ring hard-cover stand up. **$12.00**

1960's - *Kraft Cookery - Salads, Desserts, Main Dishes, Sandwiches.* 12-page pamphlet. **$3.00**

1970's - *Kraft Cheese Cookery - To Help You Serve Something Different.* 8-page pamphlet. **NCV**

1971, 1977 - *The Complete Cheese Cookbook.* Dorothy Holland, Director, Kraft Kitchens, Kraft Foods, Division of Kraftco Corp., ninth printing, 192 pages. **NCV**

1980 - *Nobody Cooks Like You.* Recipes as featured on the January Kraft T.V. Special, Kraft, Inc., 4-page flyer. **NCV**

1981 - *Cooking For You ... Or Two.* The Kraft Kitchens, Kraft, Inc. **NCV**

1982 - *Miracle Whip Cookbook - 50th Aniversary, 185 Great Tasting Recipes.* **NCV**

1982 - *Cooking With Miracle Whip Salad Dressing.* 12 Great Recipes from 50th Anniversary Cookbook. 8 pages. **NCV**

1984 - *The Nature's Fast Food Salad Recipe Book From Kraft.* Kraft Limited, Mount Royal, Quebec, Canada, 12 pages. **NCV**

1987 - *Creative Cooking With Velveeta.* Recipes developed by the Kraft Kitchens, Kraft, Inc., 33 pages. **NCV**

◊ ◊ ◊ ◊

Kroger

The Kroger Grocery & Bakery Company issued weekly "Thought for Food," tested recipes, and offered a two-ring binder to hold a collection of these weekly publications. There was a nominal charge of 25 cents for the binder. The weekly publication was published every Monday and found in the same place in your Kroger Store, at least through 1942. Jean Allen was the Home Economist for the Kroger G. & B. Company.

The following publications are what we were able to collect:

▶ Circa 1930 - *Menus and Recipes.* The Kroger Food Foundation, 10-page fold out. **$5.00**

▶ 1931 - *Canning "Do's" and Canning "Don'ts."* Bulletin No. 11. **$5.00**

▶ 1931 - *Three R's to Remember in Feeding School Children.* Bulletin No. 13. **$5.00**

1931 - *Putting the Power of Flour Into Your Daily Diet.* Bulletin No. 14. **$5.00**

1931 - *"Budget-Saving" Menus For 14 Days.* Bulletin No. 15. **$5.00**

1931 - *"Cutting Corners" on Food Costs.* Bulletin No. 16, the second issue of "Budget-Saving " Menus for third and fourth weeks, 24 pages. **$5.00**

1931 - *Stretching Your Food Dollars For the Next Two Weeks.* The third issue of "Budget Saving" Menus for fifth and sixth weeks, 24 pages. **$5.00**

1931 - *How To Get More From Your Food Dollars - Budget-Saving Menus for 14 Days Including Thanksgiving.* The fourth issue of "Budget-Saving" Menus for seventh & eighth weeks, 24 pages. **$5.00**

1930's - *Oven Dinners - Menus and Recipes.* Jean Allen, 8 pages. **$5.00**

▶ 1933 - *How to Make the Menu Please the Crowd - And Pay A Profit.* The Kroger Food Foundation, 70 pages. **$10.00**

1931 - The Kroger Food Foundation 2-ring binder to hold weekly "Food for Thought" bulletins. Embossed on cover. **$10.00**

1935 - The Kroger Food Foundation 2-ring binder. Contains Dec. 2, 1935 - Aug. 17, 1942 bulletins. **$10.00**

1935 - *The Meat Course.* The Kroger Food Foundation, 79 pages. **$10.00**

1940's - *Ways To Save Sugar.* Jean Allen, World War II flyer. **$5.00**

1940's - *Your Wartime Food - 19 Tested Recipes For Utility Beef.* Jean Allen, 8½"x11", 4 pages. **$5.00**

1950 - *7 Menus and Recipes For Chicken Dinners That Are Different.* Jean Allen tested recipes, 8 pages. **$4.00**

1950's - *The Little Cookbook.* Jean Allen tested recipe, 10 pages. **$6.00**

◇ ◇ ◇ ◇

La Choy Chinese Recipes, Now - The Art and Secrets of Chinese Cookery. 1929, La Choy Food Products, Inc., Detroit. **$5.00**

◇ ◇ ◇ ◇

Larkin Company Pure Food Specialists - established in 1875 in Buffalo, New York.

1906, 1907, 1908 - *Good Things To Eat and How To Prepare Them.* Sixth revised edition. **$16.00**

1909 - *Good Things To Eat and How To Prepare Them.* Seventh edition. **$16.00**

1915 - *The Economy of Factory to Family Dealing - The Larkin Idea.* A premium booklet, 24 pages. **$14.00**

1915 - *Larkin Housewives Cook Book.* The Larkin Company mail order products for the home. **$14.00**

▶ 1916 - *The Larkin Idea.* Larkin products and premiums including Larkin ice-cream powder, 38 pages. **$14.00**

◇ ◇ ◇ ◇

LaVille & Les Champs With Recipes. 1960, Paris, spiral, 110 pages. **$6.00**

Lawry's 'Tis The Seasoning Cookbook - Menus and Recipes for Year-Round Holiday Entertaining. 1984, Lawry's Foods, Inc., 22 pages. **NCV**

Leavitt's Farmers Almanac. 1922, Dudley Leavitt, Concord, New Hampshire, 48 pages. **$12.00**

Le Creuset Cookbook. 1970's, Irena Chalmers, Schiller & Asmus, Inc., Distributors for Le Creuset, 48 pages. **NCV**

Les Fromages De France Recipes. 1960, 110 pages. **$6.00**

Let Florence Do Your Cooking. 1934, Florence Stove

Company, makers of Kerosene Stoves, Gardner, Massachusetts. **$10.00**

▶ *Libby's Fancy Red Alaska Salmon.* 1935, in shape of a can, Libby, McNeill & Libby, Chicago, 31 pages. **$10.00**

▶ *Leibig Company's Cook Book.* 1893, contains new and original recipes written by Miss Parloa, 95 pages plus index. **$20.00**

Liebig Company's Cook Book. 1893, contains new and original recipes written by Miss Parloa, different cover, 95 pages plus index. **$20.00**

Lifetime Cooking Fun and Eating Pleasure. 1949, Ann Williams-Heller, Food and Nutrition Consultant, Lifetime Stainless Steel Cookware, established in 1909, 56 pages. **$8.00**

The Little Red Devil. 1920's, deviled ham, 30 pages. **$12.00**

Lucca. 1936, 7 million people have been served by Lucca with these recipes. The Lucca Restaurant opened in San Francisco in 1930, in Los Angeles in 1933, 24 pages. **$10.00**

Luncheons, Salads and Vegetables. 1978, Home Cooking Library, Banner Press, Inc., 62 pages. **NCV**

Magic Meals in Minutes. 1956, Betty Baker, Home Economist, American Research Kitchen, Holsum Bread, Kansas City, Missouri, 24 pages. **$6.00**

Magnolias & Ambrosia - Creole Recipes. 1967, Dorothy V. Doughty. **$3.00**

▶ *Majestic Cook Book.* 1899, compiled by The Best Housekeeper in this or any other country, Majestic Manufacturing Company, St. Louis, Missouri, manufacturers of Cast Iron Cooking Ranges, 96 pages. **$20.00**

Majestic Recipes. 1931, Dorothy Ayers Louden, Home Economics, Food Lecturer, Grisby-Grunow Company, Chicago Manufacturers of Refrigerators, 40 pages. **$10.00**

Homestead Recipes - Making Breads with Home-Grown Yeasts & Home-Ground Grains. 1974, A Garden Way Guide by Phyllis Hobson, 44 pages. **NCV**

Making Breads With Home-Grown Yeasts & Home-Ground Grains. 1979, A Garden Way Guide by Phyllis Hobson, fifth printing, 44 pages. **NCV**

Making The Most Of Your Electrolux with Practical Recipes. 1935, Servel, Inc., 48 pages. **$10.00**

Making The Most of Your Servel Electrolux Refrigerator. 1941, Servel, Inc. **$8.00**

▶ *Marion Harland's Recipe Calendar.* 1924, 56 pages. **$24.00**

Margaret Mitchell's Meal Time Magic Desserts. 1951, Wearever Aluminumware, first printing. **$6.00**

Martha Logan's Meat Cook Book. 1953, Beth Bailey, Director, Home Economics of Swift & Company, fourth printing. **$6.00**

Martha Logan's Meat Handi-Book. 1963, Martha Logan, Home Economist, Swift & Company. **$3.00**

Maylies Table D'Hote Recipes La Maison. 1930's, Maylie Esparba and Eugenie Maylie, 37 pages. **$10.00**

Mayrose Menus. 1940, St. Louis Independent Packing Company, 4"x5" booklet, 16 pages. **$5.00**

Maytag Dutch Oven Gas Range Cook Book. 1949, spiral, 118 pages plus index. **$8.00**

◊ ◊ ◊ ◊

McCall's Magazine Publications
McCall's Magazine
The Service Editor
236 West 37th St., New York City

▶ 1922 - *Time-Saving Cookery Prepared by The House of Sarah Field Splint.* Issued by *McCall's* magazine. **$12.00**

▶ 1923 - *What To Serve At Parties.* Compiled by Lilian M. Gunn, issued by *McCall's* magazine, menus and recipes. **$12.00**

1923, 1929 - *What To Serve At Parties.* Compiled by Lilian M. Gunn, issued by *McCall's* magazine, menus and recipes, second printing, 62 pages. **$10.00**

1923, 1929 - *My Own Book of Etiquette, Parties for Grown-Ups. McCall's* magazine. **$10.00**

McCall Corporation
Dayton 1, Ohio
In Canada, 133 Simcoe St., Toronto 1, Ontario

▶ 1953 - *McCall's Basic Cake Book* - 12 Perfect Recipes. **$6.00**

1956 - *McCall's Cake & Frosting Book.* New edition. **$6.00**

McCall's Cookbook Collection. By The Food Editors of McCall's, published by Advance Publishers, Inc., P.O. Box 7200, Orlando, Florida.

1965 - M1 (title unknown)

1965 - *McCall's Cassrole Cookbook.* M2, 64 pages. **$3.00**

1965 - *McCall's Practically Cookless Cookbook.* M3, 64 pages. **$3.00**

1965 - *McCall's Salads & Salad Dressings.* M4, 64 pages. **$3.00**

1965 - M5 (title unknown)

1965 - *McCall's Book of Marvelous Meats.* M6, 64 pages. **$3.00**

1965 - M7 (title unknown)

1965 - *McCall's Family-Style Cookbook.* M8, 64 pages. **$3.00**

1965, 1974 - *McCall's Company Cookbook.* M9, 64 pages. **$3.00**

1965 - M10 (title unknown)

1965 - M11 (title unknown)

1965 - M12 (title unknown)

1965 - *McCall's Fish "N" Fowl Cookbook.* M13, 64 pages. **$3.00**

1973 - McCall's Great American Recipe Card Collection, Recipe Card File. **NCV**

1974, 1975 - *McCall's Company Cookbook.* M3, 64 pages. **NCV**

The McCall Publishing Company
230 Park Avenue, New York, New York

1983 - *McCall's Cookery.* No. 1, 32 pages. **NCV**

1985 - *McCall's Cookery.* No. 2, 32 pages. **NCV**

1985 - *McCall's Cookery.* No. 3, 32 pages. **NCV**

1983 - *McCall's Cookery.* No. 4, 32 pages. **NCV**

1984 - *McCall's Cookery.* No. 5, 32 pages. **NCV**

1984 - *McCall's Cookery.* No. 6, 32 pages. **NCV**

1985 - *McCall's Cookery.* No. 7, 32 pages. **NCV**

1987 - McCall's Cookbook Collection. A plastic tray to hold them, 18 publications numbered in sequence.

◊ ◊ ◊ ◊

Meals For Small Families. 1929, Jean Mowat. **$12.00**

Meat For Thrifty Meals. 1942, U.S. Dept. of Agriculture. **$8.00**

Meals of Many Lands - A Cookbook for Children. 1978, Miriam B. Loo, spiral, 24 pages. **NCV**

Meat Selection, Preparation and 100 Ways to Serve. 1932, Dept. of Food Economics, Armour & Company, Chicago. **$10.00**

Meat Selection, Preparation and Many Ways To Serve - A Souvenir of Your Visit to the Armour Building. 1934, A Century of Progress, Chicago World Exposition 1933-34, 64 pages. **$15.00**

Meat - The Main Course. 1942, Ann King, Home Economics Director, Kingan & Company, Reliable Brands, Purveyors of Fine Meats and Other Foods since 1945, 32 pages. **$8.00**

Meat Tops the Menu. 1936, National Live Stock and Meat Board, recipes, menus, reducing menus, 40 pages. **$10.00**

Meat For Thrifty Meals. 1953, Home and Garden Bulletin No. 27. **$6.00**

Meats - Hussmann Hand Book for the Housewife. 1925, Harry L. Hussman Refrigerator Company. **$12.00**

▶ *Meletio's Home Cook Book and Encyclopedia.* 1913, 1925, Meletio Sea Food Company, St. Louis, Missouri, 32 pages. **$12.00**

Menu Booklet. 1930, 30 complete meals, each whole meal cooked all at the same time by Corning Glass Works, makers of Pyrex. **$10.00**

◊ ◊ ◊ ◊

Metropolitan Life Insurance Company Cook Books

To date the Metropolitan Cook Books when they do not show a copyright date in the front, turn to the back cover or last page on the bottom and you will see something like this: (e) 331 L.W. (e) = 1936, so (f) = 1937 and (g) = 1938, etc. This is true except for "The Family Food Supply" editions which were dated up front.

▶ 1918 - *Metropolitan Cook Book.* 64 pages. **$14.00**

▶ 1922 - *Metropolitan Cook Book.* 64 pages. **$12.00**

1925 - *Metropolitan Cook Book.* 64 pages. **$12.00**

1927 - *All About Milk.* 24 pages. **$12.00**

▶ 1928 - *The Family Food Supply.* 24 pages. **$12.00**

1934 - *The Family Food Supply.* 24 pages. **$5.00**

1935 - *The Metropolitan Cook Book.* (d) 331 L.W., 64 pages. **$5.00**

1936 - *Metropolitan Cook Book.* (e) 331 L.W., 64 pages. **$5.00**

1937 - *Metropolitan Cook Book.* (f) 331 L.W., 64 pages. **$5.00**

1938 - *Three Meals A Day - Suggestions For Good Food at Low Cost.* (g) 468 L.W., 24 pages. **$5.00**

1939 - *Metropolitan Cook Book.* (h) 331 L.W., 64 pages. **$5.00**

1941 - *Three Meals A Day.* (j) 468 L.W., 16 pages. **$4.00**

1943 - *Metropolitan Cook Book.* (l) 331 L.W., 64 pages. **$4.00**

1944 - *Overweight and Underweight.* (m) 380 L.W., 32 pages. **$4.00**

1946 - *Metropolitan Cook Book.* 56 pages. **$4.00**

1948 - *Metropolitan Cook Book.* 56 pages. **$4.00**

1953 - *Metropolitan Cook Book.* Ladle, fork and spatula on cover, 56 pages. **$3.00**

1954 - *Metropolitan Cook Book.* Ladle, fork and spatula on cover, 56 pages. **$3.00**

1953, 1955 - *Metropolitan Cook Book.* Ladle, fork and spatula on cover, black background, 56 pages. **$3.00**

1957 - *Metropolitan Cook Book.* Ladle, fork and spatula on cover, blue background, 56 pages. **$3.00**

1964 - *Metropolitan Cook Book.* Ladle, fork and spatula on cover, yellow background, 64 pages. **$2.00**

1973 - *New Metropolitan Cook Book.* 59 pages plus index. NCV

◊ ◊ ◊ ◊

Mexican Cookery For American Homes. 1923, Gebhart, San Antonio, 32 pages. **$12.00**

Mexican Cookery For American Homes. 1949, Gebhardt's Chili Powder Company, San Antonio, 47 pages. **$8.00**

Mickey Mouse Recipe Scrapbook. 1930's, premium given away by Bell Bread, each page has a block with a recipe, 4"x6", 48 pages. **$35.00**

Minnie Pearl Cooks. 1970, special author's edition, spiral, 185 pages. **NCV**

40 Miracles For Your Table. 1930, Sprague Warner & Company, Chicago, manufacturers of Canned Food Products, established in 1862, 36 pages. **$10.00**

Mirro-Matic Pressure Pan Recipes. 1946. **$6.00**

Mirro Cook Book. 1954, Mirro Aluminum Company. **$6.00**

Mirro Doughmaker and Bread Baking Kit Cook Book. 1955. **$6.00**

Mirro-Matic Directions, Time Tables and Recipes. 1961, Mirro Aluminum Company, 58 pages. **$3.00**

Mirro-Matic Pressure Pan Recipes. 1961, Mirro Aluminum Company. **$3.00**

Mirro-Matic Speed Pressure Cooker Cookbook. 1972. **NCV**

Miss Parloa's Kitchen Companion. 1887, **$30.00**

Miss Parloa's New Cook Book. 1888, Maria Parloa, limited edition to 100,000, 8½"x11", 56 pages plus ads. **$30.00**

Missouri Cattle Women Beef Recipes. 1987, 8-pages fold out. **NCV**

Missouri Farm Bureau Cookbook. 1968, spiral. **$6.00**

Mistress Prudence's Own Book of Recipes. 1931, Boston Food Products Co. **$10.00**

The Modern Hostess Cook Book. 1942, Eleanor M. Lynch, editor, contains 1,000 recipes with menus, party plans, vitamin charts, 98 pages. **$8.00**

▶ *Modern Household Helps.* Mrs. S.T. Rorer's Copyrighted Recipes, 1903, presented with the compliments of Standard Oil Company (Indiana), 18 pages. **$20.00**

Modern Household Hints. 1930's, Miles Laboratories, Inc., Dr. Miles Nervine-Alka-Seltzer, 16 pages. **$10.00**

The Modern Way to Health. 1930, Super Maid Cookware Corporation, 48 pages. **$10.00**

Moonlight Mushrooms Recipe Book. 1974, Butler County Mushroom Farm, Inc., Pennsylvania, fourth printing, 20 pages. **NCV**

Money Saving Main Dishes. April 1948, 150 Tested Recipes Especially Prepared by the Bureau of Human Nutrition and Home Economics. **$8.00**

Money Saving Main Dishes. 1955, Human Nutrition Research Branch, Agricultrual Research Service, 48 pages. **$6.00**

Morningstar Farms Cholesterol Counter Menu Planner. 1979, Worthington Foods, Inc., 24 pages. **NCV**

The Morrell Menu Maker. 1950, John Morrell & Company, 3"x5", 31 pages. **$6.00**

The Most Amazing Short-Cuts in Cooking You Ever Heard Of. 1939. **$10.00**

Mr. Peanut's Guide to Entertaining. 1960's, Planters Peanuts Test Kitchen. **$6.00**

Mrs. Morton's Cook Book. 1917, Shrewesbury Publishing Company, 142 pages plus ads. **$14.00**

Mrs. Olson's Get-Together Recipes. 1973, give-away with coffee purchase, 65 pages. **NCV**

Mrs. Winslow's Domestic Receipt Book. 1869, Jeremiah Curtis & Sons, John I. Brown & Sons, 32 pages. **$30.00**

Mrs. Winslow's Domestic Receipt Book. 1872, Jeremiah Curtis & Sons, John I. Brown & Sons, 32 pages. **$28.00**

▶ *Mrs. Winslow's Domestic Receipt Book For 1873.* 1873, Jeremiah Curtis & Sons and John I. Brown & Sons, 32 pages. **$28.00**

▶ *Mrs. Winslow's Domestic Receipt Book.* 1877, 1878, Jeremiah Curtis & Sons and John I. Brown & Sons, 32 pages. **$28.00**

My Best Recipes. 1934, Mary Hale Martin, Libby, McNeill & Libby, 87 pages. **$10.00**

▶ *My Meat Recipes.* 103 Prize Winning With Holiday Greetings from The National Live Stock and Meat Board, 1926, 46 pages plus index. **$12.00**

Mueller's Tested & Proven Recipes. 1929, Mueller's Pasta Products, 24 pages. **$12.00**

Magic Menus with Meller's Macaroni Products. 1937, C.F. Mueller Co., Jersey City, 28 pages. **$10.00**

The Myra Breckinridge Cookbook. 1970, Howard Austen and Beverly Pepper, Dedication page says "For Escoffier, Fannie Farmer and Gore Vidal," 344 pages. **NCV**

Nancy Pepper's Recipes. 1947, Electromaster Inc., 64 pages. **$8.00**

The New Art. 1933, created by General Electric Kitchen Institute. **$10.00**

The New Art. 1934, General Electric Kitchen Institute, Nela Park, Cleveland. **$10.00**

The New Art of Buying, Perserving and Preparing Foods. 1934, General Electric Kitchen Institute. **$10.00**

The New Art of Buying, Preserving and Preparing Foods. 1934, created by General Electric, Kitchen Institute, NRA, 112 pages. **$10.00**

The New Art of Buying, Preserving and Preparing Foods. 1935, created by General Electric Kitchen Institute, first edition. **$10.00**

The New Art of Modern Cooking. 1937, General Electric, spiral, 112 pages. **$10.00**

▶ *New Art Refrigerator Recipe Book.* 1940, created by General Electric Kitchen Institute, 56 pages. **$8.00**

New Breakfast Ideas. 1961, Ruth Hatheway, Home Econimics Department, Wonder Bread, Continental Baking Co. Inc., 12 pages. **$3.00**

New Calendar of Salads. 1920's, Elizabeth O. Hiller. **$12.00**

New Delights From the Kitchen - The Kelvin Kitchen. 1930, The Kelvinator Home Economics Department. **$10.00**

New England Buttery Shelf Cook Book. 1969, Mary Mason Campbell. **$3.00**

◊◊◊◊

The Perfection Stove Company

In 1897 John P. Crowell, an officer and stockholder in the American Cereal Company, purchased control of an iron-mongering firm that had patented an oil-burning stove known as the Cleveland Foundry Company, later to become the Perfection Stove Company.

The following is what we were able to collect from this company:

▶ 1895 - *New Perfection Cook Book and Directions for Operating New Perfection Oil Stoves.* 96 pages. **$20.00**

1902 - *New Perfection Cook-Book.* 70 pages. **$16.00**

1912 - *New Perfection Cook-Book.* The Cleveland Foundry Company, For Best Results Use "Eupion" Oil, 72 pages. **$14.00**

▶ 1923 - *The New Perfection Cook Book Also Instructions On The Care & Operation of New Perfection Oil Cook Stoves.* The Cleveland Metal Products Company. Other products - Perfection Oil Heaters, Puritan Cook Stoves and new Perfection Kerosene Water Heaters, 64 pages. **$12.00**

1952 - *Recipes.* Perfection Stove Company, Cleveland, Ohio, sold by Stoltz Hardware, 613 Pine St., Rolla, Missouri, 29 pages. **$8.00**

◊◊◊◊

The New Orleans Cook Book. 1957. **$6.00**

New Process Cookery. 1920's, Lorain New Process Stove Company. **$12.00**

The New Romagnoli's Table. 1975, 1988, Margaret and G. Franco Romagnoli, 297 pages. **NCV**

The New Science of Waterless Cooking. 1928, Waterless Ware. **$12.00**

New Sunbeam Cooker & Deep Fryer. 1952, Sunbeam Corp., Chicago, 25 pages. **$6.00**

The New World of Welch's. 1975, 1976 Bicentennial Welch Foods, Inc., 28 pages. **NCV**

O & C Division - Durkee Famous Foods. 1930's, 33 delightfully different recipe ideas, 8 pages. **$10.00**

Oh Boy! - RF Spaghetti, For Mom's Favorite Recipes. 1951, Glenn G. Hoskins, Chicago, 32 pages. **$6.00**

Ohio State Grange Cookbook. July 1974, spiral, 244 pages. **NCV**

The Old Farmer's Almanac Colonial Cookbook. 1982, premium edition, Clarissa M. Silitch, Yankee Books, Yankee Publishing Co., 64 pages. **NCV**

The Old Farmer's Almanac. 1988, Robert B. Thomas, planting tables, Zodiac secrets, recipes pages 200-205, 232 pages. **NCV**

Olde Family Favorites Cookbook. 1983, first edition, Favorite Recipes Press, 128 pages. **NCV**

The Olive and Its Oil. 1920's, H.J. Heinz Co., Pittsburg, factory brochure. **$12.00**

The Omaha Steaks Cookbook. 1983, Omaha Steaks International. **NCV**

One Dozen Prize Winning Recipes Calling for Frank's Jumbo Peanut Butter. 1930's, booklet. **$6.00**

▶ *100 Old Fashioned Cooking Recipes.* 1910, *The Chicago Tribune.* **$16.00**

100 Recipes for Deep Fried Foods. 1950. **$6.00**

100 Recipes Using Campfire Marshmallows and Creme. 1920's. **$12.00**

▶ *101 Ways To Prepare Macaroni.* 1949, LaRose V. Larosa & Sons, Inc., Danielson, Connecticut, Brooklyn, New York, 62 pages. **$8.00**

▶ *One Man's Family - 20th Anniversary Souvenir - Mother Barbour's Favorite Recipes.* 1952, Miles Laboratories, Inc., 48 pages. **$15.00**

One Pot Meals. 1976, Margaret Gin. **NCV**

1,000 Recipes Cook Book. 1949, *Dell Magazine*, desserts, salads, meats, candies, pies and cakes, 98 pages. **$4.00**

1,000 Recipes Cook Book. 1950, Nancy Wood featuring Fred Astaire, salads, desserts, meats, candies, pies and cakes, 98 pages. **$4.00**

1,000 Recipes Cook Book. 1953, *Dell Magazine.* **$4.00**

Operating Suggestions and Recipes. 1930's, Coldspot, Sears, Roebuck & Co. **$10.00**

▶ *Original Menus.* 1908, Curtice Brothers Company, Rochester, New York, Blue Label Brand Canners and Bottlers of Food Products. **$16.00**

Ott's Dressings and Sauces from Carthage, Missouri. 1950's. **$3.00**

Our Favorite Meat Recipes. 1935, National Live Stock and Meat Board, Dedicated to the American Housewife, 22 pages. **$10.00**

Outdoor Picture Cook Book. 1954, Bob James, spiral. **$6.00**

▶ *Papa Cribari in Cucina - Family Cooking with Wine.* 1950's, B. Cribari & Sons, San Francisco, California, 16 pages. **$6.00**

Party Recipe Ideas. 1962, Martha Logan, Swift & Company. **$3.00**

Party Cook Book. 1954. **$6.00**

Paul C. Bragg's Personal Health Food Cook Book and Menus. 1930, 1935 second edition autographed by author, Paul C. Bragg, 201 pages. **$10.00**

▶ *Peanut's Cook Book.* 1969, first printing Jan. 1970, recipes by June Dutton, United Feature Syndicate Cartoons by Charles M. Schulz, 64 pages. **$6.00**

Peanut's Cook Book Recipes. 1970, June Dutton, cartoons by Charles M. Schulz. **NCV**

Pennsylvania Angler's Cook Book. 1977, Pennsylvania Fish Commission. **NCV**

Pennsylvania Dutch Cookery. 1935, J. George Frederick. **$10.00**

Pennsylvania Dutch Cooking. 1960, The Pennsylvania Dutch. **$6.00**

▶ *Pennsylvania Dutch Cooking - Recipes For Traditional Pennsylvania Dutch Dishes.* 1960, Yorkraft, Inc., York, Pennsylvania. **$6.00**

Pennsylvania Dutch Pies and Pastries. 1963, Conestoga Crafts, Gettysburg, Pennsylvania, 16 pages. **$3.00**

Perk Up With Prevention. 1968, compiled by the staff of *Prevention* magazine. Contents - Health Foods are Gourmet Foods, Foods That Fight Fatigue, You Can Afford to Eat for Health, etc. **$3.00**

▶ *The Peter Pan Peanut Butter Cook Book.* 1963, Derby Foods, Inc., 26 pages. **$3.00**

Petro-frost Automatic Kerosene Refrigerator Operating Instructions And Recipes. Circa 1910, 16 pages. **$14.00**

The Philadelphia Inquirer Cook Book. 1936, Mrs. Anna B. Scott. **$10.00**

Photoplay's Cook Book. 1927, C. Van Wyek, editor, *Photoplay* magazine. **$12.00**

Pickle and Relish Recipes. 1944, U.S. Dept. of Agriculture. **$4.00**

Picnics For People on the Go. 1982, Paul Mason Vineyards, original recipes to compliment the convenience of the Paul Mason carafes, 6-page fold out. **NCV**

A Picnic Treasury of Good Cooking - A Tested Recipe Institute Cook Book. 1953, Demetria M. Taylor and Lillian C. Ziegfeld, 127 pages. **$6.00**

Pies & Cakes. 1978, Arlene Mueller, Nitty Gritty Productions, a 2 in 1 cookbook, 178 pages. **NCV**

A Plan For the Day's Choice of Food. 1942, General Foods Corp., 8½"x11", 4-pages folder. **$8.00**

Portable Electric Cookery. 1971, first edition, Sunbeam Appliance Service Co. **NCV**

Practical Cooking Recipes. 1920's, The Lydia E. Pinkham Medicine Co., Lynn, Massachusetts, 32 pages. **$12.00**

Preparing Foods with Reynolds Wrap Pure Aluminum Foil. 1950's, 34 pages. **$6.00**

Pressure Cooking. 1949, Ida Bailey Allen. **$8.00**

The Presto Book of Menus & Recipes. 1930's, Della Lutes, published by Cupples Company, distributors of Presto Canning Products, St. Louis, Missouri. **$10.00**

Presto Cooker Recipe Book. 1940, National Pressure Cooker Co. **$8.00**

Presto Cooker Instructions & Recipes. 1940's, time tables. **$8.00**

Presto Cooker Recipe Book. 1953. **$6.00**

Presto Fry Pan Recipe Book. 1956. **$6.00**

Preventions Better Living Cookbook. 1976, Emma Bailey, *Prevention* magazine. **NCV**

Primer for Gourmet Cooking Groups. 1969, Foods From France, Inc., New York, 30 pages. **$3.00**

Priscilla Cook Book for Everyday Housekeepers. 1913, Fannie Merritt Farmer, The Priscilla Publishing Company, Boston. **$16.00**

The Proper Method of Laying & Serving A Table. 1908, Miss Janet McKenzie Hill of the Boston Cooking School, The Griswold Manufacturing Company, Erie, Pennsylvania, booklet. **$8.00**

Purity Premier's Recipes. Circa 1910, Francis Leggett & Co. **$14.00**

Pyrex Experts Book on Better Cooking. 1925, Alice Bradley, principal, Miss Farmer's School of Cookery, Boston, Corning Glass Works, Corning, New York. **$12.00**

The Quality Cook Book. 1920's, Roberts & Mander Stove Co., Gas Range Division, 32 pages. **$12.00**

Quantity Cooking. 1927, Woman's Home Companion. **$12.00**

Quench That Thirst. 1938, Julia Lee Wright, Director, Homemakers Bureau, *The Family Circle Magazine,* June 3, Oakland, California, 4 pages for 2-ring binder. **$5.00**

Quick, Easily Prepared Recipes for Your Kenmore Electric Servants. 1948. **$8.00**

Quick Recipes - 20 Minutes or Less From Start to Serving, 83 Home-Cooked Dishes in Quick Time. 1952, *Quick* Mgazine, 64 pages. **$6.00**

Quick and Easy Riceland Rice Kitchen Tested Recipes. 1950's, Arkansas Rice Growers. **$6.00**

◊ ◊ ◊ ◊

Ransom's Family Receipt Books

Ransom's Family Receipt Book, published by D. Ransom & Son Company, Buffalo, New York. Since 1868 circulated by drug stores during the winter months.

1878 - *Ransom's Family Receipt Book.* 32 pages. **$28.00**

1880 - *Ransom's Family Receipt Book.* 32 pages. **$24.00**

1884 - *Ransom's Family Receipt Book.* 32 pages. **$24.00**

1886 - *Ransom's Family Receipt Book.* 32 pages. **$24.00**

1887 - *Ransom's Family Receipt Book.* 32 pages. **$24.00**

▶ 1889 - *Ransom's Family Receipt Book.* 32 pages. **$24.00**

1898 - *Ransom's Family Receipt Book.* Palmer Cox Brownies on back, 32 pages. **$20.00**

▶ 1906 - *Ransom's Family Receipt Book.* 32 pages. **$16.00**

▶ 1907 - *Ransom's Family Receipt Book.* 32 pages. **$16.00**

▶ 1908 - *Ransom's Family Receipt Book.* 32 pages. **$16.00**

1910 - *Ransom's Family Receipt Book.* 32 pages. **$16.00**

1911 - *Ransom's Family Receipt Book.* 32 pages. **$14.00**

1912 - *Ransom's Family Receipt Book.* 32 pages. **$14.00**

1913 - *Ransom's Family Receipt Book.* 32 pages. **$14.00**

1914 - *Ransom's Family Receipt Book.* 32 pages. **$14.00**

◊ ◊ ◊ ◊

Reasons for Using and Recipes for Preparing Woodcock Macaroni. Circa 1910. **$14.00**

Recipe Book. 1930, Wm. W. Bevan Co., makers of Liberty Paper Baking Cups. **$10.00**

Recipe Book. 1930's, Fisherman's Grotto. **$10.00**

▶ *The Recipe Book for Club Aluminum Ware with Personal Service.* 1925, Anne Hurst Harrlett, Home Managers Service, 31 pages. **$12.00**

Recipe of the Month Magazine. October 1935, Eleanor Howe, Halloween theme, Cudahy Packing Co., 16 pages. **$5.00**

Recipe Book - Gregory's Elko-Ozark, The Aristocrat of All Vinegars. 1920's, Gregory-Robinson-Speas, Inc. **$12.00**

Recipes by Worthington. 1930's, Jan Worth, Worthington Foods Kitchen, 16 pages. **$10.00**

Recipes ... Care ... Use Westinghouse Refrigerator. 1948, **$8.00**

Recipes for Hearty Salads - That's Using Your Head with California Iceberg Lettuce. 1982, Safeway - America's Favorite Food Store, 4 pages. **$6.00**

Recipes For Today. 1943, Consumer Service Dept., General Foods Corp, 40 pages. **$8.00**

▶ *Recipes For Trade Mark Pureed Fruits and Vegetables, "Van Camps - Of Course!"* 1930. **$10.00**

▶ *Recipes For War Breads.* 1917. **$14.00**

Recipes From Some of the World's Greatest Chefs and The Kitchens of Best Foods. 1967. **$3.00**

Recipes From the Kitchens of Dorothy Taylor. 1973, Series #1, The Complete Family Recipe Card Library, Collect All 15 Series, Curtin Promotions, Inc., New York City. **NCV**

Recipes. 1931, Kitchen Aid Electrical Food Preparer for the Home Department of Home Economics, The Kitchen Aid Manufacturing Co., 72 pages. **$10.00**

Recipes: The Cooking of Provincial France. 1968, *Time-Life,* spiral. **$3.00**

Recipes - Virginia Pancake Flour, Buckwheat Flour and Syrup. 1925, The Fishback Co., booklet. **$12.00**

Redbow Tested Recipes. 1967, The Graham Co., New York Dried Beans. **$3.00**

"Rex" Beef Extract. 1903, Nellie Duling Gans, The Cudahy Packing Company. **$16.00**

Rexall's 75th Anniversary Country Cook Book - 75 All Time Favorite Recipes from The Farmer's Almanac Cook Book. 1978, Rexall Drug Company, 64 pages. **NCV**

Rice - 200 Delightful Ways to Serve It. 1935, Home Economics Dept., Southern Rice Industry, New Orleans, Louisiana. **$10.00**

Riceland Rice Recipes, Delicious-Quik-Easy. 1952, Arkansas Rice Growers Cooperative Association, 28 pages. **$6.00**

Riceland Rice Kitchen Tested Recipes. 1953, Arkansas Rice Growers, Stuttgart, Arkansas, 8 pages. **$6.00**

Riceland and Rice Cook Book. 1960's, Arkansas Rice Growers Cooperative Association, Stuttgart, Arkansas. **$3.00**

Richard Simmon's Never-Say Diet Book. 1980, with his Volume Food Plan and body-correcting exercises, 212 pages. **NCV**

Richard Deacon's Microwave Oven Cookbook. 1975, 231 great new recipes. **NCV**

Ripley's Sweet Sixteen. 1898, Mrs. Owen, 16-pages booklet. **$20.00**

Rival Crock-Pot Slow Cooker Cookbook. 1982, Barbara Brooks, Home Economics Dept., Rival Mfg. Co., 48 pages. **NCV**

Robertshaw Oven Heat Control Cooking Suggestions. 1920's. **$12.00**

Robertshaw Cook Book. 1940, Elizabeth Gray, Robertshaw Thermostat Company, 94 pages. **$8.00**

Robertshaw Measured Heat Cook Book. 1940's, 94 pages. **$8.00**

Robertshaw Measured Heat Cook Book. 1949, 94 page. **$8.00**

Robertshaw Measured Heat Cook Book. 1953, 94 pages. **$6.00**

"Round The World" Cooking Library - German Cooking. 1976, Arne Kruger, 72 pages. **NCV**

The Rural Home Cook Book. St. Louis, Misouri, Thompson Printing Company. **$16.00**

The Salad Bowl. 1929, Martha Adams, The Best Foods Company, Home Economics Service. **$12.00**

Salad Ideas. 1929, Hellman's Blue Ribbon Mayonnaise, Richard Hellman, Inc., P. Co. Inc., a holding company that emerged in 1930 as General Foods Corporation, 16 pages. **$12.00**

Salad Leaves. 1920's, Harriet Meaker Osborne of the Ivanhoe Kitchens, Ivanhoe Food Inc., 35 pages. **$12.00**

Salads - Alluring and New. 1926, The Intriguing Creations of Alice Bradly Gebhardt's Chili Powder Company, San Antonio, 12 pages. **$16.00**

Salads - Favorite Recipes. 1970's, Home Economics Teachers 2,000 recipes including appetizers, Montgomery, Alabama, spiral, 384 pages. **NCV**

Salads, Sandwiches & Summer Drinks. 1927, Ethel Somers, *Liberty Weekly.* **$12.00**

Salads Well Dressed. 1970, Irena Chalmers, published by Potpourri Press, Greensboro, North Carolina, 48 pages. **NCV**

Sally Stokely's Prize Vegetable Recipes. 1933, Stokely Brothers & Co. Inc., canners of Indianapolis, 30 pages. **$10.00**

Sara and Aggies Household Handy Book. 1938, 31 pages. **$10.00**

The Saturday Evening Post Family Cookbook. 1984, Cory SerVass, M.D., Charlotte Turgeon, 112 pages. **NCV**

Savor the Seasons with Beef. 1970's, Beef Industry Council, National Live Stock and Meat Board, 16 pages. **NCV**

Savory Prize Recipe Book. 1909, published in the interest of Better Living at Less Cost. Savory roasters, double boilers, coffee percolators, bread & cake boxes, The Republic Metalware Co., Buffalo, 40 pages. **$16.00**

Savory Prize Recipe Book for the "Savory" Roaster. 1922, J.W. Clement Company. **$12.00**

Say "Good Bye" to Hand Beating! 1933, Kitchen Wizard mixer-beater, juice extractor, The New Kitchen Helper, The Fitzgerald Mfg. Company, 2-page fold out. **$6.00**

Say "Good-Bye" to Hand Beating! Magic Maid and Tested Recipes. 1934, The Fitzgerald Mfg. Company, 32 pages. **$10.00**

Scandinavian Recipes. 1940, 1944, 1945, Julia Peterson Tufford, Deer Creek, Minnesota, seventh printing, 54 pages. **$8.00**

Sea Foods With the Tang O' The Sea. Circa 1910, Davis Fish Company. **$14.00**

The Secret of Better Taste. 1961, The Angostura Cook Book. **$3.00**

▶ *Secrets of the Jam Cupboard - Jellies and Jams in Delightful New Uses.* 1930, Certo, a product of G.F. Corp., 23 pages. **$10.00**

Seventy-Five Tempting Recipes for Dainty Desserts. 1930, Lyon Manufacturing co., Inc., Brooklyn, New York. **$10.00**

The Shaker Cook Book. 1953, Caroline B. Piercy, illus. by Virginia Filson Walsh. **$6.00**

The Shaker Cookbook - Recipes & Love From the Valley of God's Pleasure. 1953, 1981, 1984, Caroline Piercy, Arthur Tolve, 176 pages. **NCV**

Shefford Cheese Recipes. 1932, Shefford Cheese Company, Inc., Syracuse, New York, 36 pages. **$10.00**

Shefford Cheese Recipes. 1938, Alberta Winthrop, Shefford Cheese Company, Inc., Green Bay, Wisconsin, 36 pages. **$10.00**

Shortcut Cooking. 1969, Meredity Corporation, first printing, 47 pages. **$3.00**

Shrimp Tips From New Orleans. 1956, U.S. Dept. of the Interior, Fish and Wildlife Service, Washington, D.C., 16 pages. **$6.00**

Simple Recipes for Home Cooking. 1910, Gaylord Du Bois, Haldeman-Julius Company, Girard, Kansas, small booklet, 64 pages. **$16.00**

Simplified Healthful Food Preparation. 1936, second edition, Century Silver-Seal Metalcraft Corporation, Jean Douglas, Food Director, 48 pages. **$10.00**

The Sister's Favortie Recipes. 1977, Orange Park, Florida by owners of this famous tea room, Bon Appetit. **NCV**

Sixty Ways To Serve a Famous Candy "Oh Henry" Candy Bar. 1925, Williamson Candy Co., Chicago, Brooklyn. **$12.00**

Something Special from Homemakers Schools. 1988, an event featuring cooking demonstrations and home management ideas cookbook, 32 pages. **NCV**

The Soup and Sandwich Handbook - How to Campbell Up Your Favorite Sandwiches. 1984, 8 pages. **NCV**

Soups, Salads and Desserts - The Story of Dick's Surprise. 1918, Burt Olney's Products, 32 pages. **$14.00**

Sourdough Jack's Cookery. 1959, Jack Mabec, spiral. **$6.00**

Southern Cook Book of Fine Old Dixie Recipes. 1935, 322 fine tested recipes. **$10.00**

Southern Cookbook - 250 Fine Old Recipes. 1965, 1967, 1971, 1972, Claire S. Davidow, Culinary Arts Press, Inc., Reading, Pennsylvania, 64 pages. **NCV**

The Sportsman's Way - How to Prepare Wild Game & Waterfowl. 1940's, Ruth Elizabeth Mills, Culinary Expert, Hyde Park Breweries Association, Inc., St. Louis, 96 pages. **$8.00**

St. Louis Globe-Democrat Stage Personalities Visit Cooking Schools. 1955, Magda Gabor, James Melton and Mary Aster, *Globe-Democrat* Cooking School, lots of recipes, 16 pages. **$6.00**

Start To Finish. 1934, 1954, Ann Batchelder, Food Editor of the *Ladies Home Journal*, Elm Tree Press, spiral, 96 pagse. **$6.00**

State of Maine Potato Cook Book - Tried and True Recipes. 1972, 31 pages. **$6.00**

The Story of Bread. 1911, International Harvester Company. **$14.00**

Success Wtih Meat - Buying, Cooking, Nutrition. 1940's, National Live Stock and Meat Board, Chicago, 6-page fold out. **$8.00**

Summer Cookbook. 1988, Michael Reese, editor, Waldbaum's Foodmart, Middletown, Connecticut, 67 pages. **NCV**

Sunbeam Mixmaster. 1957, instructions and recipe book, 42 pages. **$6.00**

Sunbeam Portable Electric Cookery. 1971, Sunbeam Appliance Service Co., 160 pages. **NCV**

Sunset Magazine

Sunset Magazine, San Francisco, California, copyright in 1934 by Lane Publishing Company, by 1967 Sunset Books and Sunset Magazine by Lane Magazine & Book Company of Menlo Park, California. By 1975 the company was Lane Publishing Company, Menlo Park, California, 94025.

The following is what we have collected or know about:

1932 - *Sunset Kitchen Cabinet Recipe Book.* 34 pages. **$10.00**

1934 - *Sunsets Favorite Company Dinners.* Genevieve A. Callahan, Home Economics Director, Sunset Magazine, fourth edition, 80 pages. **$10.00**

1938 - *Sunset's Kitchen Cabinet Cook Book.* Fifth printing. **$8.00**

1938, 1942 - *Sunset's Kitchen Cabinet Cook Book.* **$8.00**

1966 - *Sunset Cook Book of Breads.* The editors of Sunset Books and Sunset Magazine, 96 pages. **$3.00**

1966, 1967 - *Sunset Cook Book of Breads.* Editors of Sunset Books and Sunset Magazine, third printing, 96 pages. **$2.00**

1966, 1967 - *Cooking Bold and Fearless Men's Cook Book.* Regular edition. **$3.00**

1966, 1967 - *Cooking Bold and Fearless Men's Cook Book.* Gift edition. **$4.00**

1966, 1967 - *Dinner Party Cook Book.* Regular edition. **$3.00**

1966, 1967 - *Dinner Party Cook Book.* Gift edition. **$7.00**

1966, 1967 - *Spice Islands Cook Book.* **$2.00**

1966, 1967 - *Sunset Appetizer Book.* **$2.00**

1966, 1967 - *Sunset Barbecue Cook Book.* Regular edition. **$2.00**

1966, 1967 - *Sunset Barbecue Cook Book.* Gift edition. **$3.00**

1966, 1967 - *Sunset Breakfasts & Brunches.* **$2.00**

1966, 1967 - *Sunset Casserole Book.* **$2.00**

1966, 1967 - *Sunset Cook Book of Chicken & Turkey.* **$2.00**

1966, 1967 - *Sunset Cook Book of Desserts.* **$3.00**

1966, 1967 - *Sunset Cook Book of Favorite Recipes.* **$2.00**

1966, 1967 - *Sunset Cook Book of Soups and Stews.* Regular edition. **$2.00**

1966, 1967 - *Sunset Cook Book of Soups and Stews.* Gift edtiton. **$3.00**

1966, 1967 - *Sunset Quick & Easy Dinners.* **$2.00**

1966, 1967 - *Sunset Seafood Cook Book.* Regular edition. **$2.00**

1966, 1967 - *Sunset Seafood Cook Book.* Gift edition. **$3.00**

1966, 1967 - *The Sunset Cook Book.* Regular edition. **$3.00**

1966, 1967 - *The Sunset Cook Book.* Gift edition. **$8.00**

1966, 1967 - *The Ground Beef Cook Book.* **$2.00**

1974, 1975 - *Home Canning, Preserving, Freezing, Drying.* A Sunet Book, March, second printing, 96 pages. **NCV**

1975 - *Home Canning, Peserving, Freezing, Drying.* A Sunset Book, August, sixth printing, 96 pages. **NCV**

1974, 1975 Additional Sunset Cook Books:

Appetizer Book
Barbecue Cook Book
Breads
Casserole Book
Chafing Dish & Fondue Cook Book
Cooking With Wine
Dinner Party Cook Book
Entertaining
Favorite Recipes
Ground Beef Recipes
Italina Cook Book
Mexican Cook Book
Oriental Cook Book
Quick & Easy Dinners
Salad Book
Scandinavian Cook Book
Seafood Cook Book
Soups & Stews
Spices & Herbs
Vegetables

◊◊◊◊

Sunshine Festival of Foods. 1969, Fort Lauderdale News, 10th Annual All Electric Cooking School, 16 pages. **$3.00**

The Supermarket Handbook. 1973, Nikki & David Goldbeck, first printing, October 1974, 413 pages. **NCV**

The Sweet Tast of Success, Recipes by the World's Most Famous Chefs - Jacqueline Kennedy, Lady Bird Johnson, Ed Sullivan, Alec Guiness, Jennie Grossinger, Casey Stengal and Many More. First edition, 1966, by Cecil Dyer, nationally syndicated food economist, 95 pages. **$5.00**

▶ *Tables and Favors.* 1922, published by Dennison Manufacturing Co., Framingham, Massachusetts, Party Craft items, 32 pages. **$12.00**

The Taste of Country Cooking. 1976, 1978, 1982, Edna Lewis. **NCV**

Taste-Tempting Recipes for Your Automatic Electric Griddle or Skillet. 1957, 30 pages. **$3.00**

Tasty Dishes, How To Prepare Them. 1898, Pond's Extract Company, New York, 48 pages. **$20.00**

Taylor Oven Thermometer and Other Temperature Aids - Together With More Than 100 Recipes for Candy, Baking, Preserving. 1930, Taylor Instrument Company, Rochester, New York. **$10.00**

Taylor Oven Thermometers and Cake Recipes. 1931, Taylor Instrument Company, makers of Taylor Oven Thermometers. **$10.00**

Tea Goes American - The New American Attitude Toward Tea. 1939, Tea Bureau Inc., New York, 32 pages. **$10.00**

Tent & Trail Cookery. 1973, Mary L. Kibling & Stephanie Parson, published by Potpouri Press, Greensboro, North Carolina, 48 pages. **NCV**

Tested and Proven Recipes. 1933, C.F. Mueller Co., Jersey City, makers of Macaroni Products. **$10.00**

This Is So Good. 1932, Helen T. Smith, *Better Homes and Gardens.* **$10.00**

This Little Book of Suggestions for the Careful Housekeeper. 1900's, Woman's Club of Albany, Inc., Albany, New York. **$14.00**

Thousand Dollar Prize-Winning Recipes - Canned Salmon. 1927, Assoicated Salmon Packers, Seattle, Washington, 24+ pages. **$12.00**

Thousand Dollar Prize-Winning Recipes - Canned Salmon. 1931, Association of Pacific Fisheries. **$10.00**

Three Hundred Sensational Salads. 1982, Lucinda Hollace Berry, Ventura Books, New York City, 48 pages. **NCV**

▶ *Three Hundred and Ten Daily Recipes and Menus For Home and For Guests.* 1930, Virginia Vincent by Margery L. Jenkins, Instructor, Frank Wiggen's Trade Schools, 66 pages. **$10.00**

Timeless Recipes with Minute Rice - 170 Delicious Recipes. 1966, General Foods Corp. **$3.00**

Time-Life Recipes, The Cooking of India. 1969. **$3.00**

Timely Meat Recipes For Meal Appeal. 1944, 1945, compliments National Live Stock and Meat Board, 40 pages. **$8.00**

Toast Recipes - Toasted Sandwiches, Toast Dishes. 1930, foreword by Oscar of the Waldorf, Waters-Genter Company, Minneapolis, 24 pages. **$10.00**

Today's Woman Book of Salads - Over 200 Tested Salads. 1953, Mrs. Hyla Nelson O'Conner, *Today's Woman Magazine,* Fawcett Publications, Greenwich, Connecticut, 144 pages. **$6.00**

▶ *Treasured Recipes of the Old South.* 1941, Mrs. Marie Kimball, John Morrell & Co., back cover has Mr. Ham goes to town, 20 pages. **$8.00**

A Treasury of Meat Recipes. 1940, National Live Stock and Meat Board, Dept. of Home Economics, 40 pages. **$8.00**

The Tribune Cook Book. 1925, Jane Eddington, *Chicago Tribune.* **$12.00**

T.V. Guide Cook Booklet. 1970, a selection of favorite recipes that have appeared in America's favorite T.V. magazine, 30 pages. **NCV**

Twelve Dream Dishes, Yours For Delightful Class Luncheons. 1954, Francis Barton, Consumer Service Dept., General Foods Corp., 2-page fold out with 12 pages of recipes. **$6.00**

25 Tempting Recipes. 1915, compliments of Westinghouse Electric Range with the Automatic "Flavor Zone" oven, on individual 3"x5" cards in an envelope. **$7.00**

24 Delicious Recipes Waffel-ized. 1920, Westinghouse Electric Dept. of Domestic Science, 15 pages. **$12.00**

21 "None Such" Mince Meat Recipes For Winter, Spring, Summer and Fall. 1952, The Borden Company, 31 pages. **$6.00**

244 Prize Winning National Beef Cook-Off Recipes - Economical, Eye-Appealing Beef Recipes Compiled From National Beef Cook-Offs by The American National CowBelles. 1980, American National CowBelles were organized in 1952 as a non-profit association, volume 11. **NCV**

Universal Cook Book. 1899, Universal Food Chopper. **$20.00**

The "Universal" Bread Maker Cook Book. 1904, Landers, Frary & Clark Company, New Britain, Connecticut. **$16.00**

The Universal Bread Maker with Recipes. 1905, Landers, Frary & Clark Company, New Britain, Connecticut. **$16.00**

The Universal Dessert Feature - Tryphosa. Circa 1910, Rich's. **$14.00**

▶ *Unusual Meats.* 1919, recipes by Mrs. Harriet Ellsworth Coates, Swift & Company, U.S.A. **$14.00**

Unusual Old World and American Recipes. 1971, Nordic Ware Aluminum Ware, Minneapolis, Minnesota, 47 pages. **NCV**

Unusual Old World and American Recipes. 1973, Nordic Ware Aluminum Ware, 48 pages. **NCV**

Unusual Recipes. 1938, Demetria Taylor, presented by White Baking Company, bakers of White's Bread, 48 pages. **$10.00**

The Use and Care of Miracle Maid Cook-Ware, Including a Brief Treatise on Waterless Cooling. 1936, 1947, 1948, Advance Aluminum Castings Corp., 47 pages. **$6.00**

The Use and Care of Miracle Maid Cook-Ware and Recipes. 1936, 1947, 1948, 1950, Advance Aluminum Castings Corp., 47 pages. **$4.00**

◊ ◊ ◊ ◊

Van Camp Packing Company of Indianapolis, Indiana

1897 - Van Camp's Bean Cookery. Van Camp Packing Company. **$20.00**

1897, 1898 - Van Camp's Bean Cookery. **$20.00**

1923 - What To Serve and How To Serve It - Something Good for Every Meal. Mrs. Harriet Ellsworth Coates, one of the foremost authorities in America, Van Camp's, Indianapolis. **$12.00**

1923 - The Ad-Ven-Tur-Ous Billy and Betty. Van Camp's Products Company, dedicated to the Children of America, Billy Van and Betty Camp, 24 pages. **$12.00**

1930 - Recipes For Pureed Fruits and Vegetables Ideal for Infant Feeding. Van Camp's, Indianapolis, 32 pages. **$10.00**

◊ ◊ ◊ ◊

Vermont Guild Recipes for Old-Fashioned Stone-Ground Corn Meal, Wholegrain Wheat, Samp Cereal. 1942, The Vermont Guild of Oldtime Crafts and Industries, Inc., Weston, Vermont, 16-page booklet. **$8.00**

Vermont Maid Pancake Cookbook. 1968, reprint from May 1968 Good Housekeeping, 8½"x11", 10 pages. **$2.00**

▶ *Victory Cook Book.* 1943, Demetria Taylor, Lysol manufacturer, 32 pages. **$8.00**

Voyage Gastronomique. 1958, French cooking, 106 pages. **$6.00**

▶ *War Gardening and Home Storage of Vegetables.* 1917, Victory Edition, published by National War Garden Commission, Washington, D.C., 32 pages. **$14.00**

Ward's Windsor ... Pressure Cooker and Cook Book. 1930's, Montgomery Ward. **$10.00**

▶ *Warner's Safe Cook Book.* Tenth edition, 1889, Warner's Safe Yeast, Rochester, New York, over 100,000 in circulation, 500 pages. **$24.00**

▶ *Warner's Safe Cure Telephone Book Cooking Recipes.* 1893, Warner's Safe Yeast Company, 48 pagess. **$16.00**

Warner's Safe Cook Book - Cooking Recipes. 1893, Warner's Safe Yeast Company, 48 pages. **$20.00**

Wartime Suggestions To Help You Get the Most Out of Your Refrigerator - Tested Recipes. 1943, Frigidaire Division, General Motors Corp., 32 pages. **$8.00**

Waterless Cookware Instruction & Recipe Book. 1927. **$12.00**

Ways With Wine - The Paul Mason Vineyards Wine & Food Digest. 1982, 14 pages. **NCV**

"Wear-Ever" New Method of Cooking. 1926, 1928, Aluminum Cooking Utensil Company, Oakland, California. **$12.00**

"Wear-Ever" New Method of Cooking. 1929, Aluminum Cookware, Aluminum Cooking Utensil Company. **$10.00**

"Wear-Ever" New Method of Cooking For Health, For Flavor, For Economy. 1933, The Aluminum Cooking Utensil Company, 100,000 printed, 48 pages. **$8.00**

The "Wear-Ever" New Methold of Cooking. 1935, Margaret Mitchell of the "Wear-Ever" Test Kitchen, The Aluminum Cooking Utensil Company, 48 pages. **$8.00**

"Wear-Ever" New Method Cooking Instruction Book. 1950, 16th edition, Margaret Mitchell and her assistants in the Wear-Ever Kitchens, 96 pages. **$4.00**

"Wear-Ever" New Method Cooking Instructions and Recipes. 1953. **$4.00**

Weight Watchers Fast & Fabulous Cookbook. 1983, Weight Watchers International, Inc., A Plume Book, 374 pages. **NCV**

Weight Watchers Fast & Fabulous Cookbook. 1983, 1985, 374 pages. **NCV**

West Virginia Ham - 22 Ways to Win Praise. 1940's, Hygrade Food Products Corporation, New York, 18 pages. **$8.00**

The Westinghouse Refrigerator Book - Hints, Helps and Recipes. 1936, Edna I. Sprarkman, Director, Refrigeration Home Economids, 49 pages. **$10.00**

▶ *Westinghouse Refrigerators. Recipes...Care...Use.* 1948, Mrs. Julia Kiene, Director, Home Economics Institute, 48 pages. **$8.00**

What Makes Jelly "Jell"? 1945, Certo Consumer Service Department, General Foods Corporation, back cover Sure-Jell, 24 pages. **$6.00**

"What's Cooking"? 1951, Mytinger & Casselberry, Inc., manufacturers of Nutrilite, first printing 200,000, 22 pages. **$6.00**

What Have You Eaten in Norway - Popular Norway Dishes. 1959, ninth edition, Buster Holmboe, Forlag, Norway, 61 pages. **$6.00**

*When Do We Eat? First choose the Meat...*1937, Ann King, Home Economics Director, Kingan & Company, since 1845. **$10.00**

When You Entertain. 1932, Coca Cola Company. Ida Bailey Allen. **$20.00**

Where to Dine in Thirty-Nine; Guide to New York Restaurants plus Recipes of Famous Chefs. 1939, Diana Ashley. **$10.00**

White's Sandwich Book - Sunday Night Sandwich. 1935, Demetria Taylor, White Baking Company. 46 pages. **$10.00**

▶ *The Wilken Family Home Entertaining Album.* 1937, The Wilken Family, Inc., Aladdin, Pennsylvania, 40 pages. **$10.00**

Wine And Dine with Frau Held's Favorite Recipes. 1970's, first edition, Betty Ann Held, Co-owner of Stone Hill Winery, Hermann, Missouri, spiral, 72 pages. **NCV**

Winning Recipes From the Hunt's Sauce Ads. 1973, Hunt-Wesson Kitchens, Hunt-Wesson Foods, Inc., Fullerton, California, 21 pages. **NCV**

With A Saucepan Over the Sea. 1903, Adelaide Keen, recipes from the kitchens of many foreign countries. **$20.00**

◊ ◊ ◊ ◊

Woman's Day, Incorporated
Established in 1938

1958 - *Woman's Day Cook Book of Favorite Recipes.* 20th anniversary of *Woman's Day,* Woman's Day, Inc., 96 pages. **$6.00**

By 1963 *Woman's Day* magazine was published by Fawcett Books, Greenwich, Connecticut, member of American Book Publishers Council, Inc., Joseph Piazza, editor; Hyla O'Conner, Food Editor.

1963 - *Woman's Day Book of Salads - Over 200 Tested Recipes.* A Fawcett Book, 112 pages. **$2.00**

▶ 1963 - *Woman's Day Cook Book of Favorite Recipes - Over 400 Tested Recipes.* 96 pages. **$2.00**

1963 - *Woman's Day Cookie Cook Book - Over 300 Tested Recipes.* **$2.00**

1963 - *Woman's Day Cook Book of Main Dishes - Desserts.* **$2.00**

1963 - *Woman's Day Cook Book of Sandwiches, Appetizers.* **$2.00**

1963 - *Woman's Day Cook Book of Soups, Vegetables.* **$2.00**

1963 - *Woman's Day Cook Book of Salads, Breads.* **$2.00**

1963 - *Woman's Day Cook Book of Relishes.* **$2.00**

1963 - *Woman's Day Cook Book of Special Favorites.* **$2.00**

1967 - *Woman's Day Kitchen #131 - The Collector's Cook Book, Candies and Confections.* December, 22 pages. **$2.00**

1979 - *Woman's Day Kitchen #280 - The Collector's Cook Book, "The Fannie Farmer Cookbook."* 22 pages. **NCV**

1984 - *Woman's Day Cook Book #321 - Cookie Cookbook.* December 1984. **NCV**

1987 - *Woman's Day - The Healthy Foods Book.* By the Editors of *Woman's Day,* 16-page booklet. **NCV**

1989 - *Woman's Day - Summer Pleasure, the Disease Doctors Can Miss.* July, published by Diamondis Communications Inc., a wholly-owned subsidiary of Hachette Publications, Inc., 1515 Broadway, New York, New York. **NCV**

◊ ◊ ◊ ◊

The Woman's World Magazine Company, Inc.
4223-4243 West Lake Street
Chicago, Illinois

1922 - *Woman's World Calendar Cook Book*. Mrs. Ida Bailey Allen. **$12.00**

1927 - *The Candy Calendar*. Lilian Dynevor Rice, Home Economist, 50 pages. **$12.00**

1927 - *Fifty-Two Sunday Dinners*. Lilian Dynevor Rice, Home Economist, 50 pages. **$12.00**

1927 - *Cakes & Desserts - Being a Collection of 150 Tested Recipes for Home Cookery*. Lilian Dynevor Rice, Home Economist, 50 pages. **$12.00**

1927 - *Salads and Sandwiches - Being a Collection of 150 Tested Recipes for Home Cookery*. Lilian Dynevor Rice, Home Economist, 50 pages. **$12.00**

1927 - *Woman's World Cookery Calendar*. Lilian Dynevor Rice, Home Economist. **$12.00**

1929 - *The Fish Book - Over 250 Practical Recipes*. Lilian Dynevor Rice and Lily Haxworth Wallace. **$12.00**

1929 - *The Fruit Book - Over 250 Practical Recipes & Menus*. Lilian Dynevor Rice and Lily Haxworth Wallace. **$12.00**

1929 - *Woman's World Book of Unusual Cookery*. Lily Haxworth Wallace, Domestic Science Expert, magazine size. **$12.00**

1929 - *The Cookery Book*. Lily Haxworth Wallace, Domestic Science Expert, Woman's World Service Library, magazine size. **$12.00**

1929 - *The Vegetable Book - Over 250 Practical Recipes*. Lilian Dynevor Rice and Lily Haxworth Wallace, Woman's World Service Library. **$12.00**

◊ ◊ ◊ ◊

Women's Circle Home Cooking

Women's Circle Home Cooking, P.O. Box 428, Seabrook, New Hampshire, Publishers. A monthly publication. They also published Tower Press, a monthly publication by Tower Press, Inc., P.O. Box 428, Seabrook, New Hampshire. Barbara Hall Pederson, editor; Goldie P. Roscoe, food editor.

1977 - *Women's Circle Home Cooking*. Christmas special, 96 pages. **NCV**

1977 - *Women's Circle Home Cooking - Fruited Bread Braid*. December, 72 pages. **NCV**

1978 - *Women's Circle Home Cooking - Christmas Cakes, Cookies & Confections*. **NCV**

1978 - *Tower Press Christmas Cooking Special*. **NCV**

1979 - *Women's Circle Home Cooking - Christmas Cakes, Cookies & Confections*. **NCV**

1979 - *Tower Press Christmas Cooking Special*. **NCV**

1979 - *Women's Circle Home Cooking Christmas Annual*. **NCV**

1980 - *Women's Circle Home Cooking - Preserve the Tastes of Summer*. September. **NCV**

1980 - *Women's Circle Home Cooking - Christmas Annual*. **NCV**

1980 - *Women's Circle Home Cooking - Christmas Cakes, Cookies & Confections*. **NCV**

1980 - *Tower Press Christmas Cooking Special*. **NCV**

1981 - *Women's Circle Home Cooking - Christmas Cakes, Cookies & Confections*. 96 pages. **NCV**

1981 - *Women's Circle Dessert Special*. **NCV**

1981 - *Tower Press Christmas Cooking Special*. **NCV**

1981 - *Women's Circle Home Cooking - Christmas Annual*. **NCV**

1981 - *Women's Circle Home Cooking - Easter Cakes, Cookies & Confections*. NCV

1982 - *Women's Circle Home Cooking - Easter Cakes, Cookies & Confections*. **NCV**

1982 - *Women's Circle Home Cooking - "Tower Press" Christmas Cooking Special*. 80 pages. **NCV**

1982 - *Women's Circle Dessert Special*. **NCV**

1982 - *Women's Circle Home Cooking - Over 120 Recipes to Help You Plan Holiday Menus*. **NCV**

1982 - *Women's Circle Home Cooking - Christmas Annual*. **NCV**

1982 - *Women's Circle Home Cooking - Christmas Cakes, Cookies & Confections*. 96 pages. **NCV**

1982 - *Women's Circle Christmas Cook Book*. **NCV**

1983 - *Women's Circle Dessert Special*. **NCV**

1983 - *Women's Circle Home Cooking - Easter Cakes, Cookies & Confections.* **NCV**

1983 - *Women's Circle Home Cooking - Christmas Cakes, Cookies & Confections.* **NCV**

1984 - *Women's Circle Home Cooking - Chinese Foods Cookbook.* **NCV**

1984 - *Women's Circle Cookbook - Readers Tested Recipes.* Volume 1. **NCV**

1984 - *Women's Circle Home Cooking - Recipes for Children to Try.* **NCV**

1984 - *Women's Circle Sumptuous Soups #1.* **NCV**

1984 - *Women's Circle Dessert Special #4.* **NCV**

1984 - *Women's Circle Home Cooking - Christmas Snacks.* **NCV**

1984 - *Women's Circle Home Cooking - Christmas Special.* 163 recipes, 74 pages. **NCV**

1984 - *Women's Circle Home Cooking - Christmas Cakes, Cookies & Confections.* 232 pages. **NCV**

1984 - *Women's Circle Home Cooking - Holiday Cooking Across America, New England, Hawaii & Lancaster.* 63 pages. **NCV**

1984 - *Women's Circle Home Cooking - Holiday Cooking Around The World.* Recipes from: Canada, Ireland, Turkey, China, Finland, Germany, just to name a few, 63 pages. **NCV**

◊ ◊ ◊ ◊

▶ *The Wonder Sandwich Book.* 1928, Alice Adams. Proctor Continental Baking Company, Inc., 12 pages. **$12.00**

The Wonder Book of Good Meals. 1934, World's Fair Edition, Wonder Bread, Continental Baking Company, Inc. **$10.00**

Wonderful Ways to Prepare Salads. 1978, first edition, Jo Ann Shirley, Playmore Company, Inc., publishers. **NCV**

The Wonderful World of French Cheeses. 1969, Foods From France, Inc., 16 pages. **$2.00**

The Wonderful World of Welch's. 1968, Welch Foods Inc., spiral, 97 pages. **$3.00**

Your Frigidaire Recipes. 1936, Miss Verna L. Miller, Director Home Economics, Frigidaire Division, General Motors Corp., 38 pages. **$3.00**

▶ *Yacht Club Manual of Salads.* 1914, Agnes Carroll Hayward, Eminent Chicago authority on practical Culinary Art, Tildesley & Co., Yacht Club Canned Food Products, 30 pages. **$14.00**

The Year Round Turkey Cookbook. 1984, Barbara Gibbons (author of *The Slim Gourmet*), features over 300 taste-tempting recipes for turkey, 185 pages. **NCV**

Year 'Round Entertaining. 1950's, picture of two cooks and man with a camera on cover. 28 pages. **$6.00**

Chapter 7

Pocket Cookbooks

The largest and probably best-known paperback publisher is Pocket Books, founded in 1939 by Robert de Graff and supported at first by Simon & Schuster. A look at the copyright page of these cookbooks reveals an additional value. Here is found information seldom seen on the corresponding pages of a hard-cover - the cookbook's publishing history. For example:

The I Hate To Cook Book, a Crest book published by arrangement with Harcourt, Brace & World, Inc., copyright 1960 by Peg Bracken. Printing history, Harcourt, Brace & World edition published September 28, 1960, sixteenth printing, April 1964. A Better Homes and Gardens Book Club Selection, June 1964. First (pocket book) printing, January 1965.

Also:

Fannie Farmer's Book of Good Dinners by Fannie Merritt Farmer, copyright 1905 by Dodge Publishing Co., copyright 1914 by Dodge Publishing Co.,

Popular Library (pocket book) edition copyright 1972 by Pyne Press.

This is very valuable information to collectors and other interested persons.

Penguins was founded in England in the middle 1930's. The first two Penguin pocket books appeared in 1936. In 1939 the company established an American branch. January 1946 was the issue date of the first Pelican book.

These paper-cover pocket cookbooks were cheaply made, though fairly sturdy and meant to be used and when in dilapidated condition, if thrown away or lost, it was no monetary concern.

Apparently by 1942 Pocket Books published their first cookbook titled *The Pocket Cook Book* by Elizabeth Woody who was the Food Editor for *McCall's* magazine. That was the very beginning of what is now almost a flooded market on paper-cover pocket cookbooks. The following is a listing of what can be found today.

NCV denotes No Collector Value.
▶ **denotes titles found in photo section**

The All New Fannie Farmer Boston Cooking School Cookbook. 1957, 1961, 1964, 1965, 1972, Wilma Lord Perkins, A Bantam Book, 652 pages. **NCV**

America's Favorite Recipes from Better Homes and Gardens. 1966, 1971, 1972, 1973, 16th printing, 314 pages. **NCV**

Better Home and Gardens Barbecue Book. 1956, 1965, 1972, fourth printing, A Bantam Book, 2828 pages. **NCV**

Better Homes and Gardens Calorie Counters Cook Book. 1970, 1972, fifth printing, A Bantam Book, 164 pages. **NCV**

Buffy's Cook Book. 1971, Jody Cameron of Celebrity Kitchen, Inc., 176 pages. **NCV**

The Fabulous Egg Cookbook. 1979, Jeffery Feinman, 128 pages. **NCV**

Fannie Farmer's Book of Good Dinners. 1972, Fannie Merritt Farmer, Pyne Press, 270 pages. **NCV**

The Farmer's Almanac Cook Book. 1952, 1964, Missouri Ruralisi Pocket Book, 390 pages. **$4.00**

The Farmer's Daughter Cookbook by The Farmer's Daughter. 1971, Kandy Norton Henely, A Fawcett Gold Medal Book, 326 pages. **NCV**

Free "2 in 1" Cook Book - The Art of Italian Cooking, Maria Lo Pinto and The Art of French Cooking. 1948, Fernande Garvin, 362 pages. **$4.00**

Grandmother's Country Cookbook. 1966, 1971, 1972, Ted and Jean Kaufman, Coronet Communications, 352 pages. **NCV**

The I Hate To Cook Book. 1960, 1964, 1965, Peg Bracken, Crest Books, 144 pages. **$3.00**

James Beard's Fish Cookery. 1954, 1967, 1969, 1971, 1972, Warner Paperback, 416 pages. **NCV**

Let's Cook It Right. 1947, 1962, 1970, Adelle Davis, A Signet Book, 11th printing, 576 pages. **NCV**

Make-A-Mix Cookery. 1978, 1979, 1980, 1981, Narine Sliason, A Bantam Book, 264 pages. **NCV**

Martha Logan's Meat Cook Book. 1953, Beth Baily of Swift & Co., fourth printing, 440 pages. **$3.00**

The Molly Goldberg Jewish Cookbook. 1955, Gertrude Berg and Myra Waldo, 192 pages. **$6.00**

The New Ground Beef Cookbook (original title); *The New Hamburger Cookbook.* 1966, Mottja C. Roate, 158 pages. **$2.00**

Newly Revised, The Pocket Cook Book. 1948, Elizabeth Woody and members of the food staff of *McCall's* magazine, 376 pages. **$4.00**

The Pocket Cook Book. 1942, 1947, 1948, 1955, 1959, Elizabeth Woody, seventh printing, 376 pages. **$2.00**

Pot Luck Cookery. 1955, Beverly Pepper, 190 pages. **$6.00**

The Quick & Easy Cookbook. 1980, first edition, Joan Savin, Ventura Books, 176 pages. **NCV**

Selections from Better Homes and Gardens "New Cook Book." 1983, 192 pages. **NCV**

A "2 in 1" Cookbook - The Art of Salad Making, The Soup and Sandwich Cookbook. 1954, Carol Truax, compliments of Liggett & Meyers, A Bantam Book, 403 pages. **$3.00**

Whole Grain Cookery. 1951, 1961, Stella Standard, A Dolphin Book, 240 pages. **$3.00**

Chapter 8

Charity, Fund-Raising, Regional and Political Cookbooks

Charity and Fund-Raisers

These cookbooks are regional in circulation. That is, they are usually only sold in one city, town or county, or possibly two or three counties covered in one area for the fund-raiser. In some cases it is a state publishing and selling cookbooks for a particular event such as a centennial or sesquecentennial. The 1972 National Bicentennial Celebration had a cookbook for sale. Most fund-raisers are by churches, women's clubs or organizations where the proceeds help that particular group or organization. Radio stations publish cookbooks as an advertising medium to get the public involved.

One of the oldest and most successful fund-raising cookbooks was *The Settlement Cook Book* or *The Way To A Man's Heart* by Mrs. Simon Kander, first published in 1901. Originally the proceeds went to the Milwaukee Settlement House for Immigrants. This book tends to be scarce for old ones were seldom kept, even by local libraries. Many provide regional recipes not found elsewhere. The following lists some of these types of publications that we have collected.

NCV denotes No Collector Value
▶ denotes titles found in photo section

Amana Colony Recipes - Family-size Recipes of the Foods Prepared and Served in the Amana Villages for Over a Century. 1948, compiled by the Ladies Auxiliary of the Homestead Welfare Club, Homestead, Iowa, hard cover, 120 pages. **$20.00**

Argo Presbyterian Cook Book. 1959, The Ladies Aid of the Argo Persbyterian Church as a community project, Sullivan, Missouri, spiral bound, 93 pages. **$6.00**

Belgian Relief Cook Book. 1915, favorite recipes of VIP's including G.S. Porter, B. Tarkington, J. London, J. McCutchean and their printed autograph, Reading, Pennsylvania, ring bound on top. **$50.00**

The Camp Fire Cook Book. 1915, The Camp Fire Girls of Wellsville, Missouri, Optic-News Publishing Company, Wellsville, Missouri, 159 pages. **$20.00**

The Carrolton Cook Book. 1900, S.E. Simpson & Co., Carrollton, Illinois, cloth bound, 124 pages. **$16.00**

The Children's Mission Cook Book. 1937, Children's Mission, Inc. of Canton, Ohio. **$10.00**

Christian Home Cook Book. 1966, Church of God in Christ, Mennonite recipes from Canada, United States and Mexico, hard cover, 400 pages. **$6.00**

Christian Home Cook Book. 1966, 1967, 1970, 1972, 1974, 1976, 1980, Church of God in Christ, Mennonite recipes from Canada, United States and Mexico, 400 pages. **NCV**

Cook Book. 1910, arranged and published by the Women's Home Mission Society of the Westport Methodist Church, Kansas City, Missouri, 56 pages. **$16.00**

The Cook Book of St. Mary's Guild Emmanuel Church of LaGrange, Illinois. 1916, hard cover. **$25.00**

Cook Book - Sweets And Meats And Other Good Things To Eat. 1910, compiled and published by the Ladies Aid Society of the Christian Church, Rolla, Missouri, 52 pages. **$16.00**

Cook Book. 1953, The Maple Grove Extension Club by the Members of the Maple Grove Extension Club, Dittmer, Missouri, 65 pags. **$6.00**

▶ *Confessions of 211 St. Louis Housewives and Bob Hope* or *What's Going On In Their Kitchens?* 1967, Auxiliary of the St. Louis Children's Hospital, first printing, 240 pages. **$4.00**

Episcopal Women's Cook Book. 1877. **$28.00**

Everybody's Best Cook Book. 1886, compiled by the Ladies of the Macmillan Home Missionary Society of the Presbyterian Church, Mt. Pleaasant, Pennsylvania. **$24.00**

Ever-Ready Cook Book. 1931, Circle No. 2 of First M-E Ladies Aid Society of Plymouth, Michigan. **$10.00**

Foods From Truro Kitchens. 1960, Hill of Churchs, Truro, Massachusetts. **$4.00**

▶ *Golden Anniversary Cook Book.* 1949, First Presbyterian Church, Napponsee, Indiana, spiral bound. **$8.00**

Gravenhurst Ladies Cook Book. 1900. **$20.00**

Heavenly Dishes. 1977, Vichy community Church, Vichy, Missouri, this cookbook is dedicated to Mark Chambers, 122 pages. **NCV**

Helpful Hints. 1931, Jubilee Circle of the First Methodist Church. **$10.00**

▶ *Hood's High Street Cook Book.* 1887, The Ladies of High Street Church, Lowell, Massachusetts, 32 pages. **$24.00**

Household Reference Book. 1935, edited by the Loyal Circle of the Southern Methodist Church, Farmington, Missouri, art paper cover, hand bound, 28 pages. **$10.00**

▶ *The Ladies' Delight Cook Book.* 1889, No. 2, 32 pages. **$24.00**

M.E. Ladies Aid Cook Book. 1908, Mrs. W.R. Sanner, Larned, Kansas, 48 pages. **$16.00**

▶ *Lakes & Hills Cook Book.* 1936, Branson, Missouri Christian Church, 80 pages. **$10.00**

Newland Avenue Parent-Teachers Association Cook Book. 1928. **$12.00**

Our Favorite Recipes Cook Book. 1930, St. Pauls Episcopal Church Parrish, Steubenville, Ohio. **$10.00**

P.E.O. Cook Book - A Book of Tested Recipes. 1938, assembled Chapters "N" & "R" Patroness. **$10.00**

Presbyterian Cook Book. 1876. **$28.00**

Recipes To Remember. 1957, Women's Association of Grosse Pointe Memorial Church and Their Friends, Grosse Pointe Farms, Michigan. **$6.00**

▶ *Town and Country Cookie Book.* 1953, sponsored by Hillsboro P.T.A., Hillsboro, Missouri, spiral, 81 pages. **$6.00**

Unity Vegetarian Cook Book. 1955, first edition, Unity School of Christianity, Lee Summit, Missouri. **$6.00**

Win The War Cook Book. 1918, Reah Jeannette, Council of National Defense, Missouri Division, Sold for War Work or War Relief only, hard cover. **$25.00**

Women's Ministries Cookbook. 1979, Women's Ministries Department, First Assembly of God Church, Rolla, Missouri, 54 pages. **NCV**

W.P.F.A. Cook Book. 1930, Women's Progressive Farmers Association, Inc. of the State of Missouri, recipes contributed by the Farm Women of Missouri. **$10.00**

W.W.M.S. Cook Book. 1956, published by The Willing Worker Missionary Society of the First Church of God, St. James, Missouri, 114 pages. **$6.00**

Our Favorite Recipes. 1980, W.C.G. First Church of God, St. James, Missouri, 144 pages. **NCV**

Treasured Recipes. 1987, W.C.G. First Church of God, St. James, Missouri, centennial anniversary 1887-1987, 124 pages plus index. **NCV**

Regional Cookbooks

The Art of Hermann German Cooking. 1980, Sauerbraten, Jlitztorte, Schnitzbrod, Hermann, Missouri, 60 pages. **NCV**

Book Fare. 1967, first edition, by Book Fair, The Greater St. Louis Book Fair, book of recipes, 232 pages. **$6.00**

Book Fare. 1967, 1973, 1974, second edition, by Book Fair, The Greater St. Louis Book Fair, book of recipes, 232 pages. **NCV**

The Chautauqua Cook Book. 1882, 1886, 1889, 1896, sixth edition, Kate Cook, Chautauqua County, New York, stiff cover, 154 pages. **$16.00**

Christmas Cookies. 1940, Hartford Electric Light Company. **$8.00**

Connecticut Home Record Book. 1917, County Farm Bureau, small booklet. **$8.00**

▶ *Electric Cook Book.* 1910, Portland Railway, Light & Power Company, 82 pages. **$16.00**

The Forst's Catskill Mountain Smoked Turkey. 1946, Kingston, New York, 24-pages booklet. **$4.00**

From Kiwanis Kitchens. 1985, compiled by Delba Engelhardt, Mo. Ark. Division, St. James Missouri Club, 498 pages. **NCV**

"The Galloping Gourmet" Cook Book. 1983, The Edgar Springs Saddle Club, Edgar Springs, Missouri, 96 pages. **NCV**

Good Cookies. 1982, Rolla Cerebral Palsy School, Rolla, Missouri, 30 pages. **NCV**

Grandma's Mountain Cookbook. 1976, compiled by Mountain Empire Senior Citizens, Campo, California, 124 pages. **NCV**

Hermann Cook Book - Fine Old Recipes by The Brush and Palette Club. 1979, Hermann, Missouri, 32 pages. **NCV**

Hermann Cook Book. 1987, eighth edition, The Brush and Pallette Club, Hermann, Missouri, 32 pages. **NCV**

Household Guide with Recipes. 1935, Arra Stutten Mixter, Director, Homemaker Service Dept., Hartford Gas Co., Hartford, Connecticut. **$10.00**

I'd Rather Play Tennis Than Cook. 1970, Mary Kay Poppenberg and Marlene Parrish, Pittsburgh, Pennsylvania. All proceeds to go to the Smash Lannigan Home for Aging Tennis Players, 44 pages. **NCV**

The Mixing Bowl - WTIC Radio Cooking School. 1933, Florrie Bishop Bowering, Director of Home Economics, Hartford, Connecticut. **$10.00**

▶ *Murphy's Pets - Fifty Recipes for Cooking Potatoes.* 1899, Mrs. DeWitt C. Owen, Dixon Tri-Weekly Star, Dixon, Illinois, 16 pages booklet. **$10.00**

Nita Neighbor's Book of 100 Cooky Recipes. 1930's, Gretchen L. Lamberton (Nita Neighbor), Winona, Minnesota, 32 pages. **$10.00**

100 Old Fashioned Cooking Recipes. 1910, *The Chicago Tribune*, 32 pages. **$16.00**

Ripley's Sweet Sixteen Recipes for Home Made Candies. 1898, Mrs. DeWitt C. Owen, Dixon Tri-Weekly Star, Dixon, Illinois, 16 pages. **$10.00**

Rotary Ann's Recipe Book. 1964, 1966, 1968, 1969, District 597, Fayette, Iowa, sixth printing, 52 pages. **$2.00**

Sugar 'n Spice for Recipes So Nice. 1984, United Telephone Cooks, Rolla, Missouri, 118 pages. **NCV**

Political Cookbooks

The Cookbook of the United Nations. 1964, 1965, soft cover, 146 pages. **$4.00**

▶ *Favorite Recipes from The United Nations.* 1951, 1956, American Home Economics Association, 96 pages. **$6.00**

Favorite Recipes of Missouri. 1964, Family Edition, softcover spiral, 192 pages. **$4.00**

Missouri 1821-1971 Sesquicentennial Cook Book Edition. 1971, soft cover, 400 pages. **NCV**

The Missouri Sampler Cookbook. 1971, Pauline E. Pullen, soft cover, 340 pages. **NCV**

The Missouri Sampler Cookbook. 1972, 1973, 1975, 1978, 1987, Pauline E. Pullen, soft cover spiral, 340 pages. **NCV**

Sally Danforth's Cookbook. 1973, Rolla, Missouri, 44 pages. **NCV**

Regional-Radio Cookbooks

Calling All Neighbors Cook Book. 1960, Centennial Edition, KSIS, Sedalia, Missouri, 102 pages. **$4.00**

8 Years with Your Neighbor Lady. 1949, Yankton-Sioux City, WNAX 570 on your dial, 72 pages. **$8.00**

Here's Whats Cookin from KTTR's "My Favorite Recipe" Cook Book. 1973, Radio Station KTTR, Rolla, Missouri, 92 pages. **NCV**

KTTR Hotline Cookbook. 1968, Rolla, Missouri, 28 pages. **$4.00**

KTTR's "My Favorite Recipe" Cook Book. 1972, KTTR's Morning Mayors, Rolla, Missouri, 122 pages. **NCV**

KTTR "Party and Company Recipes" Cookbook. 1974, Radio Station KTTR, Rolla, Missouri, 80 pages. **NCV**

KTTR Presents "My Favorite Recipe." 1971, a program of good eating, KTTR 1490, Rolla, Missouri, 132 pages. **NCV**

▶ *KTTR Problems & Solutions Cook Book.* 1969, 38 pages. **$4.00**

KTTR Problems & Solutions Cook Book No. 2. 1970, Rolla, Missouri, 42 pages. **NCV**

▶ *Your Neighbor Lady Book.* 1956, WNAX 570 on your dial, Yankton-Sioux City, 72 pages. **$6.00**

Your Neighbor Lady Book. 1957, WNAX 570 on your dial, Yankton-Sioux City, 72 pages. **$6.00**

Your Neighbor Lady Book. 1958, WNAX 570 on your dial, Yankton-Sioux City, 72 pages. **$6.00**

Your Neighbor Lady Book. 1961, WNAX 570 on your dial, Yankton-Sioux City, spiral, 72 pages. **$4.00**

Your Neighbor Lady Book. 1962, WNAX 570 on your dial, Yankton-Sioux City, spiral, 72 pages. **$4.00**

Chapter 9

Canning, Preserving and Curing Cookbooks

NCV denotes No Collector Value
▶ denotes titles found in photo section

The Ball Corporation

In 1880 the five Ball brothers purchased a small business in Buffalo, New York, and by 1883 the company was named Ball Brothers Glass Manufacturing Company, thus the "BBGM Co." logo found on the early fruit jars. In 1886 following a fire that destroyed their plant, they relocated and built a glass plant in Muncie, Indiana. The company soon became Ball Brothers Company. Today the company is The Ball Corporation.

The forerunner of today's *Ball Blue Book* was first compiled and written in 1905 by Miss Elisabeth Ball. The earliest known version called *The Correct Method For Preserving Fruit,* was published in 1909. Later editions were called *The Correct Methods ...,* adding a plural to the word "method." The Blue Books were revised yearly or more often up to 1917, making well over 80 years of Blue Books. The following is a list of the editions that we have collected and the ones that we were able to find out about from other collectors.

1910 - *Correct methods for Preserving Fruit.* Greenish cover, 31 pages. **$40.00**

1911 - *Correct Method for Preserving Fruit.* Brown cover, 31 pages. **$40.00**

1912 - *Correct Method for Preserving Fruit.* Blue cover, 31 pages. **$40.00**

1913 - *The Ball Preserving Book.* Brown cover, 55 pages. **$30.00**

1913 - *The Ball Preserving Book.* Green cover, 55 pages. **$30.00**

1914 E - *The Ball Canning and Preserving Recipes.* 63 pages. **$30.00**

1914 F - *The Ball Preserving Book.* 64 pages. **$30.00**

1915 F - *The Ball Canning And Preserving Receipts and Spraying Calendar.* **$30.00**

▶ 1915G - *The Ball Blue Book of Canning and Preserving Recipes.* 79 pages. **$25.00**

1915 H - *The Ball Blue Book of Canning and Preserving Receipts.* 79 pages. **$25.00**

▶ 1916 J - *The Ball Blue Book of Canning and Preserving Receipts.* 79 pages. **$25.00**

no date K - *The Ball Blue Book of Canning and Preserving.* 77 pages. **$25.00**

1917 L - *The Ball Blue Book of Canning and Preserving Recipes.* 77 pages. **$25.00**

1918 K - *The Ball Blue Book of Canning and Preserving.* 77 pages. **$25.00**

no date L - *The Ball Blue Book of Canning and Preserving Recipes.* 77 pages. **$25.00**

1919 L - *The Ball Blue Book of Canning and Preserving Recipes.* 77 pages. **$25.00**

1920 L - *The Ball Blue Book of Canning and Preserving Recipes.* 94 pages. **$25.00**

no date M - *The Ball Blue Book of Canning and Preserving.* 47 pages. **$20.00**

1922 M - *The Ball Blue Book of Canning and Preserving.* 47 pages. **$20.00**

1926 N - *The Ball Blue Book of Canning and Preserving Recipes.* 56 pages. **$20.00**

1930 O - *Ball Blue Book.* 56 pages. **$15.00**

1930 O2 - *Ball Blue Book.* 56 pages. **$15.00**

1932 P - *Ball Blue Book.* 56 pages. **$15.00**

1932 P2 - *Ball Blue Book.* 56 pages. **$15.00**

1933 Q - *Ball Blue Book.* 56 pages. **$15.00**

1934 R - *Ball Blue Book.* 56 pages. **$15.00**

1935 S - *Ball Blue Book.* 56 pages. **$12.50**

1937 T2 - *Ball Blue Book.* 56 pages. **$12.50**

1937 T20 - *Ball Blue Book.* 56 pages. **$12.50**

1938 T3 - *Ball Blue Book.* 56 pages. **$12.50**

1941 U - *Ball Blue Book.* 56 pages. **$10.00**

1943 V - *Ball Blue Book.* 56 pages. **$10.00**

1944 W - *Ball Blue Book.* 56 pages. **$10.00**

1946 X - *Ball Blue Book.* 56 pages. **$10.00**

1947 X - *Ball Blue Book.* 56 pages. **$10.00**

1949 Y - *Ball Blue Book.* 56 pages. **$10.00**

1953 26 - *Ball Blue Book.* 60 pages. **$8.00**

1956 26B - *Ball Blue Book.* 64 pages. **$8.00**

1960 26C - *Ball Blue Book.* **$6.00**

1963 27 - *Ball Blue Book.* 96 pages. **$6.00**

1966 28 - *Ball Blue Book.* 100 pages. **$6.00**

1969 28 - *Ball Blue Book.* 100 pages. **$5.00**

1972 29 - *Ball Blue Book.* **NCV**

1974 29 - *Ball Blue Book.* 112 pages. **NCV**

1974 29 - *Ball Libro Azul* (Spanish.) **NCV**

1977 30 - *Ball Blue Book.* **NCV**

1979 30 - *Ball Blue Book.* **NCV**

1982 30 - *Ball Blue Book.* 96 pages. **NCV**

1983 30 - *Ball Blue Book.* 96 pages. **NCV**

1984 31 - *Ball Blue Book.* 96 pages. **NCV**

1985 31 - *Ball Blue Book.* 96 pages. **NCV**

1986 31 - *Ball Blue Book.* **NCV**

1987 31 - *Ball Blue Book.* **NCV**

1988 31 - *Ball Blue Book.* **NCV**

Other Ball publications that are known are as follows:

1915 - *Canning in A Wash Boiler.* Flyer in color. **$10.00**

1924 - *How To Use The Foods You Can.* Ida Bailey Allen, 42 pages. **$10.00**

1930's - *How to Can Fruits and Vegetables.* Published in three sizes, booklet, 16 pages. **$5.00**

1930's - *Ball Steam Pressure Cookers.* Canners cookbook with directions for cooking and canning, 68 pages. **$20.00**

1930's - *"Ideal" - "Eclipse" Pressure Cookers Cook Book.* With directions for cooking and canning, 26 pages. **$20.00**

1930's - *How To Can Meat, Game and Poultry.* 4"x7". **$5.00**

1930's - *How To Can Meat, Game and Poultry.* 5"x8¼". **$5.00**

1960 - *"From Fruit Jars to Satellites."* Edmund F. Ball speech. **$10.00**

1973 - *Ball Freezer Book.* 48 pages. **NCV**

1976 - *Ball Freezer Book.* 48 pages. **NCV**

1976 - *A Collector's Guide to Ball Jars.* William F. Brantley, hard cover. **NCV**

1980 - *A Century of Progress, 1880 to 1980.* Hard cover. **NCV**

◊ ◊ ◊ ◊

Kerr Glass Manufacturing Company

On February 19, 1903, Alexander H. Kerr incorporated the Hermetic Fruit Jar Co. of Portland, Oregon, for the purpose of selling "Economy" fruit jars. In 1904 the company name was changed to Kerr Glass Manufacturing Company. The jars were made by other glass houses. By 1909 business volume had increased to the point that it became worthwhile for Kerr to manufacture their own jars and purchased the old Altoona Co-operative Glass Co. property in Altoona, Kansas. On March 9. 1909, the Altoona factory produced its first jar. In 1912 A.H. Kerr moved to Chicago from Portland, Oregon to where Kerr Glass Mfg. Co. had maintained a sales office for several years. In the fall of 1915 Kerr's company headquarters was moved to Sand Springs, Oklahoma. Kerr Glass Manufacturing Company is still in business today.

The following Kerr Home Canning publications are what we were able to collect and research from this company.

▶ 1905 - *Modern Home Canning in Economy Jars.* Portland, Oregon Branch Office, Philadelphia, Pennsylvania, 16 pages. **$16.00**

▶ 1909 - *Economy Jar Home Canning Recipes.* Portland, Oregon Factory, Altoona, Kansas, 20 pages. **$16.00**

1915 - Kerr's four-page letter of canning instructions sent to housewives by request. **$14.00**

▶ 1916 - *Kerr Home Canning Book.* Sand Springs, Oklahoma; Los Angeles, California; Portland, Oregon, 40 pages. **$14.00**

1933 - *Kerr Home Canning Book.* Honesty, 48 pages. **$10.00**

▶ 1935 - *Kerr Home Canning Book.* San Diego Fair, 56 pages. **$20.00**

1939 - *The How and Why of Canning.* Zella Hale Weyant, 56 pages. **$10.00**

1940 - *Kerr Home Canning Book.* 56 pages. **$8.00**

1941 - *Kerr Home Canning Book.* Zella Hale Weyant, 56 pages. **$8.00**

▶ 1942 - *National Nutrition Issue - Food For Victory.* Zella Hale Weyant, 56 pages. **$8.00**

1943 - *National Nutrition Issue - Food For Victory.* Zella Hale Weyant, 56 pages. **$8.00**

1944 - *Born To Serve.* Zella Hale Weyant, 56 pages. **$8.00**

1945 - *The Why and How of Canning.* Zella Hale Weyant, 56 pages. **$8.00**

1946 - *The How and Why of Canning.* Zella Hale Weyant, 56 pages. **$8.00**

1947 - *As One "Neighbor" to Another.* Ruth Kerr, president, 56 pages. **$8.00**

1948 - *Ours Is A Great Heritage, Yours and Mine.* Ruth Kerr, president, 56 pages. **$8.00**

1950 - *Dedicated to Homemakers Everywhere.* Ruth Kerr, president, 56 pages. **$6.00**

1952 - *Dedicated to Homemakers Everywhere.* Ruth Kerr, president, 56 pages. **$6.00**

1953 - *Kerr Home Canning Book.* Dedicated to homemakers everywhere, 56 pages. **$6.00**

1955 - *And How to Freeze Foods.* Ruth Kerr, dedicated to homemakers everywhere, 56 pages. **$6.00**

1958 - *And How to Freeze Foods.* Ruth Kerr, dedicated to homemakers everywhere, 56 pages. **$6.00**

1965 - *It's Fun Planning to Can.* 56 pages. **$3.00**

1966 - *Dedicated to Homemakers Everywhere.* Ruth Kerr, president, 56 pages. **$3.00**

1971 - *Kerr Home Canning Book and How to Freeze Foods.* Ruth Kerr, president, dedicated to homemakers everywhere, 56 pages. **NCV**

1975 - Dedicated to the memory of Mrs. Alexander H. Kerr (Ruth Kerr) who had implicit faith and trust in God, 72 pages. **NCV**

1976 - *Kerr 10 Short Lessons in Canning and Freezing - Its So Easy To Can.* Kerr Research and Educational Dept., 8½"x11", 22 pages. **NCV**

1981 - *Its So Easy to Can with Kerr Jars, Caps, and Lids.* 72 pages. **NCV**

1983 - *Kerr Home Canning Book and Freezing Book.* Consumers Products Division, 80 pages. **NCV**

1984 - Ths book is dedicated to the memory of Mr. and Mrs. Alexander H. Kerr who had implicit faith in God, 72 pages. **NCV**

More of Kerr's advertising publications:

Home Canning Guide Booklets, 3⅜"x5½":
1939 - 16 pages. **$4.00**

1940 - 16 pages. **$3.00**

1941 - 16 pages. **$3.00**

1942 - 16 pages. **$3.00**

1945 - 16 pages. **$3.00**

1948 - 16 pages. **$3.00**

1960 - Freezing guide, 20 pages. **$2.00**

1965 - Freezing guide, 30 pages. **$2.00**

1966 - 20 pages. **$2.00**

1969 - 20 pages. **$2.00**

1972 - 20 pages. **NCV**

Retailer's edition, Modern Homemaker, 8½"x11" :
1938 - *To Homemaker's Everywhere.* 24 pages. **$4.00**

1941 - *Recipe Edition.* 24 pages. **$3.00**

1943 - *Victory Canning Edition.* 24 pages. **$3.00**

1947 - *Recipes, Instructions & Time Tables.* 24 pages. **$3.00**

1948 - *Help Conserve Food.* 24 pages. **$3.00**

1949 - *Lets Eat Home Canned Foods.* 24 pages. **$3.00**

1950 - *Short Cuts to Good Foods Eating.* 5¾"x8", 32 pages. **$2.00**

1951 - *Guide to Better Canning.* 32 pages. **$2.00**

1957 - *Food Treats For Keeps.* 32 pages. **$2.00**

1959 - *Taste Thrills by Canning and Freezing.* 32 pages. **$2.00**

1961 - *Top Secrets on Canning and Freezing.* 32 pages. **$2.00**

1962 - *Carefree Meals by Canning 'n Freezing.* 32 pages. **$2.00**

1963 - *Jiffy Meals, You Too Can Do It.* 32 pages. **$2.00**

1965 - *You'll Love Them Too!* 32 pages. **$2.00**

Bulletins:

1940 - *Can With Success Meats, Poultry, Game and Fish.* No. 1140. **$3.00**

◊◊◊◊

Other Canning Publications

The A B C of Canning. 1942, Demetria Taylor, 64 pages. **$8.00**

The A-B-C of Canning, Preserving-Drying-Smoking and Pickling of Foods. 1942, Ruth Berolzheimer, Director, Culinary Arts Institute, 64 pages. **$8.00**

The A B C of Canning, Preserving, Smoking, Drying and Pickling of Foods. 1942, Ruth Berolzheimer, Director, Culinary Arts Institute, 64 pages. **$8.00**

Atlas Book of Recipes. 1939, Hazel-Atlas Glass Company, Wheeling, West Virginia, 80 pages. **$10.00**

Canned Fruit, Preserves and Jellies - Household Methods of Preservation. 1917, Maria Parloa, U.S.D.A., 32 pages. **$14.00**

Canning and Preserving. 1935, eighth revised edition, Gunnar Altquist, B.A., The Gunnar Co., 30 pages. **$5.00**

Canning and Preserving. 1935, ninth revised edition, Gunnary Altquist, B.A., The Gunnar Co., 30 pages. **$5.00**

Canning and Preserving. 1887, Sarah Tyson Rorer, hard cover. **$4.00**

Facts About Freezing Foods. 1942, St. Clair Ice Company, Belleville, Illinois, 48 pages. **$8.00**

Family Circle's New Home Canning Guide. 1940's, 32 pages. **$6.00**

▶ *Finer Canned & Frozen Fruits - You'll Like the Karo Way.* 1946, Home Service Dept., Corn Products Refining Company, 32 pages. **$8.00**

Finer Canned & Frozen Fruits - The Karo Way Spells Quality. 1949, Home Service Dept, Corn Products Refining Company, 64 pages. **$8.00**

Freeze With Ease with Atlas Recipes for Home Freezing and Home Canning. 1955, Educational Dept., Hazel-Atlas Glass Co., 28 pages. **$5.00**

The Frozen Food Cook Book. 1948, Jean I. Simpson, Demetria M. Taylor, second printing, hard cover, 496 pages. **$17.50**

The Home Canners' Text Book. 1927, Boston Woven Hose & Rubber Co., 64 pages. **$12.00**

The Home Canners' Text Book. 1931, 1932, Boston Woven Hose & Rubber Co., makers of Good Luck Rubber Fruit Jar Rings, 64 pages. **$10.00**

The Home Canners Text Book. 1936, Boston Woven Hose & Rubber Co., 64 pages. **$10.00**

Home Canning - Up To Date Methods and Equipment. 1927, Zella Weyant of the Agricultural Extension Dept., International Harvester Co., 80 pages. **$12.00**

Home Canning By The Cold-Pack Method. 1924, 30 pages. **$12.00**

Home Canning By The One-Period Cold Pack Method. June 1917, May 1918, 40 pages. **$14.00**

Home Canning & Drying of Vegetables & Fruits. 1919, Victory Edition (Can The Kaiser) (The Kaiser Is Canned), National War Commission, picture of the Kaiser in a canning jar on the cover. **$20.00**

A Home Canning Guide. 1944, Extension Service, University of Missouri, Columbia. **$8.00**

Home Canning Manual for Vegetables and Fruits. 1917, National Emergency Food Garden Commission, Washington, D.C., 12 pages. **$14.00**

Home Freezing For Everyone. 1954, L. Alkire and S. Schuler, information and recipes for home freezing, hard cover. **$15.00**

▶ *Home Freezing of Fruits And Vegetables.* Circa 1947, Sugar Information, Inc. and International Harvester, 12 pages. **$8.00**

Home Pickling - Simple Instructions and Carefully Selected Recipes for Pickling, Vegetable Canning and Sauerkraut. 1909, Home Welfare Dept., The Cary Salt Company, 18 pages. **$16.00**

How To Can Finer Fruits and Save Sugar. 1945, Corn Products Refining Company, 32 pages. **$8.00**
How To Hold Fruit Over For The Winter. 1943, Wartime Fruit Home Canning, The Great Western Sugar Company, 20 pages. **$8.00**

Modern Book of Home Canning. 1938, M.G. Kains. **$10.00**

Old-Time Pickling And Spicing Recipes. 1953, Florence Brobeck, hard cover. **$15.00**

Pickling & Preserving Book, The Putting Up Book. 1953, Flora Harris. **$6.00**

The Preserving of Fruits. 1916, a handbook compiled by Dr. D. Jayne & Son, Philadelphia, 36 pages. **$14.00**

Preserving With Karo. 1912, Corn Products Refining Company. **$14.00**

Safe Home Canning. 1950's, Better Living Through Farm Improvement, 80 pages. **$6.00**

Secrets of Cold-Pack Canning. 1923, The Swartzbaugh Mfg. Co., The Conservo Steam Cooker, formerly The Toledo Cooker Co., 40 pages. **$12.00**

So Your Canning, Bring Out The Full Flavor of Fruits and Berries. 1950's, text by Demetria Taylor, Home Economics Consultant, Sugar Information, Inc. **$6.00**

Tempting Recipes for Canned Foods from the Service Kitchen of National Canners Association. 1939. **$10.00**

Use Honey for Canning and Preserving. 1945, American Honey Institute, 8-page fold out. **$2.00**

War Vegetable Gardening. 1918, National War Garden Commission, Washington, D.C., 32 pages. **$14.00**

◊ ◊ ◊ ◊

Salt Companies

Morton Salt Company
Chicago, Illinois

▶ *Meat Curing Made Easy and A New Way to Make Sausage.* 1933, Morton's Sugar-Curing Smoke Salt, Morton's Seasoning for sausage, 32 pages. **$10.00**

Recipes for Meat Dishes - The Secret's In The Seasoning. 1935, Mary Louise Marshall, Morton's Seasoning, 24 pages. **$10.00**

Home Meat Curing Made Easy, Pork-Beef-Lamb-Sausage. 1941, 112 pages. **$8.00**

▶ *Recipes for Meat Dishes - The Secret Is In The Seasoning.* 1950, Morton's Seasoning, 24 pages. **$6.00**

◊ ◊ ◊ ◊

International Salt Company, Inc.
Scranton, Pennsylvania

▶ *The Salties.* 1920's, 16 pages. **$12.00**

▶ *Salt - The Aristocrat of Minerals.* 1940, non-recipe story of salt, 22 pages. **$8.00**

◊ ◊ ◊ ◊

The Cary Salt Company
Hutchinson, Kansas
Winnfield, Louisiana

Carey's Butchering Guide With Favorite Meat-Curing Recipes. 1930's, 28 pages. **$10.00**

▶ *Home Pickling and Salting Vegetables.* 1942, 1943, A Victory Publication, 32 pages fold out. **$4.00**

Chapter 10

Chocolate

Baker's Chocolate

The Baker story began in the fall of 1764 when Dr. James Baker befriended a young Irish immigrant named John Hannon. A chocolate maker by trade, John Hannon complained that there was no chocolate mill in the new world. The doctor decided to help young Hannon. He leased a mill on the banks of the Neponset River in Dorchester, Massachusetts, obtained a run of mill stones and a set of kettles, and supplied the necessary capital.

The new industry prospered, and as early as 1777 John Hannon was advertising his product with a money-back satisfaction guarantee. Then in 1779 misfortune struck. Hannon started off for the West Indies to buy cocoa beans, but never reached his destination. He was presumed lost at sea, but his actual fate remains a mystery. Dr. Baker continued the business as Baker and Son from 1791 to 1804 with Dr. Baker's son, Edmund, as a partner. In 1818 Edmund's son, Walter, joined as a partner and after Edmund's retirement in 1824 the company became known as The Walter Baker and Company. Since that time the chocolate business has grown steadily and today Walter Baker chocolate products are famous the world over.

No better evidence could be offered of the great advance which has been made in recent years in the knowledge of dietetics than the remarkable increase in comsumption of cocoa and chocolate in this country. During the 30 years from 1860 to 1890 the population in this country a little less than doubled - from 31,443,321 in 1860 to 62,622,250 in 1890. In 1860 the amount of crude cocoa entered at the custom house for home consumption in this country was only 1,181,054 pounds; in 1890 it had risen to 28,352,822 pounds. The population in 1960 was 151,325,798 for comparison. Although there was a marked increase in the consumption of tea and coffee during the same period, the ratio of increase fell far below that of cocoa. It is evident that the up-coming American is going to be less of a tea and coffee drinker, and more of a cocoa and chocolate drinker.

In 1897 the cocoa and chocolate manufacturing establishment of Walter Baker and Company at Dorchester, Massachusetts was not only the oldest but the largest of its kind on this continent. The mills belonging to this company are situated on the Neponset River, partly in the Dorchester district of Boston and partly in the town of Milton. The plant comprises five large mills (having a floor space of about 315,000 square feet, over seven acres), equipped with all the latest and most improved machinery. The full strength and exquisite natural flavor of the raw material are preserved unimpaired in all the preparation; so that their products may truly be said to form "The Standard for Purity and Excellence."

In 1900 Walter Baker and Company had a separate building of their own in the Pan American Exposition in Buffalo, New York.

In the mid 1920's the company name changed a little to Walter Baker and Co., Inc. By 1928 the established size and cover of their recipe publications and all previous recipes were brought up to the 1928 standards. The inside format also took a change and the illustrations were modernized for that period of time.

Walter Baker and Co., Inc. was part of a group of companies who had agreed to merge or be purchased in 1927 to form Standard Brands, Inc. In 1928 the copyright appeared as Standard Brands, Inc. Since the 1981 leveraged buy-out by Nabisco Company, Inc., the company was renamed Nabisco Brands, Inc. In 1985 R.J. Reynolds, Inc. a tobacco manufacturer, performed a leveraged buy-out of Nabisco Brands, Inc. and the company was renamed RJR Nabisco, Inc.

In 1988 an investment firm of Kohlberg Kravis Roberts & Company performed a leveraged buy-out of RJR Nabisco, Inc.

The following are the publications that we were able to collect and research from this company.

NCV denotes No Collector Value
▶ denotes titles found in the photo section

▶ 1897 - *Choice Receipts by Miss Parloa.* 48 pages. **$20.00**

▶ 1901 - *Choice Recipes.* Miss Maria Parloa and Miss Elizabeth K. Burr. 48 pages. **$16.00**

1914 - *Choice Recipes.* Compliments of Miss Maria Parloa, Mrs. Janet M. Hill, Miss Fannie M. Farmer, Miss Elizabeth K. Burr, 64 pages. **$14.00**

1916 - *Choice Recipes.* Compliments of Miss Maria Parloa, Mrs. Janet M. Hill, Miss Fannie M. Farmer, Miss Elizabeth K. Burr, 64 pages. **$14.00**

1923 - *Choice Recipes.* Compliments of Miss Maria Parloa, Mrs. Janet M. Hill, Miss Fannie M. Farmer, Mrs. A. Louise Andrea, 64 pages. **$12.00**

1924 - *Choice Recipes.* Compliments of Miss Maria Parloa, Mrs. Janet M. Hill, Miss Fannie M. Farmer, Mrs. A. Louise Andrea, 64 pages. **$12.00**

▶ 1928 - *Famous Recipes for Baker's Chocolate and Breakfast Cocoa.* Maria Parloa, Janet M. Hill, Fannie Farmer, A. Louise Andrea, 64 pages. **$12.00**

1929 - *Chocolate Cookery.* Baker's G.F. Corp., Inc., 36 pages. **$12.00**

▶ 1931 - *Best Chocolate and Cocoa Recipes.* Walter Baker & Co., Inc., a Division of General Foods Corp., 60 pages. **$10.00**

1932 - *Baker's Best Chocolate Recipes.* Walter Baker & Co., Inc., A Division of General Foods Corp., 60 pages. **$10.00**

1934 - *Chocolate Cookery.* 2nd edition, Consumer Service Dept., 36 pages. **$10.00**

1936 - *Baker's Famous Chocolate Recipes.* Selected by Francis Lee Barton, Consumer Service Dept., 64 pages. **$10.00**

1938 - *My Party Book of Tested Chocolate Recipes.* Francis Lee Barton, 26 pages. **$10.00**

1938 - *Chocolate Candies You Can Make.* 24 pages. **$10.00**

1958 - *Unusual Recipes for Fancy Cooking with Baker's German Sweet Chocolate.* Samuel German's Formula, Famous since 1852, 8-page pamphlet. **$2.50**

1980 - *Baker's Chocolate and Coconut Favorites.* General Foods Kitchens, 72 pages. **NCV**

1985 - *Baker's Book of Chocolate.* Rich's, 112 pages. **NCV**

1985 - *Baker's Chocolate & Coconut Favorite Products.* Idea File, 8-page folder. **NCV**

Following are two versions of the story of
"La Belle Chocolatiere."

The famous picture of "La Belle Chocolatiere," known all over the world as the trademark that distinguishes the cocoa and chocolate preparations made by Walter Baker & Co. Ltd., was the masterpiece of Jean-Etienne Liotard, a noted Swiss painter who was born in 1702 and died in 1790. It is one of the chief attractions in the Dresden Gallery, being better known and sought after than any other work of art in that collection. There is a romance connected with the charming Viennese girl who served as the model, which is well worth telling.

One of the leading journals of Vienna has thrown some light on the Baltauf, or Baldauf, family to which the subject of Liotard's painting belonged. Anna, or Anneri, as she was called by friends and relatives, was the daughter of Melchior Baltauf, a knight, who was living in Vienna in 1760, when Liotard was in that city making portraits of some members of the Austrian Court. It is not clear whether Anna was earning her living as a chocolate bearer at that time or whether she posed as a society belle in that becoming costume. Her beauty won the love of a prince of the Empire, whose name, Dietrichstein, is known now only because he married the charming girl who was Immortalized by a great artist. The marriage caused a great deal of talk in Austrian society at the time, and many different stories have been told about it. The prejudices of caste have always been very strong in Vienna, and a daughter of a knight, even if well-to-do, was not considered a suitable match for a member of the court. It is said on the wedding day Anna invited the chocolate bearers with whom she had worked or played, and in "sportive joy at her own elevation" offered her hand to them saying, "Behold! now that I am a princess you may kiss my hand." She was probably about 20 years of age when the portrait was painted in 1760, and she lived until 1825.

It is pleasant to think of the graceful figure of the Chocolate Girl, as it appears upon Walter Baker & Co. packages, as a positive guarantee of purity and fine quality.

The Romance of "La Belle Chocolatiere"

Her story is just another version of Cinderella and Prince Charming ... He is Dietrichstein, brilliant young Austrian nobleman ... She is a waitress in a new Viennese chocolate shop, daughter of Baldauf, an impoverished knight!

One frosty afternoon in 1760, the dashing young hero commands his chaise to stop before this quaint chocolate shop, first of its kind in Vienna. He must discover for himself the merits of a rich new beverage, that romantic drink from the tropics which is the topic of conversation among all the young fashionables. He enters, seats himself at at table, orders "hot chocolate" and promptly discovers not only the glories of this mellow, fragrant drink, but also the prettiest girl in all Vienna.

Day after day, he returns for more chocolate and more demure glances. The bewildering enchantment grows and grows ... until his daily cup of chocolate becomes the most important event in Prince Dietrichstein's life. He completely forgets that a Prince may not look at a waitress ... and the rest you've already guessed!

As a betrothal gift, Dietrichstein engaged a talented Swiss artist, Jean Etienne Liotard, to paint his winsome beloved in the simple costume in which she first bewitched him. This portrait now hangs in the Dresden Museum and its well-known replica graces every can of Walter Baker's cocoa and chocolate.

◊ ◊ ◊ ◊

Lowney's

The Walter M. Lowney Company of Boston produced Lowney's premium chocolate bar and Lowney's "Always Ready" Sweet Chocolate Powder. "The Cocoa Beans we use are the best grades grown in Central and South America, Ceylon and Java. We blend them to produce the most perfect result."

The Lowney's Chocolate won two gold medals at the Pan American Exposititon in Buffalo, New York in 1901. Other products were Lowney's Cocoa, Diamond Sweet Chocolate Bar, Milk Chocolate, Malted Cream Chocolate, Tid-Bit Chocolate and Vanilla Sweet Chocolate. The following lists what we were able to collect from this company.

▶ 1904 - *Lowney's New Receipt-Book.* Lowney's Premium Chocolate, revised edition, 36 pages. **$16.00**

1912 - *Lowney's Chocolate Recipes.* Revised hard cover, 426 pages. **$25.00**

◊ ◊ ◊ ◊

Hershey's

Milton Hershey was in the caramel candy business in the early 1880's. The caramels were being made in the back room of a house in Lancaster, Pennsylvania and sold from a push cart.

In 1884 Milton Hershey had met an Englishman named Deceis, a candy importer who was enthusiastic about Hershey's "home made" caramels. He offered to introduce them in England if Hershey could manufacture them in sufficient quantity to make it worthwhile.

Financing obtained, Hershey's caramel pots were soon bubbling with candy to send to England. In 1894, Hershey was doing over a million dollars worth of business, selling caramels to all parts of the world. He realized that the United States was importing 24 million pounds of cocoa beans. At the Chicago Exposition in 1892 he had seen an exhibition of chocolate-making machinery from Dresden, Germany. It did not take Hershey long to buy the machinery, all of it, and to have it shipped to Lancaster as soon as the fair was over and dismantled.

Hershey hired two expert chocolate makers and began to produce chocolate enough to coat the famous Hershey Caramels and produce a wealth of "novelties" that sold for two cents and three cents apiece.

"Three Friends" is a rare and early example of Hershey's turn of the century promotional art. It was a "point of sale" poster, used before 1900 when Milton Hershey was still making caramels and chocolate in Lancaster, Pennsylvania.

© 1983 Hershey Foods Corporation

By now Hershey could see that the future lay in chocolate. The caramel business was sold in 1900 for $1,000,000.00 and Hershey centered his attention on making a single item, producing it in great quantity and pricing it so everyone could afford to buy it.

The object on which Milton Hershey concentrated his efforts was a simple chocolate bar. He built a factory to make them in huge quantities.

In 1907 Hershey's introduced HERSHEY'S KISSES milk chocolates. The KISS Kids helped popularize HERSHEY'S KISSES mlk chocolates in the 1920's and 1930's. This design was used on actual box labels.

© Hershey Foods Corporation

In 1920 the company suffered a temporary setback when Hershey's need for sugar exceeded the supply from all his mills. The company weathered the storm and Hershey went on to a new phase of development.

The lesson of the "bad year" in 1920 was that the Hershey Chocolate Company had grown too big and important to be administered by one man. Milton Hershey agreed to dissolve the Hershey Chocolate Company and allow three separate companies to take over. Hershey Chocolate Corporation acquired the chocolate properties; the Hershey Corporation acquired the sugar interests in Cuba; and the Hershey Estates conducted the various businesses of the town and its public services. Today the new name for the Hershey Chocolate Corporation is Hershey Foods Corporation which manufactures various food products including REESE'S peanut butter cups, HERSHEY'S MINICHIPS semi-sweet chocolate, HERSHEY'S iolk chocolate chips, HERSHEY'S semi-sweet chocolate chips and HERSHEY'S cocoa.

The following lists the publications we were able to collect and research from this company.

1923 - *Hershey - The Chocolate Town.* Compliments of the Hershey Chocolate Company, 32 pages. **$12.00**

▶ 1930 - *The Hershey Recipe Book.* Caroline B. King, Hershey Chocolate Corporation, 80 pages. **$10.00**

1934 - *HERSHEY'S Cook Book.* Hard cover, 74 pages. **$20.00**

1936 - *The Story of Chocolate and Cocoa.* Small booklet, 24 pages. **$5.00**

1937 - *HERSHEY'S Favorite Recipes.* Mrs. Christine Frederick, Hershey Chocolate Corporation, 30 pages. **$10.00**

1940 - *HERSHEY'S Bitter-Sweet Chocolate Recipes.* Booklet, 16 pages. **$8.00**

1948 - *HERSHEY'S Breakfast Cocoa Recipes.* 16-page booklet. **$8.00**

1949 - *HERSHEY'S Recipes.* Home Economics Dept., 32 pages. **$8.00**

1963 - *The HERSHEY Garden Collection.* 10 pages fold-outs, 2⅝"x4¾".
   The Milton Hershey Rose. Recipes using HERSHEY'S Cocoa. **$2.00**
   The Montezuma Rose. Recipes using HERSHEY'S Baking Chocolate. **$2.00**
   The Peace Rose. Recipes using HERSHEY'S instant cocoa mix and chocolate syrup. **$2.00**
   The Mirandy Rose. Recipes using HERSHEY'S semi-sweet chocolate. **$2.00**

1971 - Reprint of 1934 *HERSHEY'S Cook Book.* Revised and expanded with recipes brought up-to-date for use in the kitchen, 10th printing, hard cover spiral, 96 pages. **NCV**

1979 - *HERSHEY'S Cocoa Cookbook.* Hershey Chocolate Company, Division of Hershey Foods Corporation, 96 pages. **NCV**

1982 - *HERSHEY'S Chocolate Memories, Sweets and Treats Since 1895 - Through The Years Cook Book.* Hard cover spiral, 96 pages. **NCV**

1982 - *Hershey - A Man, An Industry, A Community.* Fourth printing, history only. **NCV**

1983 - *HERSHEY'S Chocolate Memories - Beverages & Sauces.* Miniature recipe book, hard cover, 18 pages. **NCV**

1984 - *HERSHEY'S Chocolate Treasury.* Hard cover, 290 pages. **NCV**

1985 - *HERSHEY's Cocoa Easy-Does-It Recipes.* 13-pages book.et. **NCV**

1986 - *HERSHEY'S Makes It Special.* Pamphlet, 8 pages. **NCV**

1987 - *HERSHEY'S Make It Chocolate! Favorite Recipes From The Hershey Kitchens.* Hard cover spiral, 126 pages. **NCV**

1988 - *HERSHEY'S Simply Chocolate.* Soft cover, spiral, 96 pages. **NCV**

(The KISS configuration and the words HERSHEY, HERSHEY'S, HERSHEY'S KISSES, MINICHIPS and REESE'S are registered trademarks of Hershey Foods Corporation and used with permission.)

◊ ◊ ◊ ◊

Nestlé

The Nestlé Company, Inc. was founded in 1938 in White Plains, New York. Their recipes were tested in the Better Homes and Gardens Test Kitchen. This means that each recipe is practical and reliable, and meets standards of quality.

In the late 1980's the company relocated to a new building complex in Purchase, New York and there they had their own test kitchen. The company name was changed to The Nestlé Foods Corporation.

The company in 1988 had a 50th Aniversary cookie tin that was free with the purchase of two 12 oz. bags of Nestlé Toll House semi-sweet morsels inside. 50 years of memories in the making. The company also manufactures the following products: Nescafé, Nestea, Nestlé Quick and Eveready.

The Toll House Cookie...How a Legend Began

The legendary Toll House Cookie got its name from a lowly old toll house on the outskirts of Whitman, Massachusetts. Built in 1709 at the halfway point between Boston and New Bedford, it became a haven where weary travelers stopped for food, drink and rest while they waited for a change of horses.

The historic old toll house was purchased by Mr. and Mrs. Wakefield in 1930 and turned into the now famous Toll House Inn. Mrs. Ruth Wakefield experimented with, and improved upon many old dessert recipes. Her incredible baked desserts attracted people from all over New England. One day she was experimenting with a favorite Colonial Cookie, the Butter Drop Do. She cut a bar of Nestlé Semi-Sweet Chocolate into tiny bits and added them to the cookie dough, half expecting them to melt. Instead the bits of chocolate held their shape, softening just slightly to a delicately creamy texture. Mrs. Wakefield named her delicious discovery The Toll House Cookie.

The cookie soon became a wide-spread favorite. Everyone wanted the recipe to make at home. So, with Mrs. Wakefield's permission, Nestlé put the recipe right on the wrapper of their semi-sweet chocolate bar.

As the popularity of the Toll House Cookie grew, Nestlé looked for ways to make it easier for people to bake the recipe. They started producing a special chocolate bar that was scored so it could be easily divided into tiny sections. Not long after, Nestlé started offering little pieces of chocolate in convenient, ready-to-use packages, and the very first semi-sweet real chocolate morsels were introduced to American bakers.

The following are publications that we were able to collect from this company.

▶ 1959 - *Nestlés Semi-Sweet Chocolate Kitchen Recipes.* 64 pages. **$6.00**

1960 - *Lets Make Something Chocolate. Make It Glorious with Nestlés Morsels!* 8-page pamphlet. **$3.00**

1962 - *Perfect Endings From The Test Kitchens of the Nestlé Company, Inc.* Hard cover spiral, 192 pages. **$3.00**

1984 - *Nestlés Presents Sweet Celebrations!* 40 pages. **NCV**

1986 - *Time for Baking Recipes from Nestlé.* Nestlé Foods Corporation, 17 pages. **NCV**

◊ ◊ ◊ ◊

Ghirardelli's

Domingo Ghirardelli was introduced to the art of chocolate making as a young boy in Rapallo, Italy. By the age of 20, he had already begun to establish himself in the chocolate trade when he opened his first confection shop in Lima, Peru. Fortuitously, the shop next door was occupied by a cabinetmaker from Philadelphia, James Lick, a man who was fated to play an important role in California history. The time was the late 1840's and the fantastic tales of the Gold Rush has raced around the world. James Lick, excited by the opportunities for wealth and adventure, packed up his belongings and, with great foresight and 600 pounds of Ghirardelli's chocolate, set sail for California.

In 1848 San Francisco was a frontier town. Basic goods were in short supply and luxuries, such as chocolate, were almost non-existent. Lick, always quick to spot a business opportunity, wrote to his friend Ghirardelli and urged him to come to California.

Soon after arriving in San Francisco in 1849, Ghirardelli opened his first general store in Stockton, and a few months later a second store in San Francisco. Business advanced so briskly that within the year, Ghirardelli was the owner of a fleet of ships which he used to transport his merchandise along the San Joaquin River, the proprietor of the Europa Hotel (one of the first erected in San Francisco), and a rich man with $25,000.00 to his name.

In those days, fortunes were made and lost virtually overnight and Ghirardelli did both. In two strokes of bad luck, his warehouses in Stockton and in San Francisco were destroyed by fire, both within four days.

Less resilient men would have been defeated by such a business catastrophe, but Ghirardelli, taking his remaining savings, returned to his original trade, chocolate making, and opened a shop on Kearny and Washington. His lucky touch returned, and as his business began to thrive, he moved to larger and larger quarters, eventually settling at 415-17 Jackson Street, the site of the Ghirardelli Chocolate Factory for the next 40 years. Luckily, the Jackson Square neighborhood was spared the ravages of the 1906 earthquake and today, the building that housed the first large Ghirardelli Chocolate Manufactury is still standing.

By the 1880's, the Ghirardelli Chocolate Company was one of the largest in the West, selling over 50,000 pounds a year. The mainstay of the business was the ground chocolate which was manufactured by a process Ghirardelli himself had invented and patented.

Having outgrown the Jackson Street location, Ghirardelli searched for a new site with sufficient space for expansion. He selected one of the prime spots in the city, one square block on North Point, overlooking the San Francisco Bay. Embarking on a spectacular 11-year building project with his sons, they constructed the buildings that became the headquarters for Ghirardelli Chocolate for more than half a century.

In 1962, the Ghirardelli Chocolate Company was purchased by the Golden Grain Macaroni Company. The North Point buildings, while charming in appearance, were no longer adequate to produce the large quantities of chocolate consumers were demanding. The new owners built a large and modern plant in San Leandro and in 1966 it became the new home of the Ghirardelli Chocolate Company.

The following publication is all that we have been able to collect from this company and we got this one from the company itself.

1986 - *Ghirardelli Original Chocolate Cookbook.* Third edition, 156 pages. **NCV**

◊ ◊ ◊ ◊

Chapter 11

Baking Powder

Dr. Price's

The Price Baking Powder Company and the Price Flavoring Extract Company was established in 1853 in Chicago to manufacture Dr. Price's Cream Baking Powder and Flavoring Extracts. We have a trade card dating in the 1860's advertising Dr. Price's Cream Baking Powder manufactured by Steele & Price of Chicago and St. Louis, manufacturers of Lupulin Yeast Gems, Dr. Price's Special Flavoring Extracts, and Dr. Price's Unique Perfumes. It can only be assumed that the Steele & Price factory in St. Louis manufactured the Lupulin Yeast Gems and Dr. Price's Unique Perfumes. It is another assumption that the partnership ceased and Steele ended up with the St. Louis factory and Price with the Chicago factory. Anyhow, by 1893 the Chicago factory was solely owned by Dr. Price.

The trade card we have has this on the reverse side: "The Contrast," trademark, a symbol with a hand holding a tall vase of fruits and leaves. Below this states, "While other Baking Powders are largely Adulterated with Alum, Ammonia and other hurtful drugs, Dr. Price's Cream Baking Powder has been kept unchanged in all it's original; Purity and Strength. The best evidence of its Safety and Effectiveness is in the fact of its having Received The Highest Testimonials from the most Eminent Chemists in the United States, who have analyzed it, from its introduction to the present time. No Other Powders show such good results by the true test, 'The Test of The Oven.' This is a Pure Fruit Acid Baking Powder."

Dr. Price's Cream Baking Powder is a cream of tartar (made from grapes) baking powder. Honors came quickly to Dr. Price's Cream Baking Powder. At both the Columbian Exposition (1893) and the California Midwinter Fair it received highest honors and gold medals. Official tests at each showed it to be purest, to possess highest leavening power, to be the most excellent and to have the best keeping properties of any baking powder made.

By 1915 the Price Baking Powder Company was acquired by the Royal Baking Powder Company and continued manufacturing Dr. Price's Cream Baking Powder. Royal Baking Powder was a cream of tartar base also. This provided a centrally located plant in the United States for Royal for additional distribution without increasing freight costs from New York.

In 1921 under ownership of the Royal Baking Powder

Company the name was changed to Price Baking Powder Factory and began making a Phosphate Baking Powder. Advertising began to appear like the following: "Dr. Price's Phosphate Baking Powder is made in the same factory in which Dr. Price's Baking Powder containing cream of tartar has been made for nearly seventy years, and embodies all the skill, scientific knowledge and great care used therein. It perfectly leavens the food and never leaves a bitter taste even if you should happen to use more than the recipe calls for."

This change enabled Royal to compete with all of the phosphate-based baking powders and continue with their New York factory with cream of tartar-based baking powder.

The following cookbooks and recipe books are what we were able to collect and research from these companies.

▶ 1893 - *Table and Kitchen*. World's Columbian Exposition Issue, 59 pages. **$20.00**

1896 - *Table and Kitchen*. 59 pages. **$20.00**

▶ 1908 - *Table and Kitchen*. Cover in color with grapevines, 59 pages. **$16.00**

1913 - *Table and Kitchen*. 59 pages. **$14.00**

1915 - *Table and Kitchen*. Royal Baking Powder Company, 59 pages. **$14.00**

1916 - *Table and Kitchen*. A Practical Cook Book. 60 pages. **$14.00**

▶ 1921 - *The New Dr. Price Cook Book For Use With Dr. Price's Phosphate Baking Powder*. Address Price Baking Powder Factory, 50 pages. **$12.00**

1921 - *How To Save Eggs by Using Dr. Price's Phosphate Baking Powder*. 21 pages. **$12.00**

▶ 1925 - *Billy in Bunbury*. Price Baking Powder Factory, Royal Baking Powder Company, illus. A child's fantasy land of all good things to eat, 20 pages. **$12.00**

◊ ◊ ◊ ◊

Royal

In 1865 Thomas M. Biddle and J.C. Hoagland began producing baking powder which they called Royal Baking Powder in a little Indiana town. They moved to Chicago in 1875, then to New York City.

American housewives were offered a combination of cream of tartar and soda, prepared commercially by careful measure and exact rule, perfectly blended, carefully sealed in cans and always ready for instant use.

It met with immediate approval for it represented a sure safe way of leavening flour mixtures, a way that abolished guess work. In recipes calling for one teaspoon of soda and two of cream of tartar, the cook was to use two teaspoonsful of Royal and leave the cream of tartar out. The result was better food and less trouble and guess work.

Since 1878, when the first Royal Cook Book was offered, millions of copies have been printed to meet the demand for this practical and trustworthy guide to good baking. Royal recipes were prized by American housewives, not only for their accuracy, but because they invariably meet the test of good eating.

In 1929, Royal Baking Powder Co., Chase and Sanborn Coffee Co., and the Fleischmann Yeast Company agreed to merge and form the Standard Brands, Inc. In 1981 a merger of Nabisco, Inc. and Standard Brands, Inc. created the Nabisco Brands, Inc., an operating company of R.J. Reynolds Industries, Inc. (The corporate name was changed to R.J.R. Nabisco, Inc.) In 1988 there was a hostile leveraged buyout of this company complex by an investment firm of Kohlberg Kravis Roberts & Co.

The following lists the cookbooks and recipe books we were able to collect and research from the above companies.

1886 - *My Favorite Receipt.* First edition, hard cover. **$45.00**

1886 - 1896 - *My Favorite Receipt.* Eighth edition, hard cover, 126 pages. **$35.00**

▶ 1898 - *Royal Baker And Pastry Cook.* Prof. G. Rudmani, late Chef of Cuisine of the New York Cooking School, 44 pages. **$24.00**

▶ 1902 - *Royal Baker And Pastry Cook.* The Chefs of the New York Cooking School, 44 pages. **$16.00**

1911 - *Royal Baker And Pastry Cook.* A manual of practical receipts of home baking and cooking, 44 pages. **$16.00**

1911 - *Royal Baker and Pastry Cook.* Receipts for home baking and cooking, 46 pages. **$16.00**

1920 - *Royal Baking Powder Cook Book.* **$12.00**

▶ 1922 - *New Royal Cook Book.* 50 pages. **$12.00**

1923 - *55 Ways to Save Eggs.* 22 pages. **$12.00**

▶ 1923 - *The Little Gingerbread Man.* Ruth Plumly Thompson. The author is the daughter of L. Frank Baum, author of the first Oz books. 16 pages. **$20.00**

1920's - *Royal Cook Book.* 50 pages. **$12.00**

1924 - *Making Biscuits.* 14 pages. **$12.00**

1924 - *My Favorite Receipt.* Hard cover. **$12.00**

1925 - *Royal Cook Book.* 50 pages. **$12.00**

1927 - *Royal Baking Guide.* Educational Department, 19 pages. **$12.00**

1927 - *Royal Cook Book.* 49 pages. **$12.00**

1927 - *Making Biscuits.* 14 pages. **$12.00**

1927 - *Any One Can Bake.* Hard cover, 100 pages. **$20.00**

1928 - *Any One Can Bake.* Hard cover, 100 pages. **$16.00**

1929 - *Any One Can Bake.* Hard cover, 100 pages. **$12.00**

1932 - *Royal Cook Book.* Standard Brands, Inc., 45 pages. **$10.00**

1937 - *Royal Cook Book.* 64 pages. **$10.00**

1939 - *A Guide to Royal Success in Baking.* 22 pages. **$10.00**

1941 - *A Guide to Royal Success in Baking.* 22 pages. **$8.00**

1950 - *Royal Cakes.* 40 pages. **$6.00**

◊ ◊ ◊ ◊

Rumford

In 1854 Eben N. Horsford, eminent Professor of Chemistry at Harvard University, made a revolutionary discovery in food science. He perfected a method by which vital dietary elements (calcium and phosphates) lost in the milling of white flours can be restored by incorporating them in baking powder.

In 1854 George F. Wilson formed a partnership with Professor Eben N. Horsford for "building up a chemical manufacturing establishment of respectability and permanency, such as shall be an honor to ourselves and our children, and a credit to the community in which it is located, and shall afford us a means of reasonable support."

In 1857 the George F. Wilson Company was moved from Providence to what is now East Providence or known then as Seekonk, and its name changed to the Rumford Chemical Works. The new name was supplied by Professor Eben N. Horsford who held the Rumford chair of the Application of Science to the Useful Arts. This Harvard Professorship had been endowed by Benjamin Thompson, a physicist who, after serving the Duke of Bavaria, returned to America and called himself Count Rumford. Benjamin Thompson had taken the name from a town, Rumford, New Hampshire, where he had taught school. Professor Horsford was the Rumford Professor from 1847 to 1863. Once Wilson and Horsford's company expanded and their mill village took shape, Seekonk would come to be known as Rumford.

The two partners complimented each other: one contributed practical skills while the other devoted his time to theory. The success of Rumford Chemical Works was built upon Wilson's business sense and knowledge of machinery and Horsford's understanding of chemistry. At first the company manufactured an entire line of chemical products used in printing and dyeing. Quite early, though, Wilson and Horsford decided to concentrate on a compound of puverulent acid phosphate.

In 1859 the Rumford Chemical Works gave the country its first phosphate baking powder called "Horsfords" and by 1894 the name was changed to "Rumford" Baking Powder which remains today the only nationally distributed calcium phosphate baking powder. Most of this acid phosphate product was used in Horsford's Baking Powder and Rumford Yeast Powder. In addition the two partners manufactured a medicinal product called Horsford's Acid Phosphate. All of these products became common in households throughout the country, and Rumford came to be called "the Kitchen Capital of the World." We have two trade cards advertising this product and they are as follows:

> 1860's - Little girl's head with pink bonnet, Horsford's Acid Phosphate For Mental & Physical Exhaustion, Dypepsia & C.
> 1860's - Little girl (the little dancer) in front of seated musician, Horsford's Acid Phosphate For Mental & Physical Exhaustion, Dyspepsia & C. On the reverse, "It makes a delicious drink with water and sugar only," prepared according to the directions of Prof. E.N. Horsford of Cambridge, Massachusetts.

Not only did the company prosper, but so did Wilson's standing in the community. Until 1861 he was a resident of Providence and, between getting his business off the ground and patenting inventions, he managed to serve an extended tenure on the school committee and two terms in the General Assembly. He moved to Seekonk in 1861 and was soon called into public service. He won four elections to the school committee and one to the town council.

Wilson had long envisioned establishing more than a factory. Perhaps one reason why he moved his company to Seekonk was because the large tracts of farming land in the "Ring of Green" area offered him an opportunity to found a self-sufficient mill village. He bought much of the acreage which had belonged to the original homesteads of Old Rehoboth and established a company farm, pasturage and dairy. When work was slack in the chemical factory employees were kept busy in the fields or at the dairy. By 1872, 325 acres of land were being farmed and 175 acres served as pasture land.

Numerous horses and oxen performed the heavy work on the farm and 150 hogs and a herd of livestock supplied the meat needs of the employees. At the beginning of 1872 Rumford officials predicted that 25,000 pounds of pork and 18,000 pounds of beef would be handled in the company's slaughter house. At the same time the dairy house processed butter, cheese and milk from a herd of company cows. All of the goods produced on the farm were sold to employees in the company store.

In addition, workers rented company houses and had use of a community buillding which Wilson erected for them on Greenwood Avenue. Small clusters of company housing were scattered along the streets surrounding the plant. At the end of Newman Avenue, for example, a number of tenements that were formerly part of the Central Mills complex housed Rumford Chemical Works employees. Other company houses, most of which are still standing, were built on North Broadway.

The company's products included the following:
Horsford's Baking Powder
Horsford's Cream of Tartar Substitute
Horsford's Bread Substitute
Rumford Yeast Powder
Horsford's Acid Phosphate
Horsford's Sulphite, for preserving cider
Horsford's Anti chlorine, for paper makers

Rumford, Rhode Island, was the location of chemical factories with their interdependencies of a repair shop, carpenter shop, machine shops, cooper shop, harness shop, one of the laboratories - all the necessary adjuncts that make up a great manufacturing enterprise of this kind. A library was also established for use by the employees.

The main offices, packing department, printing and binding departments (producing labels, circulars, pamphlets, etc. used in business), the principal and research laboratories, and other departments occupied buildings owned by the company and covered more than an entire square in the city of East Providence, Rhode Island.

The principal manufacturing plant of Rumford Chemical Works was located at Rumford, Rhode Island, and main offices and the printing department were in Providence, Rhode Island. Branches and agencies were located in Boston, New York, Philadelphia, Baltimore, Chicago and San Francisco in the U.S. Foreign offices were located in London, England; Paris, France; Geneva, Switzerland; Naples, Italy; Havana, Cuba; City of Mexico, Mexico; Rio de Janerio, Brazil; Buenos Aires, Argentine Republic; Lima,

Peru; Valparaiso, Chili; Honolulu, Hawaii; Yokohama, Japan; Sydney, Melbourne, Adelaide and Brisbane, Australia; Wellington and Auckland, New Zealand.

Lily Haxworth was born in London, England, and graduated as a gold medalist from the National Training School of Cookery of London. After graduation she was employed by the Rumford Baking Powder plant in London, England.

During the 1890's, the London plant published "Cooking Made Easy" by Lily Haxworth. This advertising recipe book had a completely different format and arrangement from the ones published in America.

The next that we hear of Lily Haxworth, she was in the employ of the Rumford Chemical Works of Providence, Rhode Island. In 1908 Rumford published a hard-cover cookbook titled *Rumford Complete Cook Book* by Lily Haxworth Wallace. I can only assume that Lily chose to come to America to work for the Rumford Chemical Works of Providence, Rhode Island because the real estate had been sold in London, England and no longer manufactured Rumford baking powder.

In 1895 the baking powder was named Rumford and was made of Horsford's acid phosphate, a pure bicarbonate, and the finest starch. Nothing else enters into its composition. It is a powder of the highest grade, prepared by an imported process, and excels all other baking preparations in wholesomeness.

Rumford continued to prosper up to and beyond World War I. Gradually in the early 20th century, Rumford Chemical officials and heirs divided, plotted and sold parts of the company's extensive real estate. Major residential development of the area, however, would not occur until the 1930's and 1940's. Throughout the years the company's baking powder carried the name Rumford far and wide. Wilson and Horsford were now long dead, but their contributions to the growth of Rumford were commemorated when two avenues running through the village were named in their honor.

Beginning in 1919, visitors traveling on Wilson Avenue near North Broadway would find a unique 165-foot water tower staring down at them. It was a monument to the inventiveness and business ability of Wilson and Horsford. The water tower was in the shape of a Rumford Baking Powder Can and was a hallmark in the area's developement as an industrial center.

By 1912 the Rumford Chemical Works had changed the company name to The Rumford Company and had established The Department of Home Economics. The listings of the manufacturing plants in foreign countries that were once on advertising material had disappeared. There was no more reference made of these foreign plants.

In a 1913 advertising recipe booklet, the inside of the back cover tells of the origin of the Rumford Chemical Works and a paragraph tells of the company holdings in Rumford, Rhode Island and another paragraph tells of the company holdings in Providence, Rhode Island, four miles away. Still no mention on any foreign holdings.

During the 1920's, it was learned that you could also cook with Rumford Baking Powder. The company Department of Home Economics went to work and developed 80 different cooking recipes. Thirty of them in their presentation had sufficient merit to put before the American housewife. The company then asked Miss Berth M. Becker, a well-known food specialist in New York, to test their recipes. She rejected six of them. In the 24 remaining was found the inspiration to publish the 1929 recipes publication titled *Several New Things Under The Sun.* Rumford All-Phosphate Baking Powder should be used with these recipes.

Also in the late 1920's the one-pound container was discontinued and the company began packaging in 12-ounce containers.

Rumford was not a stranger to advertising with premiums. The company distributed long, narrow baking powder notebooks, some with a pencil included for the housewife to make her shopping list and/or record a recipe. The Rumford buyer could send for a biscuit cutter or doughnut cutter with "Rumford" printed on top. Each pound can of baking powder had a Rumford company card inside and when the housewife saved some of these cards they could be sent to the company for premiums. Some would require 10 cards, others 25 cards. In 1929 the company premium was a recipe slide indicator that could be pulled out to select recipes for biscuits, muffins, rolls, etc. It measured 5½"x8" in size.

The Rumford Company was purchased by The Hulman & Company of Terre Haute, Indiana, and in 1966 all of the Rumford Company was packed in crates and moved to their new location in Terre Haute, Indiana. The Hulman & Company continued to manufacture and distribute Rumford Baking Powder along with their Clabber Girl Brand Baking Powder.

The following cookbooks and recipe publications are what we were able to collect from this company.

▸ Circa 1865 - *The New Horsford's Bread and Pastry Cook.* Compiled by Miss A.M. Simpson, Professor Horsford's Baking Powder, 48 pages. **$30.00**

▸ 1879 - *The Horsford Almanac and Cook Book.* 46 pages. **$28.00**

▸ 1883 - *The Horsford Almanac & Cook Book.* 48 pages. **$24.00**

1895 - *Rumford Cook Book.* Fannie Merritt Farmer, 48 pages. **$30.00**

1890's - *Cooking Made Easy.* Lily Haxworth, London, England, 24 pages. **$20.00**

▸ 1890's - *Cozinhados Saudaveis Com O Po´ De Levedura.* Rumford, 8-sided fold out. **$30.00**

1890's - *Una Raccolta Di Ricette Scelte Rumford* (Italian). **$30.00**

1895, 1907 - *Rumford Cook Book.* Fannie Merritt Farmer, 48 pages. **$16.00**

▶ 1907 - *Rumford, The Wholesome Baking Powder.* Lily Haxworth, London, England, 8 pages. **$16.00**

1895, 1907, 1908 - *Rumford Cook Book.* Fannie Merritt Farmer, 48 pages. **$16.00**

1908 - *Rumford Complete Cook Book.* Lily Haxworth Wallace, first edition, hard cover, 241 pages. **$35.00**

1895, 1907, 1908, 1909 - *Rumford Cook Book.* Fannie Merritt Farmer, 48 pages. **$16.00**

1912 - *The Rumford Way of Cooking and Household Economy.* Janet McKenzie Hill, 68 pages. **$14.00**

▶ 1913 - *Rumford, The Wholesome Baking Powder.* Compiled by well-known teachers of cookery, Miss Farmer's Sponge Cake recipe on page 5, pretty girl on cover, 12 pages. **$14.00**

1915 - *Rumford Dainties and Household Helps.* Janet McKenzie Hill, 64 pages. **$14.00**

Circa 1910 - *Rumford Southern Recipes.* Mrs. Mary A. Wilson, principal, Mrs. Wilson's Cooking School, 65 pages. **$14.00**

▶ Circa 1919 - *Rumford Everyday Cook Book For the Housekeeper and Student.* Mrs. Mary A. Wilson, Lily Haxworth Wallace, Janet M. Hill, 68 pages. **$14.00**

1919 - *Rumford Company Department of Home Economics - Dainty Desserts.* 16 pages. **$7.50**

1919 - *Rumford Company Department of Home Economics - Left-Overs.* 16 pages. **$7.50**

1919 - *Rumford Company Department of Home Economics - Good Breads.* 16 pages. **$7.50**

1919 - *Rumford Company Department of Home Economics - Meat Substitutes.* 16 pages. **$7.50**

1919 - *Rumford Company Department of Home Economics - Salads.* 16 pages. **$7.50**

1920 - *A Selection of Choice Recipes.* Cover is 'How's That Grandma?' 4-page pamphlet. **$7.50**

1920's - *Rumford Book on Home Management.* Compiled by Hannah Wing, gray cover, 64 pages. **$12.00**

1920's - *Rumford Book on Home Management.* Compiled by Hannah Wing for the Department of Home Economics, orange cover, 64 pages. **$12.00**

1920's - *Rumford Common Sense Cook Book.* Lily Haxworth Wallace, 64 pages. **$12.00**

1920's - *A Selection of Choice Recipes.* Cover pictures children baking, 4-page pamphlet. **$7.50**

▶ 1922 - *Rumford Nya Bakbok (New Bake Book).* Stockholm, Sweden, book in Swedish, 64 pages. **$25.00**

1922 - *The Rumford Modern Methods of Cooking.* The House of Sarah Field Splint, 64 pages. **$14.00**

1927 - *Rumford Fruit Cook Book.* Lily Haxworth Wallace, 48 pages. **$12.00**

▶ 1929 - *Several New Things Under The Sun.* Shows the Rumford elves on the cover and throughout the booklet, 12 pages. **$25.00**

1930 - *New Uses Giving Delicacy And Flavor To Daily Cooking By The New Use for Rumford.* 24 recipes. **$10.00**

1931 - *New Uses Giving Delicacy And Flavor To Daily Cooking By The New Use for Rumford.* 64 recipes. **$7.50**

1931 - *Attractive Meals Planned Complete.* Ann Batchelder, 32 menus, 72 recipes, 56 pages. **$10.00**

1932 - *New Use Giving Delicacy and Flavor to Daily Cooking By The New Use for Rumford.* 64 menus, 34 pages. **$10.00**

1932 - *New Use Giving Delicacy and Flavor to Daily Cooking By The New Use for Rumford.* Has NRA symbol on the cover, 34 pages. **$10.00**

1941 - *Magic Muffins - Twenty-Three Recipes.* Rumford Insured Recipes, 15 pages. **$8.00**

1908, 1918, 1926, 1929, 1930, 1931, 1932, 1933, 1936, 1938, 1939, 1940 - *Rumford Complete Cook Book.* Lily Haxworth Wallace, revised, 209 pages. **$5.00**

1941 - *Biscuits and Biscuits Glorified - Twenty-One Recipes.* 16 pages. **$8.00**

1941 - *Cakes To Cheer About - Twenty-One Recipes.* 16 pages. **$8.00**

1941 - *Captivating Cooking - Twenty-One Recipes.* **$8.00**

◊ ◊ ◊ ◊

Clabber Girl

Hulman & Company has been in existence since 1850 and is privately owned by the same founding family. This company has manufactured baking powder since 1879. The earlier production of their baking powder was marketed under various names until 1899 when they became Clabber Baking Powder. Through continuous research and re-formulation, improved baking powder came into being and in 1923 their brand was changed to Clabber Girl Baking Powder.

Farmers Pride is just one of the product lines which Hulman & Company of Terre Haute, Indiana produced. While many of its labels are familiar only to local collectors, some of the products are Farmers Pride High Grade Oil, Farmers Pride canned pumpkin, and Farmers Pride Blue Rose rice.

The following cookbooks and recipe books are what we were able to research and collect from this company.

▶ 1923 - *The Old, Healthy, Family Baking Powder.* 10 pages. **$12.00**

▶ 1931 - *The Healthy Baking Powder - Gives Appetite To All.* 14 pages. **$10.00**

1934 - *Clabber Girl Baking Book.* 19 pages. **$10.00**

1937-1938 - *Clabber Girl Baking Book.* 15 pages. **$10.00**

1985 - *Fine Baking is Family Fun!* 15 pages. **NCV**

◊◊◊◊

Calumet

The Calumet Baking Powder Company was established in 1889 by William Wright in Chicago, Illinois. Calumet has a double leavening action. Its first action begins in the mixing bowl when liquid is added to the dry ingredients. This action starts the leavening just right, getting the mixture light and spongy and ready for baking. When the cake is in the oven, Calumet's second leavening action begins. This action, scientifically proportioned to the first, continues slowly and steadily until the cake is taken from the oven perfectly leavened and perfectly baked.

By 1922 The Calumet Baking Powder Material Plant was located in Joliet, Illinois. This entire plant, comprising 43 buildings on six acres, is devoted exclusively to the manufacture of the materials used in the preparation of Calumet Baking Powder. Calumet Baking Powder Plant No. 2 was at East St. Louis, Illinois. The main plant was located in Chicago, Illinois. The three plants comprise the largest, finest, and most complete baking powder industry in the world.

The following cookbooks and recipes books are what we were able to research and collect from this company.

1906 - *Reliable Recipes.* **$16.00**

1909 - *Reliable Recipes.* 52 pages. **$16.00**

▶ 1914 - *Reliable Recipes, "Always Welcome."* 10th edition, 75 pages. **$14.00**

1916 - *Reliable Recipes.* 72 pages. **$14.00**

1916 - *Twenty Lessons in Domestic Science.* Marion Cole Fisher, hard cover, 108 pages. **$14.00**

1918 - *Reliable Recipes.* 72 pages. **$14.00**

1920 - *Reliable Recipes.* 32 pages. **$12.00**

1921 - *Childrens Party Book.* Illus. by Francis Tipton Hunter, 40 pages. **$12.00**

▶ 1922 - *Calumet Cook Book.* 80 pages. **$12.00**

1922 - *Reliable Recipes.* 16th edition, 40 pages. **$12.00**

1923 - *Calumet Cook Book.* 27th edition, 80 pages. **$12.00**

1923 - *Cakes And Pastries.* First edition, Cleve Carney, hard cover, 64 pages. **$20.00**

1927 - *Modern Baking Powder.* First edition, Juanita E. Dorrah, hard cover, 125 pages. **$20.00**

1929 - *The Calumet Baking Book - 89 Recipes Sure to Succeed.* Mary Jane Parker, The Calumet Baking Powder Co., P. Co., Inc., 31 pages. **$12.00**

1930 - *New Edition, The Calumet Baking Book.* G.F. Corp., 31 pages. **$10.00**

1931 - *New Edition, The Calumet Baking Book.* **$10.00**

1933 - *All About Home Baking.* First edition, Calumet, G.F. Corp., hard cover, 144 pages. **$10.00**

▶ 1934 - *Happy Times Recipe Book.* Calumet, 23 pages. **$10.00**

1934 - *The Calumet Book of Triumphs.* Form 1967, 32 pages. **$10.00**

1934 - *The Calumet Book of Triumphs.* Form 516, 32 pages. **$10.00**

1937 - *The Perfect Baking Combination.* Calumet & Swans Down Cake Flour, 8-page folder. **$10.00**

1940 - *Cake Making at High Altitudes.* Calumet Baking Powder, rear cover; Swans Down Cake Flour, 30 pages. **$8.00**

1983 - *The Calumet Treasury of Home Baking*. 23 pages. **NCV**

1987 - *The Calumet Treasury of Home Baking*. General Foods Consumer Center, 23 pages. **NCV**

◊ ◊ ◊ ◊

Davis

The Davis Baking Powder Company of Hoboken, New Jersey was established in 1879. Davis Baking Powder was a phosphate-based baking powder made from the most wholesome ingredients known for baking powder. These were combined under the supervision of expert chemists, insuring against errors of composition. The company also manufactured acid phosphates and corn starch.

In 1929 with the merger of a number of food companies to form the basis of what became Standard Brands, Inc., Davis Baking Powder Company was one of the acquisitions following the merger. In 1981 a merger of Nabisco, Inc., and Standard Brands, Inc., created the Nabisco Brands, Inc., and operating company of R.J. Reynolds Industries, Inc. Later the name was changed to RJR Nabisco, Inc. In 1988 an investment firm of Kohlberg Kravis Roberts & Co. performed a leveraged buyout of RJR Nabisco, Inc.

The following cookbooks and recipe books are what we were able to research and collect from this company.

▶ 1880's - *Cook Book Dry Yeast Baking Powder*. 64 pages. **$25.00**

▶ 1907 - *Davis' O.K. Cook Book - Useful Information And Budget Fun*. 64 pages. **$16.00**

1910 - *Davis Cook Book - The Pure Food Kind*. 62 pages. **$16.00**

1914 - *Davis Baking Powder Recipes*. Winifred Stuart Gibbs, consultant in Home Economics. **$14.00**

1922 - *Davis Baking Powder Recipes*. Winifred Stuart Gibbs, 48 pages. **$12.00**

1932 - *The Little Book of Excellent Recipes and Cooking - Tips by the Davis Mystery Chef*. **$10.00**

1940 - *Davis Master Pattern Baking Formulas*. **$8.00**

◊ ◊ ◊ ◊

KC Baking Powder

The Jaques Mfg. Co. of Chicago was established in 1891 for the purpose of manufacturing KC Baking Powder.

The following lists the cookbooks and recipe books that we were able to research and collect from this company.

1916 - *The Cook's Book*. Janet McKenzie Hill, 64 pages. **$14.00**

1921 - *Favorite Recipes From The KC Baking Powder Cook's Book*. Six-page fold out flyer. **$4.00**

1924 - *Favorite Recipes From the KC Baking Powder Cook's Book*. Six-page fold out flyer. **$4.00**

1933 - *Favorite Recipes From the KC Baking Powder Cook's Book*. **$4.00**

1935 - *The Cook's Book*. Janet McKenzie Hill, 47 pages. **$10.00**

1941 - *The Cook's Cook - Recipes Prepared for KC Baking Powder*. 32 pages. **$8.00**

▶ 1942 - *KC Cook's Book*. Lorna Lee, 32 pages. **$8.00**

◊ ◊ ◊ ◊

Gold Label

The Hardesty Manufacturing Company was established in 1895 for the purpose of manufacturing Gold Label Baking Powder. They were purchased by the Jaques Manufacturing Company of Chicago prior to 1926.

The following lists the cookbooks and recipe books that we were able to collect from Gold Label.

1926 - *Gold Label Recipes - Guaranteed by Gold Label Division*. Jaques Mfg. Co., Chicago, 16 pages. **$12.00**

1932 - *Gold Label Recipes - Guaranteed by Gold Label Division*. Jaques Mfg. Co., Chicago, 16 pages. **$10.00**

◊ ◊ ◊ ◊

Cleveland's

Cleveland's Baking Powder was founded in 1867 in Albany, New York, manufactured by Cleveland Brothers of Albany, New York, and then by the Cleveland Baking Powder Company of New York.

We were able to collect the following advertising cookbook by this company.

▶ 1895 - *Cleveland's Superior Receipts*. Dr. C.N. Hoagland, President, 76 pages. **$20.00**

◊ ◊ ◊ ◊

Ryzon

The General Chemical Company of New York was established in the mid-1870's. This same company developed Ryzon Baking Powder and marketing of this came about right after 1900. When the marketing began, it was soon learned that a practical manual for the use of baking powder was desirable. It was discovered that the present baking powder recipe books did not contain recipes in the best homes. The company developed the *Ryzon Baking Book.*

1916 - *Ryzon Baking Book.* Marion Harris Neil, hard cover, 82 pages. **$25.00**

1917 - *Ryzon Baking Powder.* Marion Harris Neil, hard cover, 82 pages. **$15.00**

◊ ◊ ◊ ◊

Thatcher's

The H.D. Thatcher & Company of Potsdam, New York, was founded in 1864 and manufactured the "Thatcher's" Sugar of Milk Baking Powder in 1890, and in 1891 in Canada. In the 1893 World's Columbian Exposition at Chicago, Illinois, Thatcher's Sugar of Milk Baking Powder Pavillion gave away 8,000 biscuits daily to establish its superior leavening power. It was awarded Premium with Medal and Diploma.

The following is what we were able to collect from this company.

▶ 1893 - *How To Test Baking Powder.* Thatcher's Sugar Of Milk, World's Columbian Exposition Issue, 24 pages. **$24.00**

1894 - *How To Test Baking Powder.* First patented 1890, in Canada 1891, illustrated, 24 pages. **$24.00**

◊ ◊ ◊ ◊

Others

The **Jack Frost Baking Powder Company** was established in 1883 by the F.B. Chamberlain Company, manufacturers of Food Products in St. Louis, Missouri.

The following recipe book is what we were able to collect from this company.

Circa 1900 - *Jack Frost Cook Book.* 78 pages. **$20.00**

The D.L. Slade Company of Boston was manufacturer of **Congress Baking Powder.** They also manufactured spices and extracts. They began to manufacture Congress Baking Powder in approximately 1890.

The following recipe book is what we were able to collect from this company.

1902 - *Slades Guide to Good Cooking.* 66 pages. **$20.00**

Miscellaneous baking powder companies.

1875 - Aunt Sally Baking Powder. George H. Vickery, Hyde Park Pennsylvania

1878 - Big Bonanza Baking Powder. Smith Hanway & Co., Baltimore, Maryland.

1889 - American Baking Powder. Konn B. Sayers, Cincinnati, Ohio.

As of 1893 in the year of the World's Columbian Exposition in Chicago, Illinois, the following baking powders were on the market.

Unrivaled
Taylor's One Spoon
Monarch
Snow Ball
Hotel
Yarnalls
Shepards
Bon Bon
Forest City
Crown
Schillings
Chicago Yeast

Chapter 12

Sweetners

Sugar

Have you ever realized that sugar cost more than $2.00 a pound? That was the price paid for it in London in 1842. Before that, in early days of the Roman Empire ita was even more precious. Sugar, in those days was principally for medicinal purposes. Only the fabulously wealthy could afford to sweeten things with it.

Today, sugar is one of the cheapest commodities we can buy. For a few pennies we may have a luxury that would have delighted a Roman Emperor.

Sugar cane has often been described as "looking like a corn stalk," but it really resembles bamboo more than anything else. After the cane is cut in the fields it is taken to the sugar mill. The stalks are carried by a belt conveyor to a machine that cuts the stalk into small pieces which are carried to heavy rollers that crush and extract the juice. The juice falls down the surface of the rollers into a receiver from which it flows to a strainer which removes the pieces of stalk that remain in the liquid.

The extracted juice is dark and covered with a thick white foam caused by the rising of air bubbles. This liquid is cleansed and purified by heat and filtering and is converted from a thin watery liquid to a syrup. Then in vacuum pans this syrup becomes wet, sticky crystals. These wet crystals are whirled in large baskets with screened sides until they are separated from the molasses which has adhered to them. The resulting product is known as raw sugar.

When the raw sugar comes to the refinery it is brought to a semi-liquid form by adding syrup to it. This forms a substance of raw sugar crystals and syrup.

This mixture is placed in whirling baskets called centrifugals, in this raw sugar is washed and whirled in order to remove most of the molasses sticking to the grains. This operation is called washing the raw sugar. After it is completed the washed raw sugar is placed into giant melting tanks. These tanks are fitted with mechanical stirrers which can be best described as giant egg beaters. Hot steam from steam coils melts the sugar.

Next is the step that makes the familiar glistening, snowy substance that comes to us in the package at the grocery. All that remains is for this pure, white syrup to be crystallized. This is done by drawing the syrup into vacuum pans where it is boiled until crystallization takes place. Sufficient syrup is drawn into the pans to fill them partly. The pans contain the coils which are covered by the syrup. Steam is admitted into these coils and in a few moments the syrup begins to boil. Microscopic crystals begin to form and grow larger as the boiling continues.

After the boiling is over, these crystals are drained from the pans. They flow from the pans in a heavy mixture of crystals and a liquor called the mother liquor. The next step is the separating of the crystals from this liquor. This is done by placing the mixture in the centrifugals, whirled about, the mother liquor being thus removed and leaving only wet crystals of sugar.

These white, wet crystals are then conveyed into a machine called the revolving sugar drier. This is a large machine that looks like a water-wheel with narrow shelves built upon the face of the wheel. As the drum goes around the sugar is carried upward and drops from the narrow shelves while hot currents of air are constantly played upon it.

In this way it is dried, becoming the white glistening sugar that we use as a sweetener. Next, the sugar is placed on screens which are shaken by electricity. These screens are at varying textures so that the grains of sugar are separated according to their size.

◊ ◊ ◊ ◊

Godchaux's

Godchaux's pure cane sugar refinery at Reserve, Louisiana was established in 1855. The following cookbooks and recipe booklets are what we were able to collect from this company.

1935 - *The Story of Godchaux's Pure Cane Sugar.* Household helps and excellent recipes, 96 pages. **$10.00**

1940 - *Famous Recipes From Old New Orleans Collected For You By The Makers of Godchaux's Sugars.* 64 pages. **$6.00**

1949 - *Famous Recipes From Old New Orleans Collected For You By The Makers of Godchaux's Sugars - Look for the Blue Band.* 64 pages. **$6.00**

1955 - *Famous Recipes From New Orleans Collected For You By The Makers of Godchaux's Sugars - Look for the Blue Band.* **$4.00**

◊ ◊ ◊ ◊

Domino

The American Sugar Refining Company introduced the Domino brand sugar in 1901. The American Sugar Refining company packed its first sugar cartons in 1899, in prior years sugar was sold in bulk from a barrel by the pound. Sometime between 1915 and 1920, sugar cubes were introduced and packaging included wrappers for these.

The following publications are what we were able to collect from this company.

▶ 1954 - *New Reducing Diet Menus With Domino Sugar.* 24 pages. **$6.00**

▶ 1962 - *Sugar Spoon Recipes From the Domino Sugar Bowl Kitchen.* First printing hard cover spiral stand-up, 51 pages. **$4.00**

1986 - *Brownulated Sugar Spoon Recipes.* Domino Pure Cane Sugar, 33 pages. **NCV**

◊ ◊ ◊ ◊

Others

Cane juice was processed into sugar in the tropics as early as 1543 and sugar cane culture became commerically successful in Louisiana in 1794.

Following are other advertising cookbooks that we were able to collect.

1930's - *How to Make Jellies That Jell.* Great Western Pure Sugar Company, 15 pages. **$10.00**

1943 - *How To Hold Over Fruit For the Winter.* Wartime Fruit Home-Canning, The Great Western Sugar Company, 19 pages. **$6.00**

▶ 1950's - *So You're Canning...* Demetria Taylor, Home Economics Consultant by Sugar Information, Inc., The Great Western Sugar Company, 32 pages. **$4.00**

1950's - *What Could Be Sweeter?* Interesting Sugar Facts and Fun-To-Try Recipes. Western Beet Sugar Producers, Inc., 23 pages. **$4.00**

1957 - *C&H Cane Sugar Presents "Drivert" Fondant Icings.* 28 pages. **$4.00**

Honey

Cooking with honey is an old and treasured art. We have famous recipes from the Middle East, the Far East, the Mediterranean country and even from our grandmothers - recipes for cakes and cookies, for sauce to dress meats and vegetables, for beverages and confections, all distinctive because they are made with honey. A fine honey adds great flavor to even the simplest cooking.

Honey is a natural, unrefined food - the only unmanufactured sweet readily available in stores. It is man's first sweet as evidenced by references made in earliest records of many countries. It requires no digestive changes before being absorbed into the blood stream, as it is 98% predigested when taken from the hive. For this reason it is often used as a quick energy food by many participating in vigorous exercises such as athletics, etc. It is nature's germ killer, as germs cannot survive in honey.

The color and flavor of honey depends on the flowers from which bees gather the nectar. It comes in a wide range of colors from crystal white through different shades of amber to dark amber. Flavors range from mild through sharp.

Honey may be purchased in liquid form in various sizes, usually 1, 2, and 5 lbs. Honey should be kept in a closed container in a dry place. Do not refrigerate as it hastens granulation.

To use honey in place of sugar, substitute equal amount of honey, but reduce other liquid by 1¼ cup. It is well to lower baking temperature by about 25° which prevents over-browning of honey-baked goods.

The following publications are what we were able to collect on honey.

Circa 1910 - *The Use of Honey in Cooking.* 58 pages. **$14.00**

1942 - *Honey - A Good Cook's Secret.* The John G. Patton Company, Inc. Inside cover and next page show pre-war tin containers of honey and the new victory glass jars to save metal for the armed forces. 42 pages. **$6.00**

▶ 1945 - *Old Favorite Honey Recipes.* American Honey Institute, 52 pages. **$6.00**

1945 - *Use Honey for Canning & Preserving.* American Honey Institute, 8-page fold out. **$6.00**

1950's - *Honey for Breakfast.* Qualities of honey, American Honey Institute, 6-pages fold out. **$4.00**

1960's - *My Favorite Honey Recipes.* Mrs. Walter T. (Ida) Kelly, 19 pages. **$4.00**

▶ 1963 - *Gems of Gold With Honey.* California Honey Advisory Board, 32 pages. **$4.00**

1970's - *The Vermont Beekeepers Cook Book.* 73 pages. **NCV**

1976 - *The Honey and Yogurt Cookbook.* Rena Cross, 73 pages. **NCV**

1977 - *The Wonderful World of Honey - A Sugarless Cookbook.* Joe Parkhill. **NCV**

Molasses

For hundreds of years molasses was sugar's poor relation. The brash, forth-right flavor laced the refinement to be included on the best of tables. But with natural and homespun foods currently very much in favor, molasses gains popularity daily.

The early settlers had little choice of sweeteners because, until the mid-1800's, refined sugar was prohibitively expensive. Maple sugar and maple syrup were available in some areas, but most people used thick, dark molasses in a variety of ways to moisten corn cakes, enrich baked beans, sweeten pork, and make steamed Indian pudding palatable.

Not only was molasses cheaper than sugar, it was distilled into an important commodity, potent dark rum. Molasses was shipped from the Caribbean to New England where distilleries in Massachusetts and Rhode Island converted it and then shipped it on to West Africa to be exchanged for slaves.

The molasses pitcher remained on the colonists' table until after the Civil War. But by the end of the century, just as the invention of giant rolling mills put white bread within the means of the general population, two other inventions lowered the price of sugar and thus enabled it to replace molasses. In 1840 a more efficient vacuum system of evaporation was invented, and the centrifuge was invented in the 1800's. Both the vacuum and the centrifuge are still used in the manufacture of sugar.

Molasses was never replaced by white sugar in many homes, however, but for many others it is a recent discovery in the search for good nutrition. It is rich in the Vitamin B group, while its caloric content is virtually the same as that of sugar.

The American Molasses Company and its subsidiaries was initiated in Washington, D.C. by William Taussig in 1861 and established two bakeries in our national capital.

An 1864 trade card advertisement of the William Taussig Bakeries, published by Boyd's Washington and Georgetown Directory, Washington, D.C. announced that Mr. Taussig would deliver molasses pound cakes, mince pies, molasses sheet cakes, tea cakes, molasses jumbles, sugar cakes and molasses pies.

During the course of the years, natural growth determined many changes in the business and organizing of the baking enterprise which later expanded into the molasses-and-sugar business. This development ultimately gave birth to the American Molasses Company and its subsidiaries, incorporated in 1905.

Since 1916, The American Molasses Company has maintained research and control laboratories and a practical testing bakery where products and formulas are developed and tested before their adoption and presentation to the baking industry.

The following publication is what we were able to collect from this company.

1956 - *Baking Molasses ... That Made Molasses Flavor Famous.* 96 pages. **$4.00**

◊ ◊ ◊ ◊

Brer Rabbit Molasses

The Penick & Ford, Ltd. Incorporated of New Orleans, Louisiana manufactured Brer Rabbit Molasses, made only from Southern Plantation Sugar Cane. In 1956 Ruth Jordan was the company spokesperson.

The following publications are what we were able to collect from this company.

▶ 1930's - *Brer Rabbit's Modern Recipes for Modern Living.* 48 pages. **$10.00**

1956 - *Brer Rabbit Book of Molasses Magic.* 24 pages. **$4.00**

Corn Syrup

Karo Syrup

The Corn Products Refining Company was located in New York, New York. They have manufactured Karo Syrups since 1902. The company manufactured Karo Syrup with both the red and blue label and Kingsford Cornstarch and Mazola Oil. In the 1920's Linit starch was added to the product line and the orange label Karo was developed and Argo Starch was added to the product line.

By 1950 Jane Ashley became the company spokesperson and Home Economist.

In the early 1960's Best Foods, Inc. made a leveraged buyout of The Corn Products Refining Company and the merger became a division of Best Foods, CPC International, Inc., with general offices in Englewood Cliffs, New Jersey.

The following cookbooks and recipe booklets are what we were able to collect from this company.

▶ 1915 - *Corn Products Cook Book.* Emma Church Hewitt, former associated editor of *Ladies Home Journal*, 40 pages. **$14.00**

▶ 1916 - *Corn Products Cook Book.* Emma Church Hewitt, 40 pages. **$14.00**

1920's - *Delightful Cooking With The Three Great Products From Corn.* Endorsement by Oscar of the Waldorf Astoria, 63 pages. **$12.00**

1964 - *Dainty Homemade Candies.* Jane Ashley, Home Service Department, Best Foods Division, Corn Products Co., New York, New York. **$4.00**

Chapter 13

Flour

Hecker's

The Hecker-Jones-Jewell Milling Division of Standard Milling Company of New York and Buffalo was founded in 1840 and manufactured Hecker's Superlative Flour.

The following publication is what we were able to collect from this company.

1933 - *33 Select Recipes.* 12 pages. **$10.00**

◊ ◊ ◊ ◊

Gold Medal Flour

In 1866 Caldwaller C. Washburn bought a failing Minneapolis Flour Mill with a prime location beside the Falls of St. Anthony on the Mississippi River. The mill was named Minneapolis Mill Company. Robert Smith was president and ran the business during the Civil War in the absence of C.C. Washburn. The Minnesota wheat crop grew from 2,000,000 bushels in 1850 to 15,000,000 by 1869 and the millers of Minneapolis became important merchants of the states most important crop.

C.C. Washburn served in the Army during the Civil War, first in the Arkansas campaign and later at Vicksburg. He was with the Army of the Tennessee and the Army of the Potomac. In 1865, as the Civil War came to a close, C.C. Washburn began to think of his own business. He returned to Minneapolis and built a large six-story stone mill with 12 pairs of millstones that would produce more flour than the existing markets at that time could handle. He completed the mill in 1866 and later it was named the "B Mill."

Eleven years later, in 1877, Washburn formed a partnership with John Crosby and the Washburn-Crosby Company was born. On May 31, 1880, the company entered three brands of flour in a Miller's International Exhibition in Cincinnati, Ohio. The winning flour was awarded a gold medal, so in August of 1880, the first flour was packed and shipped under the now famous trademark of "Gold Medal Flour."

In the late 1800's flour was sold in bulk, by the 100-pound sack or in a barrel. The grocer would then put it in a paper sack and weigh it. Shortly after the turn of the century the company established more sanitary packaging for their flour. They switched from fabric sacks and barrels to carton, wrapped shells and fibre cans. During World War II the packaging turned to paper bags. This is where the 5, 10, and 25-pound bags that we see today originated.

In 1880, the same year that Gold Medal flour was introduced, Washburn-Crosby Company also introduced its first cookbook, *Miss Maria Parloa's New Cook Book.* Next came a new printing of *Miss Parloa's New Cook Book* in 1888. Miss Maria Parloa was the owner of the Boston School of Cookery in Boston, Massachusetts. Next came the *Washburn-Crosby Company's New Cook Book* of 1894, then again in 1897. That was followed by the *Gold Medal Flour Cook Book* of 1900. Since that time there has been a continuing flow of cookbooks to aid consumers in their daily meal cooking.

For more information on Washburn-Crosby Company and cookbooks, refer to Chapter 14, Betty Crocker. The following are the advertising cookbooks that we were able to collect or find out about and research, up to the point of the introduction of Betty Crocker to the American public in 1917.

1880 - *Miss Parloa's New Cook Book.* Limited edition, Maria Parloa, published by Estes and Lauriat, 58+ pages. **$24.00**

1880, 1888 - *Miss Parloa's New Cook Book.* Limited edition, Maria Parloa, published by Estes and Lauriat, 58+ pages. **$24.00**

1894 - *Washburn-Crosby Company's New Cook Book.* **$20.00**

1897 - *Washburn-Crosby Company's New Cook Book.* A locomotive was pictured on the back cover and the inside cover had a picture of a railroad dining car on it. **$20.00**

1900 - *Gold Medal Flour Cook Book.* Washburn-Crosby Company. **$16.00**

▶ 1904 - *Gold Medal Flour Cook Book.* 72 pages. **$16.00**

1908 - *Gold Medal Flour Cook Book.* 76 pages. **$16.00**

1909 - *Gold Medal Flour Cook Book.* 76 pages. **$16.00**

1910 - *Gold Medal Flour Cook Book.* 74 pages. **$16.00**

1910 - *Gold Medal Flour Cook Book.* This publication is larger than the previous 1910 publication. 74 pages. **$16.00**

1916 - *Eventually Washburn-Crosby's Gold Medal Flour - Why Not Now?* **$14.00**

1917 - *Gold Medal Flour Cook Book.* Does not include Betty Crocker, 74 pages. **$14.00**

In 1937 General Mills, Inc. was manufacturing "King Flour" as well as Gold Medal Flour.

◊ ◊ ◊ ◊

Swans Down

In 1853 Levi Igleheart, at the age of 35, finding farming to be discouraging, moved to the then little town of Evansville, on the Ohio River and Erie Canal, and started a saw mill. He later took on grinding of corn and wheat grist. With this new enterprise he was so successful that in 1856 his brothers, Asa and William, established the firm of Igleheart Brothers, Millers. The business was run by Levi and William while Asa followed the legal profession later withdrawing from the firm. In 1892 the firm was incorporated and William died soon thereafter, leaving Levi and his three sons, Leslie, Addison and John, to run the business. In 1896 Addison Igleheart found a means of making flour which was of superior quality for cake baking. After experimenting and perfecting it he began the manufacture and sale of this new product called Swans Down Cake Flour.

In 1898 the Iglehearts began advertising in the *Ladies Home Journal,* hoping to expand the Swans Down name. The early cake flour business grew slowly until 1904 when Swans Down won the grand prize for cake flour at the 1904 World's Fair in St. Louis, Missouri.

In 1905 the company had ourgrown its mill and moved to a new facility with an increased production capacity of about 40%. In 1909 a fire destroyed this mill and a new mill was built using the most modern machinery available, increasing production to 1,000 barrels a day.

The business has grown from year to year and the capacity has been increased from a small mill on the canal in 1853 to a fine plant of modern construction. Every care and precaution is taken to put out a superior product under the most sanitary conditions.

By 1928 Igleheart Brothers was acquired by Post Cereal Co., Inc. to become part of a company to be known as General Foods, Inc. In 1945 General Foods, Inc. introduced the first cake mix under the Swans Down name.

By the early 1980's, General Foods, Inc. had decided that the cake flour mix category had become too costly to compete at the marketplace. On November 12, 1985, Wm. B. Reily company purchased the Swans Down Brand from General Foods, Inc.

The following are the cookbooks that we were able to collect from this company.

▶ 1915 - *Cake Secrets.* Igleheart's, Mrs. Sarah Tyson Rorer endorsement inside, 36 pages. **$14.00**

▶ 1922 - *Cake Secrets.* Igleheart's, Janet M. Hill, editor, *American Cooking Magazine,* Boston, 32 pages. **$12.00**

1926 - *Cake Secrets.* Igleheart's, Janet M. Hill. **$12.00**

1927 - *7 Selected Swans Down Recipes.* P. Co., Inc., package insert. **$2.50**

1928 - *Cake Secrets.* Francis Lee Barton, Swans Down, P. Co., Inc., Igleheart Brothers, Inc., 48 pages. **$12.00**

1928 - *Cake Secrets.* Revised edition, Francis Lee Barton, Swans Down, P. Co., Inc., Igleheart Brothers, Inc., 36 pages. **$12.00**

1929 - *Home Baked Delicacies.* Francis Lee Barton, P. Co., Inc., Igleheart Brothers, Inc., 24 pages. **$12.00**

1931 - *New Cake Secrets.* Francis Lee Barton, Swans Down, Igleheart Brothers, Inc. **$10.00**

1931 - *Home Baked Delicacies - New Edition!* Igleheart Brothers, Inc., Division of General Foods, Corp., 23 pages. **$12.00**

1934 - *The Latest Cake Secrets.* Francis Lee Barton, Consumer Service Dept., General Foods Corp., third printing, 64 pages. **$10.00**

1936 - *Bake Like A Champion, Cakes-Pies-Muffins-Biscuits-Cookies.* G.F., Corp., Swans Down Division, 22 pages. **$10.00**

1936 - *9 Party Recipes Thrifty Enough For Every Day! Made With Swans Down Cake Flour.* G.F., Corp., package insert. **$2.50**

▶ 1943 - *How to Bake by The Ration Book - Swans Down Wartime Recipes.* Cakes, quick breads, desserts, 23 pages. **$8.00**

1943 - *Recipes For Today.* Consumer Service Department, 39 pages. **$8.00**

1944 - *How to Bake By the Ration Book.* New edition, Kate Smith, Swans Down. **$8.00**

1945 - *New Swans Down Desserts & Hot Breads.* Package insert. **$2.50**

1947 - *Learn To Bake ... You'll Love It.* Consumer Service Department, 80 pages. **$8.00**

1949 - *Swiss Chocolate Cake*. Swans Down, package insert. **$2.50**

▶ 1953 - *Cake Secrets - Unveiling the Joyous Mysteries of the Loveliest of Cakes*. Francis Barton, Consumer Department, 64 pages. **$6.00**

1986 - *Swans Down Breakthrough Baking: Classic Cakes That Cut The Calories!* Swans Down Cake Flour, Wm. B. Reily & Co., Inc., 12 pages. **NCV**

◊◊◊◊

Pillsbury

The story of the Pillsbury Flour Mills company is one of the most interesting of modern business romances. It had its modest beginning in 1869, only two years after the granting of the Minneapolis city charter. The years that followed have been years of continued steady growth. The mills have grown in capacity from 150 barrels of flour a day to 40,000 by 1929. An enormous output of pancake flour, health bran, farina and corn products was also developed.

In 1869, Mr. Charles A. Pillsbury wended his way from New England to the western frontier, to what was then the village of St. Anthony, located at the falls of the same name. He took this step, which later was to mark the beginning of a singularly successful career, at the suggestion of his uncle, the Honorable John S. Pillsbury, his goal being to engage in flour manufacturing. A start was made with the purchase of a small 150-barrel-a-day mill. At this time also, the Pillsbury's Best brand was first used, the same brand that is still the world's standard for goodness and purity in flour after all of these years.

The business grew by leaps and bounds. In 1870, John S. Pillsbury, three time governor of Minnesota, Charles A. and his father, George A. Pillsbury, organized the C.A. Pillsbury & Company. Charles A. Pillsbury was the leading milling authority in the country at the time and it was he who spent two years in Hungary and brought to this country and to the Pillsbury mills, the Hungarian gradual reduction process of milling, a process of grinding wheat between corrugated rollers. This process was especially adapted to the milling of spring wheat, and with the improvements made in it since, still remains the most modern and advanced practice in the milling industry.

By this time the little mill by the falls had become the nucleus for a larger group of mills, all under the control of the Pillsbury's, and all grinding Pillsbury's Best Flour. The largest single addition to the Pillsbury mills was made in 1881, when the Pillsbury "A" mill was built. This mill, with a capacity at that time of 5,000 barrels daily, was then the largest flour mill in the world. By 1929 it had a capacity of 17,500 barrels of flour every 24 hours. The huge Pillsbury elevators, where the wheat was stored and cleaned before it entered the mill, had a storage capacity of 4,000,000 bushels.

By 1929, the Pillsbury Flour Mills Company operated mills at Buffalo, New York; Atchison, Kansas; and Enid, Oklahoma. The mills, along with the six Minneapolis mills, produced approximately 40,000 barrels of flour daily. The company had branch offices located throughout the entire United States and many agents abroad.

Pillsbury's Family of Foods included pancake flour, health bran, and farina. Pillsbury's cake flour was added to the family in the 1930's.

During the early 1940's the company name became Pillsbury Mills, Inc. In 1964, nearly a century after its beginning, the small flour mill had risen to proportions hardly dreamed of by the Pillsbury's when they started out in business. Pillsbury Mills, Inc. now employed 7,200 people in the Pillsbury Flour Mills, prepared mix plants, refrigerated food plants, formula feed plants, research and development laboratories, service centers and sales offices in key locations in the United States, Canada and South America.

Helen M. Wolcott was appointed Director of the Ann Pillsbury Home Service Center in Minneapolis in January 1962. By 1970 the Pillsbury Mills, Inc. had established a company titled Pillsbury Publications to publish their advertising cookbooks and for other companies' advertising cookbooks. Some other publications by Pillsbury Publications are as follows: *Kraft's Main Dish Cook Book, Lipton's Soup & Salad Cook Book, Armour's Meat Cook Book, Nabisco's Snack Book, Booth's Fish & Seafood Cook Book, Green Giant's Vegetable Cook Book, and Pepsi Cola's Beverage Book.*

The following are the cookbooks and advertising cookbooks that we were able to research and collect from this company.

1905 - *A Book For A Cook - Always Use Pillsbury Best Flour*. L.P. Hubbard. **$16.00**

1911 - *The Pillsbury Cook Book*. Mrs. Nellie Duling Gans, 125 pages. **$14.00**

▶ 1914 - *The Pillsbury Cook Book*. Mrs. Nellie Duling Gans, cover picture of a city, 126 pages. **$14.00**

1914 - *The Pillsbury Cook Book*. Mrs. Nellie Duling Gans, cover of Quaker couple, 126 pages. **$14.00**

1920 - *Pillsbury's Cook Book*. Edited and prepared under the direct supervision of the Pillsbury Laboratory, 46 pages. **$12.00**

1921 - *Buy This Flour Because Pillsbury's Best*. 10-page folded booklet. **$12.00**

1922 - *The Story of Flour*. The Pillsbury Flour Mills Company, hard cover, 28 pages. **$12.00**

1927 - *Pillsbury Cook Book*. Pillsbury Laboratory. **$12.00**

1927 - *100 Delicious Foods From 4 Basic Recipes*. 30 pages. **$12.00**

▸ 1929 - *Pillsbury's Cook Book*. Pillsbury's Laboratory, 46 pages. **$12.00**

1933 - *Balanced Recipes*. Pillsbury's famous aluminum-covered recipe book, spiral. **$25.00**

1930's - *Twenty-One Successful Little Dinners*. Mary Ellis Ames, Director, Pillsbury's Cooking Service, advertises the *1933 Balanced Recipes* with aluminum box, 47 pages. **$10.00**

1930's - *New Recipes For Pillsbury's Cake Flour*. Ida Bailey Allen, noted food specialist and founder of the national Radio Home-Makers Club, 10-page booklet. **$10.00**

1945 - *Bake The No-Knead Way - Ann Pillsbury's Amazing Discovery*. **$8.00**

▸ 1945 - *The Talking Millstones*. Camilla Wing, Pillsbury Institute of Flour Milling History, 78 pages. **$25.00**

1945 - *Ann Pillsbury's Higher, Finer, Textured, Better Flavored Cakes*. Sno Sheen, 16-pages booklet. **$8.00**

1945, 1946 - *Bake The No-Knead Way - Ann Pillsbury's Amazing Discovery*. Ann Pillsbury's Home Center Service, 64 pages. **$8.00**

1946 - *Baking Is Fun*. Ann Pillsbury. **$8.00**

1940's - *Pillsbury's Best Butter Cookie Cookbook*. **$8.00**

1948 - *Baking Is Fun*. Third edition, Ann Pillsbury. **$8.00**

1948 - *Adventures in Cake Craft*. Ann Pillsbury, 40 pages. **$8.00**

▸ 1950 - *Grand National Recipe and Baking Contest - 100 Prize-Winning Recipes*. 96 pages. **$20.00**

1950 - *Plain and Fancy - Pillsbury Hot Roll Mix*. Package insert. **$2.50**

▸ 1951 - *100 Prize-Winning Recipes*. Pillsbury's 2nd Grand Prize National Recipe and Baking Contest. 100 pages. **$15.00**

1951 - *Top Winners in Pillsbury 2nd Grand National*. Package insert. **$2.50**

▸ 1952 - *Kate Smith Chooses Her 55 Favorite Cake Recipes*. Ann Pillsbury, Tested Recipes from Ann Pillsbury's Famous Kitchen, first edition, 54 pages. **$6.00**

1952 - *6 "Grand National Prize-Winning recipes"* from Pillsbury's 2nd Grand National. Package insert. **$2.50**

▸ 1953 - *3rd Grand National Bake Off Prize Winning Recipes*. 96 pages. **$15.00**

▸ 1953 - *100 Prize Winning Recipes*. Pillsbury's 4th Grand National Baking Contest, 96 pages. **$10.00**

1953 - *Recipes from Pillsbury Bake Off, 1949*. Package insert. **$2.50**

1954 - *Pillsbury's 5th Baking Contest - 100 Grand National Recipes*. 96 pages. **$10.00**

1955 - *Pillsbury's 6th Grand National Baking Contest - 100 Prize Winning Recipes*. 96 pages. **$10.00**

1956 - *Pillsbury's 7th Grand National Cook Book - 100 Easy To Follow Prize Winning Recipes*. 96 pages. **$10.00**

1956 - *Fun-Filled Butter Cookie Cook Book - 50 Recipes From Ann Pillsbury's Recipe Exchange*. **$6.00**

1957 - *Butter Cookie Cook Book*. Pillsbury's Best. **$6.00**

1957 - *100 Grand Natonal Recipes - Collected For You at Pillsbury's 8th Grand National*. **$6.00**

1958 - *9th Grand National Cook Book - 100 Prize Winning Recipes from Pillsbury Mills, Inc*. 96 pages. **$6.00**

1958 - *Best Loved Foods of Christmas*. Ann Pillsbury, 65 recipes, 65 pages. **$6.00**

1959 - *10th Grand National Bake Off - 100 Grand National Recipes*. 98+ pages. **$6.00**

1960 - *Party Best Butter Cookies From Pillsbury's Best Flour, Saran Wrap, Sun Maid Raisins and American Dairy Association*. 28 pages. **$4.00**

1960 - *Short-Cut Breads*. Pillsbury's Best. **$6.00**

1960 - *Butter Cookie Booklet - 25 Cookie Recipes for Festive Eating and Treating*. Volume III. **$4.00**

1960 - *Cool Ideas Cook Book*. Pillsbury's Best. **$4.00**

1960 - *Best One-Dish Meals Cook Book From Pillsbury's Bake-Off Collection*. 53 pages. **$4.00**

1960 - *11th Grand National Bake Off - 100 Grand National Recipes*. 96+ pages. **$6.00**

1961 - *Fabulous Pies From Pillsbury*. Ann Pillsbury, 24 pages. **$4.00**

1961 - *Butter Cookie Booklet*. **$4.00**

1961 - *12th Grand National Bake Off - 100 Recipes*. 96 pages. **$5.00**

1962 - *13th Grand National Bake Off - 100 Recipes*. 96 pages. **$5.00**

1963 - *The Pillsbury Family Cook Book.* Hard cover, 5-ring binder, 576 pages. **$10.00**

1963 - *14th Grand National Bake Off - 100 Recipes.* **$5.00**

1960's - *Pillsbury's 24 Meat 'n Potato Ideas.* Adapted by Ann Pillsbury, 22 pages. **$3.00**

1964 - *15th Grand National Bake Off - 100 Recipes.* 96 pages. **$5.00**

1960's - *Any Time Quick Bread Ideas.* 14 pages. **$3.00**

1965 - *"Do-It Togerther" Butter Cookies.* 30 pages. **$3.00**

1960's - *Fun-Filled Butter Cookie Cookbook - 50 Recipes From Ann Pillsbury's Recipe Exchange.* 48 pages. **$3.00**

1965 - *From Pillsbury's 16th Grand National - 100 New Bake-Off Recipes.* 14 pies, 24 breads, 14 main dishes, 21 cookies, 8 desserts, 19 cakes. 96 pages. **$5.00**

1966 - *From The 17th Annual Bake Off - The Pillsbury Lady Bake Off Recipes.* 96 pages. **$5.00**

1966 - *Merry, Merry Shortcuts To You.* From 1966 Busy Lady Bake Off, package insert. **$2.00**

1967 - *Pillsbury's Time Saver Cookbook.* Barbara Thornton, Director, Consumer Service Kitchens, 94 pages. **$7.50**

1967 - *100 Bake Off Recipes - Newest American Champions.* **$5.00**

1967 - *18th Annual Bake Off Recipes.* 96 pages. **$5.00**

1968 - *The Nice 'n Easy Cook Book.* 171 recipes. **$3.00**

1968 - *19th Annual Bake Off - 100 Recipes.* 96 pages. **$3.00**

1968 - *Self-Frosted Yellow Cake.* Package insert offering two bake-off cookbooks for $1.00, 18th and 19th, 1967 and 1968. **$2.00**

1969 - *Cook Book Library.* Seven volumes. Each **$2.00**

1969 - *Pillsbury's Bake Off Main Dish Cook Book.* Free w/ purchase of Pillsbury's seven-volume cookbook library. **$2.00**

1969 - *20th Annual Bake Off Recipes.* **$2.00**

1969 - *Bake Off Cookie Favorites.* 64 pages. **$2.00**

1969 - *A Treasury of Bake Off Favorites.* 96 pages. **$2.00**

1967, 1970 - *Pillsbury's Time Saver Cookbook - Modern Age Cooking With A Home Made Touch.* Second edition, Barbara Thornton, Director, Consumer Service Kitchens, 94 pages. **NCV**

1970 - *21st Annual Bake Off - 100 Grand National Recipes.* **NCV**

1970 - *Pillsbury's Entertainment Idea Handbook.* Barbara Thornton, hard cover, 161 pages. **NCV**

1970 - *Pillsbury's Dessert Cookbook.* Dianne Hennessy King, Editor, Pillsbury Publications, 95 pages. **NCV**

1970 - *Party Cakes For Red Letter Days.* Package insert. **NCV**

1971 - *Pillsbury's Creative Cooking in Minutes.* Dianne Hennessy King, Editor, Pillsbury Publications, hard cover. **NCV**

1971 - *Pillsbury's Creative Cooking in Minutes.* Compliments of Disabled American Veterans, Dianne Hennessy King, Editor, Pillsbury Publications, soft cover. **NCV**

1972 - *Pillsbury's Cooking For Campers.* Dianne Hennessy King, Editor, Pillsbury Publications, 72 pages. **NCV**

1973, 1974 - *The New Pillsbury Family Cookbook.* 408 pages. **NCV**

1976 - *A New Way to Bake with Pillsbury Instant Blending Flour.* Ann Pillsbury, 13 pages. **NCV**

1978 - *Working People's Cookbook.* The Pillsbury Kitchens, 95 pages. **NCV**

1970's - *Sweet-10 Calorie-Slim Recipes from Pillsbury.* 38 pages. **NCV**

1980 - *New Pillsbury's Best Butter Cookie Cookbook.* Volume 11, 50 pages. **NCV**

1982 - *Pillsbury Creative Holiday Recipes.* 93 pages. **NCV**

1982 - *Pillsbury Kitchens Family Cook Book.* **NCV**

1982 - *Pillsbury Cookies, Cookies And More Cookies Cookbook.* 112 pages. **NCV**

1984 - *Pillsbury Cool 'N Frosty Cookbook.* Classic 42, 95 pages. **NCV**

1984 - *Pillsbury Cakes Unlimited.* Classic 44, 96 pages. **NCV**

1985 - *Pillsbury Let's Celebrate!* Classic 52, 93 pages. **NCV**

1985 - *Pillsbury Quick-To-Make Recipes.* Classic 53, 95 pages. **NCV**

1987 - *Pillsbury, The Crescent Collection.* 52 pages. **NCV**

◊ ◊ ◊ ◊

Standard-Tilton Milling Company

The Standard-Tilton Milling Company of St. Louis, Missouri was established in 1887. The company manufactured the following brands of flour: Royal Patent Flour, American Beauty Flour, "It's"-A-Bird Self Rising Flour, Table Queen Flour, and Over The Top Rye Flour. Added to the line in 1917 was "Win The War Self-Rising Mixture," a non-wheat flour.

The following are the cookbooks and booklets that we were able to research and collect on this company.

1916 - *The Standard-Tilton Recipe Book of Good Things For The Home.* 14 pages. **$20.00**

▶ 1917 - *War Time Recipes.* Back cover features "Food Will Win The War," Hoover, 22 pages. **$20.00**

◊ ◊ ◊ ◊

Robin Hood

The International Milling Company was established in 1890 with general offices in Minneapolis, Minnesota. The following is the complete line of flours milled for home baking by International Milling Company, Inc.: Robin Hood All Purpose Flour, Robin Hood Self-Rising Flour, Robin Hood Stone Ground Graham Flour, Robin Hood Stone Ground Whole Wheat Flour, Robin Hood Pure Rye Flour, and Velvet Cake and Pastry Flour (The Henkel Flour Mills).

By 1976 the Robin Hood Flour Company was known as International Multifoods, 1200 Multifoods Building, Minneapolis, Minnesota, and was introducing the "freezer dough method" of baking.

The following are the cookbooks and recipe books that we were able to research and collect on this company.

1964 - *Let's Bake The Robin Hood "No-Sift" Way.* Rita Martin Test Kitchen, 64 pages. **$4.00**

1976 - *Make Your Own Freezer Yeast Doughs with Robin Hood All Purpose Flour.* 15 pages. **NCV**

1980 - *Home Baking with Robin Hood Flour.* 71 pages. **NCV**

◊ ◊ ◊ ◊

King Arthur

The Sands, Taylor & Wood Company was established in 1790 in Brighten, Massachusetts. In 1896 they began manufacturing King Arthur Flour "never bleached, never bromated, it comes all purpose, pre-sifted and enriched naturally pure & wholesome."

We were able to find the following publication from King Arthur flour.

1985 - *A Short Course with King Arthur Flour in Baking with Yeast.* 28 pages. **NCV**

◊ ◊ ◊ ◊

Ceresota

The Ceresota Flour was manufactured by the Northwestern Consolidated Milling Company, Minneapolis, Minnesota. The following are the publications we were able to collect from this company.

▶ 1880's - *Ceresota Cook Book.* The Northwestern Consolidated Milling Company, Minneapolis, Minnesota, 42 pages. **$30.00**

1890's - *Ceresota Cook Book.* Marion Harris Neil, compliments of the Northwestern Consolidated Milling Company, 32 pages. **$24.00**

Circa 1910 - *Ceresota Household Hints.* Series 2, 32 pages. **$14.00**

◊ ◊ ◊ ◊

Enterprise

The Valier & Spies Milling Company with its general office located in St. Louis, Missouri, and mills in St. Louis, Saint Jacob, Illinois, and Marine, Illinois, manufactured the Enterprise brand of flour. The following recipe book is all that we were able to research and collect on this company.

1925 - *For All Good Baking.* Tested recipes, Enterprise Flour, two-page fold out. **$12.00**

◊ ◊ ◊ ◊

Larabee

The Larabee Flour Mills Company was established in Kansas City, Missouri. The following recipe book is all that we were able to research and collect on this company.

▶ 1931 - *Larabee's Best Flour.* Clara Alden, cover features Dutch girl with spoon which folds into a bowl when cover is in closed position, 10 pages. **$10.00**

◊ ◊ ◊ ◊

Town Crier

The Midland Flour Milling Company was established in Kansas City, Missouri and manufactured Town Crier brand of flour. The following lists the recipe books that we were able to research and collect on this company.

Circa 1915 - *Town Crier Baking Guide.* **$14.00**

▶ 1932 - *The Town Crier Baking Guide*. 30 pages. **$10.00**

1930's - *The Town Crier Baking Guide*. 24 pages. **$10.00**

◊ ◊ ◊ ◊

Aristos

The Southwestern Milling Company, Inc. of Kansas City, Missouri manufactured the Aristos Flour. The following are the recipe books that we were able to collect and research on this company.

▶ 1911 - *Aristos Flour Cook Book*. 32 pages. **$25.00**

Circa 1915 - *Household Hints - 205 Other Tricks and Tips*. Aristos The Never-Fail Flour, 31 pages. **$20.00**

◊ ◊ ◊ ◊

Albatross

The Spillers Limited (company) National Proprieties with a manufacturing plant located at 40 Mary Ave., London, E.C. 3 and general offices at 85 Gracechurch Street, London, E.C. 3, manufactured dog foods, animal feeding stuffs and Albatross Flour. We were able to find the following recipe book from them.

1934 - *The New Albatross Recipe Book*. 36 pages. **$10.00**

◊ ◊ ◊ ◊

Occident

In 1901 the Russell-Miller Milling Company with two small mills, built some years before, was operating in Valley City and Jamestown, North Dakota, manufacturing Occident Flour. They were in the heart of the hard wheat district of the Northwest, the section conceded by all experts to produce some of the finest wheat grown anywhere in the world. The general offices were located in Minneapolis, Minnesota with eastern headquarters in Buffalo, New York.

The following are the advertising cookbooks that we were able to collect from this company.

1920's - *Occident Quick Bread Recipes*. 10 pages. **$7.50**

1920's - *Occident Cookies Recipes*. 15 pages. **$7.50**

1920's - *Occident Sandwich Recipes*. 8 pages. **$7.50**

1920's - *Occident Cake Recipes*. 16 pages. **$7.50**

1920's - *Occident Pastry Recipes*. 10 pages. **$7.50**

1920's - *Occident Dessert Recipes*. 7 pages. **$7.50**

1931 - *Baking Made Easy*. Margaret B. Baker, Director, Home Economics Department, 24 pages. **$10.00**

1932 - *Baking Made Easy*. Margaret B. Baker, Director, Home Economics Department, 55 pages. **$10.00**

▶ 1936 - *Occident Flour Tested Recipes*. 24 pages. **$10.00**

▶ 1939 - *Occident Flour Tested Recipes*. 24 pages. **$10.00**

◊ ◊ ◊ ◊

Wingold

The Bay State Milling Company manufactured Wingold Wisdom Flour of Winona, Minnesota. The following listing is the only thing we were able to collect from this company.

▶ 1913 - *Wingold Wisdom*. Compliments of Bay State Milling Company, 46 pages. **$20.00**

◊ ◊ ◊ ◊

Capital Star, Red Seal

The G.H. Dulle Milling Company was established in 1853 in Jefferson City, Missouri on the banks of the Missouri River. The company produced the "Dulle's Patent, Capitol Star Flour and Red Seal Self-Rising Flour." Recipes were created, selected, and tested by Jessie Alice Cline and her class in Experimental Cookery, Department of Home Economics, University of Missouri.

The following is the only recipe book that we were able to collect and research on this company.

1932 - *Good Things To Eat Made From Missouri Soft Wheat Flour*. Tested recipes, 23 pages. **$20.00**

◊ ◊ ◊ ◊

Aunt Jemima

In 1889 Chris L. Rutt established a flour mill in St. Joseph, Missouri that manufactured a self-rising pancake flour named Aunt Jemima's Pancake Flour. Sometime later, R.T. Davis Mill & Manufacturing Company of St. Joseph, Missouri purchased the business. There was an Aunt Jemima display at the 1893 Columbian Exposition in Chicago when the company exhibited the world's largest flour barrel. Over 1,000,000 pancakes were served at the fair. Nancy Green, a Negro employed for the Exposition to represent Aunt Jemina pancake flour, became known as "Aunt Jemima."

In 1925 Quaker Oats Company acquired the R.T. Davis Mill & Manufacturing Company of St. Joseph, Missouri and thus acquired the Aunt Jemima Pancake Flour. It became known as Aunt Jemima Mills, Inc., St. Josesph, Missouri.

There were many premiums manufactured to promote Aunt Jemina, and housewives could send for syrup pitchers, salt and pepper sets, spice sets, cookie jars, vases, planters, banks, and even Occupied Japan salt and pepper shakers.

The following publications are what we were able to collect from this company.

▸ 1952 - *Aunt Jemima's Magical Recipes.* The Quaker Oats company, 26 pages. **$6.00**

1958 - *Pancakes "Unlimited."* A new style show of wonderful eating, 31 pages. **$6.00**

◊ ◊ ◊ ◊

Others

The following is a list of miscellaneous flour companies known to exist over the years.

1852 - Sperry Flour Company. They joined the world's largest flour miller, General Mills, Inc., in 1928

1886 - Prarie Flour, S.H. Cockrell & Company, Dallas, Texas

1890 - Jeff Davis Wheat Flour, Sweet Water Mill Co., Sweet Water, Tennessee

1891 - Pan-Handle Wheat Flour, Wichita Valley Mill & Elevator Co., Wichita Falls, Texas

1899 - Martha White Flour, Royal Flour Mill, Nashville, Tennessee

1901 - Kitchen Queen Flour, Cape County Milling Company, Jackson, Missouri

1905 - Western Delight Flour, John F. Meyer & Sons Milling Company, St. Louis, Missouri and Springfield, Missouri

1905 - Red Fox Flour, Sweet Springs Milling Company, Sweet Springs, Missouri

1905 - Betsy Ross Flour, International Milling Company, Minneapolis, Minnesota

1906 - Five Roses Flour, Justin Rosenthal Soden Empire, Kansas

1906 - Gopher Brand Wheat Flour, Montevidio Roller Mill Company, Montevideo, Minnesota

1906 - Jack Rabbit Wheat Flour, Pea-Patterson Milling Company, Coffeyville, Kansas

1908 - Lariat Flour, Dodge City Milling & Elevator Company, Dodge City, Kansas

1911 - Reliable Flour Co., Boston, Massachusetts

1914 - Kansas Maid Flour, Hays City Milling and Elevator Company, Hays, Kansas

1918 - Doughboy Wheat Flour, Mennel Milling Company, Toledo, Ohio

1919 - Olympic Flour, Portland Flouring Mills Company, Portland, Oregon

1924 - Drink Water Flour, Martin Milling Company, Dallas, Texas

1924 - The Heart of America Wheat Flour, Rodney Milling Company of Kansas City, Missouri

1925 - Stonewall Jackson Self-Rising Wheat Flour, Shenondoah Milling Company, Shenandoah, Virginia

1931 - Mother Hubbard Flour, Hubbard Milling Company, Mankato, Minnesota

1937 - Snow Lily Flour, Enns Milling Company, Inman, Kansas

1939 - White Dough Flour, Ismart-Hincke Milling Company, Kansas City, Missouri

1942 - Kentucky Wonder Wheat Flour, Hopkinsville Milling Company, Hopkinsville, Kentucky

Miscellaneous cookbooks:

1911 - *Biscuit and Cakes, Success Assured.* Reliable Flour Co., Boston, Massachusetts.

1929 - *Tested Recipes for Purasnow Enriched Flour.* General Mills, Inc., on the flour sack pictured, 4 pages. **$5.00**

1929 - *Purasnow Enriched Flour.* One of the 30 flour mill companies that formed General Mills, Inc. during 1928 and this is first use of the new group name. 8½x11", 2-page flyer. **$3.00**

Chapter 14

Betty Crocker

The Washburn-Crosby Company was quite successful. Between the publishing of the 1914 and the 1917 Gold Medal Flour Cook Book, things were happening and plans were developing.

James F. Bell, president of the Washburn-Crosby Company, was interested in the American housewife and what she thought. Inquiries and recipes were solicited and answered.

To publicize Gold Medal Flour, a picture puzzle ad was run in a national magazine. The puzzle was a village scene depicting customers carrying sacks of Gold Medal Flour to their trucks and wagons. When solved, the prize for working the puzzle was a pin cushion in the shape of a miniature Gold Medal Flour sack.

The response half-buried the office force. More than 30,000 people sent in the completed puzzle. Extra personnel was hired to untangle the heaps of mail and a corner of the mill was commandeered for working space.

Unexpectedly, along with the puzzle solution, hundreds of women also included chatty little questions. "How do you make a one crust cherry pie?" "What's a good recipe for apple dumplings?" "How long do you knead dough?"

The advertising staff was bewildered but rose to the occasion. Recipes from laboratory personnel and home economists (and from office personnel and their wives) were collected and each letter received a personal reply. But somehow, the letters of reply needed a woman's signature. The advertising department again went to work and came up with a surname - Crocker - the name of the popular secretary-director who had recently retired. Now they needed a first name, something cozy and familiar sounding, like Betty. Yes, Betty Crocker. A worker, Florence Lindeberg, provided the signature.

The 1917 *Washburn-Crosby Cook Book* established the existence of Betty Crocker as an advertising medium to the general public. Page 73 of this cookbook is titled "The New Gold Medal Home Service" and is signed by Betty Crocker.

Betty Crocker

Once introduced to the American public, Betty Crocker went on to be known to almost every woman in the United States, and is truly America's Lady of Food.

In 1924 Betty Crocker took to the air waves on daytime radio's first food service program. Subsequently, the Betty Crocker Cooking School of the air became a network program. Blance Ingersall became Betty Crocker's voice in 1924 when the company advertised on the radio. In 1925, 13 Betty Crockers were on radio programs in different areas of the United States.

The January 1928 issue of *The Farmer's Wife* magazine advertised "The newest thing in baking! 'Kitchen-tested' recipes with 'Kitchen-tested' flour." It shows one view of the Gold Medal Kitchens where every batch of Gold Medal Flour is "Kitchen-tested" and where they create many new and delightful "Kitchen-tested" recipes which are rapidly becoming recognized standards by Betty Crocker, Renowned Cooking Expert. This advertising was by the general offices of Washburn-Crosby Company in Minneapolis, Minnesota.

James F. Bell, president of the Washburn-Crobsy Company, had been aware that since 1926, the future of the flour business looked doubtful because there was no assurance that the supply of wheat would remain stable. He envisioned the possibility of merging with some flour mills into a corporation to stabilize the wheat supply for adequate supply of hard winter wheat and soft spring wheat and therefore establish a better marketplace.

In 1928 this plan was unfolded to the Board of Directors and by the end of 1928, General Mills, Inc. was born with the merger of approximately 34 flour mill companies. This assured a constant supply of hard winter wheat from the northern states to match a constant supply of soft spring wheat from the Midwest and southern regions. This also provided a base for growth and expansion.

The officials of Washburn-Crosby Company became likewise the officials for General Mills, Inc. and Betty Crocker remained the spokesperson and advertising medium for General Mills, Inc. Shortly after the merger was completed, a company official was doing some research in the laboratory and discovered a flour that was to become Bisquick, the nation's first prepared baking mix. This Bisquick flour was put into production in 1929.

The May 1930 issue of *American Cookery* magazine advertised "The Gold Medal Home Service Recipe Box,

100 Recipes, 'Kitchen-tested' under the direction of Betty Crocker, in the Finest Oak Box Money can Buy."

The July 1930 issue of *American Cookery* magazine advertised "Developed...'An All-Star Set' of 'Kitchen-tested' Recipes by Noted Cooking Editors in collaboration with the Home Economics Staff, Anna B. Scott, Cooking Editor of *Philadelphia Inquirer*, One of the Noted stars who collaborated with Betty Crocker in developing the All-Star Set by Washburn-Crosby Company of General Mills, Inc." The October 1930 issue advertised the same except with Mary D. Chambers, Cooking Editor for *American Cookery* magazine.

The 1931 American Cookery magazine advertised "A Practical Home Economics Service That Benefits House-wifes Everywhere." This service consisted of Mrs. F.C. Edgarton of Spokane, Washington, Mrs. Kathleen Underwood of Ellensboro, West Virginia, and 12-year old Agath Olson of Beltrami, Minnesota.

In 1931 General Mills, Inc. resumed the advertising cookbook publications with *New Party Cakes for All Occasions* featuring Gold Medal Cake Flour " Soft As Silk" by Betty Crocker.

In 1934 General Mills, Inc. published a recipe cookbook titled *Vitality Demands Energy*, 109 smart new ways to serve bread our outstanding energy food. The fly leaf reads: "The Facts about Bread as proven by Science. Its contribution to the well balanced, appetizing diet, its importance in providing endurance energy that promote vitality, as explained by nutrition authorities, noted screen stars, new and correct uses for Bread and other baked wheat products, by Betty Crocker." This recipe book has a full page Foreword by Betty Crocker including a composite drawing of her for the first time. This is the earliest composite drawing of Betty Crocker to appear in a publication.

The recipe book also has a page with a composite drawing of Emily Post and her letter to Betty Crocker, a page showing a photograph of Margaret Sullivan, a movie star, and her letter to Betty Crocker, and a page showing a photograph of Sylvia Sidney, actress, and her letter to Betty Crocker. Other pages feature Claudette Colbert, star of Cecil B. Demille's "Cleopatra" and her letter to Betty Crocker, and Oscar of the Waldorf (Louis De Gouy) and his letter. Another page shows a picture of Mary Astor, Bette Davis and Ann Dvorak, all endorsing bread.

The 1935 advertising cookbook published by General Mills, Inc., How To Take A Trick A Day With Bisquick, was "as told to Betty Crocker by screen stars, society stars, home stars and star homemaking editors." On the cover for the second time appears a composite drawing of Betty Crocker in a star with a white background, very much like the 1934 composite drawing. The letters telling Betty Crocker of a trick a day with Bisquick were from the following: Clark Gable, Countess Fal de St. Phalle, May Robinson, Mrs. Thomas J. Hilliard, Dick Powell, Nell B. Nichols, Bing Crosby, Joan Crawford, Mildred Maddocks Bently, Jean Parker and Beulah Gillaspie.

AS TOLD TO *Betty Crocker*
BY SCREEN STARS, SOCIETY STARS, HOME STARS AND STAR HOMEMAKING EDITORS

In 1939 Betty Crocker introduced Toll House Cookies through the radio series on "Famous Foods from Famous Eating Places."

On a 1940 package insert Betty Crocker announces, "General Mills All America Enriched Flour Improtant Notice: All America Enriched Flour is produced under the government emergency flour order aimed at saving wheat to help relieve the world food situation." It features a smiling composite of Betty Crocker.

In 1941 Mrs. Helen Hallbert joined General Mills, Inc. and became Home Service Director of the Betty Crocker Kitchens. This talented person and her staff of 60 including 34 home economists interpreted consumer desires to the company, developed services for homemakers, created and tested new products, developed visual teaching aids and prepared Betty Crocker cookbooks. One of her favorite Betty Crocker trainees was Suzanna Lee Elliott who graduated from Missouri University in the late 1940's.

During World War II, Betty Crocker stepped in the breech with a special radio program, "Your Nations Rations," offered through the U.S. Department of State. Betty Crocker endorsed booklets on low-cost menus and budgeting and helped the war-time family get through the hard times.

In 1950 Betty Crocker's first full-length *Picture Cookbook* became a national best seller. Its fifth edition, published in 1978, reflects the changing life styles of families in which the wife and mother are also wage earners with limited time for food preparation and greater interest in nutrition and natural foods.

In 1951 Betty Crocker and General Mills, Inc. introduced the new product "cake mix" with the publication of a recipe book titled *Betty Crocker's Cake Mix Magic, 121 Wonderful Cakes and Desserts you can make with Betty Crocker's Cake Mixes*.

In 1955 Gold Medal Four celebrated their Diamond Jubilee Anniversary (75th). The company published *Gold Medal Jubilee Select Recipes*, a treasure of favorite recipes modernized by Betty Crocker. This is a very well-done recipe book and of great historical value. At this time, Annette Calhoun was employed in the Betty Crocker Kitchens as a Home Economist and was a Betty Crocker. She retired some years later and passed away in the early 1970's at her home in Minneapolis, Minnesota. To settle the estate, an auction was held to sell everything in the house. It was advertised as an Estate Auction as so many are. This auction became known as the Betty Crocker Estate Auction. On auction day there was an enormous crowd on hand. A Minneapolis antiques dealer was the successful bidder on a large number of Betty Crocker's cookbooks and booklets.

This dealer and his wife moved to Missouri sometime after this and in September of 1987, they rented a table in an antiques show in St. James, Missouri during the annual Grape and Fall Festival. It was here that we obtained the *1955 Gold Medal Jubilee Select Recipes* book in excellent condition. Page one is marked "Desk Copy" and is signed by Annette Calhoun. She had marked each recipe with a file refererence number and in some cases she had written a different recipe title after the number.

In 1958 Betty Crocker introduced yet another innovation to baking when General Mills, Inc. published *Betty Crocker's Frosting Secrets*, Fancy Cake Decoration, New Cake Trimming Short Cuts, Fabulous Party Cake Ideas, Fun With Frostings. On the inside cover is the following:

Welcome! Come join us in the fun of frosting glamorous decorated cakes! It's surprising how easy it is, once you get the knack of it. Our fluffy Frosting Mix is a big help, it makes a decorator icing that's always smooth and easyflowing. Your very first cake will be pretty enough to be proud of! And if it isn't absolutely perfect, please don't be discouraged, the practice you've had will make you next cake much easier. To start, try the quick-as-a-wink tricks that don't need a decorator set. And try candies and desserts from our frosting mixes, easy short cuts to delicious treats!

Betty Crocker

In November of 1961 Betty Crocker Kitchens of General Mills, Inc. announced that a set of talking records for the blind homemaker had just been released. The talking records were a pioneering effort to help homemakers with loss of sight or failing eyesight who wish to continue to do their own cooking. The records replaced colored pictures in the ordinary cookbook with descriptive phrases meaningful to the blind. Instead of "Bake until golden brown," the record would say "If the biscuits feel crusty, they're done." These instructions have been worked out with the help of blind homemakers and organizations such as The American Foundation for the Blind. Titled "Tips and Talking Recipes, Directions for using Betty Crocker Mixes," all records can be used on 33⅓ rpm record players.

In 1963 Betty Crocker went international with the publication of *Betty Crocker's Continental Casseroles, For Those That Can't Go Abroad This Year*. On the inside cover appears the following:

Dear Friend,

Do you wish you were setting out on a grand tour, all packed and ready to step aboard a ship or plane for a carefree trip abroad, to explore the sights and scents and tastes of far off places? Well, if you're not going abroad this year, but only wish you were, come join our Armchair Cook's Tour and taste the flavors of many countries in Betty Crocker's casserole mixes at your own dinner table.

In 1963, the Betty Crocker Department at General Mills, Inc. extended it's consumer research and education internationally. After the American Exhibition in Moscow, Helen Hallbert reported Russian women found it hard to believe that everything to make a delicious cake could come in a small box. Before setting up a test kitchen in England, Helen Hallbert brought a British home economist to work in the Betty Crocker kitchens at Minneapolis for several months. Helen also supervised kitchens and home economists in Canada.

The following are the publications that we were able to collect from this company.

1917 - *Gold Medal Flour Cook Book*. Betty Crocker, soft cover, 74 pages. **$14.00**

1931 - *New Party Cakes For All Occasions*. Betty Crocker, Gold Medal Foods, Incorporated of General Mills, Inc., 24 pages. **$10.00**

1933 - *Betty Crocker's $25,000 Recipe*. Hard cover, spiral bound, 60 pages. **$14.00**

1933 - *Betty Crocker's 101 Delicious Bisquick Creations*. Director of Home Economics Dept. of General Mills, Inc., Miller of Gold Medal Flour, also conductor of one of the world's largest Radio cooking schools, soft cover, 32 pages. **$10.00**

1934 - *Vitality Demands Energy - 109 Smart New Ways*

to Serve Bread, Our Outstanding Energy Food. Includes a composite drawing of Betty Crocker that is the earliest known. Soft cover, 54 pages. **$10.00**

1935 - *How To Take A Trick A Day With Bisquick.* As told to Betty Crocker, includes a composite drawing of Betty Crocker very much like the 1934 drawing. Soft cover, 41 pages. **$10.00**

1943 - *Your Share.* 52 menus, 226 recipes, 369 hints, 48 pages. **$6.00**

1943 - *Betty Crocker's Soft as Silk Special Occasion Cakes.* **$8.00**

1941, 1942, 1943 - *Betty Crocker Cook Book of All-Purpose Baking.* Also included in a special war-time supplement to help with sugar, shortening and syrup problems. **$8.00**

1945 - *Betty Crocker Cook Book of All-Purpose Baking.* Also included is a special war-time supplement to help with sugar, shortening and syrup problems. **$8.00**

1946 - *New Betty Crocker Method Recipes, Easier-Quicker-Surer.* 54 party cake suggestions, soft cover, 31 pages. **$8.00**

1950 - *Betty Crocker's Picture Cook Book.* First edition, 5-ring binder, hard cover. **$15.00**

1950, 1952 - *Betty Crocker's Picture Cook Book.* Revised and enlarged, 5-ring binder, hard cover. **$10.00**

1951 - *Betty Crocker's Cake Mix Magic.* Soft cover, 27 apges. **$6.00**

1954 - *Betty Crocker Good and Easy Cook Book.* First edition, hard cover, spiral. **$6.00**

1955 - *Gold Medal Jubilee Select Recipes.* Betty Crocker, soft cover, 49 pages. **$15.00**

1956 - *Betty Rocker's Bisquick Cook Book.* Soft cover, 26 pages. **$6.00**

1956 - *How To Have The Most Fun With Cake Mixes.* Betty Crocker, soft cover, 33 pages. **$6.00**

1957 - *Betty Crocker's Soft as Silk Special Occasion Cakes.* Soft cover, 31 pages. **$6.00**

1957 - *Betty Crocker's Cookie Carnival.* Gold Medal Flour from the Famous Betty Crocker's Picture Cook Book, soft cover, 38 pages. **$6.00**

1957 - *Betty Crocker's Cook Book for Boys and Girls.* First edition, hard cover, spiral bound, 191 pages. **$6.00**

1957 - *Betty Crocker's Bisquick Party Book.* Gay new ideas and recipes, soft cover, 24 pages. **$6.00**

1957 - *Betty Crocker's Pie Parade.* Soft cover, 38 pages. **$6.00**

1958 - *Betty Crocker's Frosting Secrets - Fun With Frostings.* Soft cover, 24 pages. **$6.00**

1958 - *Betty Crocker's Party Calendar.* Soft cover, 16 pages. **$6.00**

1959 - *Betty Crocker's Guide to Easy Entertaining.* First edition, first priting, soft cover, 176 pags. **$6.00**

1959 - *Betty Crocker's Guide to Easy Entertaining.* Second printing, soft cover, 176 pages. **$4.00**

1959 - *Betty Crocker's "Frankly Fancy" Foods Recipe Book.* Soft cover, 26 pages. **$6.00**

1959 - *133 Quicker Ways to Home Made with Bisquick From Betty Crocker.* Soft cover, 27 pages. **$6.00**

1960 - *All-American Favorite Recipes with Corn Oil and Gold Medal Flour.* Betty Crocker, soft cover, 19 pages. **$4.00**

1960 - *Betty Crocker's Party Book.* First edition, first printing, hard cover, spiral, 176 pages. **$10.00**

1961 - *Betty Crocker's New Picture Cook Book.* First edition, second printing, hard cover, 455 pages. **$15.00**

1961 - *Betty Crocker's Outdoor Cookbook.* First edition, hard cover, spiral bound, 176 pages. **$10.00**

1962 - *Betty Crocker's Cooking Calendar - A Year Round Guide to Meal Planning with Recipes and Menus.* First edition, first printing, hard cover, spiral, 176 pages. **$10.00**

1962 - *The Betty Crocker's New Good and Easy Cookbook.* First edition, first printing, hard cover, spiral, 192 pages. **$10.00**

1963 - *Betty Crocker's Merry Makings.* Soft cover, 23 pages. **$4.00**

1963 - *Betty Crocker's Baking's Believing.* Soft cover, 23 pages. **$4.00**

1963 - *Betty Crocker's Continental Casseroles.* Soft cover, 12 pages. **$4.00**

1963 - *Betty Crocker's Festive Fixings with a Foreign Flair.* Soft cover, 23 pages. **$4.00**

1964 - *Betty Crocker's Bake Up A Story - A Cook's Tour Through Storyland.* Soft cover, 20 pages. **$4.00**

1964 - *Betty Crocker's Parties for Children.* Hard cover, spiral, 166 pages. **$10.00**

1963, 1964 - *Betty Crocker's Festive Fixings with a Foreign Flair.* Soft cover, 23 pages. **$4.00**

1964 - *Betty Crocker's New Dinner for Two Cookbook.* Hard cover, 156 pages. **$10.00**

1965 - *"George Your Wife's A Great Cook!" Help for the Hesitant Hostess.* Betty Crocker, soft cover, 16 pages. **$4.00**

1965 - *Betty Crocker's Holidays on Parade.* Soft cover, 23 pages. **$4.00**

1965 - *Betty Crocker's New Boys and Girls Cookbook.* Hard cover, spiral. **$8.00**

1965 - *Betty Crocker's Dinner in a Dish Cookbook.* First edition, first printing, hard cover, spiral, 152 pages. **$10.00**

1966 - *Betty Crocker's Holiday Heritage.* Soft cover, 14 pages. **$4.00**

1966 - *Betty Crocker's Cookbook.* Hard cover, three-ring. **$10.00**

1967 - *Betty Crocker's Hostess Cook Book Featuring More Than 400 Guest Tested Recipes.* First edition, first printing, hard cover, spiral, 168 pages. **$10.00**

1967 - *Betty Crocker 42 Hot Potato Ideas.* Soft cover, 15 pages. **$4.00**

1967 - *Betty Crocker's New Outdoor Cook Book.* Hard cover, spiral, 160 pages. **$10.00**

1967 - *Betty Crocker's Hostess Cookbook.* Hard cover, spiral bound, 168 pages. **$10.00**

1968 - *Betty Crocker's Pie and Pastry Cookbook.* First edition, first printing, hard cover, 160 pages. **$7.50**

1968 - *Betty Crocker's Holiday Hostess "Can Do" Recipes.* Soft cover, 14 pages. **$2.00**

1969 - *"Let's Eat Outdoors."* Betty Crocker and American Dairy Association Chicago, soft cover, 27 pages. **$2.00**

1969 - *Betty Crocker's Ways With Hamburger - 50 Recipes to Stretch Your Budget.* Soft cover, 24 pages. **$2.00**

1969 - *Betty Crocker's Cookbook.* Hard cover, five-ring binder. **$10.00**

1967, 1970 - *Betty Crocker's Piggy Bank Casseroles.* Soft cover, 24 pages. **NCV**

1967, 1970 - *Betty Crocker's Hostess Cookbook.* Hard cover, spiral, 168 pages. **NCV**

1965, 1970 - *Betty Crocker's Dinner in a Dish Cookbook.* Hard cover, spiral, 152 pages. **NCV**

1970 - *Foods That Men Like.* Soft cover, 24 pages. **NCV**

1965, 1970, 1971 - *Betty Crocker's Dinner In a Dish Cookbook.* Fifth printing, hard cover, spiral bound, 152 pages. **NCV**

1971 - *Betty Crocker's All-Time Favorites - Main Dishes ...Salads...Vegetables...Breads...Desserts.* First printing, soft cover, 160 pages. **NCV**

1971 - *Betty Crocker's Do-Ahead Cookbook From the Freezer and the Refrigerator.* Hard cover, spiral, 160 pages. **NCV**

1971 - *Betty Crocker's Bisquick Cookbook.* Hard cover, spiral inside, 124 pages. **NCV**

1971 - *Betty Crocker's Bisquick Cookbook.* Soft cover, 32 pages. **NCV**

1971 - *Betty Crocker's Beef & Potatoes Recipes.* Soft cover, 29 pages. **NCV**

1971 - *Betty Crocker - 50 Scrumptious Ways to Dessert Your Family.* Soft cover, 23 pages. **NCV**

1972 - *Betty Crocker's Do-Ahead Cookbook From the Freezer and the Refrigerator.* First edition, hard cover, spiral, 160 pages. **NCV**

1972 - *Betty Crocker's How to Feed Your Family to Keep The Fit & Happy, No Matter What.* Hard cover. **NCV**

1971, 1972 - *Betty Crocker's Bisquick Cookbook.* Supplement Two, Homemakers Recipes, soft cover, 16 pages. **NCV**

1967, 1970, 1973 - *Betty Crocker's New Outdoor Cookbook.* Third printing, hard cover, spiral, 160 pages. **NCV**

1971, 1972, 1973 - *Betty Crocker's Do Ahead Cookbook.* Hard cover, spiral, 160 pages. **NCV**

1967, 1970, 1973 - *Betty Crocker's Hostess Cookbook.* Hard cover, spiral, 168 pages. **NCV**

1973 - *Betty Crocker's Money-Saving Dinners.* First edition, hard cover, 76 pages. **NCV**

1973 - *Betty Crocker's Dinner for Two Cookbook.* First edition, hard cover, spiral, 160 pages. **NCV**

1973 - *Betty Crocker's Easy Oven Meals.* Hard cover, spiral. **NCV**

1974 - *Betty Crocker Desserts Cook Book.* Hard cover, spiral. **NCV**

1971, 1974 - *Betty Crocker's All-Time Favorites.* Soft cover, 160 pages. **NCV**

1969, 1976 - *Betty Crocker's Cakes Kids Love.* Soft cover, 24 pages. **NCV**

1976 - *Betty Crocker's Ways With Hamburger.* Soft cover, 24 pages. **NCV**

1970, 1976 - *Betty Crocker's Piggy Bank Casseroles.* Soft cover, 24 pages. **NCV**

1969, 1976 - *Betty Crocker's Cookbook.* 28th printing, five-ring binder. **NCV**

1970, 1976 - *Betty Crocker's Foods Men Like.* Soft cover, 24 pages. **NCV**

1971, 1974, 1977 - *Betty Crocker's All-Time Favorites - Main Dishes...Salads...Vegetables...Breads...Desserts.* Seventh printing, soft cover, 160 pages. **NCV**

1977 - *Cooking With The Greatest of Ease.* Gold Medal Wondra Flour, soft cover, 12 pages. **NCV**

1978 - *The Bisquick No Time to Cook Summer Recipe Book.* Better Homes & Gardens magazine, Betty Crocker, 8-pages pamphlet. **NCV**

1969, 1976, 1978 - *Betty Crocker's Cookbook.* Five-ring binder, hard cover. **NCV**

1979 - *Betty Crocker's Continental Casseroles.* Soft cover. **NCV**

1979 - *Gold Medal Century of Sucess Cookbook - The Best Gold Medal Recipes of 100 Years.* Introduction by Betty Crocker, first printing, soft cover, 112 pages. **NCV**

1982 - *The "You've Got It Made With Bisquick" Cookbook.* Soft cover, 12 pages. **NCV**

1983 - *Creative Desserts from Betty Crocker.* Soft cover, 92 pages. **NCV**

1986 - *The Weekend Chef.* Gold Medal Flour, soft cover, 48 pages. **NCV**

Betty Crocker Flour Package Inserts
The Value of Each Package Insert Is $1.00

1930 - These pictures show the difference between Betty Crocker's "Kitchen Tested" and Ordinary Recipes. Home Service Department, Gold Medal Products Company of General Mills, Inc.

1931 - Cakes Your Husband Will Boast of To All His Men Friends. A 24-page book "New Party Cakes For All Occasions" Free! Betty Crocker Home Service Dept., Gold Medal Foods, Incorporated of General Mills, Inc.

1939 - Two Naming Contests in this folder. $6,668 cash prizes. Name The Orange Rolls. Name the Inexpensive Sponge Cake.

1940 - A smiling Betty Crocker composite drawing. Betty Crocker announces: "General Mills All America Enriched Flour Important Notice: All America Enriched Flour is produced under the government emergency flour order aimed at saving wheat to help relieve the world food situation. It is less white, less fine flour than you are accustomed to."

1941 - The Betty Crocker $1,000 prize contest cake, contest entry blank. $1000.00 in prizes for naming it, $500 first prize, 10 prizes of $10 and 400 prizes of $1.

1941 - Fruit Filled Cream Puffs. Free folder of carefully tested recipes developed for those who bake their own bread, rolls and coffee cakes! "For Superior Baking Results" an endorsement by Eleanor Howe, nationally known home economist for "Kitchen Tested" recipes. A premium offer of Betty Crocker Party Favors, Set of A, one Squirrel, Penguin, gopher and Rabbit at 15 cents per set.

1941 - Series 15. Here's the Betty Crocker feature for holiday baking! Military Christmas Cookies. Extra! 20th Anniversary Special! Betty Crocker Cook Book of "All-Purpose" baking, also valuable baking and sugar-saving hints.

1942 - 1 Series 7. "Elegant," You'll Call It! French Apple Pie. "Baking Success Assured by Gold Medal Flour plus Betty Crocker recipes." writes Barbara Reid Robson, the distinguished home economics consultant. A premium offer of Betty Crocker party favors, set of A, one Squirrel, Penguin, Gopher and Rabbit.

1942 - Series 10 1. Cherries and nuts make it a "Carnival Dessert."

1942 - Series 16. Just Like "June in January" when you serve your family Betty Crocker Mid-Winter Fruit Pies. Oh! What fun it is to bake with the Betty Crocker Cook Book of All-Purpose Baking.

1942 - Series 17. Hails From "Covered Wagon" Days, Betty Crocker Four-Layer Jelly Cake. Sent for your copy yet? The Betty Crocker Cook Book of All-Purpose Baking. Thousands of women have sent for theirs.

1943 - Series 20. Spicy, fruity satisfying Applesauce Cake. Betty Crocker Holiday Cranberry Pudding. Also send for Betty Crocker's Cook Book of All-Purpose baking, with a special war-time supplement.

1944 - Series 21. Betty Crocker presents three grand recipes you can make from one basic dough, Basic Sweet Dough, Cinnamon Rolls (showing a brown teddy bear) and Swedish Tea Ring. Also send for Betty Crocker's Cook Book of All-Purpose baking, with a special war-time supplement.

1945 - Series 22. Most flavorful ginger creams make a hit with men. Tempting and unusual is this Betty Crocker reicpe for flavorful ginger drop cookies. Also send for Betty Crocker's Cook Book of All-Purpose baking, with a special war-time supplement.

1946 - Betty Crocker explains our new method for cakes that cuts your mixing time 1/2. Send for your "Picture-Frame Tray" with lovely reproduction of the famous oil painting "Company For Supper" by Dale Nichols.

1947 - Betty Crocker presents Different! Delicious! Peach Skillet Pie.

1948 - Betty Crocker announces "Lovelier cakes in less than 1/2 the mixing time.

1948 - Betty Crocker "Double Quick" new method picnic spice cake only four minutes to mix.

1948 - Betty Crocker says: "Cut mixing time over 1/2...yet get better cakes.

1949 - Betty Crocker says: "Make more than 60 cake-icing combinations from these 4 basic icings recipes and party cake mix!" Be sure to try Betty Crocker Devil's Food Cake Mix.

1950 - Betty Crocker suggests: For the happiest holiday ever three way fruit cake raisin, fig & date filled cookies, streusel coffee cake.

1951 - Betty Crocker pledges: "Exquisite cakes in less than half the mixing time."

1955 - Fresh berry pie, new, easy, tasty with Betty Crocker's Stir-N-Roll Pastry.

1957 - Try Betty Crocker's Coconut chiffon cake with blush pink icing.

1958 - Time to be fancy. Betty Crocker advertises the 1950 *Betty Crocker's Picture Cook Book.*

1950's - Betty Crocker's Food Festival Recipes. Easy to prepare.

1959 - Let's talk about brand new recipes. Betty Crocker.

1961 - Dear Friend: Don't you often look for recipes that will fit any occasion, everyday family meals or special parties? Well, here they are. Cordially, Betty Crocker.

1962 - Dear Friend: Don't you agree that baking is much more fun when you can try something new now and then? That's why we are giving you these two brand new delicious treats and an old-time favorite made new and easy the modern way. Cordially, Betty Crocker.

1960's - Dear Friend: Here they are, Butterfudge creations! We hope you'll want to make them yours, too! Cordially, Betty Crocker.

1965 - Dear Friend: Perfect pie crust every time is possible with our new "1-2-3" pie crust recipe. Cordially, Betty Crocker.

Chapter 15

Arm & Hammer Baking Soda

In 1847 the firm of John Dwight & Company was founded and the Cow Brand logo was adopted for the John Dwight & Company's Baking Soda and Saleratus. The baking soda and saleratus was a pure bicarbonate of soda. The first baking soda factory was in John Dwight's kitchen, where the product was manufactured and packaged by hand in paper bags.

Dr. Austin Church, the founder of the firm of Church & Company commenced the manufacture of baking soda and Saleratus in 1846 and first introduced it into family use in this country.

In the 1860's Dr. Austin Church's son, James, established a spice and mustard company named the Vulcan Spice Mills. Their trademark was the arm of Vulcan, God of fire, with a hammer in hand about to descend upon an anvil. In 1867 James Church closed his spice factory to join his father in his baking soda business. Although he foresaw no possible use for it, he took the sign along with him out of sentiment.

Soda was sold by the barrel in those days and along with each barrel went a supply of paper bags in which to package it. Inside each package there was a copy of Mrs. Church's own recipe for Gold Cake and later there would be a brand new recipe for Silver Cake.

But in spite of its efforts and Mrs. Church's recipes, sales lagged discouragingly behind competitors. One day James Church sat at his desk staring wistfully at the old Arm & Hammer sign that now hung in his office. Suddenly the thought struck him that here was the perfect symbol for his baking soda. It took power to lift that hammer as it took power to leaven baked goods. James Church immediately had a quantity of paper bags printed with the Arm & Hammer label and rushed them to all the stores in the area. His hunch proved right. The label was an outstanding success.

Arm & Hammer Salerauts (as baking soda was then called) quickly became the fastest selling brand on the market. With its introduction in 1867, one of the world's oldest and most widely recognized package designs in the food industry was launched.

Mined in the Green River Basin in Wyoming, Arm & Hammer Baking Soda is used today by millions of homemakers not only to get a rise out of baked goods, but also to add a shine to dull surfaces and to freshen stale air.

In 1880, Church & Company published the first edition of one million copies of *Valuable Recipes*, the first baking soda recipe booklet. They continued to offer recipe booklets until the merger in 1896, at which time a current edition of Church & Company's recipe booklet was edited to include John Dwight & Company.

In 1896, the descendants of the founders of John Dwight & Company and Church & Company merged and consolidated their interests into one firm, Church & Dwight Company, Inc.

After the merger in 1896 the then current edition of Church & Company's recipe booklet, *Valuable Recipes,* was hastily edited to include John Dwight in the new company of Church & Dwight Company, Inc. The 1897-1898 edition was edited to include John Dwight & Company, but the editing was not complete and there were paragraphs still titled Church & Company. This was finally cleared up after several years.

They printed one million copies each time, and when the supply was depleted, they would print one million copies again. By 1904, the book was in its 42nd edition. They continued to offer the recipe booklet until 1953. In 1983 the company resumed publishing a recipe booklet with recipes updated to conform to modern ingredients and mixing procedures.

The following lists what we were able to collect from this company.

1897-1898 - *Book of Valuable Recipes.* 27th edition of one million, 32 pages. **$24.00**

1904 - *Hand Book of Valuable Information.* 42nd edition of one million, 32 pages. **$20.00**

1913 - *Cow Brand Soda Cook Book.* Issue published for Canada, cow's head on cover, 32 pages. **$20.00**

1914 - *Book of Valuable Recipes.* 64th edition, 32 pages. **$14.00**

1915 - *Book of Valuable Recipes.* 68th edition, 32 pages. **$14.00**

▶ 1916 - *Book of Valuable Recipes.* 68th edition, 32 pages. **$14.00**

1916 - *Book of Valuable Recipes*. 69th edition, 32 pages. **$14.00**

▶ 1920 - *Arm & Hammer Almanac*. 29 pages. **$12.00**

1922 - *Book of Valuable Recipes*. 75th edition, 33 pages. **$12.00**

▶ 1924 - *Good Things To Eat*. 79th edition, compiled by Alice Bradley, principal, Miss Farmer's School of Cookery, Boston, 32 pages. **$12.00**

1925 - *A Friend In Need - Facts Worth Knowing About*. Small booklet, 28 pages. **$4.00**

1933 - *Successful Baking*. 32 pages. **$10.00**

1933 - *A Friend In Need - Facts Worth Knowing About*. Small booklet, 28 pages. **$4.00**

1934 - *Successful Baking*. 2nd edition, Martha Lee Anderson, 32 pages. **$10.00**

▶ 1934 - *It's All in Knowing How - New Uses for Arm & Hammer Baking Soda Introducing Mrs. Anderson*. 2nd edition, 37 pages. **$10.00**

1935 - *Successful Baking For Flavor and Texture*. 3rd edition, Martha Lee Anderson, 32 pages. **$10.00**

1936 - *Successful Baking For Flavor and Texture*. 5th edition, Martha Lee Anderson, 38 pages. **$10.00**

1936 - *Good Things To Eat - Tested Recipes*. 115th edition, 32 pages. **$10.00**

1937 - *Successful Baking For Flavor and Texture*. 6th edition, Martha Lee Anderson, 38 pages. **$10.00**

1937 - *Good Things To Eat - Tested Recipes*. 118th edition, Martha Lee Anderson, 15 pages. **$10.00**

1938 - *Good Things To Eat - My Favorite Chocolate Cakes*. 121st edition, Martha Lee Anderson, 15 pages. **$10.00**

1930's - *A Friend Indeed*. Picture of a nurse, 2⅜"x3¼" folded pamphlet. **$2.50**

1930's - *Arm & Hammer Baking Soda is a Good Dentifrice*. Picture of boy brushing teeth, 3¼"x6" giveaway. **$1.00**

1939 - *Good Things To Eat - My Favorite Hot Breads*. 124th edition, Martha Lee Anderson, 15 pags. **$10.00**

1940 - *Some of My Favorite Good Things to Eat*. 129th edition, Martha Lee Anderson, 15 pages. **$8.00**

1941 - *A Friend Indeed...* Small Booklet, 18 pages. **$3.00**

1942 - *Good Things To Eat - My "Suprise" Recipe*. 131st edition, Martha Lee Anderson featuring Mr. Baking Soda illustrations, 15 pages. **$8.00**

1942 - *Recipes to Stretch Your Sugar Ration*. Features Mr. Baking Soda illustrations, 8-page pamphlet. **$4.00**

1945 - *Arm & Hammer Baking Soda is a Good Household Cleanser*. 6"x3¼" giveaway. **$1.00**

1940's - *Arm & Hammer As a Cooking Aid*. Picture of bowl of green peas, reverse has instructions, 6"x3¼" giveaway. **$1.00**

1940's - *Good Things to Eat*. Reverse side has recipe for baking soda biscuits, 6"x3¼" giveaway, 15 pages. **$1.00**

1948 - *New Fashioned Old Fashioned Recipes*. 2nd edition, Martha Lee Anderson, 15 pages. **$8.00**

1949 - *New Fashioned Old Fashioned Recipes*. 3rd edition, Martha Lee Anderson, 15 pages. **$8.00**

1950 - *New Fashioned Old Fashioned Recipes*. 4th edition. **$6.00**

1951 - *New Fashioned Old Fashioned Recipes*. 5th edition, 19 pages. **$6.00**

1952 - *New Fashioned Old Fashioned Recipes*. 6th edition, Martha Lee Anderson. **$6.00**

1953 - *New Fashioned Old Fashioned Recipes*. 7th edition, Martha Lee Anderson, 19 pages. **$6.00**

1983 - *All-Time Baking Soda Favorites*. Arm & Hammer Division of Church & Dwight Co., Inc. 35 million printed, 14 pages. **NCV**

1985 - *Great Ideas Come Naturally With Arm & Hammer Pure Baking Soda*. Pamphlet. **NCV**

Today, Church & Dwight Co., Inc. also sell Arm & Hammer Washing Soda, Arm & Hammer Borax, Arm & Hammer Laundry Detergent, Arm & Hammer Oven Cleaner, and Arm & Hammer Deodorant for carpets and rooms.

◊ ◊ ◊ ◊

Bird Cards

From their beginning, Church and Company merged love of nature with their business and packed a nature card directly into each box of baking soda. The company has printed literally millions of Bird Cards in at least 20 different series of 10 to 15 and up to 60 cards each. The earliest of these educational card series was published around 1888 and included exotic birds of other continents as well as those of North America. The legend appearing on all of these early Brid Cards was: "For the Good of All, Do Not Destroy the Birds."

At the turn of the century following the merger of the two family companies forming Church & Dwight Co., Inc., fish, bird and dog cards were issued, printed from the works of Bufford, M.E. Eaton, G. Muss Arnolt and Hy Hintermeister, about whom little is known.

In the early 1920's, Charles T. Church, a senior officer of Church & Dwight Co., Inc. and an avid conservationist, commissioned his friend, Louis Agssiz Fuertes (1874-1927) to paint a series of original bird paintings. Fuertes painted about 90 birds for the company. Thirty song birds and 30 game birds were made into a series of Bird Cards and offered for 10¢ a set, each containing 10 cards.

Fuertes also painted 30 Birds of Prey, which are now being made into Bird Cards for the first time. They are considered by many to be among the finest birds that this renowned artist ever painted.

Forerunners of baseball cards, the nature cards or trade cards printed by Church and Dwight for over a century numbered literally in the millions and included flowers, fish and animals as well as birds.

Although Fuertes' series of song birds and game birds were in wide distribution in the early 1900's, his Birds of Prey were never before made into cards, although they were commissioned for that purpose. The paintings remained in the Church & Dwight vault for over 50 years and have retained all their brilliant color.

On the eve of the Bicentennial year of 1976 and the 130th anniversary of the company, Church & Dwight was reintroducing the Arm & Hammer Bird Cards, discontinued since 1966. With this series of 10 Birds of Prey, the Church & Dwight tradition of Bird Cards was revived. Number one in the series is the Bald Eagle, America's national bird, now on the verge of extinction.

The new cards measure 3¾"x2½" and information about each bird is given on the back. The first series of 10 cards, (the rest of the Fuertes Brids of Prey will be available in subsequent series) was available for 35¢ and a box top or proof of purchase from any Arm & Hammer product. Card sets are available by contacting Consumer Services, Church & Dwight Co., Inc., Two Pennsylvania Plaza, New York, NY 10001.

The following is an excerpt from 1924 *Good Things To Eat*, 79th edition, page 30:

"To obtain a full set of thirty pictures in color of the Useful Birds, one of which is always found in each package of Arm & Hammer Baking Soda, it is only necessary to send ten cents in stamps to Church & Dwight Company, 27 Cedar Street, New York, New York. In addition to the set of thirty now being published, we are able to furnish all three previous sets of thirty each at ten cents per set. These four sets make a collection of one hundred and twenty different birds at a cost of only 40 cents, should one desire the four full sets."

The following sets and dates that we know of are based on what trade Bird Cards we have in our collection the value of each is **$2.50.**

1900 - Set of 20; Fish, No. 4 Golden Shiner, No. 20 Red Snapper.

1902 - Set of 30; Dogs, No. 21 Pomeranian.

1908 - Set of 30; Birds, No. 1 Robin Snipe, No. 10 Spoon Bill, No. 19 Gull.

1908 - Set of 30; Birds, No. 4 Black Canada Grouse, No. 27 Passenger Pigeon.

1910 - Set of 30; Dogs, No. 18 Bienheim Spaniel.

1912 - Set of 30; Useful Birds, No. 9 Myrtle Warbler.

1922 - Set of 30; Useful Birds, 2nd series, No. 2 Tufted Titmouse, No. 6 Redstart.

1922 - Set of 30; Userful Birds, 3rd series, No. 1 Dickcissel, No. 25 Bobolink.

1922 - Set of 30; Useful Birds series by Fuertes, No. 5 Red eyed Vireo.

1922 - Set of 30; Birds by Eaton, No. 4 Varied Bunting, No. 14 Phoebe.

1924 - Set of 30; Birds by Fuertes, No. 30 Sharp-tailed Grouse.

1928 - Set of 30; Birds by Fuertes, No. 1 Redstart, No. 12 Song Sparrow.

1929 - Set of 30; Ducks by Fuertes, No. 7 Cinnamon Teal.

1930 - Set of 30 - Beautiful Birds, No. 15 Blue-throated Warbler.

1930's - Set of 60; Beautiful Birds, No. 25 Blue Long Grosbeak, No. 57 Magpie.

1930's - Set of 60; Beautiful Birds, No. 42 Wood Warbler.

1930's - Set of 60; Flowers, No. 49 Geranium.

1930's - Set of 60; Interesting Animals, No. 13 Weasel, No. 44 Zebra.

1940's - Set of 60; Birds, No. 28 Black-headed Gold Finch.

1975 - Set of 10; Birds of Prey, No. 1 Bald Eagle, No. 10 Rough-Legged Hawk.

Chapter 16

Spices And Extracts

Dr. Ward's

Dr. Ward's Medical Company was established in 1856 in Winona, Minnesota. Starting with a small line of goods, Dr. Ward's Medical Company was sold always on the basis of satisfaction guaranteed or no pay. Superior quality and big money value have steadily promoted the growth of the company. Their products included home remedies, baking powder, spices including black pepper, extracts, shaving cream, poultry tonic and hair tonic, and pickling spice.

The following publication is what we were able to collect from this company.

1915 - *Ward's Cook Book.* **$14.00**

◊ ◊ ◊ ◊

Watkins Products

Mr. J.R. Watkins established his business on January 1, 1868 in Winona, Minnesota. He was gratified to find, as the business grew, that his original methods of selling direct to the customer proved to be successful. The salesman would canvas from door to door, or in the country, from farmhouse to farmhouse, and leave a brochure or pamphlet showing and telling about the products and their uses and leave samples. Sales routes were set up all over the country in this way. The salesman in most cases called at predetermined times and in this way he could establish thousands of customers. In most cases, the products sold were collected for on the next visit. This was called "the free trial plan" and the guarantee of satisfaction before payment.

This sales method was called the wagon method. From 1868 until the invention of the motor car the salesman used a horse and wagon. Upon the arrival of the motor car, the salesman used a coupe (single seat) car, removed the rumble seat and inserted a box to hold his products. By the 1930's the motor vehicle manufacturers designed a delivery paneled-type vehicle that was very popular for home delivery.

This plan saved the customer money. Watkins claimed, "This is possible because we do not have to pay the jobber, the wholesaler or the retailer any big profits. We do not have any silk hatted drummers, riding about the country in parlor cars and putting up at the most expensive hotels. We do not spend any extravagant sums in newpaper advertising. We have not purchased any record-breaking horses or built any palaces to live in. On the other hand, we have grown steadily from year to year."

The J.R. Watkins Medical Company published the soft cover *Watkins Almanac, Home Doctor and Cook Book* to advertise and promote their products and home remedies. These incuded baking powder, chocolate, many food products, spices, extracts, toilet articles, soap products, household aids and stock and poultry preparations. Watkins claimed "We have more than 500 personal representatives daily carrying the glad news of the Watkins Way To Good Health to the people of the United States and Canada. We don't believe there is a finer set of agents in the world than the Watkins Representative. Each one of them works in his own territory, calling upon his regular customers at stated intervals.

We are making sixty-three different articles from cough cure to extracts and black pepper. We are proud of our plant and proud of the splendid patronage accorded Watkins Remedies by our half-million customers. Look for our agent and famous horse and delivery wagon on you next scheduled day. From laboratory to consumer, the largest company in the world."

Mr. J.R. Watkins died in 1911. Mr. E.L. King, son-in-law of Mr. Watkins, took over the office of president of The J.R. Watkins Medical Company.

By 1915, approximately four million families were satisfied Watkins customers. They offered 72 different articles and had nearly 3,000 salesmen in their employ.

By 1926 The J.R. Watkins Company reached from ocean to ocean with factories in New York, Chicago, Newark, Columbus, Kansas City, Winona, Memphis, Oakland, Montreal, Hamilton, Winnipeg, and Vancouver.

The following publications are what we were able to research and collect from this company.

▶ 1905 - *Watkins' Almanac Home Doctor and Cook Book.* 95 pages. **$16.00**

▶ 1907 - *Watkins' Almanac Home Doctor and Cook Book.* 96 pages. **$16.00**

1908 - *Watkins Almanac Home Doctor and Cook Book.* 64 pages. **$16.00**

1913 - *Watkins Almanac and Cook Book.* 122 pages. **$14.00**

▶ 1915 - *Watkins Almanac Home Doctor & Cook Book.* 48th year, 96 pages. **$14.00**

1917 - *Watkins Flavoring Extracts.* **$14.00**

1926 - *Watkins Cook Book.* Public Relations Dept., 64 pages. **$12.00**

1936 - *Watkins Cook Book.* Hard cover, spiral, 192 pages. **$20.00**

▶ 1936 - *Watkins Almanac and Home Book 1868-1936.* 46 pages. **$10.00**

1938 - *Watkins Cook Book.* Hard cover, 288 pages. **$20.00**

1945 - *Watkins Cook Book.* Elaine Allen, hard cover, spiral, 288 pages. **$17.50**

1946 - *Watkins Salad Book.* Elaine Allen, hard cover, spiral, 251 pages. **$17.50**

1958 - *Watkins Products - How I Use Spices.* Home shopping service since 1968, 48 pages. **$4.00**

1962 - *Watkins Products - Spices in Fine Foods.* Your Friendly Watkins Dealer, 23 pages. **$4.00**

◊ ◊ ◊ ◊

McConnon's

The McConnon & Company was established in 1889 in Winona, Minnesota. H.J. McConnon was the company's president and J.R. McConnon the vice president. The McConnon line was sold by McConnon dealers or agents by the wagon method, direct to the consumer. They also shipped by parcel post. Their products included extracts, spices, baking powder, cocoa, water softener, toilet articles, family and veterinary medicine.

McConnon states, "Since 1889 that friendly neighbor the McConnon dealer has given convenient home service to hundreds of thousands of families. His high quality products fresh from the modern McConnon Laboraties have effected great savings in time, money and convenience. His friendly home service enables you to choose more accurately the products you need in the quiet comfort and leisure of your home."

The following publications are what we were able to collect from this company.

▶ 1926 - *The Rainbow Road To Health and Happiness.* 64 pages. **$12.00**

▶ 1939 - *Aunt Jane's Cook Book 1889-1939.* 50th anniversary, 48 pages. **$10.00**

◊ ◊ ◊ ◊

Chamberlain's

The Chamberlain Medicine Company was established in Des Moines, Iowa. The company's products included extracts, toilet articles, medicines, and home remedies.

From a 1923 publication: " 'Bonnie Bird Cards' Free to all childern. Send For Them - All children should have a set of these 'Bonnie Bird' cards with their quaint alphabetical rhymes and accurate information of the character, nest and note of each bird. Children love them and they help to while away many a tedious hour. Kindergarten, first grade and Sunday school teachers regard them as useful and valuable."

The publication further states, "Ask for 'Chamberlain's Almanac' and If you send us your name and address we will mail you one now and put your name on our list for future issues."

The following is the only publication we were able to collect from this company.

▶ 1923 - *Quality Helps for Home Makers.* 12 pages. **$12.00**

◊ ◊ ◊ ◊

Rawleigh's

The business of the W.T. Rawleigh Company of Freeport, Illinois was founded in 1889 by W.T. Rawleigh who began retailing a small number of medicines and flavoring extracts to farmers. The business grew steadily in the face of keenest competition with much older, similar businesses, until it passed all its former rivals and became the largest of all such industries in the world. The W.T. Rawleigh Company also sold direct to the customer using the same wagon method as his competitors establishing their routes all over the country. This company had the largest number of employees, manufactured a larger number of products, made the largest sales, and the most modernly equipped factories, owned the most real estate, had the largest capital and resources, and imported more raw materials than all similar industries combined.

Mr. Rawleigh started as a boy without capital. He established his business on sound, practical and correct economic principles. Its growth was unparalled in the history of all such industries.

This industry, which made Rawleigh a household word, had over 800 factory and branch house employees. All Rawleigh agents were in business for themselves.

Rawleigh products include pain medicines, home remedies, extracts, spices, toilet preparations, toilet soaps, baking powder, cocoa, other food products and veterinary and poultry preparations.

The following publications are what we have been able to research and collect from this company.

1916 - *Rawleigh's Stock & Poultry Raisers Guide.* No recipes, 95 pages. **$14.00**

1920 - *Rawleigh's Almanac Good Health Guide Cook Book.* **$12.00**

▸ 1922 - *Rawleigh's Good Health Guide Almanac Cook Book.* 64 pages. **$12.00**

1923 - *Rawleigh's Good Health Guide Almanac Cook Book.* **$12.00**

1928 - *Rawleigh's 40th Anniversary Good Health Guide and Cook Book.* Her First Lesson, 32 pages. **$12.00**

▸ 1929 - *Rawleigh's Good Health Guide and Cook Book.* 32 pages. **$12.00**

▸ 1932 - *Rawleigh's Good Health Guide Cook Book and Year Book.* 36 pages. **$10.00**

1939 - *Rawleigh's 50th Anniverary Good Health Guide Almanac Cook Book.* 32 pages. **$10.00**

1943 - *Rawleigh's Good Health Guide Almanac Cook Book.* 32 pages. **$6.00**

1946 - *Rawleigh's Good Health Guide Almanac Cook Book.* 32 pages. **$6.00**

1948 - *Rawleigh's Good Health Guide Almanac Cook Book.* Our 59th Year, 32 pages. **$6.00**

1950 - *Rawleigh's Good Health Guide Almanac Cook Book.* Our 61st Year, 32 pages. **$4.00**

1954 - *Rawleigh's Good Health Guide Almanac ... Cook Book.* 32 pages. **$4.00**

1956 - *Rawleigh's Good Health Guide Almanac And Cook Book.* 32 pages. **$4.00**

1957 - *Rawleigh's Good Health Guide Almanac And Cook Book.* 32 pages. **$4.00**

◊ ◊ ◊ ◊

Blue Ribbon Malt Extract

The Premier Malt Products was established in 1917 in Decatur, Illinois and within 10 years had four modern factories with its principal office in Peoria Heights, Illinois.

Blue Ribbon Malt Extract was advertised as a valuable addition to the diet, and a delightful means of bringing new taste to everyday cooking. Malt extract had long held an important place in the industrial preparation of food. Old time bakers and chefs knew the advantages of using malt and hops, but their methods entailed considerale work. Blue Ribbon Malt Extract was available in both plain and hop flavors.

The following lists the publications we were able to collect from this company.

▸ 1927 - *Tested Recipes with Blue Ribbon Malt Extract.* 32 pages. **$12.00**

1928 - *Tested Recipes with White Banner Malt Extract.* **$12.00**

◊ ◊ ◊ ◊

Burnett's

The Joseph Burnett Company of Boston, Massachusetts was the manufacturer of Burnett's Flavoring Extracts.

The following publications are what we were able to collect from this company.

1878 - *Household Reciepts.* **$30.00**

1886 - *Household Receipts.* **$24.00**

▸ 1940's - *What's Cookin? A Cook Book for Teen-agers - And Others.* 18 pages. **$8.00**

◊ ◊ ◊ ◊

F.W. McNess

The Furst-McNess Company was established in 1908 in Freeport, Illinois. Mr. F.W. McNess, P.D., Chief Chemist and Secretary had extensive training and brilliant attainments in both chemical and medicinal pharmacy. He held a degree of Doctor of Pharmacy from the Philadelphia College of Pharmacy.

Mr. McNess took full charge of manufacturing and his name was placed on each package. Their goal was to sell only the very best quality products direct to customers through bonded dealers or agents and to sell all remedies and to furnish sample bottles to those who wish a trial. These ideas worked well and helped build a high reputation.

By 1915 the company manufactured 70 products, during the 1920's this product line was expanded to 128 products and by 1930 included 240 products. These products included extracts and flavors, baking powder, cocoa, spices, home remedies, vitamins, toilet articles, insecticides, brushes, brooms, mops and dusters.

The 1933 cookbook contains a picture product endorsement by Hedda Hopper, Hollywood's best-dressed woman and popular hostess; Estelle Taylor, glamorous screen beauty and brilliant Hollywood personality; and Leila Hyams, universal movie star.

The following publications are what we were able to collect form this company.

▸ 1915 - *F.W. McNess' Cook Book and Health Hints.* 63 pages. **$14.00**

1920's - *McNess Cook Book Recipes From "Round the World."* 64 pages. **$12.00**

1930 - *F.W. McNess Cook Book.* 30 pages. **$10.00**

1933 - *F.W. McNess Cook Book.* 63 pages. **$10.00**

1935 - *F.W. McNess Cook Book.* **$10.00**

◊ ◊ ◊ ◊

McCormick

The McCormick & Company, Inc. was established in the 1880's in Baltimore, Maryland. Wiloughby W. McCormick was the firm's founder and president until his death in 1932. The McCormick & Company manufactured spices and extracts under the "Bee Brand" label and "Banquet Brand" trademark. Their raw materials were gathered from the four quarters of the world - they were cleaned and ground in the most scientific manner and packed in such a way that they can be kept with little or no deterioration until used.

In 1938 the McCormick spice packages were redesigned to emphasize "Mc" as a design feature for easy identification of all of the McCormick packages.

The following publications are what we were able to collect from this company.

1929 - *Flavor and Spice And All Things Nice.* 30 pages. **$12.00**

1964 - *Spices of the World Cookbook by McCormick.* Mary Collins in the Kitchens of McCormick, pocket book, 495 pages. **$4.00**

◊ ◊ ◊ ◊

Jewel Tea Company

The Jewel Tea Company Inc. was established in 1899 in Barrington, Illinois. They delivered quality groceries to the consumer's door, plus offered quality premiums and interest on groceries purchased from the Jewel Tea Co., Inc.

Their products included groceries such as tea, coffee, baking powder, Jewel Jell in six flavors, quick oats, extracts and spices, peanut butter, mayonnaise, soaps, cleansers, toilet articles, and many more.

The company has been renamed "J.T.'s General Store" and is still in business today.

The following lists the publications we were able to collect from this company.

1929 - *Healthful Cookery.* Mary Dunbar, 63 pages. **$12.00**

1933 - *Jewel Tea Co., Inc. Mary Dunbar's New Cook Book.* **$10.00**

1936 - *Mary Dunbar's Favorite Recipes.* 80 pages. **$10.00**

1950's - *Jewel Cook Book - Recipes for Good Eating.* **$6.00**

◊ ◊ ◊ ◊

Dr. Price's

Dr. Price's Flavoring Extract Company was established in 1860 in Chicago, Illinois. A quote in a 1904 recipe publication reads, "Dr. Price's Extracts have been in use for nearly a half a century." They acquired world wide popularity due to the care exercised in their manufacture.

Their products included spices, extracts, food colors, ice cream sugar, jelly dessert, onion relish, and were sold in stores on two continents.

In 1915 Dr. Price's Flavoring Extract Company and the Dr. Price's Baking Powder Company were acquired by the Royal Baking Powder Company of New York and produced Royal Baking Powder and Royal Flavoring Extracts.

The Royal Extract, Baking Powder and Gelatin Companies all were a part of the merger plan to the emergence of Standard Brands, Inc. with many different food manufacturers operating as one. Each became a Division of Standard Brands, Inc. The copyright by Standard Brands, Inc. appeared on all publications in 1928. Other food companies were added in future years, to enlarge and diversify the company.

In 1981 Nabisco Company, Inc. performed a leveraged buyout of Standard Brands, Inc. The company was renamed Nabisco, Inc. and Standard Brands was a Division of Nabisco, Inc. as well as Del Monte was a Division.

In 1985 R.J. Reynolds, Inc., a tobacco manufacturer, performed a leveraged buyout of Nabisco, Inc., including the Standard Brands Division and the company renamed itself RJR Nabisco, Inc. with Nabisco, Standard Brands, and Del Monte all Divisions of RJR, Inc.

In 1988 an investment firm of Kohlberg Kravis Roberts & Company performed a hostile leveraged buyout of RJR Nabisco, Inc. Their interest was in acquiring the RJR tobacco portion of the huge conglomerate.

The following is the only publication were able to collect from this company.

1904 - *Dr. Price's Delicious Desserts Containing Practical Recipes.* 34th edition, 48 pages. **$16.00**

◊ ◊ ◊ ◊

Kitchen Bouquet

Kitchen Bouquet, the magic sauce was born in the 1870's. Kitchen Bouquet is a blend of 13 garden vegetables, herbs, and spices. It is famous for making gravy and enriching the color and enhancing the flavor of food. Kitchen Bouquet is manufactured by Grocery Store Products Company of West Chester, Pennyslvania.

The folowing publications are what we were able to collect from this company.

Circa 1910 - *How to Make Your Cooking Different - Kitchen Bouquet.* 6 pages. **$7.00**

1962 - *Cooking With Inspiration - Kitchen Bouquet Outdoors Recipe Book Indoors.* 48 pages. **$3.00**

◊ ◊ ◊ ◊

Sauer's Flavoring Extracts

The C.F. Sauer Co. of Richmond, Virginia made Sauer's Flavoring Extracts. The following publications are what we were able to collect from this company.

Circa 1915 - *50 Recipes For Flavoring by a Famous Chef.* **$12.00**

Circa 1915 - *Choice Flavoring Recipes.* **$12.00**

◊ ◊ ◊ ◊

Durkee's

The E.R. Durkee & Company of New York manufactured spices and extracts including mustard flour, pepper, poultry seasoning, steak sauce, salad dressing and baking powder. The company also manufactured the Gauntlet Brand of goods. At the Chicago World's Fair in 1893, they were awarded medals of superiority. Other items manufactured included powdered herb, pastry spice, mincemeat spice and pickle spice. They also manufactured food products such as farina, cornstarch, rice flour, flake tapioca, pearl tapioca, granulated or farina tapioca, pearl sago and pearl barley. The manufactured Challange Table Sauce and a mixed bird seed and a full line of oils, essences and family medicines.

We were able to collect the following publication from this company.

▶ 1907 - *Salads - How To Make And Dress Them.* Compliments of E.R. Durkee & Company, New York, 32 pages. **$16.00**

◊ ◊ ◊ ◊

Golden Rule Extracts

The Citizen's Wholesale Supply Company of Columbus, Ohio manufactured the Golden Rule Brand of Flavorings and other food products. The company won the Gold Medal at the Panama-Pacific International Exposition in San Francisco in 1915 for their flavorings.

The following lists what we have been able to collect from this company.

1918 - *Golden Rule Cook Book.* Mrs. Ida Cogswell Bailey Allen. **$14.00**

▶ 1920's - *Golden Rule Foods ... The Golden Rule Way.* Ida Bailey Allen, The Citizen's Wholesale Supply Co., Columbus, Ohio, 122 pages. **$12.00**

1921 - *The Golden Rule Cook Book - Menus For Every Day, Suggestions for Entertaining.* Seventh edition, Mrs. Ida Cogswell Bailey Allen, editor and lecturer, founder of Mrs. Allen's School of Cooking, over 200 tested recipes. **$12.00**

◊ ◊ ◊ ◊

Colman and French's Mustard

J. & J. Colman Ltd. manufactured Colman's Dry Mustard in London, England. The company was established in 1855. Colman's Mustard won unrivaled honors for British Mustard at International Exhibitions, London 1862, Moscow 1872, Paris 1878, Melbourne 1888, Grand Prix Paris 1900, and Grand Prix Paris 1908.

J. & J. Colman registered the Bull's Head trademark in the United States in 1886 and in the late 1800's located a distribution center in New York, New York.

By 1948, Colman's was made in the U.S.A. under license from Beckitt A. Colman Ltd., London, England, and distributed by R.T. French Company, Sales Corporation, Worchester, New York. Colman's Dry Mustard appeared in a recipe publication by the R.T. French Company, manufacturers of French's Prepared Mustared and other products.

Robert T. French founded a spice company in 1880, first in New York, New York, then in Fairpoint, New York, and finally in Rochester, New York. French's Mustard was born in 1904. Hot Dan the Mustard Man was born in 1935 for advertising purposes.

We were able to collect the following publications from this company.

1910 - *Made Dishes - Salads and Savories with French's Cream Salad Mustard.* 10th edition, package insert. **$8.00**

1910 - *Made Dishes - Salads and Savories with French's Cream Salad Mustard.* 12th edition, package insert. **$8.00**

Circa 1915 - *Recipe Book - Colman's Mustard Sharpens Appetite, Aids Digestion.* 23 pages. **$14.00**

1948 - *Dining Delights by Carol French.* The R.T. French Co., 30 pages. **$8.00**

1959 - *12 New Recipes With Colman's Mustard.* Atlantis Sales Corporation, 3166 Mustard Street, Rochester, NY. Contained in this publication: "If you would like to have this handy Recipe File Outfit consisting of an attractively colored heavy cardboard box and a set of recipe Index Cards for convenient filing. Send fifteen cents for this recipe file outfit. **$6.00**

◊ ◊ ◊ ◊

Frank Tea and Spice Company

The Frank Tea & Spice Company of Cincinnati, Ohio, manufactured the Mister Mustard Brand Dijon Prepared Mustard, America's Finest. The company also manufactured Frank's Jumbo Peanut Butter, Apple Butter, Red Hot Sauce, Dove Brand Olives, spices, extracts, and food colors. Betty K. Masters was director of the Home Economics Department.

We were able to find the following publication on this company.

1950's - *Introducing Mister Mustard Brand Dijon Style Prepared Mustard, America's Finest.* 20-page booklet. **$6.00**

◊ ◊ ◊ ◊

Gulden's

As far back as 1862 Gulden's Mustard was in constant demand for hot meats, cold cuts, and sandwich fillings. The secret blend of mustard seeds, mellow vinegar and rare spices makes Gulden's ideal as a seasoning in cooking, popular as a table mustard and delicious as a dip.

We have found the following publication from this company.

1950's - *Bouquets for the Cook.* 6-page pamphlet. **$2.00**

◊ ◊ ◊ ◊

Baker Extract Company

In the mid 1880's the Baker Extract Company manufactured flavoring extracts with laboratories in Springfield, Massachusetts and Portland, Maine. The company had a coupon system for introducing their extracts. The object in attaching the coupon to the product was to interest the customer in the flavoring extract that the company produced and get the customer to insist that her dealer stock them. The coupons purchased premiums such as, six coupons could be redeemed for a package of ginger, a box of fine face powder or a packaged game. Twelve coupons bought you a 50¢ bottle of Pola Lily, a package of fine hand cream, a set of measuring spoons, a package of fine sachet powder or one spool, 500 yards, of Warrens Best Quality Sewing Cotton.

The following lists what we were able to collect from this company.

▸ 1890's - *Baker's Pure Fruit Flavoring Extracts - Receipts For Cakes, Creams, Custards, Candies, Etc.* 24 pages. **$20.00**

1920's - *Some New Selected Recipes.* **$12.00**

◊ ◊ ◊ ◊

Herbs And Spices

The Home of the Indiana Botanic Gardens was founded in 1910 by Joseph E. Meyer and is located on the Little Calumet River on the south edge of Hammond, Indiana. A portion of the wild gardens consists of virgin soil and primeval growth inhabited by pheasants and many types of wild birds. For ages the Little Calumet has flooded much of the grounds making the soil one of the richest in the United States. Four feet below the present soil level, ancient Indian relics were found embedded in cement-like clay.

The first edition of the Herbalist was published in 1918. The first edition of the Herbalist Almanac was published in 1925, and gave weather forecasts along with health problems and herbal product information. Also included were spice cookie flavors including baking with exotic cardamon, how to make vanilla sugar, dandelion cookery, some 300-year-old recipes, pickle making, and many more recipes.

Herbals or botanicals have been used since the beginning of recorded history for their medicinal properties. Many people use roots and herbs because their knowledge and familiarity of them was carried down from generation to generation. Thousands of people use the more popular herbs and roots for their present day recognized action such as herbal laxatives, carminatives, mild diuretic influence, stomachic to increase the appetite, for example.

We have been able to collect the following on herbs and spices.

1944 - *A Practical Primer of Herbs for the American Kitchen.* Twin Trees Gardens, Inc., New York. **$5.00**

1950 - Spice Island Co. Herb Spice Vinegar. **$6.00**

1950 - *The Art of Cooking With Herbs and Spices.* Milo Miloradoirch. **$6.00**

1963, 1970 - *Cooking with Herbs and Spices.* Craig Claiborne, illus. by Alice Golden, Pocket Book, 355 pages. **NCV**

1973 - *The Herbalist Almanac.* Meyer Trade Mark, 64 pages. **NCV**

1969, 1973, 1975 - *The Book of Spices From Schilling.* Frederic Rosengarten, Jr., free with purchase of any three bottles of Schilling Gourmet Spices, Pocket Book, 480 pages. **NCV**

1977 - *The Herbalist Almanac.* David C. Meyer, info, recipes. **NCV**

◊ ◊ ◊ ◊

Chapter 17

Yeast

Fleischmann's Yeast

Charles Fleischmann and his brother Maximilian came to the United States from Austria bringing samples of the yeast used in making Viennese bread. The brothers demonstrated the effectiveness of their yeast and proposed some ideas for selling it to James M. Gaff, a well-known Cincinnati distiller and the three went into business as Gaff, Fleischmann & Company. In 1868 the company began making yeast in compressed cakes of uniform size. It was a milestone in the history of American baked goods. From that day on, the guesswork was virtually removed from baking.

The company name was changed to The Fleischmann Company after the death of James Gaff which occurred sometime between 1902 and 1910.

We have a Trade Card, copyrighted 1896, 1900 January 1st, showing a bouquet of roses on the front and on the back was advertising for Fleischmann & Co. compressed yeast cakes. It read: "Notice - Until further notice we will give in return for each lot of 50 of our Yellow Labels taken from the cakes of our Compressed Yeast by the Consumer and sent by him or her to us at 701 Washington St., N.Y. City, accompanied by a two cent postage stamp. Either, at the option of the sender, a Handsome Banner Picture, or a copy or our book 'Choice Recipes', which contains tested and approved recipes for making Bread, Cakes, etc., of various kinds. Please write plainly and state whether you want a Picture or a Book."

Fleischmann Company was part of a group of companies who had agreed to merge in 1929 to form Standard Brands, Inc. In 1929 the copyright appeared by Standard Brands, Inc. Since the 1981 leveraged buyout by Nabisco Company, Inc. the company was renamed Nabisco Brands, Inc. In 1985 R.J. Reynolds, Inc., a tobacco manufacturer performed a leveraged buyout of Nabisco, Inc., and the company renamed itself RJR Nabisco, Inc. In 1988 an investment firm of Kohlberg Kravis Roberts & Company performed a leveraged buyout of RJR Nabisco, Inc.

The following lists the publications that we were able to collect from this company.

1893 - *Choice Recipes.* Fleischmann & Co., leatherette cover, 47 pages. **$30.00**

1902 - *Choice Recipes.* 57 pages. **$16.00**

1907, 1908 - *The Teddy Bears Baking School.* Promoted with recipes and rhymes. **$25.00**

1910 - *Excellent Recipes for Baking with Fleischmann's Yeast.* **$16.00**

1913 - *Good Things to Eat Made with Bread.* Marion H. Neil. **$14.00**

1916 - *Excellent Recipes for Baking Raised Breads.* 47 pages. **$14.00**

1917 - *Fleischmann's Recipes for Baking Raised Breads.* 47 pages. **$14.00**

1917 - *Fleischmann's Compressed Yeast and Good Health.* **$14.00**

1919 - *Sixty Five Delicious Dishes Made with Bread.* Marion Harris Neil, author of several cookbooks. **$14.00**

1920 - *Fleischmann's Recipes for Baking Raised Breads.* 48 pages. **$12.00**

1921 - *The New Importance of Yeast in Diet.* **$12.00**

1922 - *Excellent Recipes For Baking with Fleischmann's Yeast.* 48 pages. **$12.00**

1924 - *Fleischmann's Recipes For Baking with Fleischmann's Yeast.* 48 pages. **$12.00**

1928 - *Recipes for Delicious Varieties of Breads - Delightful Breads and Buns and Coffee Cakes.* **$12.00**

1928 - *Delightful Breads and Buns and Coffee Cakes.* **$12.00**

1920's - *Diamalt Recipes.* Second edition, Fleischmann's Yeast, 26 pages. **$12.00**

1920's - *Delicious Recipes.* Cover shows a gathering of people in evening clothes. **$12.00**

1941 - *Giving Your Meals the Touch Of Individuality with Delicious Yeast Raised Breads*. Standard Brands, Inc., 39 pages. **$8.00**

1942 - *The Bread Basket*. Fleischmann's Yeast, 40 pages. **$8.00**

▶ 1961 - *Bake It Easy! Fleischmann's Yeast - 17 Recipes that Grandmother Couldn't Bake*. 9-page booklet. **$3.00**

1962 - *The Fleischmann Treasury of Yeast Baking*. 51 pages. **$3.00**

1962 - *Versatile Sweet Doughs - The Fleischmann Treasury of Yeast Baking*. 9-page booklet. **$3.00**

1963 - *Yeast Baking & You*. Fleischmann's Yeast & Gold Medal Flour, General Mills, Inc., & Standard Brands, Inc., 20 pages. **$3.00**

▶ 1967 - *The Young Cook's Bake-A-Bun Book*. 5-page booklet. **$3.00**

1972 - *Fleischmann's Bake-it-easy Yeast Book*. 62 pages. **NCV**

◊ ◊ ◊ ◊

Yeast Foam and Magic Foam

The Northwestern Yeast Company of Chicago manufactured Yeast Foam and Magic Foam. The scientific name of yeast is Sacchar Omyces Cerevisiae. Yeast is not made, it grows. The dry yeast plants, as found in Yeast Foam or Magic Foam, are in a "resting" state. When food and moisture are supplied, and the right amount of warmth, these plants multiply very well. Yeast has four times as much vitamins as any other known foods.

The following publications are what we were able to collect and research from this company.

1890 - *Good Bread - How To Make It*. Mrs. Nellie Duling Gans, principal of the Chicago Cooking College. **$20.00**

1890's - *Good Bread - How To Make It*. Recipes furnished by Mrs. Nellie Duling Gans, principal of the Chicago Cooking College, 28 pages. **$20.00**

Circa 1915 - *Bake Day Suggestions*. Northwestern Yeast Co., Magic Yeast, 8-sided fold out. **$14.00**

Circa 1915 - *Yeast Foam Recipes*. Colorful cover of girl in pink hat holding bread and yeast foam. **$14.00**

1921 - *Dry Yeast As An Aid To Health*. 3"x4¾" blue pamphlet, 12 pages. **$2.50**

1921 - *Dry Yeast As An Aid To Health*. 3¾"x6" black and gray pamphlet, 12 pages. **$2.50**

1923 - *Dry Yeast As An Aid To Health*. 12-page pamphlet. **$2.50**

▶ 1920's - *The Art of Baking Bread*. 20 pages. **$12.00**

1930's - *The Art of Making Bread*. 25 pages. **$10.00**

1930's - *A Book of Tested Recipes - The Art of Making Bread at Home*. 28 pages. **$10.00**

◊ ◊ ◊ ◊

Maca Yeast

The Northwestern Yeast Company of Chicago also manufactured Maca Yeast that did not need refrigeration. Advertised as "the new fast dry yeast," and "one of the most important developments in home baking in many years."

The following are the publications on Maca Yeast that we were able to collect.

▶ 1939 - *The Art of Making Bread at Home*. World's Fair edition, Fair buildings on cover, 20 pages. **$20.00**

1939 - *Oven Melodies - Recipes Using Maca, The New Fast Dry Yeast*. New York World's Fair, see the Maca Exhibit in the Food Building, 17 pages. **$10.00**

◊ ◊ ◊ ◊

Red Star

The Universal Foods Corporation of Milwaukee, Wisconsin manufactured Red Star Dry Yeast.

We were able to collect the following publication from this company.

1974 - *New and Easy Yeast Recipes - Breads, Cakes, Pancakes, Pizza and More*. 23 pages. **NCV**

◊ ◊ ◊ ◊

Chapter 18

Shortening

Cottolene

The business of N.K. Fairbank & Co. of Chicago, Illinois operated as one of the departments of the American Cotton Oil Company. N.K. Fairbank & Co. are the originators of Cottolene, the sale of which extended over all the United States and by export to foreign countries.

Cottolene is a hygenic vegetable cooking fat - a clean, pure preparation of refined and clairified cottonseed oil and beef suet. Cakes shortened with Cottolene were awarded the grand prize at the Louisiana Purchase Exposition of St. Louis, Missouri in 1904.

The N.K. Fairbank Co. also manufactured "Fairy" Soaps, "Coco Bath," "Calirette," "Santa Claus," and other soaps and Gold Dust Washing Powder.

The following are the cookbooks we were able to collect from this company.

▶ 1892 - *600 Selected Recipes.* By Miss Juliet Corson, Mrs. F.L. Gillette, Marion Harland, Mrs. D.A. Lincoln, Mrs. Francis F. Owens, Miss Maria Parloa, Mrs. Eliza R. Parker, Mrs. S.T. Rorer, and Miss Margaret Wister, 131 pages. **$24.00**

1896 - *Cottolene - What It Is and How To Use It.* Compliments of the N.K. Fairbank Company, Chicago, St. Louis, Montreal, New York, Boston, and Philadelphia, 16 pages. **$24.00**

1898 - *Home Helps.* Mrs. Sarah Tyson Rorer. **$24.00**

1900 - *Home Helps, Recipes.* Mrs. Sarah Tyson Rorer, 74 pages. **$20.00**

▶ 1907 - *Pure Food Cook Book.* Cottolene, 80 pages. **$20.00**

▶ 1910 - *Home Helps - A Pure Food Cook Book.* By Five Leading Culinary Experts. Mrs. Mary J. Lincoln, Lida Ames Willis, Mrs. Sarah Tyson Rorer, Mrs. Helen Armstrong, Marion Harland, 80 pages. **$20.00**

◊ ◊ ◊ ◊

Crisco, Fluffo

The Proctor & Gamble Company was established in 1837 in Cincinnati, Ohio. In 1908 a scientific process was discovered by Proctor & Gamble Company which made it possible to change and improve vegetable oils. For three years they experimented with this new product, In 1911 the experimental product was named Crisco and placed upon the market. Today this product comes in sanitary tins. The "Crisco Process" alone can produce this creamy white fat.

By 1956 Proctor & Gamble had introduced the Golden Fluffo Shortening, their new golden-yellow shortening. By 1963 the Crisco label was redesigned and the blue field of stars was no longer used.

The following cookbooks and recipe books are those we were able to research and collect from this company.

1912 - *The Story of Crisco.* First edition, Marion Harris Neil, hard cover, 231 pages. **$30.00**

1912 - *Crisco For Frying, For Shortening, For Cake Mixing.* Soft cover, 32 pages. **$14.00**

1913, 1914 - *The Story of Crisco.* Third edition, Marion Harris Neil, hard cover, 231 pages. **$15.00**

1913, 1914, 1915, 1916, 1917, 1919, 1920, 1921 - *A Calendar of Dinners - The Story of Crisco.* 17th edition, Marion Harris Neil, hard cover, 231 pages. **$10.00**

1916 - *Balanced Daily Diet.* Janet McKenzie Hill, soft cover, 96 pages. **$14.00**

1916 - *The Whys of Cooking.* Janet McKenzie Hill, 86 pages. **$14.00**

1921 - *200 Tested Recipes.* Olive S. Allen, soft cover, 80 pages. **$12.00**

1922 - *The Whys of Cooking.* Janet McKenzie Hill, soft cover, 86 pages. **$12.00**

1923 - *A Calendar of Dinners with 615 Recipes.* Hard cover, 231 pages. **$12.00**

1924 - *Mrs. Neil's Cooking Secrets.* Marion Harris Neil, soft cover, 128 pages. **$12.00**

1925 - *199 Selected Recipes.* Sarah Field Splint, soft cover, 64 pages. **$12.00**

1927 - *A Manual Of Cookery.* Hard cover. **$25.00**

1927 - *The Art of Cookery and Serving.* Sarah Field Splint, Food Editor of *McCall's* magazine, cloth bound, 252 pages. **$25.00**

1928 - *New Cooking Suggestions.* Sarah Field Splint, soft cover, 15 pages. **$12.00**

1931 - *New Recipes - Every Day Dishes That Are New, Simple and Different.* Sarah Field Splint, soft cover, 18 pages. **$10.00**

1932 - *Good Things To Eat From Out Of The Air - 136 Tested Recipes.* Winifred S. Carter, 71 pages. **$10.00**

1934 - *French Frying.* Winifred S. Carter, the Home Economics Dept., soft cover, 48 pages. **$10.00**

1937 - *Cooking Hints and Tested Recipes From Winifred S. Carter.* Soft cover, 32 pages. **$10.00**

1937 - *The Art of Cooking and Serving with 549 Tested Recipes.* Soft cover, bound, 252 pages. **$10.00**

1945 - *Crisco for Successful Results.* Soft cover, 64 pages. **$6.00**

1949 - *New Recipes for Good Eating.* Ann Seranne and Eileen Gaden, consultants in food and fashions, soft cover, 112 pages. **$6.00**

1956 - *Creative Cooking Made Easy - The Golden Fluffo Cook Book.* Home Economics Dept., spiral bound, 108 pages. **$6.00**

1959 - *Praise For The Cook.* Crisco, spiral bound, 120 pages. **$6.00**

1963 - *Better Baking.* Prepared by Home Economics Dept., Crisco, soft cover, 16 pages. **$3.00**

1982 - *Crisco Cooking - Over 350 Easy-To-Follow Recipes.* Hard cover, 191 pages. **NCV**

◊◊◊◊

Spry

The Lever Brothers Company of Cambridge, Massachussetts was established in 1895. In 1935 the Lever Brothers Company began manufacturing Spry shortening packaged in 1 lb., 3 lb., and 6 lb cans with a green and yellow label. During World War II, with a shortage of metals, the product was packaged in jars with the green and yellow label. In 1949 the blue and white checked label was introduced. In 1955 on their 20th anniversary, the label was changed to a red and white with two gold stripes. By 1952 the Lever Brothers Company, Spry Division was located in New York, New York.

In 1942 Spry introduced Aunt Jenny as their spokeswoman. The Spry kitchen opened in 1949 and was a proving ground for Spry's all-purpose use in cookery.

The following lists the cookbooks and recipe booklets that we have researched and collected from this company.

1930's - *What Shall I Cook Today?* 48 pages. **$5.00**

1942 - *Good Cooking Made Easy - Spry The Flavor Saver.* 40 pages. **$6.00**

1943 - *Aunt Jenny's Favorite Recipes.* 49 pages. **$6.00**

1945 - *10 Luscious New Cakes Made by Spry's Amazing New One-Bowl Method.* 6 pages. **$6.00**

1949 - *Enjoy Good Eating Every Day The Easy Spry Way.* Aunt Jenny, 48 pages. **$6.00**

▶ 1952 - *Aunt Jenny's 12 Pies Husbands Like Best.* 20 pages. **$5.00**

1952 - *10 Cakes Husbands Like Best From Spry's Recipe Round-up.* **$5.00**

1952 - *Aunt Jenny's Old-Fashioned Christmas Cookies and Other All-Time Favorites.* 21 pages. **$5.00**

▶ 1953 - *Home Baking Made Easy For Beginners and Experts.* 25 pages. **$5.00**

▶ 1955 - *Spry 20th Anniversary Cookbook of Old and New Favorites.* 25 pages. **$7.00**

◊◊◊◊

Swift'ning

The Swift & Company was established in 1855 in Chicago, Illinois. In the 1930's they began to manufacture a shortening that was trademarked "Swift'ning." The company spokesperson and Home Economist was Martha Logan.

We were able to collect the following cookbooks and recipe booklets from this company.

1940's - *Fascinating Foods with Swift'ning.* **$6.00**

1950 - *77 Recipes Using Swift'ning Make-Your-Own-Mix.* 32 pages. **$5.00**

1953 - *"It's Picture Easy" to Bake and Fry with Swift'ning Shortening.* 36 pages. **$5.00**

1955 - *It's So Good to Bake and Fry with Swift'ning Says Martha Logan, Home Economist.* 20 pages. **$5.00**

1962 - *Party Recipe Ideas.* Martha Logan. **$3.00**

1962 - *Party Plans for Food & Games.* Martha Logan. **$3.00**

◊ ◊ ◊ ◊

Snowdrift

The Southern Cotton Oil Trading Company with its general office in New York City and branches in Savannah, New Orleans, and Chicago manufactured Snowdrift.

The following publication is what we have been able to collect from this company.

1913 - *Snowdrift Secrets.* Sarah Tyson Rorer. **$14.00**

◊ ◊ ◊ ◊

Prido

Prido was an all-purpose shortening, a product of John Morrell & Company with general offices in Ottumwa, Iowa. The company's recipes were tested, tasted and approved by the Good Housekeeping Institute.

We were able to the collect the following publication from this company.

1940's - *Prido Verified Thrift Recipes.* 22 pages. **$6.00**

◊ ◊ ◊ ◊

Mazola Oil

The Corn Products Refining Company was located in New York, New York. This company manufactured Mazola Oil which is a pure, refined vegetable oil, for salad dressings and cooking. The name "Mazola" is formed from "maize," the Indian name for corn. The Indian maiden was created in 1913 to enchance their product package and advertising.

The Corn Products Refining Company also manufactured Karo Syrup both in the red and blue tins and Kingsford Cornstarch. In the 1920's Linit Starch was added to the product line. By 1950 Jane Ashly became the company spokesperson and Home Economist.

In the early 1960's Best Foods, Inc. merged with The Corn Products Refining Co. and it became a Division of Best Foods, Inc. At a later date following some other acquisitions the company was changed to Best Foods, CPC International, Inc. with general offices in Englewood Cliffs, New Jersey.

We were able to collect the following cookbooks and recipe booklets from this company.

▶ 1915 - *Mazola Recipes - Introducing the Pure Oil from Corn for Salads, Deep Frying and Shortening with Recipes.* Mrs. Lincoln, Mrs. Scott and Mrs. Wood, 24 pages. **$14.00**

1927 - *The Modern Method of Preparing Delightful Foods.* Ida Bailey Allen, hard cover, 109 pages. **$12.00**

1920's - *Delightful Cooking with the Three Great Products from Corn - Mazola Oil, Karo Syrup, Kingsford Cornstarch.* Endorsement by Oscar of the Waldorf-Astoria Hotel. **$14.00**

1929 - *The Modern Method of Preparing Delightful Foods.* Seventh edition, Ida Bailey Allen. **$12.00**

1938 - *The Mazola Salad Bowl.* The cover pictures a wooden salad bowl, 31 pages. **$10.00**

1950's - *Recipes For Your Good Health.* Six-page pamphlet. **$2.00**

1956 - *Fancy Cookies, Festive Candies - Delicious Goodies For Giving.* 16 pages. **$2.00**

1967 - *Home Baked Favorites.* Eight-page fold-out. **$1.00**

1980 - *The Fitness Connection.* Mazola Oil is a Reg. Trademark of CPC Best Foods, a unit of CPC International Inc. **NCV**

◊ ◊ ◊ ◊

Amaizo Oil

The American Maize Products Company of New York and Chicago manufactured Amaizo Oil, a wholly vegetable oil.

We were able to find the following cookbooks from this company.

1920's - *Amaizo Cook Book of Tested Recipes.* **$12.00**

▶ 1923 - *Better Foods with This Pure Oil - Amaizo Oil, Best for Salads and Cooking.* 29 pages. **$12.00**

1923 - *Amaizo "Kiddie Kookies" for Growing Children.* Pamphlet. **$12.00**

◊ ◊ ◊ ◊

Wesson Oil

The Southern Cotton Oil Trading Company with general offices in New York City and branches in Savannah, New Orleans, and Chicago manufactured Wesson Oil for salads and cooking. In 1988 an investment firm of Kohlberg Kravis Roberts & Co. performed a leveraged buyout of Beatrice/Hunt-Wesson, Inc. Today Wesson Oil is produced by Beatrice, Hunt, Wesson, Inc. in Fullerton, CA.

The following cookbooks and recipe bookets are what we were able to collect and research from this company.

▶ 1911 - *Recipes - Wesson Oil.* 54 pages. **$16.00**

1920's - *The Wesson Oil Salad Book.* 12 pages. **$12.00**

1925 - *Salad Dressings.* The Wesson Oil & Snowdirft People, 27 pages. **$12.00**

1930 - *Everyday Recipes.* The Wesson Oil People, 29 pages. **$10.00**

1932 - *Everyday Recipes - "Let's Enjoy Eating."* **$10.00**

1930's - Eight-sided folder shaped like a lady. **$6.00**

1950's - *Cooking Made Easy with Liquid Shortening - Wesson Oil.* **$4.00**

1961 - *The Cookbook of Glorious Eating for Weight Watchers.* **$3.00**

◊◊◊◊

Planter's Peanut Oil

The Planters Edible Oil Company of Suffolk, Virginia, Wilkes Barre, Pennsylvania, and San Francisco, California manufactured Planters Hi-Hat Peanut Oil. At some point after 1955, Standard Brands made a leveraged buyout of Planters Edible Oil Company and became part of Standard Brands, Inc. In 1981 Nabisco, Inc. made a leveraged buyout of Standard Brands, Inc. and the resulting company became known as Nabisco Brands, Inc. Then in 1985, The R.J. Reynolds Tobacco Company made a leveraged buyout of Nabisco Brands, Inc. and the company became R.J.R. Nabisco, Inc. In 1988 an investment firm of Kohlberg Kravis Roberts & Company performed a hostile leveraged buyout of R.J.R. Nabisco, Inc. including the Nabisco, Standard Brands and the Del Monte Divisions.

We were able to collect the following cookbooks and recipe booklets from this company.

1948 - *Cooking The Modern Way - 129 Ways to Better Meals, Home Tested and Proved.* 40 pages. **$6.00**

▶ 1955 - *They Taste So-o-o Good! Recipes, Ideas, Hints.* 48 pages. **$4.00**

◊◊◊◊

Kraft Oil

The Kraft Foods Company manufactured Kraft All-Purpose Oil. In 1986 Kraft Foods Company, Kraft, Inc. purchased The Craig Food Disturbuting Company of Salem, Missouri to extend their food outlets in the wholesale field to restaurants, colleges and food service companies. In 1988 The Philip Morris, General Foods made a leveraged buyout of The Kraft Foods Company.

We were able to collect the following publication from this company.

1955 - *20 Wonderful Cakes Made By The New Kraft Oil Method.* 20 pages. **$4.00**

◊◊◊◊

Staley's Salad and Cooking Oil

The Staley Sales Corporation of Decatur, Illinois manufactured Staley's Salad and Cooking Oil as well these other products: Honey Flavored Corn and Refiners Syrup, Maple Falvored Syrup, Crystal White Syrup, Soregum Flavored Syrup and Golden Table Syrup.

The following lists the cookbooks and recipes booklets we were able to collect from this company.

1928 - *Staley's Approved Recipes.* 30 pages. **$12.00**

▶ 1935 - *Children's Party Book.* Staley, 23 pages. **$10.00**

◊◊◊◊

Jelke Good Luck Oleomargarine

The John F. Jelke Company of Chicago, Illinois with branches in New York City, Philadelphia, Pittsburgh and Cleveland manufactured "Good Luck" Oleomargarine and "Good Luck" Mayonnaise and by 1931 the manufactured "Good Luck" Evaporated Milk.

Margarine was a French dicovery and takes its name form Mons. Megre Mouries, the originator. It was the result of the desire to find wholesome food at a low cost during the Franco-Prussian war, and patriotism, as well as hope of securing the reward offered, led to exhaustive research by eminent French scientists. Finally it was discovered that the fat of cattle could be churned directly into a pure and wholesome food. Margarine was the result of these experiments.

The John F. Jelke company was one of the first to churn margarine in the United States. To be certain of having a sufficient supply of cream of the highest quality, the John F. Jelke Company had established its own milk stations in the famous Fox River Valley, the supply coming from the noted dairy farms in that region. These modern establishments produced milk exclusively for the John F. Jelke Company.

Oleo oil is the second principal ingredient used in Good Luck Margarine, and is the oil obtained from the fat of prime beef cattle. To obtain this oil, carefully selected portions are first chilled to remove all animal heat, the fibres are then broken by cutting knives, heated and the pure oil is pressed out.

Neutral is another necessary ingredient made from selected leaf and, as its name implies, is neutral in flavor and taste.

After the proper preparation these materials are carefully weighed out in exact proportions and then churned. From the churns the margarine is conveyed into tanks of ice chilled, pure distilled water which chills it instantly and gives a fine grain and texture. The surplus moisture is worked out, and the proper amount of salt is added. It is then molded into prints or rolls of the desired size or packed solid in tubs or boxes. The rolls and prints are placed in coolers to chill properly, and from the cooler they are conveyed to wrapping machines, wrapped and then placed in cartons.

By 1931 Good Luck Oleomargarine had an appetizing appearance as it was, but the housewives who wished to color it used the capsule of artificial color furnished with each pound.

The following cookbooks and recipe books are those we have been able to research and collect from this company.

▶ 1916 - *Good Luck Recipes.* Mrs. Ida C. Baily Allen, 64 pages. **$14.00**

1931 - *Good Luck Color Scheme Parties.* Home Service Dept., 32 pages. **$10.00**

1933 - *Good Luck in Your Cooking and Baking.* Home Service Dept., 31 pages. **$10.00**

1933 - *Jelke Good Luck Oleomargarine Quick Breads.* **$10.00**

1936 - *Jelke's Good Luck Recipes.* **$10.00**

◊ ◊ ◊ ◊

Nucoa Nut Margarine

The Best Foods, Inc. of New York, New York was established in 1925 and manufactured one product, Nucoa Nut Margarine. Nucoa is made of refined vegetable oils, pasteurized skim milk, salt and added Vitamin A.

During the late 1920's Martha Adams was the spokesperson and Home Economist for the company the customers could write to her at the Best Foods Home Economics Service for Best Foods Free Library consisting of: *Scientific Meal Planning Chart, The Salad Bowl, A Margarine Monograph,* and *Old and New Ideas of Diet.*

During 1930 and 1931 there appears to have been some mergers and company buyouts to expand and diversify the Best Foods, Inc. In a brief five years, the Best Foods family had grown from one product to eight fine food delicacies which women the country over were using in ever increasing quantities. These eight food products were made in plants strategically located to insure freshness in all parts of the country at all times. They were: Nucoa Nut Margarine, Gold Medal Salad Dressing, Best Foods Relish Spread, Best Foods Fanning's Bread and Butter Pickles, Best Foods Mayonnaise, Best Foods Pickle Relish, Best Foods Thousand Island Dressing, and Best Foods Peanut Spread.

By 1931 their product line included more than 20 products including the following: Hellmann's-Best Foods Mayonnaise, Presto Cake Flour, Cereals, H-O Oats, H-O Cream Farina, Fanning's Bread and Butter Pickles, Variated Dressings, Best Foods Mustard with Horseradish, Hellmann's-Best Foods Sandwich Spread, French Dressing, Thousand Island Dressing, Hellmann's Food Tartar Sauce, Shoe Polish, All Purpose Rit Dye, Instant Rit Color Remover, and Rit Easter Egg Colors.

Following a merger and a purchase the company is now named Best Foods, CPC International, Inc.

The following lists the cookbooks and recipe booklets we were able to collect from this company.

▶ 1930 - *Three Meals A Day With Nucoa.* Nucoa Home Economics Service Dept., 32 pages. **$10.00**

▶ 1931 - *My Special Date Bake Book.* Write Your Name in tis Panel, 10 pages. **$10.00**

1939 - *Cakes and Cookies with Personality - Exciting New Recipes for Cakes, Cookies & Frosting.* **$10.00**

◊ ◊ ◊ ◊

Keyko Margarine

The general offices of Shedd-Bartusch Foods Inc. were located in Detroit, Michigan with plants in Detroit, Michigan; Lousiville, Kentucky; Elgin, Illinois; Greenville, South Carolina; and Dallas, Texas. This company manufactured Keyko Margarine as well as other products. They were: Shedd's Old Style Dressing, Shedd's Lady Betty Salad Dressing, Shedd's Lady Betty Tartar Sauce, Lady Betty Cucumber Wafers, Shedd's Peanut Butter, Shedd's Lady Betty Sandwich Spread, Shedd's Lady Betty Thousand Island Dressing, Lady Betty Prune Juice, Shedd's Ezy French Dressing, Shedd's Lady Betty Mayonnaise.

The following is the only publication we were able to collect from this company.

1951 - *Spread, Bake, Fry, Season, Cook with Keyko Margarine.* Folder. **$6.00**

◊ ◊ ◊ ◊

Blue Bonnet Margarine

Standard Brands, Inc. is the maker of Blue Bonnet Margarine with general offices in New York, New York. This product was introduced in the late 1950's.

The product we know as margarine dates back to the 1860's at the time of the Franco-Prussian War. Because France was suffering from an acute shortage of fats, Emperor Napoleon The Third offered a prize to anyone who could make a food that was as appetizing and nourishing as butter. A chemist named Hippolte Megre Mouries won the prize with a table spread of beef fat and milk which was called Oleomargarine.

Margarine was introduced in the United States in 1874 but was not widely used until the outbreak of World War I when a acute butter shortage developed. A similar situation existed during World War II and since that time the popularity of margarine has steadily grown.

Modern margarine is a table spread which consists of

highly refined vegetable oils which are partially hydrogenated and emulsified with skim milk or water. Other ingredients vary somewhat from brand to brand, but usually include salt and carotene, Vitamin A and maybe Vitamin D. Minor ingredients are also added to contribute to the perfect blending of these elements to improve the flavor, spreading, cooking and keeping qualities. The oils in margarine account for 80% of its substance. Blue Bonnet Margarine is made from a blend of cottonseed and soybean oils.

In 1981 Nabisco, Inc., through a leveraged buyout, acquired the Standard Brands, Inc. and the merger created the Nabisco Brands, Inc., an operating company of R.J. Reynolds Industries, Inc. In 1988 an investment firm of Kohlberg Kravis Roberts & Company performed a leveraged buyout of R.J.R. Nabisco, Inc.

The following are the cookbooks and recipe booklets we were able to collect from this company.

1968 - *Whats-For-Lunch Cook Book*. Pocket Book, 182 pages. **$3.00**

1970 - *The Blue Bonnet Margarine Book of Creative Cookery*. 30 pages. **NCV**

◊ ◊ ◊ ◊

Fleischmann's Margarine

Standard Brands, Inc. is the maker of Fleischmann's Margarine with general offices in New York, New York. This product was introduced in the late 1950's. Fleischmann's Margarine is made from 100% corn oil, over half of which is in liquid form. It is available in these forms: stick (lightly salted), frozen unsalted, soft and diet.

Fleischmann Company was part of a group of companies who had agreed to merge in 1929 to form Standard Brands, Inc. The Fleischmann's Company manufactured Fleischmann's Yeast. This gave Standard Brands, Inc. the right to use the name Fleischmann's (which was very famous) on their new margarine. In 1981 Nabisco, Inc., through a leveraged buyout, acquired the Standard Brands, Inc., and the merger created the Nabisco Brands, Inc., an operating company of R.J. Reynolds Industries, Inc. In 1988 an investment firm of Kohlberg Kravis Roberts & Company performed a leveraged buyout of R.J.R. Nabisco, Inc.

We were able to collect the following cookbooks and recipe booklets from this company.

1977 - *Sensible Eating Can Be Delicious - 87 Recipes*. Fleischmann's Margarines and Egg Beaters Substitute, 47 pages. **NCV**

1977 - *Cooking Hints*. Nutrition information presented by the makers of Fleischmann's Margarines and Egg Beaters cholesterol-free egg substitute. **NCV**

◊ ◊ ◊ ◊

Parkay Oleomargarine

The Kraft Food Company in Chicago, Illinois manufacture Parkay Brand Oleomargarine. In 1986 Kraft Foods Company, Kraft, Inc. purchased The Craig Food Distributing Company of Salem, Missouri to extend their food outlets in the wholesale field to restaurants, colleges, and food service companies. In 1988 the Philip Morris, General Foods Company made a leveraged buyout of the Kraft Foods Company.

The following publication is what we were able to collect from this company.

1963 - *New Recipes for Cookies, Cakes 'n Muffins*. The Kraft Kitchens, 15 pages. **$3.00**

◊ ◊ ◊ ◊

Silver Churn Butterine

The Armour Packing Company of Kansas City, in the 1880's was manufacturing a product named "Silver Churn Butterine," an oleomargarine, "On each wrapper you will see A Silver Churn, Our Guarantee."

By 1918 the company was named Armour and Company with general offices in Chicago, Illinois. The company manufactured a product named Armour's Veribest Oleomargarine for table use and cooking.

The following lists the publications we were able to collect from this company.

▸ 1880's - *Silver Churn Butterine Cook Book*. Some useful recipes for pastry cooking, 32 pages. **$24.00**

▸ 1918 - *Veribest Economy - Save and Solve the Food Problem*. World War I reference, 15 pages. **$14.00**

◊ ◊ ◊ ◊

The Federal Government passed a Tax Act on August 1, 1886 imposing a Federal Tax on the manufacture of oleomargarine. The packages had to show proof that the tax was paid, so the manufacturer had to buy the tax stamp from the government and place the stamp on each package. This Tax Act was renewed on May 9, 1902 and again on March 4, 1931. The tax was in the amount of ¼ cent per pound.

◊ ◊ ◊ ◊

Land O' Lakes Butter

The Minnesota Cooperative Creameries Association of Arden Hills, Minnesota sold butter produced by the cooperative's members and in 1924 adopted the name of "Land O' Lakes" Butter Brand and was used on all of their butter packaging and advertising.

Coincidentally in 1924 the American Stores grocery chain in Philadelphia, Pennsylvania published a soft-cover booklet titled *Alice in Dairyland*. The story is of dairyland

and a family tour and they visit "The Land of the Lakes." The story reads, "When they came to the brow of a hill and looked out over the wide view spread before them, as fas as the eye could reach, they could see bright green meadows and the shining waters of many lakes reflecting the clear blue of the skies. Basking in the golden sunlight or browsing in the shade of the trees or standing knee deep in the cool waters were thousands and thousands of cows (125,000 cows.)" Today, this company also manufactures Land o' Lakes Oleomargarine.

There may be no connection between these two companies, but the following is what we have on Land O' Lakes.

1924 - *Alice in Dairyland.* Louella Brand Butter, 19 pages. **$12.00**

Chapter 19

Nuts And Fruits

Baker's Cocoanut

In the early days of this country, cocoanuts were rare and expensive and not in common use. Housewives were reluctant to go through the tedious process of splitting open the nut, digging out the meat, then grating it. In 1896, Franklin Baker, a Philadelphia flour miller, changed all of that. Having received a boatload of cocoanuts as payment for a boatload of flour, he devised an easier way to use cocoanut. His solution, a method of packing the prepared of pre-grated cocoanut while still retaining that tree-fresh goodness, is still practiced today by the Franklin Baker Cocoanut Company. Baker's Dry Shred cocoanut is now packed in a new improved double waxed, glassine-wrapped package to retain its flavor.

In July 1929, the management of the Postum Cereal Company, Inc., which then owned 14 different companies including Baker's Cocoanut, through aquisition, decided the corporation name was no longer appropriate for this new family of companies. Subsequently, the name was changed to the General Foods Corporation.

The following are the cookbooks that we were able to collect from this company.

▶ 1911 - *Baker's Cocoanut Recipes.* 16 pages. **$16.00**

▶ 1926 - *Baker's Coconut Recipes.* Marion Hughs, 15 pages. **$14.00**

1927 - *Make it a Party With Baker.* **$12.00**

1928 - *Kitchen Calendar.* 14 pages. **$12.00**

1928 - *Cocoanut Sun-Sweetness from the Tropics.* Franklin Baker Company, Inc., P.Co. Inc., 30 pages. **$12.00**

1931 - *Cocoanut Dishes That Everybody Loves.* General Foods, Corp., 38 pages. **$10.00**

1956 - *Baker's Cocoanut Cut-Up Cakes.* Franklin Baker Division, General Foods, Corp., 28 pages. **$6.00**

1968 - *Baker's Cocoanut & Chocolate Party Cut-up Cakes.* Illustrates "LaBelle Chocolatiers" trademark used originally by Walter Baker and Company, Ltd. who manufactured chocolate, 32 pages. **$3.00**

1973 - *Baker's Cut-up Cake Party Book.* Baker's Angel Flake Cut-ups. Swans Down and Calumet are registered trademarks of General Foods Corp., Pocket Book, 127 pages. **NCV**

1980 - *Baker's Chocolate and Cocoanut Favorites.* General Foods Kitchens, General Foods Corp., 16 pages. **NCV**

1985 - *Baker's Book of Cocoanut Delights.* General Foods Corp., Division of Nabisco, Inc., R.J. Reynolds, Inc. **NCV**

◊ ◊ ◊ ◊

Dunham's Cocoanut

The cocoanut, the fruit of one of the palms, is the largest edible nut in the market and perhaps the most widely known. It is very valuable to the natives in the countries in which it is grown, furnishing not only nutritious and delicious food, but huts, mats, rope, combs, brooms, clothing, baskets and even dishes. The flesh, when young, is soft and creamy, but in this condition cannot be transported. They come to the market ripe and mature. It is the shelling and grating of the cocoanut that prevents its greater use, hence, the most acceptable form is that already shelled or grated.

Cocoanut is highly nutritious, containing 36% of fats with 8% of albumaids and a little less than 1% of mineral matter. Cocoanut oil liquifies at 80° Fahrenheit, and even at lower temperatures of 50° or 60° it is about the consistency of soft lard. It is quite easily digested, hence, valuable for invalids who are obliged to take fatty matter and cannot digest other fats.

In 1893 Dunham's Shred cocoanut advertised with trade cards, typical of that period of time. One reads, "Save the labels from packages of Dunham's Shred Cocoanut and secure a handsome premium. A complete catalogue illustrating a very large variety of attractive articles of value and interest to everyone will be mailed on application. James P. Wood, Secy., P.O. Box 3611, New York."

The following lists what we were able to collect from this company.

1880's - *Dainty Desserts*. Mrs. Sarah Tyson Rorer for Dunham's Cocoanut, 32 pages. **$24.00**

▶ 1890's - *A Few of the Delicious Desserts, Dunham's Original Shred Cocoanut.* 15 pages. **$20.00**

◊◊◊◊

Dromedary Cocoanut

The Hill Brothers Company, New York City, was the manufacturer of Dromedary Cocoanut. Cocoanut demands careful preparation and packing and the Dromedary ever-seal package was devised to retain the original freshness of the cocoanut.

We were able to collect the following publications from this company.

▶ 1914 - *Dromedary Cook Book.* 33 pages. **$14.00**

1922 - *One Hundred Delights - Dromedary.* 31 pages. **$12.00**

1923 - *One Hundred Delights - Dromedary.* **$12.00**

▶ 1925 - *Foods from Sunny Lands.* Lily Haxworth Wallace, 18 pages. **$12.00**

◊◊◊◊

Walnuts

The California Walnut Growers Association of Los Angeles was a cooperative, non-profit organization of 8,242 growers in the 1920's with a yearly production over 75,000,000 pounds. Nearly 140,000 acres of California's finest land was devoted to walnuts. From the groves, the walnuts were taken to one of the 39 packing plants of the Association, located throughout the state.

We were able to collect the following publication.

1920's - *To Win New Cooking Fame, Just Add Walnuts.* 26 pages. **$12.00**

◊◊◊◊

Bananas

The banana is one of the oldest foods known to man. In 327 B.C. the armies of Alexander the Great found the fruit growing in abundance in the valley of the Indus in southern Asia. The story of the spread of its use from Asia to Africa and then to the Americas is full of history. With the development of facilities for the distribution of this tropical fruit in the markets of North America has come a greater appreciation of its food value.

Each banana plant grows from 15 to 30 feet in height and bears one stem or bunch of fruit. When that is harvested, the plant is cut down and allowed to rot and fertilize the soil for new plants growing from the same root stock. The fruit grows with fingers up (each banana is called a finger). Bananas are harvested green, even when they are to be eaten in the locality in which they are grown.

The principal countries producing and shipping bananas to the United States are Honduras, Guatemala, Nicaragua, Costa Rica, and Panama in Central America; Columbia and Ecuador in South America; Cuba and Mexico.

The true romance of the banana lies in an explanation of its universal appeal as a food for all ages and among nationalities. Its value is greatly enchanced as we learn more of the nutritive content and the variety of delicious and attractive ways in which this fruit may be included in the diet.

Bananas come in their own germ-proof package. Bananas should not be kept in the ice box but should be kept at room temperature to enhance ripening and the development of the natural flavor. To keep sliced bananas from turning dark, dip the slices into or sprinkle them with grapefruit juice (fresh or canned), pineapple juice (canned), orange juice or lemon juice.

The name Chiquita is a war baby and was born in 1944 to give a personal face to the banana for the consumer. Chiquita is part of the Multi-national United Fruit Company of New York City. The Banana Sticker identifing each cluster of bananas was born in 1947.

The following are the publications we were able to collect on bananas.

1930 - *Guaranteed To Start Conversation - 8 New Banana Recipes.* **$10.00**

▶ 1931 - *The New Banana.* United Fruit Company, 24 pages. **$10.00**

1930's - *Bananas Take A Bow...In Attractive New Dishes For the Up-To-Date Hostess.* 22 pages. **$10.00**

1939 - *A Study of the Banana - Its Every-Day Use and Food Value.* 24 pages. **$10.00**

1940 - *Bananas...How To Serve Them.* 44 pages. **$8.00**

▶ 1940 - *Banana Salad Bazaar.* Fruit Dispatch Co., 24 pages. **$8.00**

1947 - *Tempting Banana Recipes.* Foldout pamphlet. **$4.00**

1947 - *Chiquita Banana's Cook Book.* 24 pages. **$8.00**

▶ 1950 - *Chiquita Banana's Recipe Book.* United Fruit Co., 18 pages. **$6.00**

1951 - *Chiquita Banana Presents 18 Recipes from Her Minute Movies.* **$6.00**

1947, 1959 - *Chiquita Banana's Cook Book*. 21 pages. **$6.00**

◊ ◊ ◊ ◊

Sun-Maid Raisins

Long before the "Fourty-Niners" came to California, Spanish missionaries had established a string of missions all along the California coast. The Padres brought many plants from Europe, including grapes for making sacramental wines. The first grapes were the Muscat variety.

The credit for producing the first California raisins may be awarded to T.F. Eisen, a pioneer of grape growing in 1873. The summer of that year was extremely hot and the grapes dried on the vines. Refusing to have a year's work wasted, Eisen harvested his dried grapes and shipped them to a grocer friend in San Francisco. The grocer sold the dried grapes as "Peruvian delicacies." Due to their exotic flavor they sold immediately. The new demand resulted in the raisin industry being born in the San Joaquin Valley of California and for over 100 years this relatively small area has produced all North American raisins.

Fresno county is the center of grape production, this small section being one of the very few areas of the entire world where exists the combination of soil and climate conditions essential to the production of raisin variety of grapes.

The California Associated Raisin Company was founded in 1912, a growers cooperative. In 1915 they adopted the name "Sun-Maid Raisins" for its production.

In 1915 Lorraine Collett along with two other girls, was hired to work the Panama-Pacific Exposition in San Francisco for the California Associated Raisin Company. Lorraine was to represent the company in the Raisin Parade, and a company executive called on her to tell her to be sure and wear a white uniform and blue bonnet, but she wore her red bonnet to the satisfaction of all.

E.H. Berg, owner of an advertising agency under contract to the Sun-Maid Company, viewed the Fresno Raisin Parade. It was there he first saw Lorraine Collett and was impressed by the sixteen-year-old and the red bonnet which framed her face. He formed a mental picture of her holding a tray of grapes. The mental picture later became the Sun-Maid trademark.

In early May of that year, Lorraine was asked to pose for a full-color painting. This she did, and when the painting was finished it was hung in the Sun-Maid exhibit at the Horticulture Building. When the Exposition ended in December of 1915 the original painting was presented to Lorraine. However, the full-color trademark painting (sunburst and all) remained unchanged in its basic concept for 63 years.

Lorraine Collett Peterson kept the original "Sun-Maid" painting stored away with her other souvenirs for 59 years. In 1974 she sold the painting back to the Sun-Main Company for $1,700.00.

There was apparently a buyout of Sun-Maid Raisin Company in the 1940's by H.J. Heinz Company.

The following publications on raisins are what we were able to collect.

Circa 1915 - *Recipes with Raisins*. 30 pages. **$14.00**

▶ 1921 - *Sun Maid Raisins - Their Food Value and 92 Selected Recipes*. With an endorsement by J.H. Kellogg of Battle Creek Sanitorium, 28 pages. **$12.00**

1922 - *Sun-Maid Raisins - Their Food Value and 92 Selected Recipes*. **$12.00**

1926 - *Famous Cook's Recipes for Raisin Cookery*. Miss Alice Bradley, Miss Sarah Field Splint, Mrs. Caroline B. King, Mrs. Belle De Graf, 32 pages. **$12.00**

1940's - *The Amazin Raisin - California Raisin Baked Foods Round-up*. Ernest Weil, California Raisin Advisory Board, 20 pages. **$8.00**

▶ 1949 - *Downright Delicious Sun-Maid Raisin Recipes*. Distributed by H.J. Heinz Co., 32 pages. **$8.00**

1954 - *Recipes Home Pac Brand Seedless Raisins - The World's Finest Raisins*. Fresno Home Packing Company, Fresno, California, 32 pages. **$6.00**

◊ ◊ ◊ ◊

California Citrus

In 1916, The California Fruit Growers Exchange, through which all types of citrus fruits were shipped bearing the Sunkist trademark, was a cooperative of more than 8,000 California Citrus Fruit Growers. The California Fruit Growers Exchange of Los Angeles, California published advertising recipe books. There was a two-page insert put in each package advertising " 'A Handy Recipe Card File.' The neat oak box contains 23 index guides lableled 'Pudding,' 'Pastry,' 'Sauces,' etc. Then there are 100 blank cards on which recipes may be written or clippings pasted for filing between the guides. We also include 24 cards showing a wide variety of orange and lemon recipes, each carefully tested by Alice Bradley, Principal of the Fannie Farmer School of Cookery. This series includes beverages, salads, desserts, etc. These outfits, with the orange and lemon cards, sell in most retail stores for $1.25 or more. You can get a complete outfit for 75 cents, postpaid or a set of orange and lemon recipe cards alone for 10 cents. 'Fill Out Coupon,' check the offer you wish to accept, sign your name and address and forward in envelope with stamps or coin to address below."

By 1939 The Sunkist Kitchen was developed. The primary function of the food service was originating and testing of recipes for practical everyday use in the home.

The following are the publications we have collected from the Fruit Growers Exchange.

▶ 1916 - *Sunkist Recipes, Oranges - Lemons*. Alice Bradley, California Fruit Growers Exchange, 64 pages. **$14.00**

▶ Circa 1919 - *Busy-Day Salads and Desserts.* Alice Bradley, 16 pages. **$14.00**

1931 - *Sunkist Recipes For Every Day.* California Fruit Growers Exchange, 36 pages. **$10.00**

1935 - *For Vigorous Health - Sunkist Recipes for Every Day.* 48 pages. **$10.00**

1939 - *Sunkist Lemons Bring Out the Flavor.* 32 pages. **$10.00**

◊ ◊ ◊ ◊

Dole Pineapple

It all began in a little boy's garden in Maine. In that garden, among corn and beans, the seeds of a dream was sown, seeds which have since blossomed into one of the most romantic stories yet. That little boy who labored so hard and happily in that Maine garden was James Drummond Dole, better known as Jim Dole.

Jim Dole had always loved the soil, he dreamed often of a great garden of his own, maybe in a romantic land, under tropic skies. So with boyhood and college days behind him, he turned seriously to the dreams of his youthful years. He learned of homestead lands and fortunes in coffee in Hawaii. With the lure of the tropics in his blood, he set off for Hawaii.

Jim Dole found Hawaiian coffee fortunes more bragged on than real. He discovered pineapples were even greater fun to grow than coffee, corn or beans.

Hawaiian pineapple has always been delicious, even in the semi-wild state in which Jim Dole found it. He looked ahead and saw a sunny island floating in the blue waters of the Pacific, teeming with industry, thousands of acres under cultivation, thousands of happy hands at work. And from this island he saw ships set sail, all laden with the king of fruits, Hawaiian pineapple.

So a boy had a dream, an industry was born, and the rarest of tropical fruits became an everyday delicacy, all since 1897.

In the early days, pineapple could not be picked ripe because of the long sea voyage. Consequently, the fresh fruit never reached the U.S. with its natural plant-ripened flavor. The heavy crop of pineapples came in when the fruit stands of California were laden with other fruits, and there was no adequate means of getting them to Eastern markets.

For Jim Dole to think cannery was as good as having it. It was only a little cannery, big enough to put up 45,000 cans a season. Today it packs that many cans in half an hour. Dole knew that he alone could not grow enough Hawaiian pineapple to keep an entire cannery busy, so he asked other settlers to plant also. So the kitchen that was once so little now bustles with activity as thousands of workers prepare Hawaiian pineapple for worldwide consumption.

The dream that had its beginning in a little boy's garden has come true.

The following lists what we have been able to collect from this company.

▶ 1927, 1928, 1929, 1930 - *The Kingdom That Grew Out Of A Little Boy's Garden.* 6th printing. **$18.00**

1988 - *Dole's Quick and Easy Recipes.* Dole Pineapple Company. **NCV**

◊ ◊ ◊ ◊

Florida Citrus

Florida's sun, sand and sparkling water have made her climate famous, and perhaps more important, have produced citrus crops of the finest quality and variety in the world. The state sends all over the world its bounty of delicious, health-giving oranges, grapefruit and tangerines.

Citrus was not native to the New World, however seeds carried by Spanish explorers found fertile ground near St. Augustine, Florida and south along the Indian river. The roots of citrus lie deep in antiquity in southeastern Asia and China and have been traced back through early writings as far back as 1500 B.C.

By the 1920's, then modern technology and advanced transportation opened new vistas as Citri Culture became a major endeavor. New plantings which often reach as far as the eye can see from the highway in the ridge and lake sections of Florida.

In the 1930's, Vitamin C was isolated and citrus fruits were found to be the natural source of this daily needed food element.

With the development of canned, chilled and frozen orange and grapefruit juices and sections, the availability of favorites was extended to all seasons and climates.

The Valencia orange which took its name from the Spanish city, is the most widely grown variety in the world and accounts for nearly half of Florida's orange production. Another widely grown variety is the naval orange.

The State of Florida has a Florida Citrus Commission with a Home Economics Department to develop and test recipes. The following publication is what we were able to collect from this commission.

▶ 1960 - *Favorite Recipes from Florida.* State of Florida, Department of Citrus, 48 pages. **$4.00**

◊ ◊ ◊ ◊

Prunes

The Sunsweet name is owned by the growers who belong to the California Prune & Apricot Growers Association of San Jose, California. We have collected the following publication from this association.

1950 - *Sunsweet Recipes.* 46 pages. **$6.00**

◊ ◊ ◊ ◊

Apples

The Processed Apples Institute, Inc. of New York, New York is an organization of leading manufacturers of ready-to-use apple products. Conveniently packed in gleaming glass jars, neat tin cans and shining bottles, these apple products are found on every grocery shelf from one end of America to another.

"Happy Apple" was developed to illustrate the recipes in their advertising cookbooks. They publish a happy story of economy, convenience, flavor, versatility, glamour which he tells.

The American-developed varieties of apples began with the Newton Pippin in the early 1700's, to be followed by the Baldwin soon after 1740, the Rhode Island Greening about 1748, and many others. The European varieties were not suited to the eastern and midwestern sections of the country although they later proved well adapted to the West Coast.

Big nurseries were established in western New York after that territory was opened in 1800. Nurseries in Pennsylvania and Tennessee also made huge plantings of established varieties of apples.

In the middle 1800's the American pattern of living began to change fast. Railroads, flung across the mountains and prairies, carried the fruits of farm and ranch from one end of the country to the other.

Until about 1900 apple growing remained an individual farm operation, almost every farm had its orchard. In the early 1900's, it took a full-time operation to grow apples successfully for the expanding markets.

Around 1910 Oregon's Hood River Valley became famous for its apples and the Wenatchee and Yakima Valleys of Washington came into production shortly thereafter. At least 35 states now raise apples commercially.

We were able to collect the following publications on apples.

1940's - *Design for Eating.* Dorothy W. Lewis, featuring apples from the Appalachian Area, 15 pages. **$8.00**

1952 - *All About Apples.* A Flanley and Woodward Production, 32 page. **$6.00**

1966 - *Apple Kitchen Cook Book.* Demetria Taylor, 220 pages. **$3.00**

1967 - *Basic Fruit Cookbook.* Sybil Henderson, 32 pages. **$3.00**

◊ ◊ ◊ ◊

Chapter 20

Gelatin

Cox's Gelatine

The J & G Limited Company was established in 1725 in the Gorgie Mills area of Edingurgh, Scotland. In 1842 the company began the manufacture of powdered gelatine and packaged it in bright red and black checkered boxes. In 1845 the company established an office and warehouse at 100 Hudson Street in New York City. The American company was named the Cox Gelatine Company and Cox Gelatine was imported from their plant in Scotland.

In 1914 the company published its fifth Cox's edition of *Cox's Manual of Cookery*. A statement in the recipes book says, "Our recipes have been prepared by Marion Harris Neil, as the result of a wide experience, and the directions have been studied out with a view to making the prepartation of the dishes as easy as possible for the busy housewife." Miss Marion Harris Neil was the Cookery Editor of the *Ladies' Home Journal*.

In the 1930's the company's publication included an endorsement by Mary Marshall, Home Economics Authority. "Food writer and editor, and practical housewife, Mary Marshall has for years given advice and inspiration to American homemakers. Her enthusiastic endorsement of Cox's Gelatine is based on her thorough understanding of athe dietary requirements and taste of the present-day American family."

We have collected the following publications from this company.

1906 - *Recipes for Cox Gelatine.* **$16.00**

▶ 1914 - *Cox's Manual of Gelatine Cookery.* 64 pages. **$14.00**

1920 - *Cox's Gelatine Recipes.* The Cox Gelatine Company of New York. **$12.00**

1930's - *Cox's New Simple Recipes - What To Do with Gelatine.* 31 pages. **$10.00**

◊ ◊ ◊ ◊

Dr. Price's Jelly Dessert

In 1860 Dr. Price founded the Dr. Price's Flavoring Extract Company in Chicago. A 1904 publication contained the following. "What is Dr. Price's Jelly Sugar Dessert? Dr. Price's Jelly Sugar Dessert is a new food product. It is a combination of refined sugar, refined gelatine, and lemon acid. It is prepared by Dr. Price, a Physician and chemist, whose name has never been associated with any food product that was other than pure, wholesome and nutritious. Jelly Sugar Dessert (also known as Jella) is flavored with Dr. Price's Delicious Flavoring Extracts, and colored with Dr. Price's harmless Food Colors and not with the usual amiline or coal tar dyes. In the matter of color alone it is a safe dessert."

In 1915 the Dr. Price's Flavoring Extract and Baking Powder companies were acquired by the Royal Baking Powder Company of New York City and soon was producing Royal Baking Powder and Royal Flavoring Extracts and Royal Gelatin products.

The Royal Baking Powder and Flavoring Extracts and Gelatin Companies in 1929 were a part of a merger plan to the emergence of Standard Brands, Inc. With many different food manufacturers operating as one company and each became a Division of Standard Brands, Inc. The copyright by Standard Brands, Inc. appeared in publications in 1929. Other food manufacturing companies were added during future years which included Del Monte Brands to enlarge and diversify the company.

In 1981 Nabisco Company, Inc. performed a leveraged buyout of Standard Brands, Inc., including their Del Monte Division. The company was renamed Nabisco, Inc. and Standard Brands and Del Monte were Divisions of Nabisco, Inc.

In 1985 R.J. Reynolds, Inc., a tobaco manufacturer performed a leveraged buyout of Nabisco, Inc., including the Standard Brands and the company renamed itself RJR Nabisco, Inc. with Nabisco, Standard Brands and Del Monte all being Divisions of RJR Inc.

In 1988 an investment firm of Kohlberg Kravis Roberts & Company performed a leveraged buyout of RJR Nabisco, Inc. Their main interest was in acquiring the RJR Tobacco portion of the huge conglomerate.

The following lists what we were able to collect from this company.

1904 - *Dr. Price's Delicious Desserts, Containing Practical Desserts.* 34th edition. **$16.00**

1929 - *14 New Gelatin Desserts with Royal.* Standard Brands, Inc. 14 pages. **$12.00**

▶ 1932 - *Royal Desserts.* Royal Quick Setting Gelatin, Royal Chocolate & Vanilla Puddings. 32 pages. **$10.00**

1940 - *Royal Desserts Recipes.* "A Treat As Thrilling As A Burst of Applause" Says Ginger Rogers of Royal Desserts! 23 pages. **$15.00**

1942 - *Royal Recipe Parade.* Royal Gelatin and Puddings, 171 recipes, Tapioca Puddings, 48 pages. **$8.00**

1950's - *Time Tested Royal Recipes.* Gelatin molds & Parffae's, 31 pages. **$6.00**

1950's - *Time Tested Royal Recipes.* Standard Brands, Inc., 31 pages. **$6.00**

1980's - *Royal Gelatin Dessert.* Nabisco Brands, Inc. **NCV**

◇◇◇◇

Plymouth Rock Gelatine

The Plymouth Rock Gelatine Company of Boston, Massachusetts manufactured Phosphated Gelatine which was patented on March 5, 1889.

The 1901 advertising recipe book published by this company contains "The Story of Plymouth Rock," from the arrival of the Mayflower ship in Cape Cod Bay and the historic landing party on December 11, 1620 to 1880 when it was carried back to its original position at the water's edge. The story is interspersed with recipes. On the inside of the back cover is this notice: "Send us three two cent stamps to pay postage, and we will send you one of these beautiful books and a sample package of Plymouth Rock Phosphated Gelatine large enough to make one pint of delicious jelly."

The following lists what we were able to collect from this company.

▶ 1901 - *The Story of Plymouth Rock.* 40 pages. **$16.00**

▶ 1910 - *Plymouth Rock Gelatine Dainties and Household Helps.* 10 pages. **$16.00**

◇◇◇◇

Knox Gelatine

Knox Gelatine was founded in 1890 when an enterprising knit goods salesman from Mapletown, New York, Charles B. Knox, moved to Johnstown, New York and started a small processing plant as Charles B. Knox Gelatine Company, Inc. Gelatine has been known to exist as far back as 1682. It is a protein substance which is derived from the collagen bearing portion of skin, bone or white connective tissue of animals. It is tasteless, odorless, and when dissolved in water, transparent.

Formerly, gelatine came to the market in sheets, and the housewife had to dissolve it in water before she could use it. Those who didn't buy it made their own from beef bones, a long laborious process.

At the turn of the century (1800) housewives used to cook bones for soup and skim off the resulting gelatine released from the bones from the top of the pot. This was then used for making salads and light lesserts used primarily in convalescent diets.

Charles Knox had watched his wife prepare gelatine and decided that there should be a market for a gelatine to which only water need be added. This, he reasoned, would be more convenient for the housewife and therefore would find a place on the pantry shelf of every home. Johnstown, New York was located in Fulton County and the necessary raw material was available from local tanneries, in addition to an excellent water supply.

Mr. Knox's business thrived as a result of very bold advertising which was years ahead of the drum-beating publicity campaigner of the early part of this century. One of the slogans originally used to introduce the product was, "Its Not Like Pie, It's Healthy." In 1904 Knox had a booth at the St. Louis World's Fair.

When Charles Knox died in 1908 his company was an important part of Johnstown's economic future. Although she was advised to sell the company, his 50-year-old widow, Rose Markward Knox, assumed complete control of the firm.

Gelatine, Mrs. Knox reasoned, was bought by women and women were more interested in cost, nutrition, and ease of preparation than in election stunts and airships. She set up an experimental laboratory and developed hundreds of recipes which were printed on the products box, in leaflets and in illustrated cookbooks. They also appeared in newspapers and magazines under the heading, "Mrs. Knox says..."

During the years of 1928, 1929, and 1930, Recipe Cards showing a picture of a dessert made with Knox Gelatine with the recipe on the back. Yes, trade cards. One of these recipe cards was put into each box of Knox Gelatine for the housewife. Other advertising encouraged the housewife to collect an entire set. These trade cards were in color.

Mrs. Knox operated the company for 40 years. She became America's foremost woman industrialist and the company prospered. In 1946 Mrs. Knox, then 88, turned the presidency of the company over to her son, James. Upon the death of his mother in 1950, James Knox became chairman of the board of directors and his 32-year-old son was made president.

In 1972 the Knox Gelatine Company, Inc. was acquired by Thomas J. Lipton, Inc., manufacturers of Lipton Soup Base Mixes.

The following publications are those we were able to collect and information furnished to us by the Thomas J. Lipton, Inc., from the Archives of the Knox Gelatine Company, Inc.

1896 - *Dainty Desserts for Dainty People.* Cow's head in upper right corner of cover. **$20.00**

1898 - *Dainty Desserts For Dainty People.* Cow's head in right corner of cover. **$20.00**

1900 - *Dainty Desserts For Dainty People.* On cover is entrance to large building framed with four very tall columns and steps in the middle. **$20.00**

1909 - *Dainty Desserts for Dainty People.* Compiled by Rose Markward with cow's head centered near bottom of cover. **$16.00**

1909 - *Dainty Desserts for Dainty People.* Revised edition, free on request, pint sample for a 2¢ stamp. **$16.00**

1910 - *Dainty Dishes Made of Knox Gelatine.* Package inserts, shows cow's head, 2½"x3¼". **$2.50**

1910 - *Dainty Dishes Made of Knox Gelatine.* Shows smaller cow's head with a white and a Negro boy on each side. **$2.50**

1910 - *Dainty Dishes Made of Knox Gelatine.* **$16.00**

1910 - *Food Economy, Recipes for Left-Overs and Plain Desserts.* Plain gray cover, 30 pages. **$16.00**

1915 - *Knox Sparkling Gelatine.* Package insert, cow's head with a white boy and a Negro boy on each side, 2½"x3¼" folded into three sections. **$2.50**

1915 - *Dainty Desserts for Dainty People.* **$14.00**

1915 - *Mrs. Knox's Recipe Book.* **$14.00**

1918 - *Food Economy Recipes for Left-Overs and Plain Desserts.* Mrs. Knox, 30 pages. **$14.00**

1923 - *The Health Value of Knox Sparkling Gelatine.* 21 pages. **$12.00**

1923 - *Food Economy Recipes for Left-Overs, Plain Desserts and Salads.* Mrs. Knox, 30 pages. **$12.00**

1924 - *The Health Value of Knox Sparkling Gelatine.* 23 pages. **$12.00**

▶ 1924 - *Dainty Desserts For Dainty People.* Knox Gelatine, 41 pages. **$12.00**

▶ 1927 - *Knox Gelatine Dainty Desserts - Salads - Candies.* **$12.00**

1920's - *Knox Recipes for Anemia.* **$12.00**

1920's - *Moo-calfie Knox Gelatine.* **$12.00**

1920's - *Reducing Diets with Knox.* **$12.00**

1920's - *Diabetic Recipe Book.* **$12.00**

1928 - *Food Economy Recipes for Left-Overs, Plain Desserts and Salads.* Checkered gray cover, 35 pages. **$12.00**

1929 - *Your Electric Refeigerator and Knox Sparkling Gelatine.* 25 pages. **$12.00**

1931 - *Knox Gelatine Dainty Desserts, Candies, Salads.* 47 pages. **$10.00**

1932 - *Meals for Three.* **$10.00**

1933 - *Quantity Serving Recipes Illustrating the Profit Building Use of Knox Sparkling Gelatine.* 48 pages. **$10.00**

1933 - *Knox Gelatine Desserts, Salads, Candies and Frozen Dishes.* 71 pages. **$10.00**

1936 - *Dainty Desserts - Salads - Candies.* **$10.00**

1937 - *Quantity Serving Recipes Illustrating the Profit Building Use of Knox Sparkling Gelatine.* 48 pages. **$10.00**

1930's - *Diet Dial.* **$10.00**

1938 - *Knox Quickies.* **$10.00**

1938 - *Entertaining Round The Calendar.* **$10.00**

1939 - *Be Fit Not Fat.* **$10.00**

1941 - *Knox Gelatine Desserts, Salads, Candies and Frozen Dishes.* 55 pages. **$8.00**

1942 - *Reducing Diets and Recipes.* 30 pages. **$8.00**

1942 - *Mrs. Knox's Top 20 Salads and Desserts.* **$8.00**

1943 - *13 Wonderful Knox Recipes Children Love.* 8-page folder. **$5.00**

1943 - *Knox Dishes Are Good Eating That's Good For You!* Package insert, 2⅜"x3¼", 10-page foldout. **$2.50**

1943 - *24 "Firsts" New Original Recipes for Salads and Desserts Made with Knox Gelatine.* 8-page folder. **$5.00**

1943 - *Salads, Desserts, Pies, Candies.* Large size. **$8.00**

1945 - *Salads, Desserts, Pies, Candies.* Small size, 27 pages. **$8.00**

1940's - *Brand New Dessert Idea!* Package insert, 3½"x 4¼", folded once, 4 pages. **$2.50**

1946 - *The Protein Value of Plain Unflavored Gelatine.* Package insert, 4-page folder. **$2.50**

1952 - *Knox Gelatine Recipe Book - Eat and Reduce Plan.* 39 pages. **$6.00**

1955 - *Knox Eat And Reduce Plan Including Choice-Of-Foods Chart.* 34 pages. **$6.00**

1955 - *Meal Planning for the Sick and Convalescent with Menus and Recipes.* 31 pages. **$6.00**

1950's - *Help With the Diet in Colitis and Digestive Disorders.* 10 pages. **$6.00**

1957 - *Gel-Cookery Recipe Book.* Over 40 ways to give that "Something Special" touch to your meals with Knox desserts, salads, main dishes, 34 pages. **$6.00**

1959 - *Gel-Cookery Recipe Book.* Over 40 ways to give that "Something Special" touch to your meals with Knox desserts, salads, main dishes, 34 pages. **$6.00**

1959 - *Knox Eat And Reduce Plan Including Choice-Of-Foods Chart.* 34 pages. **$6.00**

1959 - *Silhouette Recipes, Low-Calorie Desserts... Salads...Main Dishes in Modern Knox Gel-Cookery.* 13 pages. **$6.00**

1959 - *Individualized Low Salt Diets.* 35 pages. **$6.00**

1960 - *Meal Planning for the Sick and Convalescent with Menus and Recipes.* 31 pages. **$6.00**

1961 - *Fabulous Foods That Are Fun To Fix - Salads , Main Dishes, Desserts.* Knox Unflavored Gelatine. 12 pages. **$3.00**

1961 - *Bland Diets For Gastritis and Peptic Ulcer.* 27 pages. **$3.00**

1961 - *Do You Really Want to Lose Weight? Then Here's The Knox Eat and Reduce Plan.* 52 pages. **$3.00**

1962 - *Knox On-Camera Recipes - A Completely New Guide to Gel-Cookery.* 48 pages. **$3.00**

1963 - *Knox On-Camera Recipes - A Completely New Guide to Gel-Cookery.* 48 pages. **$3.00**

1965   *Family Album Diamond Jubilee Year - 75 Years of Knox Gelatine.* **$20.00**

1960's - *Fresh Tasting Great Looking Gel Dishes So Simple with Knox.* Package insert, 2⅜"x3", folded, 18 pages. **$1.00**

1960's - *Dishes That Fly.* **$1.00**

1977 - *The Knox Gelatine Cookbook - Fun Beginnings, Endings, and In Between.* Hard cover. **NCV**

1986 - *Best of the Blox - Prize-winning Recipes From The Knox Blox Recipe Contest.* **NCV**

1986 - *Knox Blox Finger-Size Gelatine Snacks.* **NCV**

1988 - *Knox Blox Finger-Size Gelatine Snacks.* **NCV**

1988 - *Knox For Nails - The Knox Plan For Finger Nail Improvement.* **NCV**

◊ ◊ ◊ ◊

JELL-O

In 1682 a French chemist developed a means of isolating the tasteless, odorless pure protein material "gelatin."

In 1845 Peter Cooper obtained a patent for a dessert he described as a "transparent, concentrated substance containing all the ingredients fitting for the table use in portable form and requiring only the addition of hot water to dissolve it." For over 50 years the patent remained undeveloped and unused.

It was not until 1895 that Pearl B. Wait, a cough medicine manufacturer, entered the packaged food business with an adoption of Cooper's gelatin dessert. His wife coined the name "JELL-O," and in 1897, production began. There did not appear to be any public interest aroused for the use of JELL-O.

In 1898 Wait sold the JELL-O name and formula for $450.00 to Francis Woodward, owner of Genesee Pure Food Company, at that time known for the manufacture of a roasted cereal beverage, "Grain-O." Woodward was determined to make JELL-O a household word.

In 1904 Francis Woodward hired artist Franklin King to design a trademark for JELL-O. Elizabeth, his blonde daughter became the model for the JELL-O girl. Elizabeth was visible on all JELL-O advertising from the magazine ads to the recipe booklets until 1908.

In 1908 Rose O'Neill was employed by JELL-O and she revised the drawing of Elizabeth King to the now-famous JELL-O Girl. In 1915 O'Neill introduced "JELL-O and the Kewpies," and she also was the artist for the 1916 JELL-O. In 1922, the artist was Norman Rockwell. The 1924 JELL-O artist was Maxfield Parrish.

During the 1920's, the company name was changed to The JELL-O company, Inc. of Le Roy, New York. This appeared on the advertising recipe booklets in 1924-1926. In 1928 a recipe booklet contained an offer by The JELL-O Company Inc., but on the inside of the cover appears the copyright by P. Co. Inc. At this time Postum Cereal Co., Inc. renamed to form the General Foods Corporation. In 1929 the JELL-O recipe booklet was copyrighted by the G.F. Corporation.

In 1915 The Genessee Pure Food Company had been purchased by the Post Cereal Co., Inc. After 1930 there were other food companies added to the corporation by purchasing them to make General Foods Corporation even larger and more diversified.

In 1985 Phillip Morris, Inc. performed a leveraged buyout of all of the General Foods Corporation stock from the stockholders to take over the ownership of the company. Later the General Foods Corporation became a division of Phillip Morris, Inc., along with Miller Beer, Marlboro Cigarettes, and Sealtest Ice Cream.

In 1988 Phillip Morris, Inc., along with General Foods, performed a leveraged buyout of Kraft Foods, Inc., which created the world's biggest consumer products company.

We were able to collect the following recipe booklets from JELL-O.

▶ 1904 - JELL-O booklet, picture on cover looks like playing cards only with an illustration of a JELL-O dessert on each of the cards. This is believed to be the first advertising recipe booklet by JELL-O, free for sending in your name and address. 14 pages. **$100.00**

▶ 1905 - *JELL-O The Dainty Dessert.* "The JELL-O Girl," Nellie Duling Gans, 14 pages. **$75.00**

▶ 1906 - *JELL-O Ice Cream Powder.* "The JELL-O Girl," 14 pages. **$65.00**

▶ 1908 - *JELL-O The Dainty Dessert.* Nellie Duling Gans, 10 pages. **$60.00**

1908 - *They Wanted JELL-O.* Illustrated by Rose O'Neill, no signature. **$60.00**

▶ 1909 - *Desserts of the World.* 22 pages. **$60.00**

▶ 1912 - *What Six Famous Cooks Say of JELL-O.* Illustrated by Rose O'Neill, 18 pages. **$55.00**

▶ 1912-1913 - *"Yes, JELL-O Please."* Illustrated by Rose O'Neill, 14 pages. **$55.00**

▶ 1913 - *"Even If You Can't Cook, You Can Make a JELL-O Dessert."* Illustrated by Rose O'Neill, 17 pages. **$55.00**

▶ 1914 - *The JELL-O Girl Entertains.* Signed Rose O'Neill, 20 pages. **$55.00**

▶ 1914 - *The JELL-O Girl Gives A Party.* Signed Rose O'Neill, 20 pages. **$55.00**

▶ 1915 - *JELL-O and the Kewpies.* Signed Rose O'Neill, 20 pages. **$55.00**

▶ 1916 - *JELL-O America's Most Famous Dessert.* The Bride and Her Task (featuring the six Famous Cooks), 20 pages. **$50.00**

▶ 1917 - *All Doors Open to JELL-O.* Rose O'Neill article, 20 pages. **$50.00**

▶ 1918 - *New Talks About JELL-O.* 16 pages. **$14.00**

1918 - *New Talks About JELL-O.* Stamped on upper right hand corner, "2 packages 25 cents," 14 pages. **$14.00**

▶ 1920 - *For Economy Use JELL-O.* 14 pages. **$12.00**

1920 - *Many Reasons For JELL-O.* Greer is artist, 14 pages. **$15.00**

1921 - *JELL-O America's Most Famous Dessert of What and How Made.* 8 pages. **$30.00**

1922 - *JELL-O America's Most Famous Dessert at Home Everywhere.* 16 pages. **$15.00**

▶ 1922 - *"It's So Simple" - JELL-O America's Most Famous Dessert.* Cover by Norman Rockwell. **$15.00**

1923 - *JELL-O Rhymes - America's Most Famous Dessert.* 22 pages. **$15.00**

1923 - *JELL-O America's Most Famous Food.* **$15.00**

1924 - *A JELL-O Year - America's Most Famous Dessert.* 16 pages. **$15.00**

1924 - Cover of book has picture of JELL-O box on railroad tracks and a train coming, 18 pages. **$15.00**

▶ 1924 - *Polly Put the Kettle On We'll All Make JELL-O.* Illustrated by Maxfield Parrish, 20 pages. **$45.00**

▶ 1925 - Cover of book has picture of a JELL-O box on railroad tracks and train coming, 20 pages. **$15.00**

1925 - *JELL-O America's Most Famous Dessert.* Shows a table setting on the cover, 2-page folder, insert in 1925 ice cream powder. **$15.00**

1925 - *JELL-O America's Most Famous Dessert.* Picture of George Washington on cover, 18 pages. **$15.00**

1925-1926 - *New JELL-O Recipes.* 18 pages. **$15.00**

1925 - *JELL-O Ice Cream Powder Makes Ice Cream, Ices and Puddings.* With 2-page JELL-O insert, 6 pages. **$15.00**

1926 - *The Charm of JELL-O.* Lady in green dress with tray and JELL-O mold. **$15.00**

1927 - *Through the Menu with JELL-O.* 20 pages. **$15.00**

1928 - *Today...What Salad...What Dessert? JELL-O Brings Dozens of Answers.* 22 pages. **$15.00**

1929 - *The Complete JELL-O Recipe Book.* 48 pages. **$15.00**

1930 - *New JELL-O Recipes Made with The New Flavor, Lime.* 11 pages. **$12.00**

1930 - *Quick Easy JELL-O Wonder Dishes.* 23 pages. **$12.00**

1930 - *The New JELL-O Book of Surprises - Salads - Desserts.* 23 pages. **$12.00**

1931 - *Thrifty JELL-O Recipes to Brighten Your Menus - Desserts, Salads.* 23 pages. **$12.00**

1931 - *The Greater JELL-O Recipe Book.* 47 pages. **$12.00**

1931 - *Want Something Different? 48 New JELL-O Entrees - Relishes, Salads, and Desserts.* 23 pages. **$12.00**

1932 - *Try The New JELL-O - You Make It Without Boiling Water - 48 New JELL-O Recipes.* 23 pages. **$12.00**

1933 - *What Mrs. Dewey Did With The New JELL-O.* 23 pages. **$12.00**

1933-1934 JELL-O Oz recipe booklets
▶ *Tiktok and the Nome King.* 31 pages. **$50.00**
Ozma and the Little Wizard. **$50.00**
Jack Pumpkinhead and the Sawhorse. **$50.00**
The Scarecrow and the Tin Woodsman. **$50.00**

1934 - *Gayer Mealtimes with New JELL-O.* **$12.00**

1934 - *Now JELL-O Tastes Twice as Good...Enjoy These Tempting Recipes.* 23 pages. **$12.00**

1935 - *Desserts.* Institution Department, 32 pages. **$20.00**

1935 - *Recipes for Luscious Ice cream - JELL-O Ice Cream Powder.* **$12.00**

1936 - *What Your Can Do With JELL-O.* Fifth edition, second printing, 26 pages. **$12.00**

1936 - *Recipes For Delicious Ice Cream - JELL-O Ice Cream Powder.* **$12.00**

▶ 1937 - *Jack & Mary's JELL-O Recipe Book.* Second edition, Jack Benny and Mary Livingstone, 23 pages. **$35.00**

1940 - *A Calendar of Desserts - 365 New Ideas And Recipes.* 48 pages. **$8.00**

1941 - *New Desserts.* Institution Department, 48 pages. **$15.00**

1944 - *Dessert Magic (JELL-O).* Sixth printing, 26 pages. **$8.00**

1953 - *Its Dessert Time - You Can Do Wonders With JELL-O.* 33 pages. **$6.00**

1961 - *Joys of JELL-O - The Story of JELL-O and Why It Grew.* First edition, 95 pages. **$3.00**

1961, 1962 - *Joys of JELL-O - The Story of JELL-O and Why It Grew.* Fourth edition, 95 pages. **$3.00**

1961, 1962, 1963 - *Joys of JELL-O - The Story of JELL-O and Why It Grew.* 95 pages. **$2.00**

1961, 1962, 1963, 1964 - *Joys of JELL-O - The Story of JELL-O and Why It Grew.* Fifth edition, 95 pages. **$2.00**

1966 - *Sweet Moments Desserts - JELL-O and Dream Whip Topping Mix.* 44 pages. **$3.00**

1972 - *Make Someone Happy - Make Someone JELL-O Brand Gelatin.* 6 pages. **NCV**

1973 - *The New Joys of JELL-O Recipe Book.* 128 pages. **NCV**

1977 - *Amazing Magical JELL-O Desserts.* Hard cover, 95 pages. **NCV**

1978 - *JELL-O Gelatin - Rainbow Cake Recipes.* 6 pages plus folder. **NCV**

1979 - *Easy Homemade Desserts with JELL-O Pudding.* Spiral bound, 96 pages. **NCV**

1980 - *The JELL-O Gelatin Salad Selector.* Large Dial-a-Recipe cards. **NCV**

1981 - *Joys of JELL-O Gelatin.* First edition, hard cover, spiral bound, 128 pages. **NCV**

1980's - *Your Favorite Meals Have Met Their Match.* Gelatin Flavor For Salads with Poultry, Ham, Chicken & Pork. **NCV**

1984 - *Simply Delicious Recipes from Sugar Free JELL-O Gelatin.* 24 pages. **NCV**

1987 - *JELL-O Brand Gelatin Desserts.* Favorite Producer's Idea File. **NCV**

1987 - *The JELL-O Pages from JELL-O Gelatins & Puddings.* **NCV**

1988 - *JELL-O Fun and Fabulous Recipes.* **NCV**

JELL-O Package Inserts
Value for each insert is $2.50

The Mothers of Whatsis Declare Their Independence
The Dove Princess
The JELL-O Girl at Lake Louise No. 6

The JELL-O Girl at Grand Canyon No. 12
The Four Winds, an American Fairy Tale No. 7
The JELL-O Girl in April
The JELL-O Girl in May
The JELL-O Girl in June
The JELL-O Girl in July
JELL-O Vegetable Salads, 1927, Postum Cereal Co.
JELL-O Pudding Recipes, Delicious, 1927, Postum Cereal
    Co.
(Inside) A Brief History of Plum Pudding
Family on Veranda (inside) JELL-O Salads
Miss JELL-O Visits Spain
Miss JELL-O Goes to Alaska
JELL-O...(in blue), on the back, The Easy JELL-O Way No.
    8, Marion Harland's Pineapple Bavarian Cream
Same as above, No. 11, Macaroon Velvet JELL-O
Same as above, No. 6, cherry JELL-O, on back, A Marion
    Harland's JELL-O Dessert, Lemon JELL-O Whip
Same as above, No. 7, Delight JELL-O, on back, Janet
    McKenzie Hill's Raspberry JELL-O Supreme
Same as above, No. 2, Almond Cherry, on back, Mrs.
    Rorer's JELL-O Jambolaya
Same as above, but on back, Chocolate JELL-O, No. 10
Same as above, but on back, Grape Juice Frappe, No. 12,
    Pineapple Mousse
JELL-O...in red, No. 11, JELL-O Relish
JELL-O...in solid red, No. 5, Glorified Rice
JELL-O...gray outlined in black, No. 3, Strawberry JELL-O
JELL-O in blue, No. 5, Neapolitan JELL-O on cover, on
    back, Stuffed Tomato Salad
JELL-O in black, No. 5, Neapolitan JELL-O on cover, on
    back, Stuffed Tomato Salad

JELL-O in black, No. 9, Orange JELL-O on cover, on back,
    Roman Sponge made of cherry JELL-O
JELL-O in red, No. 10, Nut Frappe on cover, on back,
    Beautiful Salad
JELL-O in red, No. 12, Thrifty Salad on cover, on back,
    Delmonico Dessert

◊ ◊ ◊ ◊

Minute Gelatine

The Minute Tapioca Company of Orange, Massachusetts manufactured gelatine as well as Tapioca and Star Brand Pearl Tapioca.

We have collected the following publication from this company.

1926 - *Minute Gelatine Cook Book.* 16 pages. **$12.00**

◊ ◊ ◊ ◊

D-Zerta

The D-Zerta Food Company of Rochester, New York manufactured D-Zerta Perfect Jelly Dessert as well as Quick Pudding and Ice Cream Powder. D-Zerta Perfect Jelly Dessert came in five flavors: raspberry, strawberry, lemon, orange and cherry.

We have collected the following publication from this company.

▶ 1890's - *All Eyes on the New Creation.* 4-page flyer. **$2.50**

Chapter 21

Milk

Milestones In The History of Milk in The U.S.

1611   Cows arrive for Jamestown Colony

1624   Cows reach Plymouth Colony

1841   First regular shipment of milk by rail, Orange County to New York City

1878   Continuous centrifugal cream separator invented by Dr. Gustave DeLaval

1884   Milk bottle invented by Dr. Harvey D. Thatcher, Potsdam, New York

1886   Automatic bottle filler and capper patented

1890   Tuberculin testing of dairy herds introduced. Test for fat content of milk and cream perfected by Dr. S.M. Babcock

1892   Certified milk originated by Dr. Henry L. Coit in Essex County, New Jersey

1895   Commercial pasteurizing machines Introduced

1908   First compulsory pasteurization law (Chicago) result of Dr. Bundeson's long fight

1911   Automatic rotary bottle filler and capper perfected

1914   Tank trucks first used for transporting milk

1932   Methods of increasing Vitamin D in milk

1932   Commercial introduction of homogenized milk in U.S.

1938   First farm bulk tanks for milk begin to replace milk cans

1942   Every-other-day milk delivery started (war conservation measure)

1946   Vacuum pasteurization method perfected

1948   Ultra-high temperature pasteurization introduced

1950   Milk vending machines win place in distribution

1955   Flavor control equipment for milk introduced commercially

Borden's

Gail Borden was born in Norwich, New York in 1801. He applied for a patent for evaporated milk and the same was granted on August 19, 1856. The first works were established at Wolcottville, Connecticut in 1856, and the second at Burrville in 1857. Deceased in January 1874, he was succeeded by his son, John G. Borden, whose inventive genius contributed many valuable mechanical improvements to the manufacturing department of the business. John was an earnest, Christian character with nobel generosity and devotion to the welfare of others. He passed away October 20, 1891 and H. Lee Borden, eldest son of Gail Borden, became president of the company.

The village of Wassaic, New York has a brick building bearing prominently upon its front the name of the New York Condensed Milk Company and also the world-reknowned trademark, "Gail Borden Eagle Brand." The Eagle Brand name for Borden's Condensed Milk had been adopted in 1866.

Elsie the Cow was introduced to the public in the late 1930's and appeared "in person" at the Pet Milk display at 1939 New York World's Fair.

Today the company name is Borden, Inc.

The following lists the cookbooks and booklets that we were able to collect from this company.

▶ 1892 - *Eagle Brand Milk.* Columbian Exhibit in the 1893 Columbian World Exposition, New York Condensed Milk Company, Agricultural Building, soft cover, 56 pages. **$25.00**

1911 - *Unusual Recipes.* Borden's Malted Milk Department, soft cover, 14 pages. **$16.00**

▶ Circa 1919 - *Borden's Evaporated Milk Book of Recipes.* Soft cover, 32 pages. **$14.00**

1920's - *Borden's Condensed Milk Prize Recipe Album.* Prize-winning recipes from the contests conducted by the Borden Company, hard cover, 72 pages. **$20.00**

▶ 1931 - *New Magic in the Kitchen.* Soft cover, 55 pages. **$10.00**

1932 - *Amazing Short-Cuts.* Soft cover, 37 pages. **$10.00**

1932 - *Magic Recipes Quicker, Easier, Surer to Succeed.* 34 pages. **$10.00**

▶ 1933-1934 - *108 World's Fair Recipes from Borden's.* Chicago Exposition, soft cover, 33 pages. **$10.00**

1935 - *Magic Eagle Brand Magic Discoveries for Quicker, Easier Cooking.* Soft cover. **$10.00**

1936 - *Borden's...Milk announces Recipe Quintuplets.* Soft cover, 10 pages. **$10.00**

1940 - *Elsie, The Borden Cow Suggests...Try These Magic Recipes.* Soft cover, 28 pages. **$8.00**

1946 - *Borden's Eagle Brand Magic Recipes.* Soft cover, 28 pages. **$8.00**

1952 - *Borden's Eagle Brand 70 Magic Recipes.* Soft cover, 26 pages. **$6.00**

▶ 1952 - *Elsie's Cook Book.* By Elsie the Cow with Aid of H. Botsford. Hard cover, 374 pagse. **$20.00**

▶ 1953 - *Starlac Presents Food in Fiction.* In The American Tradition From "The Song of Hiawatha" to "The Yearling." Soft cover, 20 pages. **$6.00**

1952, 1956 - *Borden's Eagle Brand 70 Magic Recipes.* Soft cover, 24 pages. **$4.00**

1969 - *The Dessert Lover's Hand Book.* Soft cover, 31 pages. **$3.00**

1980's - *Its So Easy with Eagle Brand Sweetened Condensed Milk.* Soft cover, 18 pages. **NCV**

1986, 1987, 1988 - *Borden Recipe Collection.* Soft cover, 96 pages. **NCV**

1980's - *Classic Desserts.* Soft cover. **NCV**

◊ ◊ ◊ ◊

Pet Milk

The Pet Milk Company was established in 1885 in the small town of Highland, Illinois. The name Pet came years later. At first, the company was Helvetia Milk Condensing Company after the Swiss farming community (Helvetia is Latin for Switzerland). John E. Meyenburg, a young Swiss, brought from his homeland the idea behind condensing and preserving milk without the use of sugar. Meyenburg left the company and the remaining investors succeeded in perfecting the processes.

The company prospered with Latzer as president. The growing process and success of evaporation led to the use of many brand names. The name "Our Pet," introduced around the turn of the century, was the most popular brand. In time it became so popular that the company took the name and became the Pet Milk Company.

One early cookbook gave these instructions for preparing Pet Milk for whipping: "Strip label from can and place on a block of ice...let it stand overnight." In the days before the electric refrigerators became common, that was the best way to chill food. Food preparation techniques have changed, but many of the recipes found in those early cookbooks, like the famous 75-year-old Pet recipe for pumpkin pie have probably remained a part of the family tradition.

The company's earliest ads included simple recipes.

Test Kitchens were established and a spokesperson was developed in the name of Mary Lee Taylor who was introduced to the public in the early 1930's and started radio cooking classes and brought recipes to the housewife. "The Mary Lee Taylor Program" aired every Saturday morning. Another Pet Milk radio show, "The Pet Milkyway" was broadcasted directly from the Woman's Magazine of the Air Kitchen by Ann Holden.

Pet moved their headquarters to St. Louis, Missouri and they built dozens of milk condensaries throughout the Midwest, east and south. In 1925 expansion into the western markets was accomplished with the acquistion of Sego Milk Products Company of Utah and they developed their first powdered milk for the bakery trade.

It wasn't until after World War II that the company diversified into non-dairy fields. In 1955 a small frozen pie business with the name of Pet-Ritz was acquired. In 1963 they added another emerging frozen food business, Downyflake Foods, Inc., makers of frozen donuts and waffles. Another fine food company came under their wing in 1961, the prestigious Whitman's Candy Company, maker of The Whitman's Sampler. In 1968 El Paso Canners of Mexican foods became another promising addition to the Pet Company and by this time the name was changed to Pet, Inc. That move reflected Pet's commitment to providing a whole family of quality food products: Sego diet foods, Heartland cereals, Downyflake frozen waffles, Compliment cooking sauces, Orleans canned seafood and Aunt Fanny's bakery goods, among others. By 1970, they had added the Wm. Underwood Company, a Boston firm for over 150 years. Underwood products included Ac'cent Flavor Enhancer, B&M Baked Beans and Brown Bread, and Richardson & Robbins Plum Pudding.

Today, Pet is a large and diverse company, Pet, Inc., an I.C. Industries Company.

The following lists the cookbooks and booklets we were able to collect from this company.

▶ 1923 - *Pet Milk Company Recipe Book.* Emily T. Chamberlin, cover has mother holding cake, two children play baking, 36 pages. **$12.00**

1926 - *You Can Save On Your Milk Bill.* "Where butter can be saved," by Sarah Field Splint; "In ice creams and desserts," by Alice Bradley, 40 pages. **$12.00**

1932 - *Pet Recipes.* Two-ring looseleaf, soft cover, 164 pages. **$10.00**

1933 - *Candies.* 21 pages. **$10.00**

1930's - *To Satisfy Winter Appetites.* Mary Lee Taylor, six-page booklet. **$8.00**

1930's - *Good Food at Lower Cost for 2 or 4 or 6.* 16 pages. **$10.00**

1930's - *Tempting Dishes the Easy Way for 2 or 4 or 6.* 16 pages. **$10.00**

1939 - *Meals at Their Best for 2 or 4 or 6.* 34 pages. **$10.00**

1939 - *Delicious Wholesome Meals for 2 or 4 or 6.* 34 pages. **$10.00**

▶ 1940 - *Tempting Low Cost Meals for 2 or 4 or 6.* 34 pages. **$6.00**

1941 - *67 Fail-Proof Recipes for 2 or 4 or 6.* 32 pages. **$6.00**

1941 - *More Wholesome Food at Lower Cost for 2 or 4 or 6.* 32 pages. **$6.00**

1941 - *Mary Lee Taylor's Meals That Please for 2 or 4 or 6.* 32 pages. **$6.00**

1942 - *Food for "Fitness" for 2 or 4 or 6.* 30 pages. **$6.00**

1942 - *Your Baby Tested Recipes for Baby's First Solid Foods and Dishes Suitable for Young Children.* 64 pages. **$12.00**

1944 - *Centennial Cook Book.* **$12.00**

1940's - *Deliciously Yours Recipes.* 16 pages. **$6.00**

1949 - *Good Food for 2 or 4 or 6.* 16 pages. **$6.00**

1951 - *Good Meals for Lazy Days for 2 or 4 or 6.* 16 pages. **$4.00**

1953 - *Time-Saving Tips to Good Eating with Recipes for 2 or 4.* 16 pages. **$4.00**

1950's - *Plain and Fancy Recipes from Pet Milk Company.* 16 pages. **$4.00**

1955 - *New Recipes by Mary Lee Taylor Using Instant Pet Nonfat Dry Milk.* 30 pages. **$4.00**

▶ 1957 - *Cookbook for Young Moderns.* Recipes by Mary Lee Taylor, 16 pages. **$4.00**

1960 - *Sweet and Simple.* 75th Anniversary 1885-1960, 8-page booklet. **$4.00**

1960 - *Carefree Cooking.* 16 pages. **$3.00**

1961 - *Good and Nourishing.* This cookbook free with this package of Pet Instant Nonfat Dry Milk, 16 pages. **$3.00**

1961 - *The Festive Touch.* Pet Milk and Nestlé chocolate, 9-page booklet. **$3.00**

1984 - *A Celebration of Cooking in America.* Hard cover, 224 pages. **NCV**

◊ ◊ ◊ ◊

Carnation

The Carnation Company was located in Milwaukee, Wisconsin and Toronto, Ontario, Canada. Their famous slogan was "From Contented Cows." At a later time their Home Service Department was located in Los Angeles, California. In 1923 Carnation Condensed Milk was introduced.

We were able to collect the following cookbooks and booklets from this company.

▶ 1934 - *100 Glorified Recipes*. Mary Blake. **$10.00**

1940's - *Selected Family Favorites*. Carnation Velvet Blend Recipes. **$8.00**

1942 - *Carnation Cook Book*. Mary Blake, Director Home Economics. **$8.00**

▶ 1942 - *Growing Up With Milk*. Eating and drinking the Carnation Way. **$8.00**

1940's - *The Velvet Blend Cook Book - Milk Rich Carnation Recipes*. Mary Blake, Home Service Dept. **$8.00**

1951 - *The Cooks Handbook*. Mary Blake, Home Service Director. **$6.00**

▶ 1953 - *Baking Secrets*. Mary Blake, 8 pages. **$6.00**

1954 - *Mary Blake Favorite Recipes*. 16 pages. **$6.00**

1956 - *Carnation's Family Favorites*. Mary Blake, 16 pages. **$6.00**

▶ 1959 - *Teen-time Cooking with Carnation*. 16 pages. **$6.00**

1961 - *38 Answers to What's Cooking*. Mary Blake, 24 pages. **$3.00**

▶ 1967 - *Fun to Cook Book*. Introducing Mary Blake's daughter, "Margie Blake," 48 pages. **$3.00**

◊ ◊ ◊ ◊

Golden Key

The Golden Key Milk Products Company in Madison, Wisconsin, produced Golden Key Brand Evaporated Milk. The company held a Golden Key Recipe Contest in 1925 in Madison, Wisconsin and Tampa and St. Petersburg, Florida. The first, second and third prize recipes from each contest are included in the booklet listed below.

We have collected the following publication from this company.

1925 - *Golden Key Recipe Book - A Booklet of Delicious Foods*. 16 pages. **$12.00**

◊ ◊ ◊ ◊

Milnot

The Carolene Products Company of Litchfield, Illinois manufactured Milnot Condensed Milk.

We have collected the following publications from this company.

1948 - *Tested Milnot Recipes for Thirfty Cookin*. Mary Elizabeth Wright, 48 pages. **$8.00**

1969 - *Tested and Tasted Economical Recipes*. Presented by Milnot, 2nd edition, 48 pages. **$3.00**

◊ ◊ ◊ ◊

Quality Dairy

Quality Dairy Company is an old, respected company that was established in 1857 in St. Louis, Missouri. This company also produced "Good Rich" salad dressing as well as margarine and Fondalac, a full-bodied buttermilk from cultured whole milk. They also produced Riviera Continental Ice Cream.

By 1964 the Quality Dairy Company had expanded their production of food items to include packaged cookies, instant coffee, jams and jellies, peanut butter, fresh eggs, sour cream and dips.

The following lists the cookbooks and booklets we have been able to research and collect from this company.

1957 - *Quality Dairy Company "None Better" Recipes*. Second edition, soft cover, 48 pages. **$4.00**

▶ 1964 - *King Quality Presents the VIP Stand Up Cook Book*. Jeannette H. Elliott, soft cover, 126 pages. **$3.00**

◊ ◊ ◊ ◊

Pevely

Casper H. Kerckhoff came to this country from Germany in 1841. He settled near St. Louis, and during the Mexican War, manufactured bullets for the U.S. Army. Shortly after the close of the war, he purchased a section of land in Jefferson county in Missouri. Casper is said to have had the first cream separator and the first herd of registered Jersey cows west of the Mississippi. Upon his death in 1899, the old homestead was split up and his son, Martin, and his brother, Jacob, retained an interest in one of the farms into which the homestead was divided.

In those days the supply of dairy products to city-dwellers was on a rather uncertain basis. Butter was made on the farms, and city folks were always glad for a chance to get fresh country butter whenever they could. Martin Kerckhoff had started a butter route to St. Louis back in the early 1880's. As his trade increased his customers began buying milk shipped to him by railroad by relatives from Pevely, Missouri, located 30 miles south of St. Louis. This product was known as Pevely Milk.

In 1887 the Pevely Dairy Company was formed in a

little building on Seventh Street. The business prospered and before long the milk routes were several in number. Martin's son, Daniel, was a young boy at the time the dairy was founded, but in those days boys started work early in life. At the turn of the century, plans were being made for the Louisiana Purchase Exposition, better known as the St. Louis World's Fair in 1904. Young Dan by this time was quite experienced in the dairy and he managed to get the milk concession for the Fair. It was the Kerckhoff's first real break.

Meanwhile, they had outgrown their original plant and built a larger dairy at 3301 Park Avenue in St. Louis. A plant of this size meant taking considerable risk, but the Kerckhoff's had faith in the future of the dairy industry. A period of growth followed and shortly after the outbreak of the first World War, father and son began plans for the present plant at Grand and Chouteau. This plant began operation in 1917, the year after the death of the founder of the dairy, and Dan took over the management.

In 1928 Pevely Dairy Company had established a milk receiving plant in St. James, Missouri at the (then) Dunmoor woolen and flour mill place built by William James in 1869. The owners of Pevely Dairy Company worked with the St. James Chamber of Commerce to hold a free barbecue and parade of cattle as a promotion. For five consecutive years the annual September dairy show was held featuring free barbecue, a banquet and parade of cattle, school children and business floats. In 1934 the depression caused a slump in the company's profits, and Pevely had to close this milk receiving plant.

Spokeswoman "Prudence Pevely" was Jeanette Elliott, a local Home Economist who directed a cooking school for newlyweds at the Pevely auditorium during the late 1920's and up to World War II (1942). Pevely used the auditorium to produce the Pevely Playhouse Party from 1954 to 1973, featuring Russ David.

Today the Pevely Dairy Company is operated by the grandsons and great grandsons of Martin W. Kerckhoff. The company product line includes fluid milks, ice creams, cottage cheeses, novelties, egg nog, dips, whipped cream, sour cream products and fruit drinks.

The following lists the cookbooks and booklets we were able to collect from this company.

1930 - *Selected Recipes - The Best Milk, Pevely Selected Milk.* 52 pages. **$10.00**

1937 - *Delicious Dairy Dishes - Tested Recipes, Tempting Menus.* Meta Given and Ruth Cooper, Specialists in Home Economics, 62 pages. **$10.00**

1939 - *Prudence Pevely's Pantry.* Dedicated to "Culinary Artists," 64 pages. **$10.00**

1939 - *Prudence Pevely Says.* 4-page mailer folded, makes 8 pages. **$4.00**

◊ ◊ ◊ ◊

Sealtest

The Sealtest Laboratory Kitchen, located at 30 Rockefeller Plaza, Radio City, New York, was part of the Sealtest System Laboratories, Inc. Miss Bealah V. Gillaspie was Director, formerly Food Research Editor of *McCall's* magazine, assisted by Miss Julia Bliss Joyner, formerly Food Editor of *Pictorial Review Magazine.* In 1939 the Sealtest Laboratory Kitchen moved to 230 Park Avenue, New York.

We have collected the following cookbooks and booklets from this company.

1936 - *150 New Ways to Serve Ice Cream.* Sue Moody, 64 pages. **$10.00**

1939 (Fall) - *The Sealtest Food Adviser.* Bealah V. Gillaspie, 16 pages. **$3.00**

1940 (March-April) - *The Sealtest Food Adviser.* Bealah V. Gillaspie, 16 pages. **$3.00**

1945 (Winter) - *The Sealtest Food Adviser.* Mary Preston, 12 pages. **$3.00**

1946 - *Sandwich-Salad Suggestions.* The Sealtest Laboratory Kitchen, 16 pages. **$8.00**

1940's - *The New Sealtest Book of Recipes and Menus.* 96 pages. **$8.00**

1954 - *641 Tested Recipes From the Sealtest Kitchens.* National Dairy Products Corp., Pocket Book, 256 pages. **$6.00**

◊ ◊ ◊ ◊

Knudsen Creamery Company

The Knudsen Creamery Company of California, established in 1919, is now a subsidiary of the Foremost Dairy Products. 1949 was the first edition of the *Knudsen Recipe Book.*

1961 - *Knudsen Recipes.* Knudsen Dairy Products, The Very Best, 12th edition, 64 pages. **NCV**

1962 - *Knudsen Recipes.* Knudsen Dairy Products, The Very Best, 13th edition, 64 pages. **NCV**

◊ ◊ ◊ ◊

Highland Dairy Farms Company
Highland, Illinois

▶ 1935 - *Aunt Sally's Favorite Recipes.* Compiled for Highland Dairy Farms Company, 32 pages. **$10.00**

◊ ◊ ◊ ◊

Windsor Farm Dairy
Denver, Colorado

1922 - *New Ways of Serving Windsor Farm Dairy Ice Cream.* By Fraderick C. Mathews Company, 12 pages. **$6.00**

◊ ◊ ◊ ◊

Iowana Farms Milk Company and
Iowa Dairy Industry Commission
Des Moines, Iowa

1950's - *Cottage Cheese Recipe Book - Appetizers, Salads, Salad Dressings, Breads, Main Dishes, Desserts.* This cottage cheese recipe booklet is made available to you by your milkman and the Iowa Milk Dealers' Association. 30 pages. **$6.00**

◊ ◊ ◊ ◊

The American Dairy Association

The American Dairy Association with offices in Chicago, has served as the voice of the dairy farmer in the marketplace of America since 1940. The American Dairy Association in the source of authentic information about dairy products. Their home economist supervised the development of recipes that are used in food photographs, publicity releases, cookbooks and dairy products information leaflets, and offered to newpapers and magazines, radio and television.

The following are examples of the materials produced and circulated to encourage the use of dairy products.

1950's - *"Lets" Eat Outdoors.* Recipes and ideas for picnics, etc., 28 pages. **$6.00**

1966 - *Modern Approach to Everyday Cooking.* Over 500 recipes, Home Economics Dept., spiral, 223 pages. **$3.00**

Chapter 22

Desserts

The White Mountain Freezer Company

The White Mountain Freezer Company of Nashua, New Hampshire manufactured ice cream freezers. Their advertising recipe book *Frozen Dainties* was published to promote the sale of the freezers and one was given with each freezer sold. They manufactured ice cream freezers in sizes from two-quart to 25-quart.

We were able to collect the following publications.

▶ 1899 - *Frozen Dainties*. Mrs. Lincoln, author of the *Boston Cook Book*, 32 pages. **$20.00**

▶ 1905 - *Frozen Dainties*. Mrs. Mary J. Lincoln, author of the *Boston Cook Book*, 32 pages. **$16.00**

◊ ◊ ◊ ◊

The North Brothers Manufacturing Company

The North Brothers Manufacturing Company of Philadelphia, Pennsylvania manufactured hardware specialties for household use. One such item was Shepard's Jumbo Lighting ice cream freezers, 14 and 20 quart capacity, and Shepard's Lightning ice cream freezers of sizes from 1 quart to 14 quart. The advertising recipe book *Dainty Dishes* was used to promote the sale of the ice cream freezers and one was given with each freezer sold.

We were able to collect the following publications from this company.

▶ 1895, 1897 - *Dainty Dishes For All The Year Round*. Mrs. S.T. Rorer, principal, Philadelphia Cooking School, 64 pages. **$20.00**

1895, 1900 - *Dainty Dishes For All The Year Round*. Mrs. S.T. Rorer, 64 pages. **$20.00**

▶ 1895, 1905 - *Dainty Dishes For All The Year Round*. Mrs. S.T. Rorer, 64 pages. **$16.00**

Others:
Circa 1915 - *Ice Cream and Other Desserts - 84 Approved Recipes for Use with Your Hand-Operated Freezer*. 32 pages. **$14.00**

▶ 1914 - *Cardui Dessert Book*. Selected Recipes by Famous Cooks. Blank space for your own recipes, Chattanooga Medicine Company, St. Louis, 24 pages. **$14.00**

1916 - *Desserts of Quality - How to Prepare Them*. Emma E. Curtis, Miss Curtis's Snowflake Marshmallow Creme, Melrose, Massachusetts. **$14.00**

1918 - *Heller's Guide For Ice Cream Makers*. 6th edition, B. Heller and Company, 154 pages. **$14.00**

◊ ◊ ◊ ◊

Hip-O-lite Marshmallow Creme

1920's - *The Book of Caterer's And Chef's Professional Recipes*. Explains how Madam herself may don an apron and add a professional touch to home desserts. Irene B. Cushing, Department of Home Economics, 16 pages. **$12.00**

1920's - *Simplified Candy Making As It Is Done with Hip-O-Lite*. 15-page booklet. **$8.00**

1930's - *Home Desserts And Confections of All Kinds Made From Professional Recipes*. Hip-O-Lite, 12 pages. **$10.00**

◊ ◊ ◊ ◊

Nabisco

In 1792 in the seaside village of Newburyport, 30 miles north of Boston, John Pearson established America's first commercial bakery. It flourished and in 1898 joined with dozens of other bakeries to form the National Biscuit Company, forerunner of Nabisco, Inc.

In 1801 in Milton, Massachusetts, a former ship's captain named Josiah Bent devised several types of crisp, light, unsweetened biscuits that he called "crackers." While his wife and children did the baking, he did the selling, traveling from town to town on horseback and dispensing his crackers from saddlebags. His business continued until it was absorbed by the National Biscuit Company in 1905.

In Arlington, to Boston's west, Aretemas Kennedy

started the Kennedy Biscuit Company in 1805, which was to continue in operation until it was absorbed by the National Biscuit Company in 1905. The cracker barrel stood for years, hospitality open, convenient for sampling in every store. In 1898 the National Biscuit Company began putting their Uneeda Soda Crackers in family size, patented, moisture-proof packages.

Nabisco Brands was a name change that occurred in 1981 through a merger of Nabisco, Inc. and Standard Brands, Inc. Then in 1985 through a takeover, Nabisco Brands became an operating company of R.J. Reynolds Industries, Inc. In 1985 R.J. Reynolds Industries then assigned its Del Monte unit to Nabisco Brands and later changed its own name to RJR Nabisco Inc.

In 1988 an investment firm of Kohlberg Kravis Roberts & Co. performed a leveraged buyout of RJR Nabisco, Inc. and maintains business with the same name.

We were able to collect the following publications from this company.

1937 - *50 Delicious Desserts.* Helen S. Kentzing, Director, Home Economics Department, 16 pages. **$10.00**

1940's - *Delicious Desserts.* Mary Ellen Baker, Director, Home Economics Division, 16 pages. **$8.00**

1957 - *75 Delicious Desserts.* Mary Ellen Baker, Director, Home Economics Division, 28 pages. **$6.00**

◊ ◊ ◊ ◊

Minute Tapioca

In 1894 the process of ground tapioca was developed. In 1895 John Whitman bought the rights to use the process of ground tapioca. In 1895 he formed the Whitman Grocery Company and produced Tapioca superlative. A year or so later, the name was changed to Minute Tapioca.

We were able to collect the following from this company.

1909 - *The Minute Man Cook Book.* Minute Tapioca, 34 pages. **$16.00**

1915 - *Minute Cook Book.* Minute Tapicoa Co., edited by Mrs. Derby, Orange, Massachusetts. Mrs. Derby has been recipe editor for 18 years. 32 pages. **$14.00**

1920's - *The $20,000 Cook Book of Minute Tapioca Recipes.* **$12.00**

1927 - *Prize Winning Recipes to Vary Your Menus. Have Your Tried Minute Gelatine?* 32 pages. **$12.00**

1929 - *30 New Recipes From the $20,000 Cook Book.* Manufacturers of Minute Tapioca, Minute Gelatine and Star Brand Pearl Tapioca, P. & Co., Inc., 20 pages. **$12.00**

1931 - *A Cook's Tour with Minute Tapioca.* Published by Minute Tapioca Company, Inc., Division of General Foods Corp, 46 pages. **$10.00**

1938 - *Miss Dine-About-Town - Marvelous Meals with Minute Tapioca.* Minute Tapioca Co., Inc., Division of General Foods Corp., 24 pages. **$10.00**

1948 - *Miracles with Minute Tapioca.* Frances Barton, Consumer Service Dept., General Foods Corp., 22 pages. **$8.00**

1980 - *Minute Tapioca Meal Time Magic.* General Foods Consumer Center, 25 pages. **NCV**

◊ ◊ ◊ ◊

Junket

Charles Hansen's Laboratory of Copenhagen, Denmark and Little Falls, New York, manufactured Junket. The laboratories also manufactured Extract of Vanilla and a product line of Pure Food Colors. By 1929 the laboratories were making both the Junket Rennet Tablets and Junket Rennet Powder in flavors and Junket Brand Food Colors. By 1938 they made Junket Brank Buttermilk Culture.

The following lists what we were able to find from this company.

▶ 1902 - *Have Some Junket.* A Collection of Valuable Recipes for Milk Desserts and Ice Cream, Janet McKenzie Hill, Emma H. Crane and other experts in cookery, 32 pages. **$16.00**

▶ 1926 - *Junket Recipes.* 17 pages. **$12.00**

1929 - *Delicious Quick Desserts.* Mary Mason, "The Junket Folks," 24 pages. **$12.00**

1936 - *Recipes by Mary Mason.* "The Junket Folks." **$10.00**

1938 - *How to Make Rennet Custards and Ice Cream.* Mary Mason, Director, Home Economics Dept., "The Junket Folks," 31 pages. **$10.00**

▶ 1941 - *How To Make Tempting Nutritious Desserts.* Mary Mason, Director, Home Economics Dept., "The Junket Folks," 30 pages. **$8.00**

◊ ◊ ◊ ◊

My-T-Fine

In 1910 the D & C Food Products Company began manufacturing My-T-Fine packaged desserts. The company also manufactured D & C Lemon Puddings and D & C Self-Rising Flour.

We were able to find the following publication from this company.

1928 - *Good things To Eat Made With D & C Quality Food Products.* The D & C Co., Inc., Brooklyn, New York, 16 pages. **$12.00**

◊◊◊◊

Miscellaneous

1920's - *Mrs. Beatty's Strawberry Dainties and Other Recipes.* 18 pages. **$12.00**

1949 - *Nescafe - 24 New Coffee-Flavored Desserts.* The Nestle´ Company, Inc., 14 pages. **$8.00**

1981 - *Mmmm in Minutes - Mouth-watering Pies to Remember From Cool Whip.* General Foods Corporation, 16 pages. **NCV**

1984 - *Simple Desserts Made Simply Sensational with Cool Whip.* General Foods Corporation, 8 pages. **NCV**

1986 - *Dessert Recipes From Around The World.* Hallmark, 12 pages. **NCV**

Chapter 23

Cereals

Oatmeal

In 1854 Ferdinand Schumacher set up a hand mill for grinding oats in the rear of his little grocery store in Akron, Ohio. The Schumacher oatmeal was a cheap protein, not merely for breakfast and was called Avena.

In 1873 John Stuart and his son, Robert Stuart, migrated to Cedar Rapids, Iowa from a small oat mill in Canada. They purchased a large warehouse that fronted on the Red Cedar River to manufacture oatmeal. Robert Stuart later opened a second mill in Chicago to manufacture oatmeal and other grain cereals.

In 1882 Henry P. Crowell entered the milling trade when he purchased a small mill at Ravenna, Ohio, 16 miles from Akron, and called the mill "The Ravenna Oatmeal Mill." By 1886 his mill was producing and marketing steel-cut oats under the brand name of "Quaker."

Oatmeal was sold and shipped in 180-pound barrels at first. The 180-pound barrel could be found in all the city and country stores. Schumacher began shipping also in wood crates of two-pound jars. Crowell packaged his Quaker brand in two-pound packages with cooking directions on the cartons. Crowell was also the first to advertise his Quaker brand of oatmeal. He advertised in large city newpapers and large billboards. His Quaker package showed a picture of a man in Quaker garb, holding a scroll that showed the word "Pure." This type of advertising worked very well.

A company called Consolidated Oatmeal Company formed in 1887 but it did not last past 1888.

By the later part of 1888 the seven largest cereal manufacturers formed under a holding company which became The American Cereal Company and jointly manufactured and marketed their various brand-named cereals.

In 1891 The American Cereal Company was reorganized as an operating company under Ohio law. At last an effective merger of seven large manufacturers had been successful. This new company's president was Ferdinand Schumacher, Henry P. Crowell was vice-president, and Robert Stuart was secretary-treasurer.

A cookbook from The American Cereal Company, Chicago, edited by Sarah Tyson Rorer, states, "Our goods are packed in cartons; under two principal proprietary brands, the 'Quaker' and 'F.S.' or 'F. Schumacher.' Under the Quaker brand we put up Quaker Rolled White Oats and other cereal foods. Under the Quaker brand we put up Quaker Rolled White Oats and other cereal foods. Under the 'F.S.' brand we put up 'F.S.' (Schumacher's) Rolled Avena, 'F.S.' Rolled Wheat, 'F.S.' Cooked Wheat, Farina, 'F.S.' Parched Farinose, 'F.S.' Hominy, 'F.S.' Grains of Gold, and other cereal products from oats, wheat, corn, rye and barley."

The Quaker Oats Company was set up as a holding company in 1901. By now all brands and manufacturing had been consolidated in the Quaker name. Robert Stuart and Henry P. Crowell and some friends with American Cereal company had pledged their holdings or stock in the new Quaker Oats Company.

The following are the recipe books we have collected from this company.

▶ 1899 - *We Feed The World - Cereal Foods And How To Cook Them.* Fifth edition, The American Cereal Company, Chicago, edited by Sarah Tyson Rorer. Cover shows a picture of Pettijohn's Breakfast Food, Given Highest Award at World's Fair, Chicago, 1893. 68 pages. **$25.00**

1963 - *'Round the Clock Recipes From Mary Alden.* Cover has picture of Quaker Oats and Mother's Oats, 48 pages. **$3.00**

1975 - *All-Time Any Time Recipes - Its Quick and Old Fashion Quaker Oats.* Special recipes for instant oatmeal, 48 pages. **NCV**

1980 - *The Quaker Oats Wholegrain Cookbook.* Seventh printing, 63 pages. **NCV**

1981 - *The Quaker Oats Wholegrain Cookbook.* Eight printing, 63 pages. **NCV**

1982 - *Stretching Food Dollars - Meal Planning Hints & Budget-Wise Recipes.* 37 pages. **NCV**

During 1900, 13 of the largest independent millers banded together as the Cereal Bureau. In 1901 a group revealed itself as The Great Western Cereal Company with production about half that of Quaker, and a brand called Mother's Oats.

◊ ◊ ◊ ◊

Shredded Wheat

Henry Perky found a way to press wheat into strips, forming a biscuit, and baking them. By 1892 he was operating a small bakery in Denver, making shredded wheat biscuits and he operated a restaurant where they were served. There were also salespeople in the area selling Shredded Wheat door to door.

Business grew rapidly and a larger bakery was built in Roxbruy, Massachusetts. This bakery could not keep up with the sales and a much larger plant was built in Worcester, Massachusetts. Still faced with growth problems, Henry Perky decided to build a new plant in Niagara Falls, New York. By 1900 The Natural Food Conservatory became successor to The Shredded Wheat Company, located in a new two-million dollar complex in Niagara Falls, New York, 10 acres with a 900-foot frontage on the upper Niagara Rapids. The main building was devoted to the manufacturing of Shredded Wheat and Triscuits, a shredded whole wheat wafer. Shredded Wheat took awards at the 1895 Louisiana Purchase Exposition and took the Gold Medal at the Paris World's Exposition in 1900.

By 1924 The Shredded Wheat Company had expanded and had built plants in Oakland, California, The Canadian Shredded Wheat Company, Ltd., in Toronto, Canada, and The Shredded Wheat Company, Ltd., in London, England.

In 1928 the National Biscuit Company acquired The Shredded Wheat Company of Niagara Falls, New York. This acquisition put the National Biscuit Company in the ready-to-eat cereal business.

We have collected the following publications from this company.

▶ 1898 - *More Light*. Series V, 20-page booklet. **$20.00**

1898, 1900 - *More Light*. Series V, 20-page booklet. **$20.00**

▶ 1899, 1906 - *The Vital Question*. And The Answer with a Comprehensive Treatise on the Principals of Cooking with 100 Recipes For Making Simple, Palatable and Nutritious Shredded Wheat. 68-page booklet. **$16.00**

▶ 1924 - *Fifty Ways of Serving Shredded Wheat Including The Dishes That Won Gold Prizes*. 20 pages. **$12.00**

1924 - *50 Ways of Serving Shredded Wheat*. 22 pages. **$12.00**

▶ 1933 - *Recipes for New and Delicious Energy Dishes*. Shredded Wheat National Biscuit Company, 17 pages. **$10.00**

1950 - *Delicious Nourishing Dishes for Breakfast, Luncheon & Dinner*. Nabisco Shredded Wheat, Nabisco Co., Inc. **$6.00**

◊ ◊ ◊ ◊

Cerealine

The Cerealine Manufacturing Company of Columbus, Indiana manufactured Cerealine Flakes for cooking, for breakfast, or any meal.

The following lists what we have collected from this company.

▶ 1886 - *Cerealine Flakes - This Book Contains 200 Recipes For Cooking Cerealine Flakes*. Third edition, second printing, 31 pages. **$25.00**

1886 - *Cerealine Flakes - This Book Contains 200 Recipes For Cooking Cerealine Flakes*. Third edition, second printing, 31 pages. **$25.00**

◊ ◊ ◊ ◊

Cream of Rice

The Cream of Rice Company established a subsidiary company named "Home Magazine of Chicago" to advertise their product of Cream of Rice Cereal. They advertised dolls, Daisy Dimple, Dolly Dimple and Dora Dimple. It was easy to get the Dimple Dolls - "send two Cream of Rice Trade-Marks and 16 cents and we will send the three dolls postpaid, also one full years paid subscription to the Home Magazine of Chicago." Premiums in the form of pictures and postcards were also offered, "2 magnificent pictures in beautiful colors for only 7 cents and two trademarks." This type of advertising proved very successful for the Cream of Rice Company.

The following publication is what we have been able to collect from this company.

▶ Circa 1890 - *Cream Of Rice - The World's Best Food*. 27 pages. **$25.00**

◊ ◊ ◊ ◊

The Kellogg Company

The General Conference of the Church of the Seventh Day Adventists decided to establish the Western Health Reform Institute in Battle Creek, Michigan. They purchased a two-story farmhouse on eight acres of ground in the western-most outskirts of Battle Creek. There, on September 5, 1866 the institution opened with two physicians, two bath attendants, an untrained nurse and some helpers. In 1867 the Institute was incorporated but some years later the stockholders relinquished their dividends and made it a non-profit institution.

In 1868 Merritt Kellogg attained his M.D. degree and returned to Battle Creek and served for several months on the Sanitarium staff before returning to California.

In 1871 John Harvey Kellogg (Merritt's younger brother) became Physician in Chief of the institution which was to become the Battle Creek Sanitarium.

In 1880 Will Keith Kellogg (John's eight-year younger brother) was a bookkeeper in the employ of Dr. John

Harvey Kellogg at the Battle Creek Sanitarium.

In 1878 a five-story building capable of housing 200 patients was built. By 1897, there had been many additions built.

In February 1902, fire destroyed the main building, the hospital and the annex (the original building). A new building was built and dedicated on May 31, 1903. It was six stories high and 550 feet in length and designed in the Renaissance Style.

Dr. John Harvey Kellogg had invented and made many types of health foods for the Sanitarium and had established a number of food manufacturing companies to supply the Sanitarium with their products, and then to supply mail-order service to previous patients and also to supply the public through grocers and health food stores. Such early products included Granola, Zwieback and toasted corn flakes. Some of the food companies were Sanitarium Food Company, Battle Creek Health Food Company, Sanitas Food Company, Sanitas Nut Food Company and Sanitas Nut Food Company, Ltd., and briefly Kellogg Food Company.

The Sanitas Food Company was established in 1894 by Dr. John Harvey Kellogg who held 75% of the shares, and Will K. Kellogg who held 25% of the shares. On May 31, 1894 Dr. John Harvey Kellogg filed an application for a patent on "Flaked cereals and the process of preparing same." The product was named Granose and was packaged in 10-ounce size, selling at 15 cents a package.

About 1900 the Sanitas Nut Food Company was created to market the new nut-foods and products. One of the products invented was peanut buttter and Nutolene (coconut oil shortening). By 1902 Sanitas Nut Food company and the Sanitas Food Company were merged to become Sanitas Nut Food Company, Ltd.

In 1904 Dr. John Harvey Kellogg, manager of the sanitarium, and the Seventh Day Adventists General Council parted company when the Church wanted to move the sanitarium to Washington, D.C. Dr. Kellogg made arrrangements to purchase the sanitarium from the Church. Dr. Kellogg managed and/or owned the sanitarium for 67 years until 1943.

Will Kellogg parted company with his brother and quit his employment at the sanitarium and devoted his attention to operating the Sanitas Food Company for his 25% shares and 22½ years at the sanitarium. Following the 1902 fire, W.K. Kellow returned to the employ of the sanitarium to help rebuild it and was there for the dedication of the new building in May of 1903.

W.K. Kellogg started his own company in 1906, manufacturing Sanitas Toasted Corn Flakes following purchase of right to manufacture from his brother in 1905. The name was soon changed to "Kellogg's Toasted Corn Flakes" and in 1925 the official company name became "Kellogg Company" and the packages contained the signature of W.K. Kellogg in red. The company soon added Shredded Wheat and All Bran to its products.

The following lists the publications we were able to collect from this company.

▶ 1934 - *The Sunny Side of Life Book - To Keep Happy, Keep Well.* Barbara B. Brooks, Home Economics Department, 32 pages. **$10.00**

1937 - *The Housewife's Year Book of Health and Homemaking.* 36 pages. **$10.00**

1938 - *The Housewife's Almanac - A Book For Homemakers.* 36 pages. **$10.00**

1971 - *Kay Kellogg's Creative Cookery.* Department of Home Economics, 64 pages. **NCV**

1970's - *Bran For All Occasions Featuring Kellogg's Bran Greats.* Public Affairs Department, 20 pages. **NCV**

1980 - *Bran For All Occasions Featuring Kellogg's Bran Cereals.* Public Affairs Department, 20 pages. **NCV**

1980 - *The Kellogg's Cookbook - 270 Exciting Recipes.* **NCV**

1981 - *Cooking With Kellogg's - A Collection of Tempting Recipes To Enjoy.* 8 pages. **NCV**

1981 - *The Kellogg's Cookbook - 270 Exciting Recipes.* **NCV**

1982 - *Breakfast Is A Healthy Habit - A Guide For People Who Skip Breakfast.* Kellogg Company Nutri-Grain, 12 pages. **NCV**

◊ ◊ ◊ ◊

Battle Creek Food Company

Will K. Kellogg left the Battle Creek Sanitarium in 1903 to operate the Sanitas Food Company and in 1905 he purchased from his brother the rights to manufacture "Toasted Corn Flakes." In 1906 he established his own company.

Dr. John Harvey Kellogg became the owner of the Sanitarium after his brother's departure. In 1904 he established the Battle Creek Food Company to manufacture the various health foods used by the sanitarium and to sell through grocers, etc. These food products included Zo, a Vitamin Breakfast Food, Zwieback, Branola and Granola cereal foods, Vita-Bits Breakfast Food, Granose Flakes, Toasted Rice Flakes, Cero-Vits, Granose Biscuit, Bran Biscuit, 40% Gluten Biscuit and many other products.

We have collected the following publication from this company.

1918 - *Healthful Living.* Fundamental facts about food and feeding, 47 pages. **$14.00**

◊ ◊ ◊ ◊

Postum Cereal Company

One of the patients who arrived at the Battle Creek Sanitarium in 1891 was a businessman who, in a greatly emaciated condition, was conveyed about the premises in a wheelchair. He had suffered reverses as a salesman, agricultrual implement dealer and hardware retailer.

However, after some months away from his business worries and under good medical care, his health improved and he regained 40 to 50 pounds. During C.W. Post's stay at the sanitarium, one of the principal health foods manufactured was a cereal coffee substitute, "Carmel Cereal." The formula was no secret and there was no apparent effort to cloak the method of its production from the public.

Following his departure from the sanitarium and his subsequent establishment of the LaVita Inn near Battle Creek, Mr. Post, in late 1894, began making a cereal Coffee which he called "Monk's Brew." This beverage did not have immediate success. He changed the product name in 1897 to Postum Cereal and established the Postum Cereal Company, Limited.

With the aid of a Chicago advertising agency, Post then launched a vigorous advertising campaign. Postum packages carried the phrase "Makes Red Blood." With some financial aid from the Fuller Company, Mr. Post was able to bridge the early lean years and by 1900 was said to be very successful.

In 1898 Post produced a product, Grape-Nuts, which bore some resemblance to Granola, a granulated cereal food which the Battle Creek Sanitarium had been making for nearly 20 years.

The following lists the publications we have been able to research or collect.

1904 - *The Road To Wellville*. This little book of recipes in each package of Grape-Nuts. **$12.00**

1914 - *There's A Reason*. Postum Cereal Company, Grape-Nuts, Postum, Post Toasties, etc., 48 pages. **$14.00**

1924 - *101 Prize Recipes That Cost $7,550.00 in Prize Money*. Grape-Nuts, Postum Cereal Company. **$12.00**

◊ ◊ ◊ ◊

Ralston Purina

The Ralston Purina Company Checkerboard Square, St. Louis, Missouri, manufactures Instant Ralston and Regular Ralston, Whole Wheat Cereals with extra wheat germ added; Wheat Chex, Bite Size Shredded Wheat Biscuits, Rice Chex and Ry-Krisp.

We were able to find the following publication on this company.

▶ Circa 1940 - *Breakfast Around The World*. 12 pages. **$8.00**

◊ ◊ ◊ ◊

Cheerios

General Mills, Inc. manufactures Cheerios breakfast cereal food. We were able to collect the following publication from this company.

1977 - *The Cheerios Recipe Booklet - Powerful Good Snacks, Main Dishes, Desserts*. Betty Crocker, 16 pages. **NCV**

◊ ◊ ◊ ◊

Cream of Wheat

In 1893 the Diamond Milling Company in Grand Forks, North Dakota was owned by Emery Mapes and George Bull and they manufactured wheat flour. In this year they experimented with the unused hearts of the wheat. The resulting porridge for breakfast was named "Cream of Wheat." By 1894 Cream of Wheat was so successful that a Cream of Wheat Company was established in Minneapolis. A solid advertising campaign helped the growth of the cereal.

At some point and time, the expanding National Biscuit Company acquired the Cream Of Wheat Company.

We have collected the following publications from this company.

1920 - *Diamond Cook Book - Compiled From Tested Recipes*. Cover illustrates a negro chef in a circle with a large ladle over his shoulder. **$12.00**

1982 - *New Recipes with Cream Of Wheat Cereal - As Good As You Remember...and More!* 19 pages. **NCV**

◊ ◊ ◊ ◊

Books on Antiques and Collectibles

Most of the following books are available from your local book seller or antique dealer, or on loan from your public library. If you are unable to locate certain titles in your area you may order by mail from COLLECTOR BOOKS, P.O. Box 3009, Paducah, KY 42002-3009. Add $2.00 for postage for the first book ordered and $.25 for each additional book. Include item number, title and price when ordering. Allow 14 to 21 days for delivery. All books are well illustrated and contain current values.

Books on Glass and Pottery

1810	American Art Glass, Shuman	$29.95
1517	American Belleek, Gaston	$19.95
2016	Bedroom & Bathroom Glassware of the Depression Years	$19.95
1312	Blue & White Stoneware, McNerney	$9.95
1959	Blue Willow, 2nd Ed., Gaston	$14.95
1627	Children's Glass Dishes, China & Furniture II, Lechler	$19.95
1892	Collecting Royal Haeger, Garmon	$19.95
2017	Collector's Ency. of Depression Glass, Florence, 9th Ed.	$19.95
1373	Collector's Ency of Amercian Dinnerware, Cunningham	$24.95
1812	Collector's Ency. of Fiesta, Huxford	$19.95
1439	Collector's Ency. of Flow Blue China, Gaston	$19.95
1961	Collector's Ency. of Fry Glass, Fry Glass Society	$24.95
2086	Collector's Ency. of Gaudy Dutch & Welsh, Schuman	$14.95
1813	Collector's Encyclopedia of Geisha Girl Porcelain, Litts	$19.95
1915	Collector's Ency. of Hall China, 2nd Ed., Whitmyer	$19.95
1358	Collector's Ency. of McCoy Pottery, Huxford	$19.95
1039	Collector's Ency. of Nippon Porcelain I, Van Patten	$19.95
1350	Collector's Ency. of Nippon Porcelain II, Van Patten	$19.95
1665	Collector's Ency. of Nippon Porcelain III, Van Patten	$24.95
1447	Collector's Ency. of Noritake, Van Patten	$19.95
1038	Collector's Ency. of Occupied Japan, 2nd Ed., Florence	$14.95
1719	Collector's Ency. of Occupied Japan III, Florence	$14.95
2019	Collector's Ency. of Occupied Japan IV, Florence	$14.95
1715	Collector's Ency. of R.S. Prussia II, Gaston	$24.95
1034	Collector's Ency. of Roseville Pottery, Huxford	$19.95
1035	Collector's Ency. of Roseville Pottery, 2nd Ed., Huxford	$19.95
1623	Coll. Guide to Country Stoneware & Pottery, Raycraft	$9.95
2077	Coll. Guide Country Stone. & Pottery, 2nd Ed., Raycraft	$14.95
1523	Colors in Cambridge, National Cambridge Society	$19.95
1425	Cookie Jars, Westfall	$9.95
1843	Covered Animal Dishes, Grist	$14.95
1844	Elegant Glassware of the Depression Era, 3rd Ed., Florence	$19.95
2024	Kitchen Glassware of the Depression Years, 4th Florence	$19.95
1465	Haviland Collectibles & Art Objects, Gaston	$19.95
1917	Head Vases Id & Value Guide, Cole	$14.95
1392	Majolica Pottery, Katz-Marks	$9.95
1669	Majolica Pottery, 2nd Series, Katz-Marks	$9.95
1919	Pocket Guide to Depression Glass, 6th Ed., Florence	$9.95
1438	Oil Lamps II, Thuro	$19.95
1670	Red Wing Collectibles, DePasquale	$9.95
1440	Red Wing Stoneware, DePasquale	$9.95
1958	So. Potteries Blue Ridge Dinnerware, 3rd Ed., Newbound	$14.95
1889	Standard Carnival Glass, 2nd Ed., Edwards	$24.95
1814	Wave Crest, Glass of C.F. Monroe, Cohen	$29.95
1848	Very Rare Glassware of the Depression Years, Florence	$24.95

Books on Dolls & Toys

1887	American Rag Dolls, Patino	$14.95
2079	Barbie Fashion, Vol. 1, 1959-1967, Eames	$24.95
1749	Black Dolls, Gibbs	$14.95
1514	Character Toys & Collectibles 1st Series, Longest	$19.95
1750	Character Toys & Collectibles, 2nd Series, Longest	$19.95
2021	Collectible Male Action Figures, Manos	$14.95
1529	Collector's Ency. of Barbie Dolls, DeWein	$19.95
1066	Collector's Ency. of Half Dolls, Marion	$29.95
2082	Collector's Guide to Magazine Paper Dolls, Young	$14.95
1891	French Dolls in Color, 3rd Series, Smith	$14.95
1631	German Dolls, Smith	$9.95
1635	Horsman Dolls, Gibbs	$19.95
1067	Madame Alexander Collector's Dolls, Smith	$19.95
2025	Madame Alexander Price Guide #15, Smith	$7.95
1995	Modern Collectors Dolls, Vol. I, Smith	$19.95
1516	Modern Collector's Dolls V, Smith	$19.95

1540	Modern Toys, 1930-1980, Baker	$19.95
2033	Patricia Smith Doll Values, Antique to Modern, 6th ed.,	$9.95
1886	Stern's Guide to Disney	$14.95
1513	Teddy Bears & Steiff Animals, Mandel	$9.95
1817	Teddy Bears & Steiff Animals, 2nd, Mandel	$19.95
2084	Teddy Bears, Steiff Animals & Annalees, 3rd, Mandel	$19.95
2028	Toys, Antique & Collectible, Longest	$14.95
1648	World of Alexander-Kins, Smith	$19.95
1808	Wonder of Barbie, Manos	$9.95
1430	World of Barbie Dolls, Manos	$9.95

Other Collectibles

1457	American Oak Furniture, McNerney	$9.95
1846	Antique & Collectible Marbles, Grist, 2nd Ed.	$9.95
1712	Antique & Collectible Thimbles, Mathis	$19.95
1880	Antique Iron, McNerney	$9.95
1748	Antique Purses, Holiner	$19.95
1868	Antique Tools, Our American Heritage, McNerney	$9.95
2015	Archaic Indian Points & Knives, Edler	$14.95
1426	Arrowheads & Projectile Points, Hothem	$7.95
1278	Art Nouveau & Art Deco Jewelry, Baker	$9.95
1714	Black Collectibles, Gibbs	$19.95
1666	Book of Country, Raycraft	$19.95
1960	Book of Country Vol II, Raycraft	$19.95
1811	Book of Moxie, Potter	$29.95
1128	Bottle Pricing Guide, 3rd Ed., Cleveland	$7.95
1751	Christmas Collectibles, Whitmyer	$19.95
1752	Christmas Ornaments, Johnston	$19.95
1713	Collecting Barber Bottles, Holiner	$24.95
2018	Collector's Ency. of Graniteware, Greguire	$24.95
2083	Collector's Ency. of Russel Wright Designs, Kerr	$19.95
1634	Coll. Ency. of Salt & Pepper Shakers, Davern	$19.95
2020	Collector's Ency. of Salt & Pepper Shakers II, Davern	$19.95
1916	Collector's Guide to Art Deco, Gaston	$14.95
1753	Collector's Guide to Baseball Memorabilia, Raycraft	$14.95
1537	Collector's Guide to Country Baskets, Raycraft	$9.95
1437	Collector's Guide to Country Furniture, Raycraft	$9.95
1842	Collector's Guide to Country Furniture II, Raycraft	$14.95
1962	Collector's Guide to Decoys, Huxford	$14.95
1441	Collector's Guide to Post Cards, Wood	$9.95
1716	Fifty Years of Fashion Jewelry, Baker	$19.95
2022	Flea Market Trader, 6th Ed., Huxford	$9.95
1668	Flint Blades & Proj. Points of the No. Am. Indian, Tully	$24.95
1755	Furniture of the Depression Era, Swedberg	$19.95
2081	Guide to Collecting Cookbooks, Allen	$14.95
1424	Hatpins & Hatpin Holders, Baker	$9.95
1964	Indian Axes & Related Stone Artifacts, Hothem	$14.95
2023	Keen Kutter Collectibles, 2nd Ed., Heuring	$14.95
1181	100 Years of Collectible Jewelry, Baker	$9.95
1965	Pine Furniture, Our Am. Heritage, McNerney	$14.95
2080	Price Guide to Cookbooks & Recipe Leaflets, Dickinson	$9.95
1124	Primitives, Our American Heritage, McNerney	$8.95
1759	Primitives, Our American Heritage, 2nd Series, McNerney	$14.95
2026	Railroad Collectibles, 4th Ed., Baker	$14.95
1632	Salt & Pepper Shakers, Guarnaccia	$9.95
1888	Salt & Pepper Shakers II, Guarnaccia	$14.95
2096	Silverplated Flatware, 4th Ed., Hagan	$14.95
2027	Standard Baseball Card Pr. Gd., Florence	$9.95
1922	Standard Bottle Pr. Gd., Sellari	$14.95
1966	Standard Fine Art Value Guide, Huxford	$29.95
2085	Standard Fine Art Value Guide Vol. 2, Huxford	$29.95
2078	The Old Book Value Guide, 2nd Ed	$19.95
1923	Wanted to Buy	$9.95
1885	Victorian Furniture, McNerney	$9.95

Schroeder's Antiques Price Guide

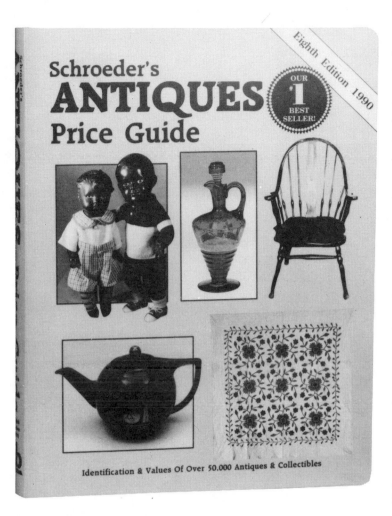

Schroeder's
ANTIQUES
Price Guide

Eighth Edition 1990

OUR 1 BEST SELLER!

Identification & Values Of Over 50,000 Antiques & Collectibles

Schroeder's Antiques Price Guide has climbed its way to the top in a field already supplied with several well-established publications! The word is out, *Schroeder's Price Guide* is the best buy at any price. Over 500 categories are covered, with more than 50,000 listings. But it's not volume alone that makes Schroeder's the unique guide it is recognized to be. From ABC Plates to Zsolnay, if it merits the interest of today's collector, you'll find it in Schroeder's. Each subject is represented with histories and background information. In addition, hundreds of sharp original photos are used each year to illustrate not only the rare and the unusual, but the everyday "fun-type" collectibles as well -- not postage stamp pictures, but large close-up shots that show important details clearly.

Each edition is completely re-typeset from all new sources. We have not and will not simply change prices in each new edition. All new copy and all new illustrations make Schroeder's THE price guide on antiques and collectibles.

The writing and researching team behind this giant is proportionately large. It is backed by a staff of more than seventy of Collector Books' finest authors, as well as a board of advisors made up of well-known antique authorities and the country's top dealers, all specialists in their fields. Accuracy is their primary aim. Prices are gathered over the entire year previous to publication, from ads and personal contacts. Then each category is thoroughly checked to spot inconsistencies, listings that may not be entirely reflective of actual market dealings, and lines too vague to be of merit.

Only the best of the lot remains for publication. You'll find *Schroeder's Antiques Price Guide* the one to buy for factual information and quality.

No dealer, collector or investor can afford not to own this book. It is available from your favorite bookseller or antiques dealer at the low price of $12.95. If you are unable to find this price guide in your area, it's available from Collector Books, P. O. Box 3009, Paducah, KY 42001 at $12.95 plus $2.00 for postage and handling.

8½ x 11, 608 Pages

$12.95

COLLECTOR BOOKS
A Division of Schroeder Publishing Co., Inc.